Babine

Pierce Clegg & Peter McMullan

Foreword by Mark Hume

Artwork by Dave Hall

Babine

Pierce Clegg & Peter McMullan
Foreword by Mark Hume
Artwork by Dave Hall

Frank Amato
PORTLAND

Brian Pol: A Dedication

There is no greater tragedy than a life cut short for any reason. I dedicate my part in this book to Brian Pol, an assistant angling guide for Norlakes who drowned in Babine Lake during the summer of 1988 (see pages 58-60). I could have been this tragedy many times over. Love for the Babine can be all-consuming to the point of death. The unexpected life and times of living in a wilderness setting can take the best of us by surprise. Brian found a part of what he was searching for on the Babine. Part of what the Trout Lodge and Steelhead Camp stand for is searching, finding, casting and loving. Brian and many others have found such a place. May it be honoured and remembered until the end of time.

I would also like to include in my dedication the Babine Watershed Monitoring Trust (www.babinetrust.ca). The legacy of stewardship or lack thereof can be found in the many land-use plans but the trust by itself is the only testimony of follow-up to see if the most at-risk values and objectives of the plans are being protected.

All book profits will go to the trust making it and the Babine River Foundation (www.babineriverfoundation.com) the trust's only private funders. Putting our funds where our mouths and hearts are is the ongoing legacy that angling can accomplish, something that should be the end result of all sports fishing.

—Pierce Clegg
Smithers, B.C.

All inquiries should be addressed to:
Frank Amato Publications, Inc.
P.O. Box 82112
Portland, Oregon 97282
www.amatobooks.com
(503) 653-8108

Cover and book design by Tony Amato

HB ISBN-13: 978-1-57188-462-6 HB UPC: 0-81127-00302-0
LIMITED HB ISBN-13: 978-1-57188-463-3 LIMITED HB UPC: 0-81127-00303-7

Printed in China

1 3 5 7 9 10 8 6 4 2

Contents

Part IV

Guest Memories...90

Part V

Listening to the Guides...126

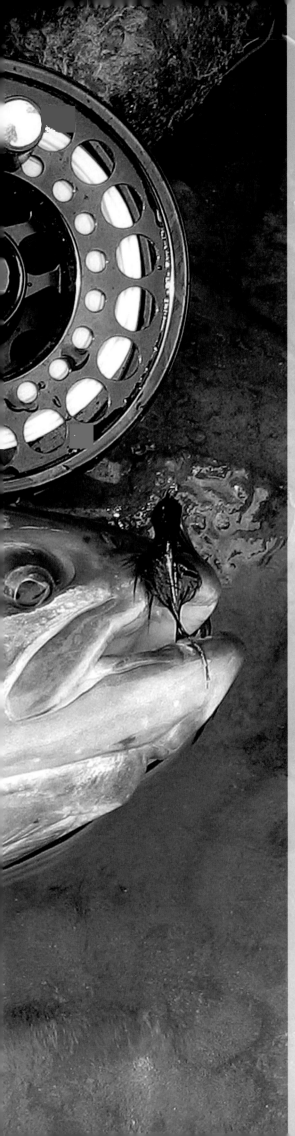

FOREWORD

On Saving a Sacred River

ivers are sacred and none more so than those that have the holy trinity of salmon, grizzly bears and steelhead. This book, a collection of tales on fishing, companionship and the power of dreams, is about one of those special rivers.

The Babine spills out of a long lake with the same name in central British Columbia, north of the small town of Smithers. It cuts a ragged arc through the remnants of a once great forest, gathering flow from water pouring off the Sicintine and Atna mountain ranges, before turning south to join the great Skeena River system, which ties it to the Pacific.

The mighty Skeena, second in Canada only to the Fraser in terms of salmon production, is the pathway the migratory fishes follow as they return from their epic journeys across the north Pacific. If they make it through the ocean fisheries, past the fleet of commercial boats that mass in the estuary to strike at them, and then run the gauntlet of sports and native fishermen in the main river, they eventually enter the mouth of the Babine. Here they pass into a special place—one of the few watersheds left anywhere in the Pacific Northwest that has not been stripped of timber to the riverbanks.

Because of the work of some of those whose writing appears in this book, a narrow corridor of forest shelters the Babine. As it flows between those green, cathedral walls, carrying the salmon and steelhead back to their natal waters and giving tantalizing life to the flies cast by fishermen, the river seems a blessed, protected place, a river that somehow, miraculously exists as it always did. But that dreamlike quality could easily be lost, for the strip of forest that buffers the river is precariously thin, as you will see if you look at satellite images. From that high perspective one can see the ever-spreading network of resource roads that have fragmented what used to be a sweeping, old growth forest. The bone white patches left by clear cut operations are drawing perilously close to the Babine and there are fears that logging on tributaries could soon damage this holy place, by sending waves of silt to choke the

spawning beds, or that new roads could destroy the wilderness atmosphere by providing uncontrolled access. Oil, gas, and mineral activity are constant threats—and there is always the danger that mismanagement of the commercial fishery at the mouth of the Skeena (where nets are set for more prolific stocks of salmon) could decimate the Babine's incredible steelhead run.

Those who have contributed stories to this book know what a remarkable, fragile place the Babine is. Their love for the river, for the bears—and most especially for the steelhead—resonate in every tale.

The Babine, and the lodge that gave generations of anglers access to the sacred waters, come to life in these pages. There are some great fishing stories, but this is far more than a book about fishing. It's a book about what's important in life. It's a book about a beautiful, wild river and the dream that it can be saved as it is, forever.

The Babine is a place where the worlds of bears, salmon and steelhead flow together, entering the hearts of the men and women who make pilgrimages there.

Some of those who contributed to this book, or who are characters in its pages, have died and their ashes have been scattered on the waters of the Babine. But others have stepped up to take their place, not just wading the baptismal pools in search of the great steelhead, but also adding their voices to the struggle to save the river.

And after reading their stories you will want to join them.

The economic forces aligned against the Babine are great. Are the hearts of those who love the river greater? After turning these pages, I think you'll see that they are.

This is a sacred river and it cannot be lost.

It can be saved, but only if enough people care. After you've read this book press it into the hands of someone young. Tell them, "You should know about this place. Together we're going to save it."

—Mark Hume
Vancouver, B.C.

Mark Hume is an award-winning Canadian journalist and author well-known for his writings on environmental issues. He is also an ardent fly-fisherman and founding editor of the website www.ariverneversleeps.com. His books are: River of the Angry Moon, *with Harvey Thommasen,* Run of the River *and* Adam's River.

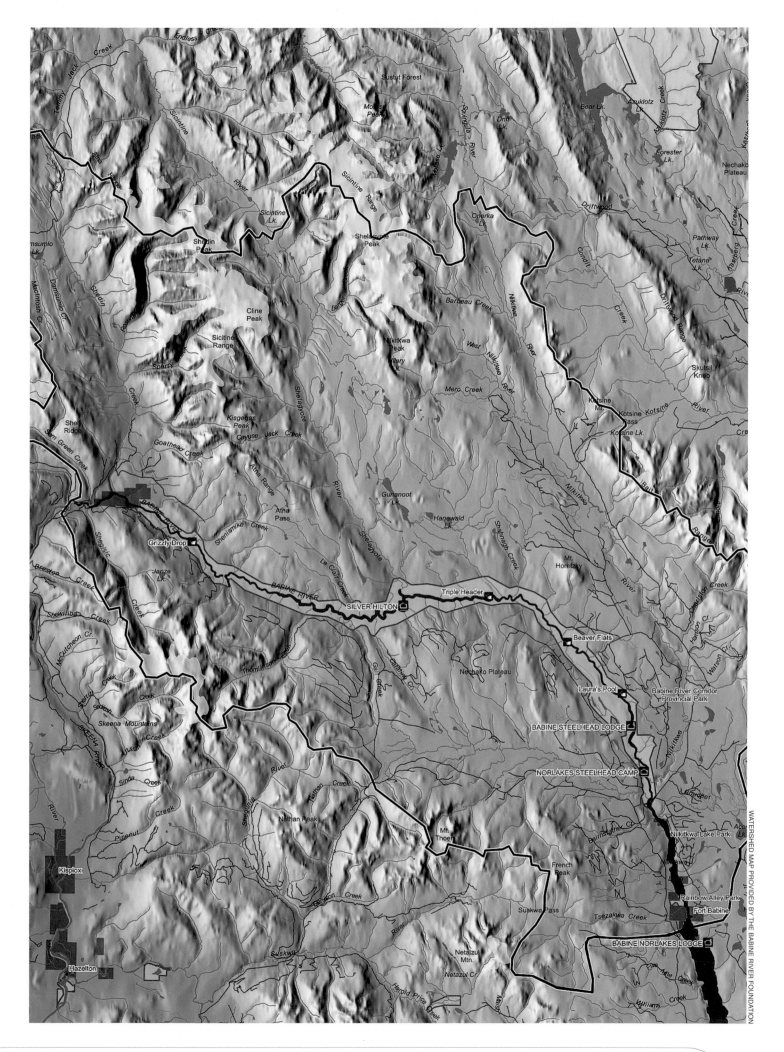

WATERSHED MAP PROVIDED BY THE BABINE RIVER FOUNDATION

PART I

Authors' Notes

The Magic of the Babine

This is definitely not your typical fishing book. Rather it is a richly illustrated tribute to a great river and a measured plea for its future conservation. In the main it's the story, most often told in their own words, of two families, the pioneering Madsens and then the Cleggs, who have done so much to introduce north central British Columbia's Babine River to generations of sports fishermen, all eager to explore and experience fresh challenges.

Part oral history, part anthology, part anglers' odyssey, it is also the story of the Babine and its fish, especially its quite magnificent steelhead trout, as told by guides and visitors from different places and backgrounds, drawn to return time after time by the combined appeal of an historic riverbank camp, lakeside trout lodge and sturdy log cabins, all in a remote wilderness setting.

This cherished location has changed little in more than half a century. It's one where guests step back in time to an era long before the advent of the Internet and cell phones, jet drive outboards, flush toilets, electricity on demand, double-handed rods, disc drag reels, hooks without barbs, Bubbleheads, Bombers and Intruders and, most significant in terms of the future of the fishery, universal catch and release for steelhead on the Babine and the other rivers that comprise the great Skeena system.

For me it's a story that came together initially by chance and then steadily, page by page, cast by cast, starting with a cancelled mid-winter steelhead trip to B.C.'s Queen Charlotte Islands and the subsequent need to identify a new destination in which to invest precious airline points. Trout fishing in June, on the Babine River's famous Rainbow Alley, staying for a week with my wife, Daphne, in a log cabin on the lakeshore, presented itself as a worthy alternative and a possible setting for a magazine feature.

Soon, Pierce Clegg's vivid story-telling convinced me that the Babine and its often huge-beyond-words steelhead, fish 10 years and more in age that can weigh well in excess of 30 pounds, if you are sufficiently skilled and lucky enough to land them, had the makings of far more substantial narrative.

Over the course of a fish-rich quarter century on the system, as accomplished guide and, with his wife Anita, Babine Norlakes Trout Lodge and Steelhead Camp owner, Pierce has established his credentials as a most eloquent and supremely determined advocate for the river, its fish, its wildlife and its important angling heritage.

Indeed his willingness to stand up and be counted has likely won him as much admiration on the part of the sports fishing and environmental community, as it has attracted the enmity of those government, mining and forestry interests more concerned with the extraction of the area's natural resources.

The Norlakes' traditions have deep roots and a proud history that reach back to the early 1950s when Ejnar Madsen, then a young, newly-arrived migrant from Denmark, found himself helping to build a fishing lodge and cabins on the shores of Babine Lake, a truly isolated destination in those days and even today accessible only by boat or float plane.

Peter and Daphne McMullan with Pierce Clegg on their first visit to Trout Lodge and the cabin called Sunset Cove.

It was not long before he became a partner in the venture. He also met and soon married Joy Hinter, then only 18, and just out of her Fraser Valley high school and 12 years younger than Ejnar. Together they developed the business, mostly for American guests, as was and is still largely the norm, and raised their three children before Ejnar was taken far too soon by cancer in the fall of 1983.

Joy, whose own careful telling of the Madsen story is such an integral part of both this book and of Norlakes' history, sold the lodge and steelhead camp to the Cleggs in 1986. Despite its far-away location, many fishermen and women from as diverse countries as the USA, Japan and Europe, were and are regular year-after-year visitors, enjoying a unique, backcountry lifestyle on lake and river.

She has continued a close association with the area and she and her second husband, Thornton Jenkins, enjoy their own Babine lakeside cabin and property, visiting every summer from California and continuing to fly-fish for the resident rainbow trout, an unchanging delight for her dating back over more than 50 years.

Then there are the guests and the guides, some no longer with us, whose skills with wonderfully evocative words and images have helped to enhance the story beyond measure. The pleasures they have derived from the river speak clearly of a very special place and we are left to hope that theirs will be a legacy still recalled and enjoyed in another 50 years.

Pierce and I want to acknowledge all those who have become involved in this project over the past few years. They are identified individually and in more detail as our story unfolds. All of them are totally passionate fishermen whose work for this book mirrors their own deep love of the river.

In particular we wish to thank artists Dave Hall and Gary Flagel for their original illustrations, publisher Frank Amato and his team for their most meaningful support for the whole concept and the idea to use it as a fund-raiser for the Babine Trust, and journalist and author Mark Hume for his Foreword.

For my part, I have to thank most sincerely Pierce and Anita Clegg for their many kindnesses and the trust they placed in me to undertake the telling of this story, Joy (Madsen) Jenkins, for her vivid recall of events long ago, and provincial government senior steelhead biologist Mark Beere, for sharing a wealth of valuable information. Then there's my own family, my wife Daphne, who has encouraged my angling passions for so very many years, and our two sons, Richard, my essential book project computer consultant, and Conor, infrequent but always most welcome fishing partners when time allows.

That's for now: perhaps there will be a future occasion where their children, our grandchildren Sarah, Finn and Jack, also have the good fortune to experience what is truly the magic of the Babine, a river where the opportunity to cast a fly is always a priceless privilege.

—*Peter McMullan*
Nanaimo, B.C.

Salmon, People Need a Healthy Ecosystem

Change comes quickly, even to the greatest of watersheds. With all the great stories it is easy to forget that the Skeena and all its many famous tributaries was once a far greater fishery. In reality, it is only a remnant fishery that we enjoy today. Records show that once upon a time there were millions more salmon. Where there were once 85 canneries at the mouth of the Skeena, there is now one. The early years of Norlakes offered only a taste of what the fishing could be like in those pioneer years yet that taste was sensational.

Some of the earliest magazine articles about Norlakes and some of the stories told by the original guests at Norlakes, speak about a time of much more wilderness value and quality and much greater fishing results, even considering how little of the fishery was accessible at that time. One of the greatest learning experiences of being able to work and live in a wilderness setting that supports a great salmon run, is that you learn the importance of the relationship between the salmon and the ecosystem.

In my short 25 seasons on the Babine I have seen a sharp decline in the salmon run and lower catch rates for trout to the point that it has affected the viability of my trout fishing business. All the trout operations associated with Rainbow Alley have struggled to the point of not operating. The days of taking guests out for a day of trout fishing, or sending them out on their own to easily have a great day of fishing, has been replaced by days of intense guiding and learning the intricacies of the fishery.

In my early years guiding, I and our other guides were referred to more as boatmen than guides since the fishery was so user-friendly. Nowadays the value of a guide is measured by his experience since the fishery demands more intense evaluation.

The greatest testament to a failed salmon run on the whole entire Skeena watershed was and is the federal government's Salmon Enhancement Projects (SEP), located on Fulton River and Pinkut Creek, tributaries flowing into Babine Lake. These SEP programs basically quadrupled the population of sockeye salmon in the Babine watershed system. If the Babine Lake SEP had not been created, there would have been a complete collapse of the Skeena watershed-based commercial salmon fishery. From abundance to scarcity, Norlakes in its infancy saw just a glimpse of what was a truly great wild salmon population.

In many great Pacific salmon watersheds, large lakes supporting slow, natural tail water watersheds had great former salmon runs. Babine Lake is the longest natural fresh water lake in B.C. The Babine watershed is the most important salmon-bearing tributary of the Skeena watershed but look what has happened so quickly. The race to unsustainably harvest salmon, steelhead, trees and copper has already left a legacy of a wild watershed not nearly as wild as when Norlakes began to pioneer the sport fishing of the Babine.

The context of my involvement in fighting logging bridge proposals and overall logging development, is very much the end game of stewardship, one where a remnant world-class river watershed is still capable of delivering angling satisfaction. It's a sad chapter in the Skeena watershed stewardship battle that we are fighting over the last salmon and steelhead runs, the last un-logged values

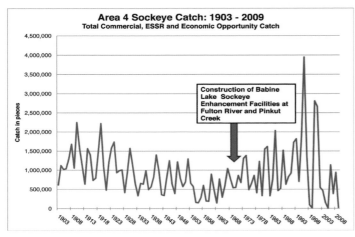

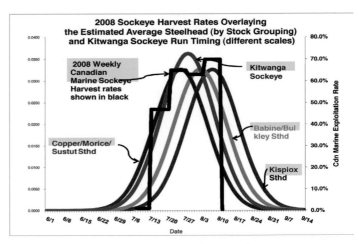

Graphs prepared by First Fish Consulting using DFO catch data. ESSR = Excess Salmon to Spawning Requirement.

and mountain passes, the last untouched mountain tributaries supporting wild fish.

It's also a sad chapter that continued developmental plans are under foot for coal bed methane mining, more logging and new copper mines. There are also hydroelectric interests called run-of-river projects, small stream water diversion projects that promise electrical power over wild ecosystems.

There are good people employed in logging, mining and the other ever-productive models of our economy. It's so easy to pit tree huggers against redneck chainsaw operators, which totally detracts and misses the real stewardship issues. We can do selective harvest of salmon. We can do sustainable and ecosystem-based logging. We can design and deliver good mining projects that don't leave a mess of acid rock drainage for somebody else to clean up.

We choose to accept commercial operations that cut costs in order to maximize profit when in reality the short-term business prospects, made attractive by lower costs, later become hindsight or short sightedness. Wild watersheds like the Skeena or Babine represent a chance to do it differently, to learn from our mistakes in other watersheds and yet we just can't seem to be different. It's the human condition so the fight is always on... they call it competing interests with different perspectives rather than what it really is.

There is a group called the Wilderness Tourism Association (WTA). They are the only organized group in B.C. trying to represent operations like Norlakes, which depend upon wild ecosystems for their tourism product. The business of wilderness has merits beyond the wild in providing the pure economics of employment, GDP and other contributing factors to healthy communities. But the world system of product delivery and development is not based on the protection, conservation and healthy economic development of our overall environment.

We are all becoming painfully aware of our now global responsibilities to be better stewards of our environment. The consequences of not valuing, recognizing and delivering on clean water, clear air, clean oceans and better systems of waste disposal all threaten our very existence on this planet as never before. On the Babine, I have learned these lessons through the bridge fights and the numerous land-use planning exercises in which I have participated. The land-use planning table of competing interests was always charged with delivering on a plan that would

allow everybody to continue on with their interests. They still call it win-win but is it really what it sounds like?

Is the commercial harvest of salmon using a gillnet selective, as the Federal Fisheries would have us believe? Is the Annual Allowable Cut, set by the Chief Forester of B.C., really sustainable for individual watersheds like the Babine? Don't we make social decisions to remove wild watersheds because we believe that logging and mining are more socially beneficial? Can we really have it all in terms of competing interests and still call it wild? Can there be a mix of development and wild watersheds? How do we restore the Skeena and Babine watersheds to a former state of salmon abundance, or is it even possible given the fact that Federal Fisheries continually denies that we even have a problem with salmon?

Sea lice caused by fish farms, really? Tyee Test Fishery numbers overstated, really? Coal bed methane drilling and development not a problem for the headwaters of the Skeena, really? The WTA has valid comments on these political and social decisions to change wild watersheds in the name of economics. The good science is in and the lessons learned on other watersheds across the planet all say that stewardship of the Skeena and Babine watersheds could and should include a different model and policy of development.

Bucking the system of short-term thinking to one of long-term, holistic and ecosystem-based economics is the business of stewardship. Wilderness watersheds and wild ecosystems have value. Even a watershed in a big city has value. There can be good economics, employment and healthy communities surrounding and located in wild watersheds. I learned a great view of land management from Ric Careless, who helped the Babine greatly in establishing protection resulting in the Class 'A' Provincial Park designation supporting numerous land-use plans. Ric is a great proponent of zonation for land-use planning.

Ecosystem-based land-use planning also uses zonation to link watershed values so that the overall watershed can continue to function and renew its sustainability. Stewardship is about the choice to make economic decisions that value wild ecosystems as healthy bases on which development can co-exist. Hard industry, highway and transportation networks, agricultural and food production and housing for population movement and expansion can all be achieved in concert with stewardship of the land and

water. We just are not used to doing it that way so we fight for every fish, bear and tree.

Another negative factor of our human condition is to use economies of scale to increase productivity and reduce cost. Both in our salmon harvest and log-harvest areas, we have believed that harvesting more with less human involvement reduces costs and increases harvest output. Well that strategy did indeed work but to the point of over-harvest with associated by-catch or by-product waste. Now we realize that value-added processes have been all but abandoned in favor of putting salmon in a can, and exporting whole logs for manufacturing elsewhere.

We are now moving away from a future of saw logs and moving to a future of fibre-based production. Old-growth forests have been undervalued and little understood in terms of the values they support and how those values came to be. Also, we have learned that our non-selective harvest techniques have resulted in a by-catch of non-target salmon and steelhead. The Babine Salmon Enhancement Program (SEP) has only added to the by-catch because of the non-selective harvesting techniques. This downward spiral has finally come to a crossroads where the over-all salmon fishery of the Skeena watershed is truly threatened.

On the logging side, huge mills with productive capacities beyond our timber supply have also threatened the old-growth inventories. The best saw log species are now in inventory numbers not large enough to support large mills and the annual allowable cut set by the Chief Forester of B.C.

Where does this leave the Babine watershed and what is the future of stewardship there? There has been an incredible amount of attention given to the Babine watershed since I first started guiding there. The bridge fights moved into land-use planning committees and final planning documents. These local community-endorsed plans moved into the Protected Areas Strategy of the 1990s.

Finally the Babine River Corridor Park and one more land-use plan have formed a multi-layered confusion of land-use plans, designations, zones and management guidelines that take much research and understanding to implement, monitor and amend.

With support from Norlakes guests and the two other steelhead tourism businesses on the Babine, the Babine River Foundation and the Babine Watershed Monitoring Trust were born. They are under-funded but make the attempt at honouring all the land-use plans and park designation work. This is a great testimony to the many individuals who gave their time and money to practice stewardship for the Babine watershed.

While the ideal of preserving a wild watershed is tempered by the limitations of money and manpower, we all have bought some valuable time in giving the Babine watershed a chance to restore its greatness in the future. This single victory of buying time is our beachhead to greater efforts of stewardship.

In evaluating whether we should log or not….in evaluating whether we should mine or not…in evaluating whether we should gillnet or not, I believe we should say 'no' to those kinds of activities if they cannot be sustained in the long-term and still provide a water base and land base for wilderness values. When we evaluate a road, a clear-cut, a strip mine or the associated acid rock drainage pond, we should be asking ourselves if that economic benefit can be sustained long after the logs are gone, the fish are harvested and the mineral is depleted.

It's what we have left over and the associated economic value therein that counts for future generations. It's disappointing and infuriating to see the closed mills, the former mining sites leaching acid rock and sterile, once-salmon-bearing watersheds become the end result of over-harvest and a total disregard for the wild ecosystems, on which we depend, to sustain life on earth.

If it costs the timber industry too much to protect watersheds and their fish and wildlife values, then I say 'no' to logging. If it costs too much to selectively harvest salmon and protect steelhead on the Skeena River approach waters, then I say 'no' harvest at all. If it costs too much for a strip mine or coal bed methane project to protect the water quality of the watershed in which they mine, then I say 'no' to mining. This status quo of approving such projects has put the Skeena and Babine watersheds in a threatened state in which restoration and recovery investment would be huge.

We must somehow reverse the trends and return to the approval of projects and industries that enhance our watershed values, not take them away, far from our communities. Saying 'no' to greed will not get us in any worse shape in terms of high unemployment rates, suicide rates and other recent developments that we have witnessed in our watersheds due to short-term, cost-cutting greed over long-term stewardship. A government system of giving away our resources with little consequence for over-harvest is a stupid system in need of overhaul.

Specific to the Babine watershed, we need to do a better job of assessing our fishery and the many streams, creeks and tiny waterways that make the river rich in fish and wildlife. We need to do a better job of creating value-added economic projects that provide employment and leave most of the production and processing in our local areas. We need to fully understand that the value of the Skeena watershed is primarily based on the health of the salmon run and not by the number of saw logs we can harvest.

Some of the best old-growth trees are directly dependent on salmon…this is something little understood by many. The relationship between salmon and all levels of the wild ecosystems of the Skeena watershed is also little understood but failing that understanding leads to a wrecked economy and social structure. We still have a chance to get it back and should seize upon the time we have left to make a difference now.

Apathy won't work and the continued support of the status quo won't work either. By supporting groups that are working to restore our salmon runs we will buy some valuable time to work on the other projects of employment, growth and development of healthy communities and a future for our children.

In discovering the Babine, it is hard to overlook not only the salmon resource but also the evidence of the people who used to live there so many years ago. Part of our rediscovery of healthy salmon populations should also be the re-discovery of the dependence upon salmon in order for us to be a healthy people. Archaeology on the Babine demonstrates that there was once upon a time, a healthy relationship between salmon and people. We should strive to get that back.

—*Pierce Clegg*

Riverside reflections at Deadman's Pool.

PART II

1953-1986: The Madsens

Joy (Madsen) Jenkins Looks Back

*Joy (Madsen) Jenkins with Dave Hall's portrait of Ejnar Madsen
which hangs in the dining room at Trout Lodge.*

Joy (Madsen) Jenkins' account of life and times over her 30 years at Norlakes Lodge, on Babine Lake, provides a unique and very personal picture of a family-owned and operated sport fishing enterprise in an even now far-away, wilderness area of north-central British Columbia. Joy Hinter, a Canadian, and Ejnar Madsen, from Denmark, were married in 1956. She was only 18 and just out of school, he was 30 and together they ran the lodge, and later a steelhead camp on the Babine River, until he died in 1983. With the help of her two sons, Karl and Erik, and her daughter, Karen, she stayed on for another three years before selling the business to the Cleggs. In 1987

she married Thornton Jenkins, a lodge guest after Ejnar's death, and lives in Sonoma, CA. This is her story.

It's followed by the recollections of Lee Richardson, in his day an acclaimed outdoors writer and author, and professional forester Gary Quanstrom, who recounts his experiences as a teenage camp cook. The chapter continues by sharing extracts from a fascinating exchange of letters between Ejnar and Clarence 'Strom' Stromsness, a distinguished and outstanding angler who came to the Babine for almost 30 years. Dick Andersen, who also fished with Ejnar and Pierce Clegg, rounds out the Madsen story.

Ejnar Madsen was born on a farm in Denmark in 1926. He was 15 when he left home and put himself through schools in Denmark, England and Sweden. He wanted the adventure that comes with living in a bigger country and applied for a visa for Australia. He was turned down so he applied to Canada and was accepted in 1952, boarding a ship and arriving in Halifax after being seasick throughout what was a very rough voyage.

He had asked one of his shipmates where he should go to find a job on a farm. He was advised to try central British Columbia so they looked at a map and decided that Vanderhoof was about the centre of the province. The Canadian National Railway took him across Canada and he was amazed at the vastness of the country compared to the Denmark of his youth.

Ejnar found work on a farm and stayed there until freeze-up, before moving on to a sawmill for the winter and early spring.

He knew that was not how he wanted to spend his future in sub-zero winters so he found a carpenter's job in Burns Lake.

It was there he first met Tom Stewart, who soon asked Ejnar to work with him on a government contract, building a Potlatch Hall for the Indians at Fort Babine, at the north end of Babine Lake. One day Mac Anderson was in a passing boat, taking some fishermen to the river, when the presence of the two white men caught his attention.

Mac, the man who created Norlakes Lodge, re-named Babine Norlakes in 1986, was struggling to fund his dream of creating an international fishing lodge on the shores of the remote Babine Lake.

He had bought the land, some 120 acres, from the government for the amount of back taxes owed to them by the previous owner, an old prospector who had died. The Indians often talked about 'the old man' and what a wonderful garden he planted every

summer. They liked to visit him, and he would send them home with some of his prized vegetables. Ejnar chose this same plot of land to plant our vegetable garden, knowing how fertile it was.

Mac then began building cabins and by 1953 he had completed three, helped by local Indians, John Madam (see page 62) and Jimmie West. He approached Ejnar and Tom and asked them if they would consider joining forces with him in fulfilling the dream he had for a fishing lodge. They agreed, and the three of them formed an equal partnership and began to complete what Mac had started.

The three partners built the lodge and the other cabins for a total of 10, all still standing to this day as is the original lodge. Every cabin and structure was built without the help of heavy equipment and each log was set in place by hand. Pius West, from Fort Babine, hand cut the shakes for the cabin roofs, all from locally felled trees.

In 1952 Wayne Coe, from Portland, OR met Mac and heard about his plan to build a fishing lodge. Wayne was very enthusiastic about this plan and supplied enough funds for Mac to continue the project, including in it a cabin for Wayne and Harriet Coe. The understanding was that the cabin would revert back to the lodge when they no longer used it. They spent 30 happy summers there and it was through them that we came to know as friends Lee Richardson, the American outdoors writer, and Cecil Brown, who was both a guest and sometime guide and partner.

I was born to Fred and Joy Hinter in 1938 in Summerland, B.C. and christened Ellen Joy Hinter, the third girl in a family of six girls and three boys. My father struggled through the 'hungry thirties' to keep food on the table as the babies kept coming and work was hard to find.

Pius West, a Fort Babine Indian born without legs, was a skilled craftsman and hand cut all the roof shakes for the 10 cabins at Trout Lodge.

He was hired to work in orchards, moving on as the fruit ripened in different places throughout the Okanagan Valley. Then he had carpentry jobs, riding atop the trains as so many men did in those hungry years, trying to find small jobs wherever possible. As times got a little better and jobs were not quite so scarce as the war years neared, the family settled in North Vancouver where he worked in the shipyards. In 1949 we moved to Langley Prairie in the Fraser Valley, now a big suburb of Vancouver called Langley. It was here that I graduated from high school in 1955.

This early 1950s lunch group includes Mac Anderson, original owner of Norlakes (far right).
Mac was never seen without his fly-festooned tam-o-shanter, lost when he drowned on the Bear River in 1957.
Tom Stewart, third left, and Ejnar Madsen joined Mac as equal partners in 1953.

The Madsen family and three young Trout
Lodge staff members. From left, Connie
Simmons, Ejnar, Joy and Karen, Wanda Plewis,
Gary Lopaschuk, Erik and Karl.

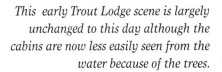

This early Trout Lodge scene is largely
unchanged to this day although the
cabins are now less easily seen from the
water because of the trees.

Tom Stewart was also living there with his family. He had posted a job description on the school bulletin board looking for a helper at a very remote fishing lodge on Babine Lake. My father heard about the job posting and was determined to send me there for the summer. Our family was poor and my father saw the job as an opportunity for me to work in a remote region where I couldn't spend any money but could help with finances at home.

He had me 'phone Tom to tell him I would take the job if we could meet him for an interview first. He spent half an hour with us outlining what my work would be and I agreed to go. Tom explained that I would take the Canadian National Railway from Langley Prairie and that I would travel for two days to a place called Topley. There, I would meet a man waiting to drive me to Topley Landing, where I would be picked up by boat for a five- or six-hour ride on Babine Lake to Norlakes Lodge.

After committing to a summer at this remote fishing lodge I had one month to finish my final school year, graduate, and prepare for this great adventure into the British Columbia wilderness. I spoke to my geography teacher and asked him to help me find out more about Babine Lake. We looked it up on a map but could not learn much about it other than it was 110 miles long and thus the longest natural lake in British Columbia. We both realized it was pretty remote but nothing prepared me for what I found.

When I left Langley Prairie for the lodge, I was the only passenger boarding the train at 10 o'clock at night. The conductor inquired where I was going and I replied Topley. I will never forget him asking me, "where the hell is Topley?" I was so terrified I started

to back off the train, but dad gently pushed me back on. I rode that train for two days with only $10 and some sandwiches in my pocket. Topley wasn't even a town. It was just a 'whistle stop.' I knew no one and was traveling solely on trust. I arrived around noon and a man was waiting there to meet me and drive me to Babine Lake. I did not know him but he knew my name. A fisherman who had been on the train was also coming to the lodge.

It was a bumpy 90-minute drive to Topley Landing and Ejnar was the one who was there to pick us up. He had the bluest eyes I had ever seen and the most delightful Danish accent. He was 12 years older than me and, by late summer, we had fallen in love and were married the following year.

Although I realized I was going to a remote area, nothing prepared me for what I found. This place was totally a wilderness of thick underbrush through which you could not see or penetrate without a machete. It was a dense forest of huge trees of every imaginable colour of green, with shorter bushes and shrubs growing right to the water's edge. The cabins and the central portion of the main lodge had been crafted from local trees, beautifully situated on hand-cleared land along the shore of this glorious setting at the north end of Babine Lake.

"Welcome to Norlakes Lodge." For the next 31 years I would offer this greeting to countless fly-fishermen and women from all over the world. Thus began for this naïve and innocent young girl an adventure of a lifetime in an untamed area of British Columbia. This was to become both my home and an education far removed from textbooks in a city college.

When I first arrived at the lodge there was a male cook, Jack Roy, who lived in one of the upstairs staff bedrooms. A French Canadian, he spoke as much French as he did English, especially if he was upset about something. When he was happy he loved to quote Shakespeare to anyone who would listen.

Jan Anderson, Mac Anderson's 27-year-old sister, was also there. We became great friends and shared another bedroom upstairs. In my first days at the lodge she got me through some homesick moments.

I had a boyfriend back home named Eddie, who wrote many letters to me that summer. He was very distressed when I accepted the job. To be sure I would return to him, he gave me an engagement ring for graduation. My father disapproved of this but it made Eddie happy. I had made it clear to Eddie that I would not marry any man until I had more education and a career.

Grocery shopping was done once a month in the early years, and mail was only picked up then too. That is when I would receive Eddie's letters. Until the supplies arrived after a 90-mile boat trip, we would sit in the dark on our beds awaiting the mail. Once the letters were in hand we each lit a candle and read the letters by precious candlelight.

Jan would open each letter and sort them by date, handing them to me in the right order. As I finished each letter, I'd hand them to her to read, and she would hand me the next. We were thrilled with his love letters and we would tell each other our favourites.

She had suffered a great loss early that year when her fiancé had been killed in an accident. Perhaps reading Eddie's letters with me helped her imagine they were from her lost boyfriend. When I wrote Eddie, I warned him that sometimes Jan read his letters, too, but it seemed fine with him and he continued to write.

By August I knew I would not marry Eddie. It was difficult to tell him my decision. He was hurt and angry, but as it turned out he married another girl about the same time I married Ejnar. I hoped he was happy.

My duties were varied and many, from cleaning the cabins and the lodge, and washing endless amounts of dishes, pots and pans, to doing the laundry in a wringer-washer powered by a Briggs and Stratton gas motor—just like a lawn mower—that had to be hand pulled to get it going. Three long lines were strung up above the vegetable garden for the clothes to dry, and we spent a great deal of time praying for sunshine and no rain.

Occasionally an extra big wind would come up and one or more of the lines would break loose and deposit the heavy flannel sheets onto the garden. I would be so unhappy, as it meant gathering them up from the dirt and laundering them all over again, while Ejnar would be equally upset that his beautiful leaf lettuce would be crushed.

It was a challenge to keep the floors looking nice without the use of a vacuum cleaner. The many cottonwood trees in the area created a lot of white, fluffy debris that could not be easily removed with a broom. One day, while I was cleaning on my hands and knees under one of the log-framed beds, someone called to me. In my haste to get out from under the bed I failed to clear the log above me, which resulted in a severe blow to my head that knocked me out. It was a full day's journey by boat and truck to the nearest town, Burns Lake, to reach medical help, which was quite primitive at best.

The Indians from Fort Babine used dugout canoes until the Madsens gave them their first outboard motor.

They created a makeshift brace to keep my head upright and, with icepacks, sent me on my way with instructions not to do any physical work until it healed. After two days of rest and icing my neck, I had to get back to work since we had no other help. After suffering for many years I was diagnosed with two broken vertebrae. A neurosurgeon in Vancouver replaced the broken vertebrae with beef bone. The surgeon was a fly-fisherman and the following year came to the lodge as a guest.

I had planned to return to Langley in September, but I decided to stay until November. That was the year we had an early freeze-up on the lake. Mac Anderson was taking his wife and children to Vancouver Island and the only way we could get out was after a Morse code message was sent by Bill Henry, from the Hudson's Bay Company, asking for someone to come and get us with a 'plane.

An old Fairchild with floats flew in with the one pilot who would agree to make the risky trip. We had to walk out on the ice that had formed close to shore to board the plane and Ejnar had to chop all the ice off the pontoons while we got in. Mac's wife and children and Ejnar and I flew out to Topley Landing. Not long afterwards, that 'plane crashed.

Mac was to follow us by boat to Topley Landing with a young man who was logging on the lake and on their way they got frozen in the ice. They set a fire to send out a signal. A priest down the lake saw it and he was able to get a crew to come to the rescue. It was a close call for them both.

Following our harrowing departure in 1955, I traveled back to Langley Prairie with Tom Stewart and Ejnar. It was too late for me to enroll in college so I took a position as a receptionist in a medical/dental practice. Some friends offered me room and board close to my job and it worked out well. Ejnar boarded with Lucy and Tom Stewart and the two men built two 'spec' homes in White Rock during the winter and following spring.

By Christmas, Ejnar and I had decided to get married and return together to Norlakes in the late spring. My father approved of our plans but insisted that we wait until I was 18 years old and 'mature' enough to make such a big decision. In February I turned 18 and Ejnar turned 30. By April I had saved my wages and Ejnar and Tom had sold both 'spec' houses so we were in a good position

Joy Hinter and Ejnar Madsen found time for a picnic shortly before their marriage in 1956.

to get married. On May 25, 1956 we had a small wedding and honeymooned in the Okanagan where I was born.

We arrived as newlyweds at Norlakes Lodge at the end of May and began our life together in that beautiful and very remote spot in the wilderness. With help from the Fort Babine Indians over the previous two summers, Ejnar had built a log cabin up on a hill just south of the lodge. Much still remained to be done inside to complete it, with the kitchen cabinets yet to be installed, but together we made a very cozy home for ourselves.

To quote 'Uncle' Lee Richardson: "There is something about a log cabin that cannot be denied, something fine and enduring, becoming more beautiful and mellow with the seasons as it is truly part and parcel of its environs, formed from the same trees that enfold it." For six months of every year for the next 27 years this was our refuge in the woods.

In the early years we used Coleman lanterns as our light source. These were fueled by highly volatile Naphtha gas and, once filled, had to be pumped full of air and then lit with a match. Soon two propane lamps were brought in for use in the kitchen. They were much easier to light and did not require filling with gas. Then we got a gas generator and the lodge and six cabins were wired for electricity.

It was exciting to have such a modern convenience, enabling the fishermen to use their electric shavers. By 1962 these six cabins also had indoor bathrooms with full plumbing. Later, indoor bathrooms were added to three more guest cabins, but our own cabin never had electricity or plumbing ("And that's the way it still is," says Pierce.)

Ejnar, Mac and Tom had already named some of the more productive fishing pools and holes on the upper river, identifying them with attractive wooden signs. Just above where the present bridge now stands, there was a footbridge for the Fort Babine people to use. By the time I arrived, in 1955, most of it had washed away but the footings were still visible.

Where a part of it stood upright, the men had attached a hand-painted wooden sign reading 'Golden Gate Bridge.' The stretch of river just down from this sign was an excellent place for finding large rainbow trout. Further down river, and over on the right bank, was another wooden sign for 'Poor Jenny's Pool,' to remember the spot where an unfortunate native woman had either fallen down or collapsed and tragically frozen to death.

Joy (Madsen) Jenkins, seen fishing for rainbow trout off Smokehouse Island, with the retreating Mt. Thoen Glacier in the background, has come back to her Babine Lake cabin every summer for more than 50 years.

In 1963 a log cabin (right) was built near Trout Lodge for Allen and Helen Phillips. Unfortunately it burned to the ground that same year and was replaced by a pre-fabricated version on the same site the following year.

There was an old wooden cross on the ground there with her name and the date of her death carved on it along with the words 'Poor Jenny him froze to death.' I think the reason this was such a popular fishing run was because of its name.

On down the river was a long stretch we called Rainbow Alley with an appropriate sign. This has always been my favourite area and I still spend many hours there every summer, drifting in my red boat and casting a dry fly as I spot a rise. It's unbelievably beautiful on a sunny day and very peaceful.

Next, where the shallow water suddenly becomes deep, there was a sign reading 'Drop Off'. If you could float a fly just at that drop-off, you had a great chance of hooking into a big rainbow and, once it took off into deeper water, you had a real fight on your hands.

The river turns slightly now, and then again a little further down, and then an island comes into view. Here you found posted a sign 'Smokehouse Island' and, on the island, was a smokehouse owned by Antoine Williams and his family. The river flowing from well above the island, and all the way alongside it, was also a very popular fly-fishing location.

While these pools and runs were the ones considered productive enough to have posted name signs, in those early days there were hungry rainbows looking for a meal throughout the upper river.

Over time the various pools and runs we fished from Steelhead Camp were given their own special names. For example Allen's Pool was called after Allen Phillips who, with Ejnar's help, caught a 30-pound steelhead there on November 5, 1969. We had a group of fishermen in camp that had fished with Allen and Helen before. They decided to take his steelhead home, carefully wrapped in dry ice, and had it mounted as a gift to Allen. It was a beautiful mount and it hung over the fireplace at Trout Lodge until we sold the business to the Cleggs in 1986. It's now displayed over our fireplace in Sonoma, CA.

It was Allen who brought the first outboard jet unit up from California for us. After being lodge guests for two summers they leased a piece of land from us at the north end of our property. With help from the Fort Babine Indians, they had a log cabin built on the property and stayed there for two or three months every summer.

JET DRIVES BRING CHANGE

The arrival of the first jet drive in the mid-1960s changed everything. Now Ejnar could take fishermen well down the river without having to worry about hidden rocks damaging his outboards and their propellers.

Joy recalls: "Allen heard about the jets and found out they were made in Berkeley, CA and sold by a company in El Cerrito. He immediately knew that the jet unit was something that Ejnar could use to run the fast water below the weir. He contacted him and asked would he like to have one brought up when he and Helen next came to their summer cabin on the lake. The rest is history."

Ed Ober, who was in partnership in an electrical company with Allen's son, Richard, and who brought his own son and grandson to experience Trout Lodge in 2009, adds more details: "Allen was looking for two things, the best deal as usual and getting it for Ejnar. The company making the jets would not sell to him direct as an individual so he established Phillips and Ober as an outlet. We joked later about him being a wholesaler for the jet with only one salesman, Al, and one customer, Ejnar. Richard thought we should get a mark-up. Al squelched that."

In 1963, the summer the Allens' beautiful cabin was finally completed, they had a big fire and it burned to the ground. The land on which it was built contained mostly peat moss, which is highly flammable; it can smoulder un-noticed for many hours before bursting into flames. It is thought that one of the workers, while raking around the cabin, dropped a cigarette butt and that likely started the fire.

Mac Anderson (left) and cook Jack Roy working on a combined laundry and store room beside the newly-built Trout Lodge.

The fire was so hot that they had to call in a water bomber from Smithers to put it out. All they saved was Allen's wallet and he risked his life running into the burning building to get it and his car keys.

They stayed for a couple of days with us and then sadly returned to their home in Napa, CA. On their drive back they noticed a big sign on a building in Quesnel, B.C. advertising pre-fabricated log cabins. They went in to make an enquiry and ended up buying one on the spot, making arrangements for the following year to have it transported to Pendelton, at the south end of Babine Lake.

From there it was put on a barge and towed up the lake to the site where their old cabin had stood. In the summer of 1964, again with the help of the Fort Babine Indians, they put it together according to the instructions and, once again, had a new home in the woods.

This time they were very careful to store the cylinders of propane gas, which were used to run their cook stove, water heater and refrigerator, a little distance from the cabin. It was the propane that had caused the fire to get so hot and spread so quickly.

Helen and Allen spent every summer in their cabin. After going home in September to take care of their grape harvest, which Allen really enjoyed, they would return to the Steelhead Camp for the last week in October for some good steelhead fishing. They were like parents to Ejnar and I and considered our children to be their grandchildren. They always referred to us as their 'Canadian family' and we loved them very much.

Cecil Brown, who Joy (Madsen) Jenkins recalls "hated the cold more than anything else" was a Trout Lodge guide in 1957 and soon became a partner, retiring in 1965. He also travelled extensively to promote the business in the USA.

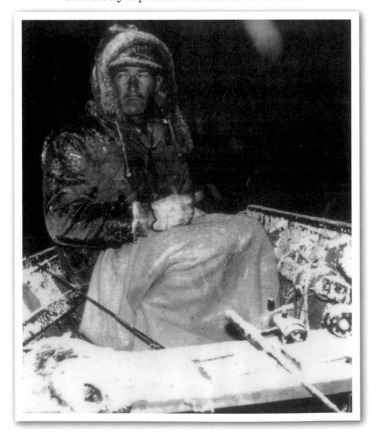

The three men operated the lodge together until 1957, when Mac decided to venture further north with the idea of opening another fishing camp on Bear Lake, northeast of Babine Lake and not far from the Sustut River. Cecil Brown was hired to guide at the lodge since Mac would not be there for that summer.

In June of that same year, in a tragic accident, Mac's boat flipped over in the rapids on the Bear River. It's thought he was struck on the head by the boat and never surfaced or was seen again. In September of that year his body was found many miles downstream. This left Betty with three young children: Jock, six years old, Janet (five), and Jamie (two). Mac was only 33 and his death was a terrible loss.

Later that summer Tom Stewart took his wife, Lucy, and their children—Jimmie (six) and Suzie (three) back to Langley so Jimmie could begin school. This was where they spent their winters.

On October 31, 1957 Ejnar and I were listening to the late-night news on an old battery-operated radio we had in our cabin, when we heard that Tom Stewart had been killed in a car accident that afternoon. We were shocked. At first we thought this could be another Tom Stewart, but once they gave his age as 37, we knew this had to be our friend and partner. Now Lucy, too, was left to raise her young children without their father, and we were suddenly left with no partners and an overwhelming sense of sadness.

The following year Cecil Brown and Ejnar became partners in the business when they bought the Norlakes Lodge shares from the two widows, Betty Anderson and Lucy Stewart. They operated together until Cecil, who we always called 'Brownie', decided to sell his shares and retire.

Brownie was a handsome bachelor who lived with his mother in the Oak Bay suburb of Victoria. He was an accomplished fly-fisherman and enjoyed teaching how to cast a fly exactly where you wanted it to land on the water. Guiding was what he did best; physical work around the camp was not his 'cup of tea.'

In the winter Brownie would travel to San Francisco to speak to various men's organizations and service clubs about Norlakes and the amazing fishing to be enjoyed on the Babine River. He stirred up business, word spread quickly among fly-fishermen, and we thrived. Brownie and I became great friends; he always called me 'half pint'.

Concerned about the lodge staff keeping costs down, Brownie tried to encourage us to eat as little as possible. His favourite food for us was baked beans, as they were cheap, but we got pretty tired of them in short order. One day Ejnar and I went into his cabin when he was out fishing and planted dry beans in all his pockets, in his underwear drawer, between his sheets and under his pillow. He never said a word about them, but never again insisted we cook beans every day.

Once he had been complaining so much about the cold seat in the outhouse, Ejnar decided to solve this problem. He took part of an old black bear hide and lined that seat with it. The next time Brownie went in, we all stood back waiting for his reaction. He walked out with a smile on his face muttering a typical Brownie response, "The bastards got me again."

In 1965 Jim Price bought Brownie's half of the business and became Ejnar's new partner. Together they got a lot accomplished. It had been hard on Ejnar shouldering most of the camp work and

now he had someone to share the load. Jim was a hard worker and enthusiastically tackled any work that had to be done. The fishermen enjoyed him very much and he was a good partner for Ejnar. His wife, Camilla, was a great companion for me while she was there.

Ejnar and I had close friends, Dorothy and Harry Beddoes, in Smithers. Harry was a builder and he agreed to help Ejnar build a full camp on the river below the counting fence. Thus began our Steelhead Camp. Harry spent a lot of time down there once Ejnar had secured a lease on the land from the government and together they built a main cooking cabin with indoor shower, bathroom, and four guest cabins. Ejnar was excited about it and Jim Price helped him put it all together. Because of its location, and the distance from the lodge on the lake, we did not attempt to install plumbing in the guest cabins at the camp for fear of frequent freeze-ups.

In the late 1960s, our cook was Olga Beck. She cooked for us for a couple of years at both the lodge and the camp. Then she was at the Steelhead Camp for two more years when I took over at the lodge. She was an unforgettable woman and all the fishermen loved her. She was six feet tall, as big as most of the fishermen, and she could cast a lure from a rock on the edge of the Camp Pool all the way across the river to the other side.

Whenever she had time between her baking and cooking in the kitchen, she would go out and cast her line. She would always have a story to tell the guests about the big steelhead she landed and was often top fisherman of the day. The guests always arrived with gifts for her; waders, a warm jacket, gloves, hats, anything they thought she could use to keep warm. Usually she would just stand at the Camp Pool in her slippers and apron and fish from 'Olga's Rock,'

She was killed in a car accident one winter and the fishermen at Norlakes mourned her death as did Ejnar and I. She could not read or write much but she knew most of the Bible by heart and was filled with a deep faith in God. She had great wisdom in getting through life and taught me many valuable lessons about living and loving.

As the years went by we made changes and improvements. The camp was a big success, and we were able to bring in more steelhead fishermen. Previously, we had to boat them down from the main lodge on the lake to the federal government's fish counting fence on the river. There they boarded another boat, with a jet unit on the motor, to take them the few miles from below the fence down river to the new camp. This made for a long, cold ride by the time October came, and Thermos flasks of coffee, spiked with an adult beverage, were an essential in every boat.

The 14-mile trip from the lodge included a seven-mile run down Nilkitkwa Lake, a shallow body of water known for the plentiful weeds that easily became caught in the propeller if the guide strayed from the proper channel.

One late October a cold spell hit and the temperature dropped to well below zero. Ejnar knew Nilkitkwa Lake would freeze over, preventing everyone from returning to the lodge on the big lake. In the morning, after the cook had made coffee and had a nice fire burning in the wood stove, Ejnar told her to put the fire out, pack up the food and get ready to leave camp.

Olga Beck was an unforgettable Steelhead Camp camp cook in the late 1960s. A good six feet tall, she would fish with great success in the Camp Pool wearing her slippers and apron.

He gave orders for all the fishermen to gather up their clothes and fishing gear and head for the boats as the camp was to be evacuated immediately. After many trips to the counting fence, the cook and the fishermen were transferred to the other boats, above the fence, and taken back to the lodge. Transportation to Smithers was arranged and they were all sent home. Nilkitkwa Lake did freeze solid that day, and some of them would not have been able to leave if Ejnar had not realized the importance of evacuating so quickly.

Not too many years after that incident the local logging company pushed a road all the way through to the counting fence. That allowed us to transport our steelhead fishermen by car and van without having to go through Nilkitkwa Lake by boat.

Our son Karl was born in 1960 and our life was enriched beyond measure. Second son Erik came along in 1962 and daughter Karen in 1966—three beautiful blonde, blue-eyed 'Scandihoovians' to complete our life as a wilderness family. As the children grew they had the privilege of learning how to live in a wild environment and to appreciate all that nature provides—the names of each flower and tree that grew around them, the many species of birds and animals that lived in the same woods, and an ability to be self-sufficient in a life apart from radio and television and the 'modern' conveniences of city or town.

The woods and the lake were their playground. They were creative in finding things that captured their imaginations and kept them busy and happy every day. As the years went by they became an integral part of the operation of Norlakes, working alongside Ejnar and I in all aspects of keeping things running smoothly—from cleaning cabins, washing dishes, doing laundry, guiding fishermen, cutting and piling firewood, and talking with and keeping our guests happy and comfortable.

It was a life in which our clients were actually guests in our home, this place where we lived and conducted our business. It was a privilege for us to have that interaction with so many fine and diverse people whose influence played a major role in developing the character of our children.

Due to the remote location of the lodge, education of the children became a challenge for the three months they missed public schooling each year. Thanks to the government of B.C., we qualified for the Home School Program offered to students living in remote areas of the Province. Each day the children would spend four hours at the kitchen table doing their assignments, which were mailed to the Home School Department of Education to be corrected.

Jim Price's wife, Camilla, was a schoolteacher and a great help in getting Karl started in the first grade. He delighted in skipping down the trail to Jim and Camilla's cabin to 'go to school'. Camilla gave Karl recess just like at real school where he enjoyed climbing trees and playing around their cabin. Although Erik was only four years old, he wanted to learn too, so Camilla worked with him in a kindergarten program. When Erik started grade one in Smithers he was quickly moved up to second grade because he was already reading well and was ahead of the first grade students.

The following year I took over their Home School Program, which proved to be very rewarding to me. It was an excellent program and each year, when they returned to the public school in Smithers, they were ahead of the rest of the class. The program gave them more depth in their studies and this made the work more interesting. When Karl and Erik reached seventh grade we boarded them with friends in Smithers because they wanted to attend the woodwork and metal shop classes that were part of the public school program. Karen also boarded in town at the same time so she could be with her brothers.

We used a Coleman iron for the pillowcases. They were about the only things we ironed because it was impossible to keep the iron from getting so hot that it burned everything else.

Erik Madsen was both a keen trout
and steelhead fisherman and a popular guide.

It operated in the same way as the Coleman lanterns. The flame could be adjusted to high or low, which took both skill and a lot of luck, and the iron had to be moved constantly to prevent it from getting too hot.

One summer Sheldon Coleman and his young wife were among our guests. He had never seen one of the irons being operated and asked me to demonstrate how it worked. I started it up and ironed a cotton pillowcase before Mrs. Coleman asked if she could try it. She rushed off to her cabin and came back with a delicate item of night attire and placed it on the ironing board. I warned her not to try anything so flimsy and offered a pillowcase instead. It was not to be. She placed the iron on her piece of clothing and it immediately melted onto the iron's base, producing a terrible smell and a mess that took much cleaning to remove. She looked at her beautiful nightgown in utter astonishment, took what was left of it and never again asked to use that wonderful Coleman family invention.

After a few years I became the full-time cook. We had a large wood stove with an oven that would hold 13 loaves of bread. I would alternate making white bread one day and whole wheat the next; I always made 12 loaves at a time. Most days I made cinnamon buns with raisins in them, and these were a big favorite with my kids and the young helpers we hired.

Another favourite among the fishermen and the hired help were the chocolate brownies, which were so sought after that I had to hide them or they would all be gone before I had a chance to put them on the buffet lunch table. No matter how well I thought I had hidden them, someone would find them, so with Karen's permission I stored them in tightly covered cookie tins under her bed, where nobody thought to look. It surprised me how tight-lipped she was about this, but she found it fun to share the secret with me, and to be able to fool even her big brothers.

Cooking on a wood stove is far different than cooking on a gas or electric stove; the more wood that you feed into it, the hotter it burns. The side of the oven nearest the firebox got much hotter then the side farthest away. It took careful planning to gauge how many pieces of wood to put in at a time, and the size of the pieces made a difference to the amount of heat it gave out out.

Whatever you put into the oven must be moved around often to prevent burning, and it became a real science to regulate the temperature at all times. With my short arms, it was quite a task to reach to the back of the oven and my hair was regularly singed from the heat as I moved the food around. The whole top made a wonderful cooking surface and again it was a delicate balance between hottest and coolest areas. Soups, stews and anything that needed slow cooking tasted wonderful when placed on the back of that huge, steel monster. I loved it like a man loves his special car and I took pride in keeping it clean.

Much time was spent splitting and carrying in the wood to keep the stove burning. It was a team effort trying to keep the box next to the stove full. When Karl and Erik were young they were in charge, but as they got older and had other tasks it fell to Karen. She used to fill up her red wagon with pieces she could handle and pulled the wagon into the kitchen, where she unloaded it into the box.

Everything was made from scratch and one of the favourites was the donut. I made both yeast and cake donuts and it

took extra wood to keep the stove hot enough for deep-frying. My little kitchen was like a sauna on those days. The aroma of the donuts filled the whole lodge and was the first thing the fishermen smelled when they returned in the boats from a long day on the river. The cookies were another favourite and I always made at least 12 dozen at a time.

Every day I got up at 4:15 a.m. and was over at the lodge at 4:30 to light the stove. It took 30 minutes to heat up enough to begin boiling water to make the coffee, which was the most important item each morning. All guests were served coffee in bed, and the wood heater was started to warm up the cabin before they got up. Gallons of coffee were consumed in a day, and the guests always said that it tasted so delicious when made on the wood stove.

Each morning I prepared large amounts of bacon in the oven and kept it hot in the warming oven above the stove. Next I made a large pot of hot cereal, popular with the fishermen and the guides. I mixed my pancake batter and had it ready for when it was needed. We used the top of the stove to make toast and it was always a difficult task to avoid burning it. A hearty breakfast was always served before the fishermen left in the boats for a day of fishing.

Ejnar would arrive each day in the kitchen at 5.45 a.m., sit on a stool next to the big stove while he drank his coffee, and we would discuss the plans for the day while I was preparing breakfast.

Apart from the full-time cooking, the heaviest work I had to do was setting up camp each year when everything had to be lifted and put in place. I remember Ejnar asking me to help him carry a water heater. It was old and very heavy and I said, "I can't lift my end." He replied: "I want you to understand something right now. There is no such word as can't."

Ejnar was a good man with amazing integrity. He never forgot anything he read or anything he was told. He was very complex, and had an incredible mind. He was a strong Scandinavian man who was often teased about his accent. He enjoyed the fishermen and had a great camaraderie with them. There was no subject he could not talk about, and he had a very dry sense of humour. The fishermen loved him and were delighted by his funny jokes.

Life at our lodge was not all work and no play. A great example of this was the joke that he played on Ted Jacobsen and his group of Mormon fishermen at the Steelhead Camp one fall. Many came down with an intestinal bug, which they suspected was from the drinking water. They diligently filled two small glass bottles with samples of the water and set them aside in order to take them home to Salt Lake City to have it tested in a lab. When they were out fishing one day, Ejnar partially emptied

the sample bottles and refilled them with fine vodka. The following year when they returned nothing was mentioned about the drinking water or the results of the lab test.

Another example of Ejnar's humour was one summer when a large group of fly-fishermen, who were known as 'The International Royal Order Of Laughing Hyenas', returned for a week's trout fishing at Norlakes Lodge. They required one cabin just for their meeting hall where they could display their club emblem, a mounted hyena's head. They were so secretive about their meetings that Ejnar decided to add a little levity to one of their sessions.

It was a typical cool evening and their wood heater was burning. Ejnar gave Jim Price a couple of firecrackers and together they climbed quietly up on the roof of the cabin and dropped them down the chimney. They quickly climbed down from the roof and hid close by to watch the action. When the firecrackers hit the stove there was a hell of a bang and the lid flew off the heater. You can almost picture 25 men trying to exit the only cabin door at the same time. Despite this near calamity, they did return several times.

Apparently Ejnar had a few firecrackers left. One morning without my knowledge while I was cooking breakfast, he dropped them into my stove. There was a terrific explosion and one of the heavy stove lids blew up and landed on the kitchen floor very close to my feet. It was so hot it started burning a hole in the floor. Ejnar did quite a dance trying to lift up the hot lid, and finally dashed out to his shop to find a tool to enable him to pick it up and put it back in place, while the flames were shooting out through the open top. I failed to see any humour in this prank, and I told him how lucky it was that it was early morning and we were still alone in the kitchen. Nevertheless, he kept a low profile around me for a few days and there were no more firecracker episodes.

Many of the fishermen delighted in playing tricks on each other. At the Steelhead Camp we had one central shower room attached to the kitchen cabin. The fishermen had to walk across an open area in order to get to the shower from their cabins. One fall afternoon, I observed a fisherman, whose only attire was a towel over his head, hurrying back to his cabin from the shower. Apparently one of his fishing buddies had slipped into the shower room and removed all his clothing leaving only one towel. At dinner that evening, all the fishermen were discussing the streaker. He turned to me and asked me if I had seen him. With a smile I replied, "Yes and I have a question for you: Why did you put the towel on your head?" He answered: "So no one would recognize me."

In our early years the Fort Babine Indians built the boats we used at the lodge. When I arrived in 1955, the Indians used only dugout canoes made from trees they cut locally. It was a silent world

as they made their way up and down the river and on the lake and they were skilled on the water. There was one large, plank-built boat with an outboard motor, built by Jimmie West for the Hudson's Bay Company Store at Fort Babine. It was known as the freight boat and was used twice a year to go down Babine Lake to Topley Landing or Pendleton Bay to pick up supplies for the store.

Ejnar asked Jimmie to build boats for the lodge. Using a chain saw, he built heavy, 26-foot-long plank boats from green wood. They were flat-bottomed and sturdy enough for the guests to stand up in and fly fish. They were chinked between the planks and then spread with hot, black tar that dried and helped to keep them from leaking too badly.

This work had to be done every year before they were put back in the water for the fishing season. Getting them in and out was a big job because of their excessive weight, so we would have one or two of the Indians walk a horse to the lodge from Fort Babine. They put a harness on the horse, attached a rope to the boat and instructed the horse to 'pull' until the boat was far enough up on the land to remain dry for the winter.

The first time I witnessed this procedure was in the fall of 1955. Ejnar was in charge and when he was ready for the horse to pull he would yell "giddie up." The horse just stood still looking straight ahead. After trying two or three times he glanced across to where Jimmie West was holding his sides laughing.

Ejnar humbly stepped aside and said: "Okay, you try." Jimmie spoke one word to the horse in his own language and the horse started walking and pulling and got that boat clear up on the beach in no time. It was apparent to all of us that if you plan to use an Indian's horse, then you better learn enough words in the Carrier language so the horse understands what you want it to do. Just swatting it on the rear end and yelling wasn't enough. Ejnar told that story about himself many times over the years and always laughed heartily as he recalled it.

After several years the Fort Babine Indians were building boats and buying used outboards, mostly from the lodge, and the beautiful dugouts quickly became a legend. Sometime in the late 1960s, Ejnar decided to try building his own boats from marine plywood. He replaced the used ones with newer ones and the Indians would buy the old ones from us. The new ones were much lighter and did not need caulking every spring, just a fresh coat of paint. He painted them red outside and green inside and that became the standard boat color for all the years we were there.

Ejnar became known for his well-built boats and completed at least one new one every winter and often two a year. To this day I know you can still find a few of them in use on Babine Lake. When he was dying he made a blueprint of the boat and asked me to give it to Phil Anderson, a close friend in Smithers, who Ejnar knew could continue to build them as he had.

We had many friends at Fort Babine. Ejnar respected the Indians and enjoyed trying to converse with them. We used to visit when time allowed and they enthusiastically made us very welcome. They would bring out their 'home brew', made from raisins and sugar purchased from the Hudson's Bay Company Store, in trade for furs. It took courage to politely sip the bubbling, sweet liquid with the raisins plumped up and floating on top. At that time it was illegal to give any liquor to a native, so the Indians were only used to their own brews and we never saw them drunk. The big change, sad to witness, happened when it became legal for them to purchase real alcohol.

Most years we had a cook down at Steelhead Camp. I stayed to look after the Trout Lodge as there were plenty of hunters about in the fall and Ejnar felt someone should always be there. I did all the laundry and much of the cooking and baking. I would drive the boat down to the weir and he would meet me. I would also pick up groceries in town once a week and take them down as well.

This meant I was living at the lodge entirely alone, without even a dog for company. The bears definitely worried me a lot and Karl taught me how to shoot a .22-calibre rifle. At first I lived upstairs in the lodge but I found it too big and too scary and moved back into my cabin. Although he knew that I was not going to kill a bear with that calibre rifle, he felt just hearing the shot would discourage any man or beast.

One summer at the lodge we had a bear in the laundry room and the door latched behind it. The guests were all at the dining room table and we could hear it banging about. We always sat in the staff room and, when I told Ejnar there was a bear in the laundry room, he did not believe me and said: "Oh such nonsense, Joy. You are always thinking you hear a bear." Then he walked out the back door, leaving it open, and threw open the door to the laundry room. This huge black bear stood up on its hind legs and roared so loudly that it scared everyone. When I saw the bear, I ran into the lodge and slammed the door behind me.

I knew Ejnar was still outside but I did not want the bear getting in where the fishermen were all eating dinner. Everyone laughed at me for years afterwards for shutting the door on Ejnar. I knew he could take care of himself and I was not at all sure what those of us inside would do if the bear charged in. That surely would have been the end of us. Happily, the bear ran the other way and Ejnar said I had done the right thing. However, he was very quiet for the rest of the evening.

A few times we had bears that came up the steps and looked in the window of our cabin. All my life I have had a very keen sense of hearing and, on one occasion, when I said to Ejnar: "Wake up, there's a bear on the porch," he told me to go back to sleep. I got up anyway, and with the flashlight in hand I looked out the window. I could see the bear with its nose pressed against the glass. I had thought it might be around the corner but there we were, nose to nose, with just one thin pane between us. I let out a shriek and the bear made a fast get-away. I think I scared him more than he scared me.

Almost all of our nuisance bears at the lodge were black. The grizzlies seemed to stay down where the salmon were in the lower river. Once we did have a grizzly around our cabin but generally they never bothered us. The biggest bears I have seen are black, although I have seen big grizzlies as well. The grizzlies were the ones that really plagued us at the Steelhead Camp.

Another story about wildlife: Randy Barto worked for us for two years, in 1970 and again in 1971, when he and I traded jobs. He came up to Trout Lodge, care-taking and harvesting the garden, and I went to Steelhead Camp. One morning he heard crashing in the woods. He knew it was rutting season and suspected it was moose. He very quickly climbed up onto the roof of his cabin and, as he watched, three bull moose, all with very large antlers, came out of the bush and walked side by side through the shallow water at the edge of the lake.

He could still hear some thrashing in the woods and thought it might be one or two cow moose that the bulls were after. He said it was an amazing sight, one he will never forget as long as he lives.

I still love to fish but for years I had no time to enjoy that. For many years at the lodge I went without picking up a rod. The year I came I was taught how to cast by some guests from San Francisco, and I was given a beautiful little Hardy St. George fly reel. One of the fishermen gave me a fly rod and I learned to fish that year with my own prized equipment. Until I had the children I tied my own flies, but I never thought they were tied well enough for me to share them. I did get better at tying wet flies and, as time went by, I shared them with other fishermen, and was delighted when they reported back to me that they had caught fish on them without the fly coming apart on the first one.

Although we had a full-time cook and housekeeper, I still did much of the baking at my cabin in the first few years. The original three partners, Ejnar, Mac and Tom, had a rule that the women could not have anything to do with the actual running of the lodge. At the time it was probably wise, and the other two women had children and had plenty to keep them busy.

Christopher (Kit) and Hazel Clegg, Pierce Clegg's father and mother, had been coming to the lodge from California for 25 years and, although I did not know it at the time, Kit had told Ejnar: "If you ever decide to sell, would you let me be the first to know." I did not find this out until the year we decided to sell. Together the kids and I had decided it was time to sell the lodge. It was never the same for any of us after Ejnar had died, and I felt 31 years was long enough for me to be there.

Ejnar died of cancer in 1983 and my oldest son Karl and I ran the lodge for another three years, with the help of Erik and Karen, before we decided it was time to leave. Before he died, Ejnar's instructions were that he be cremated and his ashes scattered in the Lower Forty Pool of the Babine River.

Not all fishermen come face to face with a Babine moose but, when they do, it's an experience not soon forgotten.

Three weeks before he passed away, Ejnar prepared a note for all his friends and guests. It was his farewell and read:

"This is my goodbye to all of you who have been our guests at the lodge for the last 30 years. It was not my plan to make this early departure but it was the way it was to be. Many thanks to every one of you for all the friendships we have built up over the years, tight lines and happy fishing in the future. God bless you."

Afterwards I sent on his words to all the people on our mailing list adding the following comments from myself, Karen, Karl and Erik:

We regret to inform our friends that Ejnar lost his battle with cancer on September 13, 1983. His passing marks the end of an era at Norlakes Lodge that will be remembered by fishermen, outdoorsmen and friends around the world for many years.

Ejnar was born in Denmark and put himself through schools in Denmark, Sweden and England before coming to Canada in 1952. His first year in Canada was spent working on a farm in Vanderhoof, B.C. and in a sawmill and the logging industry around Burns Lake. While working as a carpenter in 1953, Ejnar met Mac Anderson and Tom Stewart and the three men built Norlakes Lodge on the remote north end of Babine Lake.

In 1955 a girl named Joy came to work for a summer at the lodge. She returned in 1956, married to Ejnar, and together they raised two sons, Karl and Erik, and a daughter, Karen.

Building and operating a lodge in a remote area called for hard work and ingenuity and Ejnar loved the challenge. While honing his skills as an outdoorsman and fisherman, he also became a self-taught carpenter, plumber, electrician, mechanic and accountant. As his partners left, Norlakes Lodge evolved into a family business with all members of the Madsen family working with Ejnar to achieve his dream of creating an internationally popular fishing resort on the Babine.

Although large fighting trout were the initial reason people visited the Babine River, it was Ejnar's quiet warmth that kept them coming back. He was a man who listened more than he spoke but a crinkle at the corner of his eyes and a silent smile betrayed the humour for which he was so well known.

Many fishermen remember his brief advice and his wit has livened many streamside gatherings. Although this quiet and gentle man will no longer guide the angler to his favourite pools, his memory will continue to guide those of us who remain. We will continue to maintain Norlakes Lodge in the same fine tradition established by Ejnar during the past 30 years.

Our sincere thanks go out to all of you who wrote such wonderful letters of support during Ejnar's illness, and sympathy after his death. We wish there was time to reply to every one individually. Also, our thanks for your donations to the Cancer Fund in Ejnar's memory.

—Warmest wishes, Joy and Karen, Karl and Erik

In 1985, each week when our guests arrived, we told them that we had decided to sell the business. We preferred to tell them personally before we listed it for sale. When we told Kit and Hazel they were surprised, but once they had time to think about it they told us their desire to buy the lodge and the camp. It was wonderful for us to be able to sell to friends who had been coming for so long, and had known Ejnar as well. It made the process easier for us, and I felt that Ejnar would have approved.

It was very important to Ejnar and I that our children have the opportunity for a good education. Karl and Erik had completed two years of college and one year at the University of British Columbia (UBC) the summer that Ejnar was so ill. Karen had completed her junior year of high school in Smithers. We knew we would have to find someone to run the Steelhead Camp by the beginning of September, so we began looking for a qualified fishing guide.

Todd Stockner had been guiding for us that summer at the Trout Lodge, and planned to stay for the steelhead season. He had worked for us the previous year and Ejnar had been a real mentor to him, teaching him how to run the jet boats through that swift river, around the big rocks and through the shallow areas. He was only 19 years old, but learned quickly. By the end of the season he was comfortable with the guiding and Ejnar was very pleased with his capable performance.

However we needed another person. After discussing it, Karl and Erik decided what we would do. Although Karl had not worked at the Steelhead Camp, Erik had spent one fall there working with his dad, and Karl announced that he would miss that first semester at UBC and run it himself. He knew that he could learn to manoeuvre the jet boats up and down that lower river as well as anyone new we might hire. Erik showed him the channels and the low areas to avoid, and did all that he could help him with in advance, and then he returned to Vancouver to go back to UBC.

With Todd's expertise, and our wonderful friend and cook, Marie Darter, who had cooked for us for several seasons, running the kitchen, Karl kept the Steelhead Camp going until the season ended in November. Sadly, Ejnar died less than two weeks into the season, and though it was difficult for everyone there, the steelhead were in the river and the fishermen enjoyed some great fishing.

The fishermen and women who visited the lodge over the many years became like family to us. Many of them came every year for 20 to 25 years and some, like Bill Fife, came for 30 years, never missing a year. In 1955 we had a group of men from Walt Disney Studios. One was Milt Kahl, the chief animator. He drew pages of animations of the characters and animals in the Disney movies for me. For years I would see his name listed before each movie, and sometimes he would appear on the screen. They got some of their hunting trophies for Disneyland from the Babine Lake area.

Herbert and Lawton Flieshhacker travelled up for many years. Ejnar built a row boat for them and William Duncan, from Fort Babine, would guide them on the river. Herb taught William how to fly-fish and he was the only Indian who ever fished with flies on the Babine. San Francisco's Flieshhacker Zoo bears the family name to this day and, at one time, had a huge lion named Herbie.

Steve and Betty Bechtel also came to us for many years. They would fly up in their Lear jet to Smithers and their pilot always brought gifts for the kids and I. The most treasured gift each year was a bag of Meyer lemons. They became very special

to our family and, over the years, they brought their children with them and then their grandchildren. One year George Schultz, a member of the U.S. President's Cabinet, came with them.

We had Jesse Stienhart and his wife, for whom San Francisco's Stienhart Museum is named. Mrs Stienhart and I used to have long visits in front of the fireplace in the lodge and she offered some good suggestions to me on raising children. I was still young, and she seemed so wise and experienced, and I always remembered her advice. Willmar Smith, who was a dentist, and his wife, Solly, fished with us for 28 consecutive years and we still write letters to each other at Christmas.

One year Claude Batault, the U.S. Ambassador to France, was at Steelhead Camp. He was so tall that, when he was wading in the river, he would only be waist high in the water while the other fishermen around him were chest high. He had a great sense of humour and kept everyone in camp laughing. Ejnar enjoyed him very much.

Mr and Mrs Peavey Heffelfinger were among our guests for a couple of summers. His family invented the peavey and he was so happy when he saw Ejnar using one to roll fallen trees up the beach from where they were floating in the lake. We often beach-combed along the shore in the early summer and it saved us from having to cut down trees for firewood. The peavey was a great help for the job.

We had Richard and Charlotte Guggenhime, from San Francisco, for over 20 years and their sons, Rich and David, came many times too. They continued coming after Ejnar died but it was never the same for them.

Richard (Dick) Andersen (see pages 44-45), a doctor from the Seattle area, was among the long-time steelhead fishermen we wel-

Joe Brooks, widely read and travelled author of numerous fishing books and magazine articles, visited Trout Lodge and Steelhead Camp and helped introduce Norlakes and the Babine to an American angling readership hungry for new adventures.

comed each fall. When Ejnar was in the hospital in Vancouver, after he was diagnosed with cancer, Dick drove up to visit with us and he talked to the hospital doctors to find out if he was getting the best care available. He seemed to be satisfied that he was, especially after hearing from the doctors that they were constantly in touch with the Anderson Clinic, in Texas, for advice on his condition. Dick's visits were a great pleasure and comfort to both Ejnar and I.

Joe Brooks, the author of many books about fly-fishing, was at Steelhead Camp every year, often having his birthday there in September. The cook always baked a cake for him and the other guests were brilliant with the birthday gifts and special songs they wrote in his honour. It was usually a pretty raucous evening.

Arthur and Phyllis Oppenheimer fished with us for many years, often with Greer and Renee Sugden, Fred Greenlee and his wife, Roberta, and Lee Richardson, the fishing author. Arthur was a real perfectionist, always fixing things or changing them around. Each summer we would put him in a different cabin and when he and Phyllis left, there would inevitably be something added to or repaired. He always brought heavy, black plastic with him to cover the windows as he could not sleep when it was light for almost 20 hours a day in the summer.

One morning, when we had a whole table of anglers in a hurry to have breakfast and get out fishing, Arthur was sitting looking at my big wood stove in the kitchen. It was very hot and I was cooking several orders for bacon and eggs and trying to keep up with the requests that were coming. He suddenly jumped up from the table, rushed out to Ejnar's tool shop, came back with a crow bar and proceeded to pry up one end of my stove.

He had a little piece of wood in his hand, which he gave to me and instructed me to get down on my hands and knees and

Dr. Jack Callahan prepares bait as his final chore before it's time for bed.

Greer and Renee Sugden with a trout from Nilkitkwa Lake. They were regular Trout Lodge visitors and Renee still keeps in touch with Joy by 'phone and mail.

shove it under the corner of the hot stove he was holding up with the crow bar. While everyone looked on, I did as he instructed. Then he slowly moved the crow bar and let the stove rest back down. Then he said: "There you go, Joy. Now your stove is level."

I still keep in touch with Renee Sugden by mail and phone. We have had many laughs over those days at the lodge and the funny things Arthur did. Phyllis was always telling him what to do, or what to eat, but he just did what he wanted and never seemed to hear her.

There were many other memorable guests, among them Dr. Robert Cutter and his brother, Ted, from the Cutter Laboratory, in Berkeley, which developed the Salk polio vaccine so many years ago, and Charles and Mollie Barfield, from San Francisco.

Charlie was instrumental in sending lots of fly-fishermen to Norlakes from the famous Golden Gate Casting Club. Edmond (Eddie) Meyer was a Coca Cola distributor from San Rafael, CA and always arrived with lots of Coke for everyone. He liked to tell all of us to "buy low and sell high" and loved to entertain with stories of his past. Chuck Davis, from Warren, PA came steelheading for 25 years or more and became both a fine steelhead fisherman and a great friend to Ejnar and I.

We also had many Canadian fishermen who were regular guests over many years including Chick and Marilyn Stewart, special friends who later bought Bob Wickwire's camp downriver from ours. Victor Rempel came on an annual basis, sometimes with his son. Also 'Chunky' Woodward, of Woodward Stores and H.R. MacMillan, who was very well known in the lumber industry, and Fraser and Gladys Wright, from West Vancouver, who loved the 'dish gardens' I used to make for their cabin when they visited.

All of the fishermen who fished with us at Norlakes added special qualities to our life and we were blessed by knowing them.

I have kept up my close ties with the Babine ever since we sold Norlakes. We live there for two months each year in our own cabin overlooking Babine Lake. I have never missed a summer on the lake, and 2009 was my 55th year in succession.

Thornton, my second husband, came as a Trout Lodge guest in the summer of 1985, two years after Ejnar died. He came again in 1986, the year we were selling. I was his guide that year after Karl and Erik, in their great wisdom, said: "Get out of the kitchen and do some guiding."

It was when I was guiding Thornton that we realized how much we had in common. We were married in 1987 and have shared 21 wonderful years together in Sonoma, CA, Although very different from Ejnar, he, too, is a good and honest man, and shares my love for fly-fishing and the Babine.

—*Joy (Madsen) Jenkins, Sonoma, CA*
as told to Peter McMullan

This well-dressed group of Trout Lodge guests are typical of the fishermen who arrived each year in search of Babine rainbows and comfort in the wilderness.

Norlakes' History in Ejnar's Words

Ejnar Madsen was the driving force at Norlakes Trout Lodge and
Steelhead Camp between 1953 and 1983. Dr. Dick Andersen says,
"Ejnar came to the Babine with just an axe and a dream."

As a boy, Mac Anderson had fished the Babine in the 1930s, and in the fall of 1951 he and his wife Betty and their children came up with the idea of starting a fishing camp. In the spring of 1952 he bought the land where the Trout Lodge now stands and, with the Indians' help, built the first three cabins nearest the Lodge, also the Coe cabin. He called it 'Highlands' Cabins. He only had 15 or 20 guests that entire season, among them Wayne Coe, George Straith and Cecil Brown.

The following winter he began work on the Lodge and that was the year, 1953, Tommy Stewart and I got into the picture. Tom and I were working in Burns Lake. He knew Mac well and because he was short of both money and help, we went up to give him a hand and that fall (1953) we incorporated as Norlakes Lodge (Babine) Ltd.

The name Norlakes was a contraction of 'Northern Lakes' as it was Mac's intention to supply services to other lakes in the region. In 1956 he thought we should extend up to Bear Lake and, since Tom and I were not in accord, he did it on his own. You may recall he was drowned there in 1957, the year Tom was killed in an auto accident and Cecil (Brown) became part of the establishment.

The tent frame at the weir, that you will remember, was built to accommodate parties arriving by private plane, like Frank Fuller, Don Graham, Spike Gardiner etc. who fished the lower river during the late forties. In 1946-47 B.C. Fisheries built the counting fence making it impossible for the rainbows to move freely up and down that part of the river as they always had.

This account was provided by Ejnar in 1962 to the author, Lee Richardson, and was made
available for use in this book by the Washington State Universities Libraries, Pullman, WA.
On his death, all Richardson's extensive papers were donated to the university and are held
in the Manuscripts, Archives and Special Collections.

Lee Richardson Remembers

Lee Richardson, another prolific writer on fishing and other outdoor pursuits, got to know the Madsens well over a number of years and was once described as "a skilled, if refined, practitioner of the sporting life..."

The late Lee Richardson was a prolific and widely traveled outdoors writer and very good friend of the Madsens. He was the author of two limited-edition fly-fishing books, You Should Have Been Here Yesterday *(Touchstone Press, 1974) and* Lee Richardson's British Columbia: Tales of Fishing in British Columbia *(Champeog, 1978).*

As a young man, then attending the U.S. Naval Academy in Annapolis, he won an Olympic gold medal in 1920 as a member of the eight-oar rowing team. His extensive papers, 34 boxes occupying more than 30 feet of shelf space, were donated by his daughter, Caylee Richardson, to the Washington State Universities Libraries, Pullman, WA.

A WSU description of the Lee Richardson Papers includes the following background information: "Richardson viewed himself as a skilled, if refined, practitioner of the sporting life, a man who enjoyed the camaraderie of like-minded men, whether in elegant hotels or in the woods, lakes, streams and rivers that provided the backdrop for their hunting and fishing excursions."

The detail of his first visit to Norlakes is taken from a story outline entitled 'The Beginning 1952' and is reprinted with the permission of the Washington State Universities Library. It reappears in a greatly expanded form as Hail the Babine, Chapter V of his book, You Should Have Been Here Yesterday.

I first heard about Norlakes in the spring of 1954 when Mac Anderson and Tommy Stewart called at my office in Seattle with pictures of some enormous catches of trout and steelhead taken at a new lodge on Babine Lake. Someone had told Mac if he could "get a chap named Lee Richardson on his team" he would soon have plenty of fishermen from both Seattle and San Francisco. "He has quite a following," they said.

I was already booked for that fall, but subsequently made a date for three San Francisco friends and myself for late September 1955, our principal interest, steelhead on a fly.

In those days it was usual for fishermen arriving from the south to overnight in Vancouver, taking Canadian Pacific's early flight to Terrace, there being no facilities at Smithers to accommodate even Convairs or similar aircraft. Situated as it

is, completely hemmed in by enormous mountains, Terrace is a tricky place to land at best. Only the day before, the stewardess informed us, they had been obliged to land at Sandspit in the Queen Charlottes; Terrace and Prince Rupert, socked in. 'But today we were lucky,' says my diary.

We were met (at Terrace) by pilot Tommy Speechley flying a Widgeon bearing the insignia 'Pacific Western Airlines'. This was originally an amphibious charter service started by one of Canada's most distinguished bush pilots, Russ Baker, with headquarters in Kamloops,

Tommy made it through the pass to Norlakes despite the horrible weather, and we taxied to the float shortly after noon to be assigned one of the three original cabins next to the lodge. It had upper and lower bunks, a wood stove, but no indoor 'plumbing', which consisted of an outhouse next to the woodshed. A bucket of hot water rested on the stove and one of spring water outside the door that 'Catto's Gold Label' made palatable.

Beside our party—Bill Hudson, Fred Greenlee, Kenny White and myself—there were Turner Clack and Tommy of Spokane, who later moved to the new Honeymoon Cabin across the bridge. There were also two couples from Chicago, and at the new Coe cabin down the shore were Wayne and Harriet Coe and my old friend, Cecil Brown. A light plant served the lodge and cabins when it worked, but frequently the poker or gin rummy game ended with candlelight, using sinkers or matches in lieu of chips.

At lunch we were introduced to the staff: Jan Anderson, a sister of Mac's; Joy, a happy little brunette who waited on table (later to become Mrs. Madsen); and Helen the cook, a darn good one too. Also, Napoleon, her husband, who kept our water buckets and woodpile full and occasionally joined Bill in a game of cribbage.

Turner informed us that though the steelhead had not yet shown up (they arrived the day we left), there were plenty of trout, and ducks were beginning to arrive."

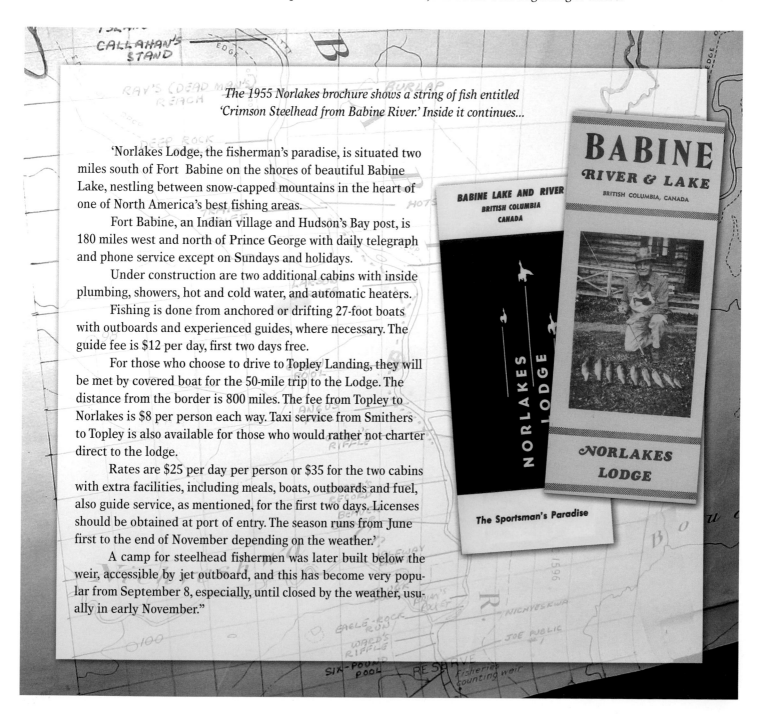

The 1955 Norlakes brochure shows a string of fish entitled 'Crimson Steelhead from Babine River.' Inside it continues...

'Norlakes Lodge, the fisherman's paradise, is situated two miles south of Fort Babine on the shores of beautiful Babine Lake, nestling between snow-capped mountains in the heart of one of North America's best fishing areas.

Fort Babine, an Indian village and Hudson's Bay post, is 180 miles west and north of Prince George with daily telegraph and phone service except on Sundays and holidays.

Under construction are two additional cabins with inside plumbing, showers, hot and cold water, and automatic heaters.

Fishing is done from anchored or drifting 27-foot boats with outboards and experienced guides, where necessary. The guide fee is $12 per day, first two days free.

For those who choose to drive to Topley Landing, they will be met by covered boat for the 50-mile trip to the Lodge. The distance from the border is 800 miles. The fee from Topley to Norlakes is $8 per person each way. Taxi service from Smithers to Topley is also available for those who would rather not charter direct to the lodge.

Rates are $25 per day per person or $35 for the two cabins with extra facilities, including meals, boats, outboards and fuel, also guide service, as mentioned, for the first two days. Licenses should be obtained at port of entry. The season runs from June first to the end of November depending on the weather.'

A camp for steelhead fishermen was later built below the weir, accessible by jet outboard, and this has become very popular from September 8, especially, until closed by the weather, usually in early November."

A Camp Cook's Tales

Steelhead fishermen always expect a hearty breakfast, being prepared here by a young camp cook, Gary Quanstrom, with an equally youthful Stacy Barto in the background.

A chance meeting at Smithers' Farmers' Market introduced me to local resident and silviculture forester Gary Quanstrom. His unique and continuing association with the Babine and Norlakes dates back to 1974 when he was hired by Joy Madsen to cook at Steelhead Camp. Then an 18-year-old high school graduate, he had inherited an interest in cooking and entertaining from his mother and had already decided that sawmill work was not in his future after a log-yard accident had left him on crutches for six weeks. He has vivid memories of those days for he has kept not only his original, hand-written diaries, recipes and photographs but also some of the notes Joy sent down to him at the camp along with the regular deliveries of groceries. Gary's diary explains how he was encouraged to apply for the Norlakes cooking job by Gordon Hetherington, co-founder of the local Hetherington and Hooper clothing store, and continues:

---

*G*ordon had a cabin near the north end of the lake and trusted me enough to lend me the keys and a boat so I could cross the lake to be interviewed at the lodge by Joy. She took the chance and offered me the job subject to three weeks of training, learning special recipes and being tested by her.

I worked at the Steelhead Camp between September 11 and October 26, 1974, 14-hour days starting at 5.30 a.m. with a cold shower. Then I lit the lamps and got the stove going with coffee ready by 6:00 a.m. Breakfast was bacon, sausages, porridge, eggs, toast, pancakes, juice, coffee, tea, hot chocolate and even fish for those that wanted and had caught some.

Clean-up came next and then baking for lunches and dinners and preparing the desserts, soups, meats, vegetables and salads. Between 3:00 p.m. and 5:00 p.m. was my time for some exercise—50 push-ups and 50 sit-ups—and a nap. Supper followed with ringing the big dinner bell at 7:00 p.m. and I would be in bed by 10:00 p.m. after tidying up again and preparing the lunch table.

Dinners were simple with basic, home-style cooking but they were hot and hearty. The highlights, that folks seemed to really enjoy, included Joy's stew and fresh buns, which was the Welcoming Dinner, cornbread, fish chowder—made from stock that included heads, eyeballs and all—and the weekly baked steelhead.

At night the guests were expected to make up their own lunches for the next day. One fellow mistook a large bowl of very hot, home-made mustard for peanut butter. His buddy watched him prepare the sandwich without saying a thing but later made sure he was nearby when his friend took the first bite.

Near the end of September, all my sleeping dreams were about camp and I was feeling pretty tired so I asked Ejnar for three days off. He would not take me into town for fear I'd never return, so he brought me up the lake to Trout Lodge, which was not being used at that time of the year. As he was about to leave he mentioned that, if I was taking time off, he expected the garden, or at least the carrots, to be harvested, cleaned and stored in sacks upon his return.

Chris Barto, from Seattle, was the fishing guide that year at Steelhead Camp and his brother, Stacy, was the bull cook, responsible for cleaning cabins, splitting firewood, pumping

water and other general duties. As we were the closest in age, and spent the most time in camp, we became friends. In the afternoons, Stacy would fish the pool directly in front of the camp. When he hooked a good steelhead he'd holler and I'd run out and play it.

It seems to me that most of the guests were business people from the US and there were also some from Canada and Germany. They included doctors, lawyers, a Supreme Court judge, writers, dam builders, football players and fishing rod manufacturers. All had a passion for fishing and getting away, relaxing and having fun.

One night the son of US President Gerald Ford's doctor was joking around with his buddy and I was listening in while trying to count strips of bacon for the next morning's breakfast. I was laughing so hard I had to recount the bacon five times and finally ended up sitting on the floor with tears streaming down my face.

Ejnar usually did not allow alcohol in the dining room. However, on Columbus Day (October 13) a guest brought in a supply of Champagne. One particularly large man was sitting on a bench and I could not reach round him to fill his glass. While wearing my white dress shirt for the special occasion, I was trying to catch a drip with a white towel draped over my arm. I was distracted and managed to continue pouring—right down the back of his pants. He jumped up and screamed as half a glass of ice-cold bubbly ran into his underwear. Luckily, everyone involved, including Ejnar, was in wonderful spirits and laughed it off.

My most memorable visitor was Helen Phillips. She and her husband, Allen, were long-time guests of the Madsens and owned vineyards in California's Napa Valley. I can't guess how old she was when I met her—perhaps around 70—but she left strong and fond memories with me, often coming to the sink to help me. Her dish washing was certainly appreciated but that was not as important as her support, encouragement and friendship.

The only other female I saw on the river that fall was Cynthia Wickwire. She was about seven at the time and was floating past in a boat on her way to her parents' lodge further downstream.

I slept on a plywood bed in the pantry, off the kitchen, while Ejnar slept in the attic of the cookhouse. He had a portable, battery-powered tape recorder that he played when he went to bed. He used to keep kept the volume so low that I had to stand on big cans of peaches and really stretch my ears if I wanted to hear any music at all.

On my last day, Chris Barto took me up the river with two boatloads of guests and let us off at the bridge below the weir. A taxi van had been ordered to bring everyone to Smithers. Instead they sent a car so I ended up being left behind. Chris said he would check back before dinner but, after waiting for about five hours, thinking all the time about the grizzlies, I finally caught a ride back to town with a logger.

My experiences at that time, meeting so many interesting people, in particular Mrs. Phillips and Stacy Barto, all helped me to decide what I really wanted to do with my life. The following year I embarked on the educational path that led me towards my current career as a silviculture forester.

—*Gary Quanstrom, Smithers, B.C.*
as told to Peter McMullan

Trout Lodge Recipes

Home cooking is a Norlakes' tradition and Joy (Madsen) Jenkins provided these examples of her recipes from her many years in the kitchen at Trout Lodge.

Bannock

Blend:	1 tsp soft shortening or butter
	1/4 cup sugar
Combine:	1 tsp baking soda, one cup raisins
	4 cups white flour
	1 tsp baking powder
	1/4 tsp salt, two tsp caraway seeds

Add dry ingredients to above. Then add 2 1/2 cups of buttermilk. Beat with wooden spoon. Pour into heavy iron skillet, 9" or so, that has been well greased and floured. Bake @350° F about 1 1/4 hours. Turn out while hot and cool on rack or clean towel for 30 min. or more.

Rhubarb Crisp

3 1/2 cups diced rhubarb
pinch of salt
1 1/2 cups sugar
1 egg—well beaten
2 tbsp flour
1/3 cup brown sugar
1/4 tsp mace (I use grated orange rind)
2/3 cup flour
1/4 cup butter

Combine sugar, flour, mace and salt. Add egg—mix with rhubarb. Place in greased baking dish. Combine br. sugar, flour and butter until crumbly and spread on top. Bake @350° F—45 min.

Trout Lodge Recipes

Wacky Cake (chocolate)

Sift into bowl
- 1 1/2 cup flour
- 1 cup sugar
- 1 tsp baking powder
- 1 tsp baking soda
- 1/2 tsp salt
- 3 tsp cocoa

Make three "wells" and add
- 1 tsp vanilla
- 1 tbsp vinegar
- 1/3 tbsp melted butter

Pour 1 cup warm coffee or water over all and blend. Pour in 8"x 8" inch pan—bake @ 350° F for 30 min. Ice as desired.

Bread Pudding

Put: 5 cups torn bread in pan
Add:
- 2/3 cup sugar
- 1 cup raisins
- sprinkle of nutmeg

Beat:
- 3 eggs and to them add
- 4 cups milk. Pour over bread

Bake @ 350° F for about one hour. Serve with a lemon or vanilla sauce (hot).

Delicious Butter Tarts

- 1 cup currants
- 4 tbsp or more butter
- 2 eggs
- 2 cups brown sugar
- few tsp rum flavoring
- chopped nuts

Soak currants in boiling water for a few minutes until they are plump. Beat butter until creamy, add eggs and brown sugar and beat until foamy. Add rum flavoring, chopped nuts and currants. Pour into uncooked tart shells (use a rich pastry rolled thin). Bake at 375° F for 15-20 min., or until brown. Cool slightly before removing gently to a wire rack.

Notes from Joy

Extracts from Joy (Madsen) Jenkins' hand-written notes to 18-year-old camp cook Gary Quanstrom emphasize her attention to detail, as essential today as it was then to the smooth running of a wilderness fishing camp:

Hope everything is going all right for you. Anything you want to know send me up a note with Ejnar. I'll try and keep you well stocked with cakes and loaves for your lunch table—use the store cookies..... Be sure not to heat the stew too fast and don't boil it—just be sure it's good and hot..... There's one bag of Saskatoon berry muffins for the lunch table on Sunday morning. Put them on instead of cake..... Try and save yourself time and effort by taking short cuts in your cooking. Don't dirty so many dishes and pots and pans... When you use the canned apples in a pie remember they are not sweetened so be sure to add sugar.

Strom's Letters from Ejnar

Clarence 'Strom' Stromsness was a truly famous Babine steelhead fisherman, recognized as such by Ejnar who named Strom's Pool in his honour. He came to the river season after season between 1967 and 1993.

*N*ot long before Clarence Stromsness, known to all in the fishing fraternity as Strom, succumbed to cancer in 1994 he was invited to spend the first week of September at Steelhead Camp as the Clegg family's special guest. At the time Pierce wrote: "I certainly wish this invitation was under better circumstances. I know you love the river as I do, and what better place to spend one's last days than on the Babine."

While the invitation had to be declined, it was a fitting tribute to a distinguished angler who had come to know and cherish the river as few others over the course of 27 years and 22 visits and many, many Babine steelhead dating back to 1967. Strom's Pool has honoured his name for years and, as Pierce told him in his letter: "It has become one of my favorite upstream runs. I don't know that many clients from the '60s who have had runs and pools named after them therefore I will always think of you when I cast a line into Strom's Pool."

Pierce's letter is one of a number kept by Strom's son Chris, then 25 and his fishing partner on that very first trip, a dedicated steelheader and an eighth-time Babine visitor in 2009. The majority of the letters are from Ejnar Madsen and these extracts help to flesh out the story of the Norlakes' Steelhead Camp, or River Camp, as it was originally known, almost from its earliest days.

There is also one of Strom's own letters, dated *October 13, 1986*, to Chris, his wife Sharon and their sons Rune and Bjorn. It describes his eighteenth Norlakes trip, one during which he landed 22 of 39 steelhead hooked. "No big fish this year. I had one buck that may have gone 20 pounds. He was 39 inches long."

Strom, in his time a district attorney and, for 12 years, mayor of Tehama, CA, continues: "Because of various cancellations there were just nine in camp and really only seven as the other two were a professional guide and a photographer

making a movie of the fishing. That meant considerable leeway to move around.

"Unfortunately it rained hard on Sunday and Monday so the river below the Nilkitkwa was out. Fortunately, because of the small number of fishermen, we had room upstream at Angus, Gravel Bar, Olson's, Strom's, Hansen's Corner or Halfway. Even fished Six Pound Pool a couple of days. Caught fish every day ending up 22/39." Every fisherman knows the numbers equate to landing 22 of the 39 fish he encountered over a seven-day period—superb statistics by any measure, anywhere.

"The greatest day was Thursday. I was alone at Strom's until about 11:00 a.m. During that time I hooked nine fish and landed six. Caught one more at the Gravel Bar so I had seven fish on the bank that day, mostly females. All in all, aside from the rain, it was a fabulous trip. The first day it was about 50° F early in the morning and 60° F during mid-day. That went down during the week and the last morning it was 28° F."

Fishing was in Strom's blood from an early age. Kristian, his father, owned a fishing boat, trolling for chinook salmon off the mouth of the Columbia River in the summer and crabbing in the winter. He lost his life when his boat went down crossing Willapa Bar in 1931.

Chris, from Dunsmuir, CA continues: "Dad grew up around water and boats and fish. So he just naturally helped with the boats and fuel and fish in 1967. That's why Ejnar invited him up to help and fish with no money involved for so many years. Later, he went as a regular guest for a few years before driving a camper up and staying near the weir, fishing the upper river and usually being invited down for dinner at the camp."

Years later, reflecting on his working relationship with Ejnar, Strom wrote: "I offered to help out for three or four weeks a year if they would let me fish half a day or so. Thus it developed that, for a number of years, I was a bull cook. Make beds, cut wood, make sandwiches, or do anything useful. Also, fish half a day or so unless detailed to go up to the landing for gasoline. That (camp) economy moves on fuel and it is all either brought in by boat, or carried in, depending on the location. Any way, I loved it."

Prior to his first Babine experience, in late September of 1967, Ejnar advised Strom: "We have about 12 miles of beautiful river to fish, most of which is only accessible by jet boats.

We have two of these and also two cabins on the lower part of the river where we often spend the night when fishing there. There are fine stretches of fly water and good pools for spin and bait fishing. The boats are mostly used for transportation on the river and waders or hip boots are necessary for fishing.

"The fish are strong and good tackle is needed. In 1966 the largest one taken was 29 pounds and there were about a dozen over 25 pounds. Most of them are eight to 14 pounds, very few smaller ones."

Of that first visit Chris still remembers meeting Joe Brooks, the renowned outdoors writer, and also watching his father cooking steaks over an open flame that roared out of the hole in a wood stove on their one night at the River Camp. "The next year dad brought a Hibachi and showed the camp how to barbecue a steak."

The 1967 trip was a success and Strom, then living in Corning, CA brought home a trophy steelhead. In December of that same year Ejnar wrote: "The fishing continued good and the weather was fairly mild into November. The last guests left on November 6 and Jim (his partner, Jim Price) and I spent most of that month cutting firewood and getting ready for next year.

"There were a number of fish taken over 25 pounds—one of them 28 pounds. We covered a lot of water and, after the river cleared, did most of our fishing as far as seven miles below the cabins. There are many good pools and also fly water there that can be waded but the Cabin Pool (*later renamed Ejnar's Pool in his memory*) is still number one.

"I wish to thank you for your generous offer of cooking at the cabins for us next October—we certainly appreciate it. For the last two years we have been working toward expanding the facilities down there so we can sleep eight or 10 and not have to go back to the lodge at all—at least not (until) the latter part of October. This would call for larger kitchen facilities and also for a full-time cook for about two months. In any event, I will write you later this winter (about) how things progress and perhaps we can work something out where you can also get in some fishing."

Thereafter a close friendship developed between the two Scandinavians, Ejnar from Denmark and Strom, whose Norwegian-born parents met in South Bend, WA after emigrating separately in the early 1900s.

Chris again: "My grandfather's name was Kristian Johan Martin Mikklesen. As was not uncommon in those days, he took the name of Stromsness, his tiny village, when he left Norway around 1905. His boathouse remains there to this day."

In a letter dated *March 21, 1968* Ejnar told Strom: "We recently got a lease on the land on the river where our cabins are. We now feel secure in building more cabins so we can sleep eight guests down there and have a cook from early in September 'til the beginning of November. We don't have one yet and I don't know whether you would want to tackle it.

"If you feel you would like to come up, we have three busy weeks, from September 21 to October 13, when we could use an extra hand and would be glad to have your help. It wouldn't likely be as a cook, but helping us on the river in a general way and perhaps running a boat for us now and again. I am sure it is something that you would feel at home at, and it would also give you an opportunity to do some fishing yourself."

The offer was obviously to Strom's liking for, on *September 6, 1968* Ejnar remarked: "We look forward to seeing you again and I hope you will enjoy your weeks here. We finished a new cabin on the river for cooking and eating and have a woman cook arriving later this week. If you would help Jim and I with the daily chores and perhaps run a boat now and again, I am sure you will get a

good deal of fishing in and, at the same time, help us out greatly to make the wheels turn.

"The week September 21 to 28 is very busy and will probably appear a bit confusing to you, but after that it will be smooth sailing. Please bring warm clothes and rain gear. The woman at the lodge will, of course, take care of your laundry. There are a good number of steelhead in the river and we have taken several, but are still fishing dry flies for trout as well."

The arrangement obviously worked well for all concerned with Ejnar thanking Strom warmly in a letter dated *November 5, 1968*. "Your assistance to us was of great help and I hope that the chores left you enough time for fishing. We have not made any definite plans for next fall but I am sure that a similar arrangement will be fine with us.

"We have only four guests this week and they will be leaving on November 8. The weather and fishing are still great. Last week there were 13 steelhead over 20 pounds landed. Olga Beck (the camp cook at that time) is still fishing from her porch and has taken several steelhead. In fact, I believe she can out cast and out fish some of our guests."

Olga, who retired in 1971, was credited by writer Ed Zern, in an April 1973 *Field & Stream* feature, with catching some 70 steelhead from the Cabin Pool in the four years she worked for Ejnar with all but four of them released. What became known as Olga's Rock was her favorite fishing stance.

Ejnar continues: "The week after you left one of our guests dropped dead on the riverbank. He was 74 and the cause was judged to be a coronary or massive heart attack. We knew him quite well, as he had been coming for about 10 years, and everyone thought it was a wonderful way to pass away. Aside from that, our only excitement has been the fishing and it has been sufficient."

On *March 14, 1969* Ejnar wrote: "We have enjoyed sunny and mild weather the last three weeks. I had half a moose hanging in the carport since December 10. It was completely frozen until a few days ago when I finally skinned it out and cut it up for the freezer. I was at the lodge earlier this week, shoveling snow off the roofs, and everything looked fine. There were many tracks of moose and wolves around the place and one morning I counted four wolves on the ice in the bay to the south. They are hard on game in the winter but seldom bother people."

Jim Price, Ejnar's partner at that time, describes himself as 'the world's worst letter writer' in correspondence with Strom dated *January 14, 1970* and goes on to say that he was able to stay at the lodge until mid-December as the weather was 'so mild'.

"Ejnar was with me for part of the time. Because of the mild weather we were able to put new foundations under the main lodge. Big job, we were very lucky to get it done. We also finished the wood, cleared all those willows and alders from the little creek by the lodge, put new foundations under Cabin 1, and tore all the old porch off my cabin and put new foundations under that as well. The weather really gave us a jump on things for next year."

That June, Ejnar had told Strom that he had not been able to purchase plastic propellers similar to the ones he had brought up the previous fall for use with the 15hp and 20hp Johnson outboards. "Perhaps I could prevail on you to mail one or two to Jim and I and we will square with you later."

Strom was back again in the fall of 1970 with Ejnar advising him in early September to bring "plenty of Oki Drifters" as a new regulation banning fishing with roe as bait was now in force. In August he had told Strom: "We have just finished the other cabin at the River Camp and built another cabin 15 miles

further down the river so we have more elbow room. Joy and the children will be at the lodge until November, the boys taking school lessons by correspondence."

A week after season's end, on *November 16, 1970*, Ejnar explained that he and Jim Price were still at the lodge, taking care of a few moose hunters and doing a little fishing.

"I went down to close up the lower cabin a few days ago and caught a nice steelhead right in front. The cabin was not used for the last two-three weeks as we pretty well had the river to ourselves because of (Bob) Wickwire not having any guests.

"Fishing was good, even without the roe, and there was one 33 1/2 pound fish taken and several in the 25 to 30-pound class. We only caught about 10 tagged fish—mostly small ones—and it will be interesting to see what (they) get out of the figures we faithfully collected.

"Joy and the children were at the lodge until a couple of days ago and the boys are starting school today. It all worked out well and I don't think they have missed out on anything of importance.

"Olga left on November 8 and was glad to see the end of the season. She was in good spirits all fall and I hope that she will come back again next year. I also hope that we will see you again. We will likely do some more improvements and fishing downstream."

Strom came back to the Babine each year between 1967 and 1993 missing only five seasons. In that time Chris says his dad's catch records show he landed more than 400 steelhead with a high of 63 ('68) and 62 ('71) and lows of two ('79), when he also suffered an aneurism, four ('81) and five ('82).

Of the 1979 heart incident, Chris recalls: "Dad would almost certainly have died in Smithers except that Joy Madsen, by sheer force of her personality, convinced the Vancouver airport to allow a mercy flight plane to land despite an air-traffic controller strike there."

This event prompted Strom to move his law office from Corning to his home in Tehama, CA, on the Sacramento River. Later he moved house again with Barbara, Chris' stepmother, to Kingston, WA.

Through the years Ejnar maintained his side of the correspondence with Strom by way of a succession of reports and comments, nearly all of them neatly typed by Joy. Success on the river always took pride of place along with news of the family and day-to-day events on the water.

December 27, 1971: "The fishing continued good with many fish in the river. There were some cold days at the end of October and about the 5th of November when it was uncomfortable to be on the river and the steelhead took poorly. There were a number of large ones caught, up to 26 pounds, but none larger. As usual, we had good fly-fishing above the weir in October.

"From the time you left, Bob Wickwire only had three guests for a few days and then closed his camp so we had the river to ourselves and didn't fish downriver very far. Unfortunately the cold weather early in November forced us to close the River Camp a few days early. It went down to zero a couple of nights and the lower end of Nilkitkwa Lake froze so we had to use the logging road and truck to get out with the last guests."

At that time Strom was considering buying Jim Price's shares in the business and Ejnar commented: "If you are serious about it, please write to me soon so we can try to work something out...I want to emphasize that there is a lot of work involved in keeping the place running but apart from that it is a good life."

He closed this letter by saying that Joy and the children were fine adding: "The boys were actually ahead on most of their work in school so they have had an easy time since they went back."

December 29, 1971: "The week after you left we had a group of four from Seattle who caught 84 steelhead. They only kept four, two 25-pounders, one 24 pounds and a small one for dinner. The two 25-pounders were caught by one person and he wanted them both mounted for his twin sons, which his wife had last year when he was up here fishing and, incidentally, was skunked. The first weeks after you left were very good with over 30 steelhead landed per day on several occasions and probably 175 fish landed per week.

"I expect to go to Vancouver early in January to see Jim and find out about his plans and desires. If you have any ideas please write or give me a 'phone call."

March 30, 1972: "The Forestry is making some headway with the bridge by Six Pound Pool. Whether it will be finished by this year is another question and there is not much on the other side to go across for. The big sawmill at Houston, which cut timber up there, finally went broke after losing $60 million and the pieces have been picked up by another company.

"Jim has still not found a buyer at his price. I know of a couple who are interested but at a more reasonable figure."

September 9, 1972: "The weather is still fairly warm and dry and we are fishing mostly for trout. Both salmon and steelhead seem to be late. The salmon run is big but there are not enough steelhead to make fishing for them very interesting. We have six jet motors running and I hope we won't have as much trouble this year as last."

November 13, 1973: "The fishing continued good and I reckon that the fellows in the week following you landed at least 150 fish and probably close to 200. One of them landed 45 and another 30. The Log Jam was one of the hot spots. In three days it came up with 28 fish and seven consecutive ones were over 20 pounds. But none of them was kept.

"The weather continued mild and we had hardly a night's frost and no snow at all before November. Since then it has been plenty cold and all the small lakes and much of Babine Lake have frozen over (in) the last few days.

"I hope to have time to make some general improvements to the River Camp cabins next spring. I am afraid the rates for steelhead fishing will have to be raised to keep step with the costs but I don't know yet by how much."

September 27, 1974: "It is a late fall up here and fishing has been the slowest I have ever seen it up until now. We are only hooking five to 10 steelhead a day and not landing all of them either. Weather is beautiful and sunny and the river is perfect, just not many fish in it yet.

"We moved one of the front cabins back in line with the duplex and put a ceiling and oil heat in it as well as insulation. It

The two spacious, sprawling pools known as Upper and Lower Trail, seen here from an upstream vantage point across from Jean's Island, are among the most popular and productive locations on the upper river. In September, 1988 the B.C. government cancelled plans for a controversial bridge that would have crossed the river at Lower Trail, destroying for ever its precious wilderness character.

was a good improvement and the other cabin will be moved back next year.

"Chris Barto and his younger brother Stacy are helping this fall and we have a young man (Gary Quanstrom, see pages 34-35) cooking for a change. It is hard to find anyone to do the job these days."

November 13, 1974: "Sorry to learn from your letter that you didn't become judge—better luck next time, Strom. Fishing was slow right into October but the last half of that month was very good. The total number of steelhead landed came to slightly over 550 with only 72 killed, both figures a little below normal.

"The camp was busy and I am glad that Chris was here again as well as his younger brother. There was a record run of cohoe (cct), which helped the fishing, and we made some very successful trips up to Smokehouse Island fishing for them."

August 2, 1975: "Regulations are pending which will require all non-resident steelheaders to be with a registered guide but it likely won't be the rule this year. Karl and Erik have been doing much of the guiding (for trout) this summer and are getting good at catching fish themselves."

Next from Chris' file comes a hand-written note dated *November 18, 1977* in which Ejnar comments: "The last steelheader left on November 7, the last moose hunter on November 12 and I left on November 15. It was a good season and a long one. Our guests landed a total of 750 steelhead but only killed 41."

A letter dated *November 11, 1980* strikes a high note with Ejnar reporting: "Steelhead fishing was the best and most consistent since the '60s and we landed over 1000—one thousand—with fewer guests than last fall."

It begins: "First off I want to tell you that we had no heart attacks but there were about half a dozen cases of the trots which can be serious when you happen to have a top bunk. We had a very good cook, Marie, who is somewhat like Olga in that she has a very good disposition and likes to catch steelhead—not just fish."

Ejnar adds that many of his guests had been asking about Strom. "I said that you would be back next year but, please note, I don't want you to come unless you are absolutely sure you can take it.

"We opened the camp on September 6 and the fish were there in numbers and never left us, even for a day. One guest landed 26 on flies the first week and I think almost everyone caught more fish than any other year. Nobody got skunked. One odd thing was that fishing by the bridge was poor and very few people fished there. Neither were there many large fish over 20 pounds but there were certainly enough small fry, 10 to 16 pounds, to compensate for this. Fishing on most other rivers around here was good and attributed mainly to the early closure of the (commercial) salmon fishing because of small runs."

While the ultimately successful battle to stop the proposed bridge continued, the approach road was driven through the forest all the way to the river's edge at Lower Trail.

Such dramatic numbers speak clearly to the reputation of what, despite many pressing challenges, remains one of the world's greatest steelhead rivers, albeit one where present day catches can never be expected to match those of the 'sixties and 'seventies. Those were the glory days. What's gone is gone but the memories remain, wonderful reminders of what still is, by any standards, a truly exceptional fishery.

Strom and his friends continued to come to Steelhead Camp each year until 1988 when he decided to make his own arrangements, camping and fishing on the Babine, the Buckley and the Kispiox. Of the Babine he wrote to Chris: "Walking is very possible to the Halfway Hole (Drift), Hansen's Corner and even to the Nilkitkwa (Gravel) Bar as well as to Strom's. I feel honoured to have a pool named for me, incidentally."

He also expressed his concerns at that time over the possibility of a new bridge being built to cross the river near Trail Drift, a famous and lengthy stretch of water now better known as Upper and Lower Trail. This logging-related proposal was fought to the bitter end by Pierce and others and was eventually cancelled by the provincial government. (See related stories pages 69-75)

Strom commented in the very detailed diary he kept of his October, 1987 trip: "They have cleared the road area, about 100 yards wide, and have pushed the road bed right to the river's edge. It is ugly. Pierce thinks he can stop it, on the basis of what is best for the economy, tourism vs. timber, but we think he is fighting a lost cause.

If the road goes in I think there will be a lot of people (drifting) down from the weir to the new bridge, assuming there is a new bridge, fishing the good spots on the way down. In that wilderness I doubt the ban on fishing from boats will be observed for long. How would the catch and release program be observed? There are a lot of places where a bright steelhead could be consumed over a campfire without being seen. Enhancement would be an almost impossible task and I can even imagine there would be those who would use roe."

In his final report, dated *October 12, 1993*, Strom advised Chris: "I have come to the reluctant conclusion that I have fished my last time on the Bulkley or Babine. There is a lack of interest, hard as that might be to believe, and a great lack of physical ability. I find that moving about on the slippery rocks in the river is getting to be a real effort, even with a staff."

Then he suggested a possible summer trip with his own boat and motor to fly fish the upper Babine River. "That is fun, not physically exhausting, and holds much promise," he wrote. Sadly, Strom died the following June.

Hopefully Anna Babine Stromsness, Strom's great granddaughter, Chris and Sharon's granddaughter and daughter of Bjorn, who fished there in 2004, and Elizabeth, will some day be the fourth generation of Strom's family to know and appreciate this special river.

During the Cleggs' early years, Strom was one of the true Norlakes old guard, one who Pierce felt lucky to have met and from whom he learned much about the river commenting, "My father made a trip to Norlakes in 1965 and Strom was looking after the Beaver Flats cabin, cooking and guiding the guests. He saw me as a greenhorn, changing things and raising prices, but he loved the river and the Norlakes traditions, which I was striving to maintain.

When he died Joy (Madsen) Jenkins and I placed his ashes in the pool that bears his name. Now his son is carrying the family tradition on the river but as a fly-fisherman whereas his father was a great gear angler."

—compiled by Peter McMullan
with lots of help from Chris Stromsness

Dick Andersen Bridges Madsen, Clegg Eras

Dick Andersen, a retired doctor from Bellevue, WA has most certainly earned all the respect due to a truly veteran Babine steelheader, more especially one who had many, many opportunities to fish with both Ejnar Madsen and Pierce Clegg over a span of almost 30 years.

Dick Andersen (left), and his friend Max Wilson were among the guests who enjoyed outstanding fishing with the Madsens.

*D*ick, now in his late seventies, went to the Babine for the first time in 1963 with his close friend, Dr. Jack Callahan, after whom the famous Callahan's Pool is named. "We went back and fished there every year over the same first week in October until 1991. My daughter was married in 1992 and in 1994 I had a very serious car accident that came close to costing me my life.

I have never been back and, while I would truly love to go there again, I think that health and visual problems would hinder that. However, the memories are great and they will have to sustain me." Prior to his first visit to Norlakes, Dick recalls going to Seattle Tackle to buy a "nice" steelhead rod and a Pflueger Supreme reel and line.

"We also got double hooks tied with an egg loop and different colours of yarn as well as everything else we needed. The hooks were rolled up in sets of a dozen or so. " In those days bait, either preserved salmon or steelhead roe, was widely used as were spoons and it was not until much later that catch and release, fly-fishing for steelhead, with both dry and wet patterns, won the widespread acceptance it enjoys today.

To reach Smithers in time for the still traditional early Sunday pick-up meant leaving Seattle on Thursday for what was always an interesting and sometimes challenging drive north.

"The roads were fine to Quesnel but from there on they were mostly one way with turn-outs and lots of gravel and rocks. There was not much traffic and the bridges were either Bailey or one way with planks that could be frosty first thing in the morning.

It was about a three-hour drive to Smithers Landing and the Tukii Lodge dock where Ejnar would meet us with this big red boat with a cabin on it. The guests from the week before us would get off and the first time I went there I met an older guy, Joe Brooks, a very famous writer and a very competent and capable fly fisherman.

He had more gear than I would have expected to see with 10 fishermen, about 30 rods he was testing in their cases along with boxes of flies and reels and lines—more reels than Pierce could have used in many years. I helped him to move his stuff to his vehicle and he gave me $5 and said 'thank you very much, son. I appreciate that and hope you have a good time down there guiding.' I said I'm not a guide, I'm a guest and gave the $5 back.

We would stay at Trout Lodge where there were three or four cabins. Each would take four fishermen and they had indoor plumbing and were beautiful. I remember most vividly the Hudson's Bay blankets on the beds. Getting in under them was like climbing into the most comfortable, soothing place you could imagine.

One night I woke up and there was a rat on the blankets between myself and the wall. I was able to crush it and threw it at Jack Callahan and he tossed it out the window."

The daily routine for the Norlakes fishermen—hot breakfast and then pack lunch boxes and flasks—has changed little over the years although, in those distant times, they would often both get up and return in the dark after a long, chilled two-way boat trip from the lodge to the weir and the river by way of Babine Lake, Rainbow Alley and Nilkitkwa Lake.

"Each morning the generator would start, the lights would go on and Ejnar , who I always said came to the Babine with just an axe and a dream, would come into the cabin with a little wooden tray with a curved handle made from a branch with pots of tea and coffee and also a bucket of river water to heat up on the stove. Really, nothing changes but why change a good thing?"

From the weir the guests would be taken downstream in a second boat as far as Six Pound Pool where the only logging road bridge was built some years later—in the early 1970s. "We would fish there until we got too cold and then we would walk for 15 or 20 minutes down the

trail to Half Way Pool and a fire pit. We used to call that Middle River."

Jack Callahan was responsible for keeping count of the often double figures daily catch and noted each fish hooked on a piece of cardboard "the sort you find inside a new shirt". He would list them under three headings 'caught', 'beached' and 'blown' and Dick remembers the fishing as being "excellent from top to bottom."

He says the fee for the week at the lodge was in the region of $600 to $700 while a steelhead licence cost around $10 or $12. The punch card was free and a limit of three fish a day and three days' catch in possession allowed each guest to take home nine steelhead. "I like my fish and in those early days there were so many darned steelhead no one thought about it. Ecology really wasn't a word we used or worried about.

Later we realized we had to stop killing all these fish if there were to be any left for our kids and our grandkids and we had decided to do a lot of catch and release, even before Pierce came along. He probably has an ecology gene in his chromosomes and definitely does not like killing fish. He's the man and he kind of grows on you like a fungus. He's gone ultra-conservative and stopped them building bridges and roads which is a fine, fine thing for anyone to do."

Speaking about the long ago rivalry between Ejnar's camp and the one owned by Bob Wickwire, another Babine legend, Dick said: "It was some times like a war. You would get to the river in the cold and the dark and light a fire and sit there freezing watching Wickwire's boat go past. Eventually peace was agreed between them with Log Jam Pool the boundary until noon and that worked reasonably well."

Bob Wickwire, 'Babine Bob', came to the Babine from Oregon in 1961 and, with a friend, bought Last Resort 30 miles up Babine Lake. It proved to be too far from the river so he and his wife, Jerrie Lou, purchased a partially completed camp known as Babine River Resort at the outlet from Nilkitkwa Lake, close to the site of the former sockeye smolt counting trap and close to the start of the river.

Later in the '60s they built Babine Steelhead Lodge, down river from the Norlakes Steelhead Camp, and finally, in 1984, this remarkable family established Silver Hilton Steelhead Lodge, from which they retired in 1998.

Dick still remembers seeing Bob and his guests heading downstream with guests and oil drums and commented: " We really had no reason to go that far for there were fish everywhere. We had it all worked out, like the tides. I liked to start at Corner and to be at Callahan's between 2.0 and 3.0 p.m. and then finish up at Angus before dark."

In 1964 or 1965 Dick was one of the first guests to stay at Steelhead Camp, then "just a cabin with a stove, a table and three or four bunks. For the first few years we would still be at the lodge and a couple of us would go down to the camp with Ejnar or Jim Price.

I remember we used to have what I call a five prop week for there was a rock just above the weir that Ejnar would seem to hit three out of four times. There was lots of paint on it and I had to wonder about his vision. " The introduction of outboard jet dives around that time was critical to the full development of the fishery not to mention the well-being of the motors.

He still recalls the day Ejnar died and how Bob Tindel, one of his fellow guests, played Taps on a trumpet after dinner in camp that night, just a few days after he had been to visit him in hospital. "I said a few words at his funeral and will always remember Joy as one of the toughest, strongest people I have ever met, a wonderful, wonderful person."

Dick also tells the story of a 33-pound steelhead that he hooked and played for 55 minutes on a Little Cleo spoon in the pool in front of the camp. "I finally had it where I could almost touch it when the hook straightened and it turned right and then just sat there out in the pool. I called Vic Rempel to come down and boom, he had it on in one cast, fairly hooked in the mouth. He landed it and I said he should take it as he was the one who had landed it so he had it mounted."

Pierce notes the weight of this great fish is confirmed by the lodge formula and matches what was for years the world fly-caught record, set by Kaul Mauser in October 1962, on another famous Skeena tributary, the Kispiox. "It's cool that there are actually three Babine 33-pounders, caught on a spoon, a wet fly and a dry line. They just have not been publicized like the one from the Kispiox."

Later Vic's mount was returned to the Steelhead Camp where it's displayed on the wall to this day, a memorable 42" x 24" trophy that helps to confirm, if confirmation is needed, the Babine's reputation as one of if not the world's greatest steelhead river. Dick Andersen supports the latter view.

—As told to Peter McMullan

....Spoons, Umbrellas and Cigars

Pierce has the highest regard for Dick and his exploits over the years. " In my years guiding them he and his other fishing pal, Kent Williamson, were quite the pair. They both used short, plug flipping bass rods to cast Little Cleo Wigl spoons and landed such ridiculous numbers of steelhead that only legend would believe.

When it rained they brought umbrellas and cigars and cast their spoons to take fish after fish. Kent and Dick knew the river's secrets and where the steelhead were likely to hold and we would go quickly from pool to pool to see how many we could catch, They would be high fiving and having

Dick Andersen and his friends were among many Babine fishermen who, for years, enjoyed great success with Little Cleo spoons.

fun like no two other steelheaders I have ever met. I was just the young, new owner and they were laughing at my youngness.

Kent was the southern gentleman and Dick was the humourist, a great pair of personalities from whom to learn how to guide and respect. Kent continued to come after Dick's accident and, when he had cancer in all but a quarter of one lung, he returned with his son, Dr. Kent Jr., and said his goodbyes to the river. Kent Sr. was also pals with Bill Russell and it was usually the three of them in Steelhead Paradise cabin with Bill, the fly fisherman who never minded Dick and Kent taking steelhead all around him on spoons.

Kent Sr. always traded his spoon rod for a fly rod to spend one day upstream of the weir. That last season, 10 or more years ago, the walk was a challenge and his son and I would often have to wait for him to catch up. It was only then that I realized what an effort it was for him."

PART III

1986–2010: The Cleggs

*When the snow flies there is nothing easy about the life of a steelhead guide. Just ask
Pierce or any of the guests who brave the worst of the late-season weather.*

From crossing the U.S.-Canada border on the night of a Stanley Cup Final, to taking over and owning and guiding, as an admitted greenhorn, at a wilderness trout and steelhead lodge, Pierce introduces the reader to a wonderfully rich cast of characters and adventures. It's never been an easy life but it is one that he has relished and defended with a rare sense of determination. Pierce's wife, Anita, and his daughter, Nicole, contribute from different but related perspectives and then Pierce highlights his defining challenge, the ultimately successful fight to prevent the provincial government from allowing the logging industry to build additional bridges over the Babine, thus providing easy road access to what thankfully remains a true wilderness

and still largely inaccessible world-class fishery. He also mourns the recent death of John Madam who helped to build the original lodge and cabins (see page 62). The history of an old and fading river map from Ejnar's days and the background to the names given to many of the pools on the upper and middle river round out the Clegg contribution to the still evolving history of the Babine. Then Smithers-based professional forester Gary Quanstrom offers some interesting perspectives on the relationship between the forest industry and the environmental movement leaving Pierce to review the situation on the Babine watershed today now that the bridge battles have been consigned to history.

Pierce Clegg: From Banking to the Babine

*E*verybody has a story about how they ended up where they are. Some seem to be destined by design at an early age. Others fumble and stumble their way along and just take the opportunities as they present themselves. And some people get a wild urge to do something totally different without really realizing what the future will bring. I was the latest of the three types.

Perhaps I was running away from my past or perhaps I was searching for a new life. I am not sure which, but coming to Canada was a surprise move considering my career path up to that point.

As a father of four, I have watched three of my children go through the challenging age of 15. I know 15 was difficult for me. And so this age is where I would like to start my own perspective and opinions about the Babine, angling, life and death. These four topics all seem related so I can't dismiss any of them and write fairly about how the Babine has come to symbolize a journey years before I actually arrived there.

Once while attending Pacific Lutheran University (PLU) in Tacoma, WA during the late 1970's, I took a course on death and dying. It was an elective course and I thought I had some

experience with the topic and wanted to face it once again. My own prerequisite experiences were the near death of myself at age 15, and the death of my grandfather, Rev. Julius Hansen, in 1978. Having six per cent chance of living will put the fear of death in anyone, and losing such a man as Rev. Julius Hansen will put the fear of God in anyone, or should.

My own near-death hospital experience, following major internal surgery, was not significant to anyone other than my immediate family, but I felt more than willing to give up the ghost due to the pain I endured. Julius's death, however, was truly significant because he was a great man and had lived a great life. In my own case, I wanted to die, and in Julius' case, I wanted him to live. Neither of us had any choice in the matter. My choices were yet to begin, and Julius had made all his choices.

Without going into great detail about Julius, it is fair to say that he was trained by a farm life with his parents and brothers in Camrose, Alberta. The work was hard to the point of creating the Hansen brothers, Olympian in strength and endurance. The Hansens were also notable in their day for their skills as ice hockey players. Their Augsburg College, MN, team was selected to represent the USA at the 1928 Winter Olympics team with Julius Hansen, my grandfather, as captain. It proved to be a brief moment of glory for, just before they were to board a 'plane on their way to face the Russians, politics intervened and they were all disqualified.

These Hansen brothers went on to become the famous hockey Hansen brothers. Some of them played in the National Hockey League, but Julius felt a calling to become a Lutheran minister. His first posting was Hogeland, MT. A church and a hockey rink were built and so Julius began a new chapter of mixing his hardwork ethic and hockey fame for the Lord's purposes and glory.

By the time I was old enough to understand, Julius was to me a most loving grandfather with many amazing stories. His heart began to fail him and so he retired from the Lutheran ministry. His last church was in Santa Rosa, CA.

On Second Thought
By JOHN F. McGOVERN

OLYMPIC PROGRAM DISTURBED

PREPARATIONS for the departure of the Augsburg hockey team to represent the United States in the Olympic games, received a temporary set back yesterday when Nick Kahler was startled by the receipt of a wire from William S. Haddock, chairman of the Olympic hockey committee, informing him that the Olympic committee had refused to certify the Augsburg team. The reason ascribed was that the committee felt that the Augsburg six was not representative.

Mr. Haddock, who has been chairman of the Olympic hockey committee for several years and who made previous selections of American teams, was indignant at the action of the committee. He will endeavor to obtain a reconsideration by the committee which has acted hastily and without knowledge of the facts. Haddock wired Nick Kahler last night as follows:

"Have wired McArthur and Rubien demanding reconsideration. Decision arrived at through talking with some New Yorkers who never heard of Augsburg team. It is outrageous; will do utmost."—Haddock.

The situation is about this: The Augsburg team was invited to represent the country after several other teams declined. The first proposal was to appear in a playoff. The Augsburg team assented to this. The playoff idea was abandoned. The sextet was then offered the opportunity to make the trip and play in the games if certain perquisites were met. These included raising $4,500 as a share of the expenses.

Raising that amount of money is not a job for boys in these times. There was only a week in which to raise the money. The limited time precluded the idea of many benefit games or performances. Nick Kahler, who has played as much hockey as any American and who knows hockey teams and hockey players as well as anyone in the country undertook to coach and manage the team and to raise the money needed for the trip.

The quota was assured. The seat sale for the benefit game with Fort Snelling Saturday night was progressing in a highly satisfactory manner. Passports were obtained. Reservations were made on the boat. The departure was set for Sunday night. Then came the wires last night. As a result things are in something of a muddle today.

An effort was made to get in touch with General McArthur and F. W. Rubiens of the Olympic committee but neither could be reached. Haddock was reached at Pittsburgh. He was doing everything possible to influence the committee to reconsider and urged that pressure be brought to bear from Minneapolis.

Wires were sent to Ching Johnson early today in New York. Ching called on the committee and told them something about the Augsburg team and the caliber of the players who were on it. Murray Hulbert, former president of the A. A. U., was talked to on the telephone by friends in Minneapolis and the matter explained to him. This should clear up the situation and ensure the trip for the team.

Fishing has to be in the Clegg family's blood. This early 1900s family photo finds Pierce's grandfather, Rev. Julius Clegg, with a very substantial catch of what are most probably pickerel.

I remember him taking one last calling to Trinity Lutheran Church in Oakland, CA where he did some preaching and assisting with the services there. His strongest ministry was visitation and many times he would take me on road trips to visit the many people he had ministered to over the years. Like my grandfather on my father's side, Dr. Harding Clegg, they both outlived the people they served and enjoyed a full life serving the old-fashioned way.

As grandfathers go, both of mine were the most loving and kind souls that any grandchild could ask for. Julius' stories about farming in Alberta, and the harsh winters there could be a book in itself. The hockey stories were also good but I was too young to appreciate what he and his brothers had accomplished so long ago.

What I remember the most about Julius and his wife, Hazel, was that their home was always a good place to be. There was good food, good times, lots of love and firm discipline, and lots of books and learning. Their home was holy ground just like the Babine in some ways. So when Julius suffered his fifth and final heart attack while I was attending PLU for my first year, I was lucky to make it back to see him one last time.

Julius' death was exceptional in that he had some out-of-body experiences in the spiritual sense of the word. I learned more about these types of experiences in the death and dying class at PLU. Only with Julius, this was far more real to me personally. Julius was the type of man that I or anyone could trust. I never knew him to lie and so I had two questions to ask him on his deathbed. My first question was, 'are you surprised to be back?' My mother had told me that he was not to recover from this fifth heart attack, and that he had gone to the other side a number of times.

His most significant witness was to meet with deceased family and to meet and speak with Jesus Christ himself. So my next question was, 'Did you see Jesus?' To both questions all he could do was to nod 'yes'. I was 17 at the time and Julius was 79. From that moment on, I had many more questions to ask about life and death. And the more questions that any of us ask about any topic the more we will learn. Ask and you shall receive. Knock and the door will be opened to you. These biblical statements hold true not only with God, but also with many other causes, which are all around us.

Asking questions and fighting for life is what I learned at an early age, and it is what I have applied to the best of my ability on the Babine. The Babine has become for me the place where the tool of angling has been used to ask questions and experience life and death. So here I am today, still asking questions and the Babine is the place where I have learned much about life and death through angling and living the Norlakes' traditions.

I was lucky to have a father, Christopher (Kit) Clegg, who loved me and loved the outdoors. Although he lived a business life in the city of San Francisco, CA he was most happy fishing, hunting or just working in the soil of this earth. He taught me to fly-fish in the high-mountain lakes and streams of California's Sierra Nevada, and he taught me to hunt ducks, geese and pheasants. For a high school graduation present, our family traveled to Norlakes Lodge Babine Ltd. in June of 1977. He, his parents and his uncle had been to Norlakes before, but this was my first

trip. We found ourselves in the earlier part of June on the famous Rainbow Alley of the Babine River.

Our family included my brother, Peter, my mother, Hazel Dell, my grandfather, Dr. Harding Clegg and a friend of the family, Jack Mussey. Ejnar Madsen and his family were running the Trout Lodge. The fishing was good, the weather was good and a fine time was had by all. Three never-to-be-forgotten memories stand out in my mind. At this point in my angling and backpacking career, I had already had some great trout and bass fishing in California, or at least I thought so. The Babine changed all that thinking.

Back in the 1970s the sport fishing history of the Babine was already in its fourth decade. Fort Babine was still an isolated Indian village with a culture of living off the land still very much a part of daily life. And here were the spoiled Californians not realizing the rich cultural history of the area but enjoying some great fishing and lodging at Norlakes.

Ejnar's son, Erik, took my brother and I on a hike to Haul and Tahlo lakes, which are located east of Fort Babine. There was an old trail that led from Fort Babine to Takla Lake. It's amazing to realize how many old First Nation trails there are peppered throughout the bush that were once used by thousands of residents. Where there were thousands, there are now only hundreds, or even fewer, so almost all trails have been reclaimed by the wilderness they once opened up. This same trail Erik, Peter and I used in 1977 is now a power line connecting residents at Takla with the power delivered to Fort Babine from Granisle on Babine Lake. The Haul and Tahlo lakes area is now heavily logged, but in 1977 had never been touched.

My father lent me his hiking boots, which quickly produced blisters within the first hour of the hike. So I took them off and wore just my socks. I was used to running around in bare feet, and the forest floor behind Fort Babine was moist and marshy, perfect moose habitat. I'd never seen so many animal tracks in all my backpacking to that time. When we stopped occasionally the silence was amazing. I quickly realized that we were the noisiest critters in the bush and could be easily detected. In other words, our chances of sneaking up on anything but fish were slim. And we didn't want to stop long anyway because the insects were more numerous than the animal tracks

There were times where the trail was not so obvious and we found ourselves wading through swamps, me in my socks, but we finally arrived at both lakes. We were dry fly fishing, caught a lot of small trout, had some lunch and I dropped my pocket instamatic camera into the water twice but the photos still came out. When we returned to our boat at Fort Babine, my legs were spent and I would never forget my first venture into some real wilderness.

My next memory from that 1977 trip to Norlakes owes everything to Ejnar Madsen. He took his son, Erik, and I to fish a small lake called Starvation Lake. This was a lake loaded with hungry rainbows averaging in size about 15 inches. Ejnar was a man of few words so there wasn't much talk and it was my only time with the pioneer of Norlakes. The fishing was ridiculous with trout caught with just about every cast. I had only experienced that once before with guess whom, Rev. Julius Hansen. Starvation Lake featured an inlet infested with lily pads, across from a forest recreation site. That day I lost all sense of time in that little inlet. Ejnar and Erik paddled by on their way back

Pierce's parents, Hazel Dell Clegg, a keen trout fisher to this day, and the late Christopher (Kit) Clegg, were annual Norlakes guests for more than 25 years and introduced their son to trout fishing on the Babine's Rainbow Alley and Nilkitkwa Lake. Pierce built his parents a cabin where each year his mother and her friends still enjoy stunning views across the lake.

to the recreation site and suggested that I follow due to a thunder storm moving in. It was hard to pull away but the impending weather was a good motivator.

The best recollection of 1977 came from an evening of angling on the Rainbow Alley. There is a place where it flows into Nilkitkwa Lake. Just before the river reaches the lake, its flow divides around Smokehouse Island. The left hand split is often too shallow to motor through so most anglers motor or drift to the right split. At the point where you pass the island on your left and view Nilkitkwa Lake, this is the place where I fell in love with the Babine.

One evening at that spot I was fishing from a Norlakes flat-bottomed, wooden riverboat following another boat containing my father and Ejnar. This was my first view of a northern sunset, the kind that lasts for hours, its colours highlighted and mirrored upon the waters of Nilkitkwa Lake in a scene of indescribable beauty. I dropped my rod to the floor of the boat and said, 'Oh my God'.

Years later I was able to secure a recreation lease close by this place, and had a log cabin built there so my parents could visit with us during the Trout Lodge seasons. This area of the river is a place of life with a scenic and auditory quality of great value. It is also a time and place where the change of seasons signal immense ecosystem changes that are priceless to witness. This precious part of our world is the Babine at its best.

All this brings us to 1985. Since Julius' death, I had finished a Bachelor's degree in Business Administration with two minors in Economics and Religion from PLU. I then worked for Household Finance International (HFC) as a banking branch manager after completing a two-year training program. I quit the banking business and moved to Corvallis, OR the place of my birth, and completed the first year of a two-year Master's program in Business Administration at Oregon State University (OSU). I had married by this time but things weren't going too well. My parents thought a break in the studies and marriage would help and invited me on another trip to Norlakes.

Ejnar had passed away from cancer in 1983, and his wife, Joy and children Karl, Erik and Karen were running Norlakes in keeping with all the established traditions. Joy was also suggesting to all the 1985 season guests that it was time for a change in ownership. For me, it was information that went in one ear and out the other.

At this point in my life I was searching for a career but lacked the vision to know what that career should or could be. I think I was using HFC to gain experience and training, which I thought could be a stepping-stone to working for my father and the family business. Before moving to Oregon in 1985, there was another turning point for the Clegg family. The sale of the family-

owned and operated business, M&T Inc., to Kolberg, Kravis and Roberts (KKR) forced a new career direction plan for me. I no longer could envision myself working for the family business so the move to Oregon was a new direction.

KKR is now a multi-billion dollar, leveraged take-over type of business. Back in 1985, KKR was just starting out and got its feet wet with the purchase of M&T Inc., the first of many such transactions. Unfortunately our family business was ripe for the take-over for many reasons. My father and I, among others, voted against the $1500 per share offer from KKR, but 80% of the family stockholders wanted out and so any aspiration I had of working for the family was over. My father continued on with the new ownership until his retirement but I think it broke his heart to see it all go down.

If there was anything good to come from the sale, it was the resources that my father and I were able to use for the purchase of Norlakes in 1986. In a twisted hand of fate, the $1500 per share offer by KKR gave me the funds to invest and my father the chance to work with his son after all.

So back to the 1985 trip to Norlakes and Joy's announcement to the guests that new blood was desired for the future of Norlakes. One morning our family and family friend, Jack Mussey, were walking from our two cabins to the main lodge. These two cabins were number seven and number eight, now named Apens and Sunset Cove. Our friend Jack is a great investor and I think he saw the possibilities for my father and I so he suggested to me that I should partner up with my dad and buy Norlakes. That's when the lightbulb finally went off in my little brain. I walked ahead a little faster until I joined my dad to relay Jack's idea. His answer, "Are you serious?" I was indeed serious about doing it at that moment without the slightest idea of what it might entail for either of us. When I returned to Oregon, I wrote to Joy stating our interest and asking for all the financial details.

Joy phoned instead of writing back. She said there was an opening for a guide at the Steelhead Camp that I had never visited during my two previous trips to the Trout Lodge. In fact, I didn't really even know what a steelhead was. Joy thought that I should experience the camp and then I would know whether to buy Norlakes or not. I jumped at the opportunity, dropped all studies at OSU, ignored a then marriage separation, and traveled to the US-Canada Border on the way to Smithers.

Being my naïve self with no tips or advice from Joy, I proceeded to the border agent and the usual questions they have for travelers. They asked me what was the purpose of my visit to Canada and I told them I was going to work for a fishing camp. Well my customs card got marked for further investigation and off I went to stand in another line, the kind of customs line you don't want to be in. At that time arriving travelers could be met at the luggage pick-up so Joy was there waiting to meet me.

She quickly asked why I was in the dreaded customs line number two. When I told her she was, of course, distressed since hiring Americans was no longer allowed as it was in the 1970s. It was time for a little white lie and I said to customs agent #2 that customs agent #1 must be mistaken, that I had said I was coming to Canada to 'work real hard to catch a fish', and not to work at a fish camp. They bought my little white lie, asked me if I had any felonies on my record and let me go through.

Well that was the best lie I have ever told in my life because for the next month the Babine River captured my heart as it did on Rainbow Alley in 1977. Only this time, the mighty steelhead and the thrill of the wilderness for the month of September 1985, sealed my unknowing fate and destiny to this day.

My first and only job working for no wages at the '85 Norlakes' Steelhead Camp was to assist Karl Madsen, Todd Stockner, Marie Darter and a housekeeper/cook's assistant whose name I can't remember. I started by mostly doing camp chores and painting the exterior of all the camp buildings. I did have some experience painting so I was good at that but the rest of the tasks were new adventures. Karl and Todd were busy guiding up to 18 guests each day so the sooner they could train me to run a jet boat the better.

Little by little I assumed more and more jet boating responsibilities. It started with helping to deliver the coffee by 10:00 a.m. to the guests located at runs and pools close to camp. Coffee delivery led to assisting with the movement of guests to the various runs and pools and then eventually I was able to help some guests, giving them very tiny bits of advice on where to cast, and so on. The river was full of steelhead and happy guests so I thought the operation looked good as an investment. Little did I know how truly great the river was and still is. For my naïve state of mind at the time, British Columbia could be full of Babine Rivers.

I caught my first steelhead on the fly, a 36-inch female, bright and early in the season of '85. The photo of that fish and a young Pierce Clegg is still on the back of the cookhouse door. I remember catching that fish behind a guest, Dr. Jeff Reese, in the pool called Allen's. I was using a 30-foot shooting head sink tip with a natural Muddler Minnow fly. This beautiful female was in very shallow water, or had followed the fly in to about shin-deep water right next to Jeff's feet. In fact, when the water around his feet blew up, as is usually the case, Jeff was startled and was looking around his wading area wondering at first what was going on. That was the first quest that Karl and Todd gave me, to catch my first steelhead on the fly.

Then Todd handed me his drift rod with a level-wind reel and a pearl corky lure and weight attached, and told me I must now try that method and get to know the bottom structure using what we still call 'bottom-bouncing'. The day I used this set-up, I was guiding Leonard Ely on a run called Dead Man's. Yes, an angler had died there after landing a large steelhead while fishing with his friends, or so the story goes.

I didn't know how to use a drift rod with this sort of reel so I was trying to figure that out. I was standing in shallow water in the upper gravel bar section of the run. I pressed the button releasing the spool, dropped the lure straight down at my feet, and a female steelhead grabbed it, took off upstream, jumping numerous times then spitting out the hook, all in a matter of seconds.

As if the Dead Man's experience was not enough for a rookie like me, my third, fifth, ninth, 12th and 15th casts put more steelhead on the line so I will never forget my first drift-rod experience on the Babine. I was amazed and in shock that such a set-up could be so deadly. I handed the rod at day's end to Todd, remarking on how effective it was. He advised me that I must now catch more on the fly so I spent the rest of my chances that month using fly-only methods. The learning curve for the fly is steeper but the rewards are greater in terms of the thrill and experience of the fight.

It doesn't take too many Babine steelhead to either ruin your life or complete your angling ambitions. The problem is you can never get enough of it, kind of like a good woman. So I returned to Oregon and told everybody that I was going to move to Canada and own and operate a fishing lodge and camp. They thought I was crazy but they already thought I was nuts so it was nothing new. I told my estranged wife that I was going to Canada with or without her. We were having troubles but she decided to join me anyway.

The next adventures were negotiating the sale of Norlakes, which included a big-game hunting territory, applying to the Canadian government for Landed Immigrant Status, and finding agreement with the Madsens, the lawyers and accountants. I wasn't ready to give up my American citizenship so the only other way was to apply under the Entrepreneur Act of Canada and become a Landed Immigrant. I filled out the application and received a quick reply, 'no.'

To make a long story short, we hired a Vancouver, B.C. law firm named Lawson, Lundell, Lawson and MacIntosh. They had some experience helping Americans buy guide outfitter territories so I was next. They quickly said that they wished I hadn't applied on my own and received my 'no' answer, but they said there was nothing in law that stated I could not apply again. So re-apply I did and little over six months later, my wife and I received the green light and it was time to pack up and drive to Seattle and pick up our papers from the Canadian Embassy.

Before stuffing our belongings into a U-Haul truck and car trailer, it had been an up and down, emotional roller coaster ride in re-applying to immigrate. It didn't seem to matter that I had Canadian roots through my great uncle, Chester Ronning, a former ambassador for Canada. It didn't seem to matter that I was the grandson of a famous Canadian hockey player. It seemed to matter, and now I understand, that I give up my American citizenship and become a new citizen of Canada. Canada also didn't like our proposed American corporate structure.

Another law firm, Pillsbury Madison and Sutro of San Francisco, CA advised my father and I to form a California Sub Chapter S Corporation. Canada kept resisting our overall application, we kept calling our Canadian lawyers for updates, and a lot of waiting went on. Eventually we received word that the last step in the process was at hand. Finally and barely in time for the upcoming 1986 Norlakes season, we drove north on I-5, headed for Seattle from Corvallis, OR.

Part of the success of my decision to move to Canada came from my complete disregard for taking the risk. In other words, I didn't plan for nor know much about anything. I had some recent experience with that type of decision making when I graduated high school, having played no school sports, and then tried out for football, baseball, diving, ski team and water polo at PLU. My chance for success in those sports was slim to none but I wanted to try despite the odds and had some success despite my lack of experience. Moving to Canada seemed easier in comparison so what the hell, eh?

If you have ever driven parts of Seattle, you'll know it's like parts of San Francisco on a smaller scale. There are steep parts, basically not the best place to be driving a large size U-Haul pulling a car trailer. It was also close to the end of the working day rush-hour, and we weren't familiar with the directions to get to the Canadian Embassy. The U-Haul had a manual clutch transmission so some of the hills meant hoping for all green lights. My last effort at breaking U.S. law before moving to Canada was running a couple of red lights on steep hills, wife screaming and other motorists flipping me off. It was Canada or getting busted but we made it to the embassy and there was a nice long parking spot along the curb right in front of the place.

T. Bording was her name, and she was the last stop to getting our landed papers. T. Bording was your vision of a tough old army boots bureaucrat, one you didn't think was happy to see you. First shot out the bag, she didn't like our corporate structure, and looking back, she was right and we should have listened. Anyway, she required a small change in the structure, which we accommodated although my wife was in tears in the hallway while we waited for the changes to arrive from our lawyers' offices. It seemed that we were not going to make it past T. Bording after all we had done to get to that point, but she called us to her office one more time. Our final discussion centered on us pleading with her that we were going to be good folks in Canada, that we wanted to raise a family there and run a good business. She softened just a little it seemed, and let us go, landed papers in hand.

We left Seattle intimidated by the whole experience and feeling we had one more government hurdle to clear, the border crossing. We felt we would be pulled over with all of our belongings to be searched. Lucky for us 9/11 hadn't happened yet, and luckier still, it was springtime, May 24th, 1986, to be exact and the Stanley Cup hockey play-offs were in full swing.

Not knowing it was the play-off finals, and not knowing what to expect, I thought this would be another layer of T. Bording type of scrutiny including the entire unloading of our vehicles. At the drive-through booth, we were directed to park and I braced myself and walked into the customs office. I opened the door to three different TV sets, all showing the same hockey

game, all fully engaged with a fight on the ice. It was your classic hockey fight with gloves off, one player holding the other player's jersey over their head while pummeling punch after punch.

The customs guys took one short look at me and my U-Haul with car trailer, looked at each other as if to say they'd rather watch the game, and signed off my papers. That was instant relief and I felt Julius' presence with a hockey fight our introduction to crossing the border. Perhaps that was the spirit of the future because there would be many more fights to come only I would be in them next time.

So we left the USA at the Sumas crossing and quickly checked into the nearest hotel, overjoyed to be in Canada. Time was of the essence though since the Madsen family had already begun opening up the Trout Lodge for the 1986 season, and we, the new owners, weren't there yet. So we drove to Smithers, found an apartment, threw all our stuff into it, un-packed and headed for the lodge to start working alongside the Madsens and their staff with the first guests arriving by June 1.

It was a strained time for the Cleggs and the Madsens to work together for the spring and summer of 1986. By prior agreement, everyone wanted the transition to go well for all concerned, including the guests, so the thought of working together sounded like the best plan. I had worked for one month at the Steelhead Camp the previous September, so that formed the basis of experience for running that operation, but I had not worked at the Trout Lodge and needed some instructions on how that was done.

The Madsens were trying to let go of so many experiences, memories, blood, sweat and tears. The Cleggs were thrust into a new life based on Norlakes' tradition and many adventures yet to come. We were young, inexperienced, new to the country, marriage struggling and really didn't have the foggiest idea how to own and operate a tourism business on the Babine.

The Trout Lodge goodwill left to us by the Madsen ownership era was based on years of backbreaking work and traditions. Our job, in part, was to keep the traditions going and not make too many changes. So traditions were our training and the many guests that had been fishing the Babine since before I was born were still there. The most gracious aspect of the Babine in the 1980s and early 1990s was the consistently great fishing and great weather. Weather is everything to good angler success and the weather and water conditions in our early years at Norlakes were stellar.

To write about Babine, one must try and capture the trinity of river, angler and wilderness spirit. How does the Babine capture or 'catch' its followers, the pioneers who came to turn sport-fishing dreams into reality? Rational thought often fails to explain the bond that is created between the river and the pioneer angler. Providing access, facilities, services and the spirit of not giving up at a time in history when the north was very remote, makes for many stories and countless memories.

Unfortunately, many if not most of us sport-fishing pioneers were not very good at keeping diaries or journals that would recall all the interesting details. I never kept much other than the annual Christmas letters and the required reporting forms to government. There are photos, video, some weekly fishing reports, but going into my third decade on the Babine, there is so much I can't remember. On the other hand, there is much that is remembered about certain things, the type of things that stand out as unforgettable and I will do my best to share them.

That first season of ownership in 1986 began a new life and bond with the Babine that was life-changing and permanent. Angling on the Babine leaves the rich, the intelligent, the physical or the frail to consider the un-explained but spiritual truths that don't fit into the preconceived fishing trip planning. There can be the PhD type of angler or the self-abusive social deviant, both being faced with a spiritual experience on the Babine. Some see it, feel it and know that they are in a place beyond their pre-trip planning and dreaming. They are the ones who develop the bond. Words are cheap and short in description where seeing is believing, feeling is more real than seeing, and direct contact becomes life-changing and possibly prolonging of the spirit to return again and again.

Five anglers' ashes consigned to the Babine on my watch confirm the completion of the 'spirit to return again' scenario. We return to a place where we feel closer to the Babine spirit than any other place we have traveled to on earth. This compliment to the river is a testimony to the end justifying the means, the cast resulting in the record, the spirit of the land, water and beast calling the angler to a higher realization.

Few hear the call. Few can express that they have been called, and few take the opportunity to share it. My first season as owner of Norlakes began a journey of meeting these pioneer Babine anglers who, I now realize, were returning again and again to get their fix for many reasons, but above all, to feel the love of a river and place of highest angler esteem.

I've often said that if I were to write another book about the Babine, it wouldn't be about the fishing, but about all the staffing stories and challenges over the years. Our first season in 1986, like most others, was far different than working for a bank in the big city, or attending university classes. The Madsens and Cleggs had joined forces and commitment to keep the traditions going into a new ownership era. Marie Darter was the cook and centerpiece of a happy, main lodge eatery.

I once had a guest, Dave Brubaker, who always asked what he considered the most important question upon his arrival at the airport, and that was: 'I just want to know one thing, Pierce. How is the food?' Marie's motto in life was killing them with kindness and she was as kind as they get. I've since learned that if the cook isn't happy, nobody is happy. Marie was great, always starting and ending a day with good food and a positive outlook no matter what.

Then there was Karl Madsen. I had worked for him the previous fall at Steelhead Camp. Looking back now I can understand how stressed out Karl then was due to factors beyond his control. I was worried that he might be stressed out again at the Trout Lodge, but just the opposite. We meshed well and he was a great aid to my training in the Norlakes' traditions. Then there was the assistant angling guide, Ron Lamperson, who had just returned from a holiday in Amsterdam where he had been left for dead, having had his nose crushed into his brain in some sort of altercation. He looked fine but he hadn't seen a doctor since the injury and was suffering depression and who knows what else so he had to leave just weeks into the job.

On top of this, my wife and Joy were not getting along so Karl and I made an agreement that we would do the work, ignore the distractions and look after around 18 guests a day for three months. Marie and the housekeeper/cook's assistant would look after the food service and cabins, and Karl and I would hustle like madmen. Marie later commented that she didn't know what I was doing half the time, but things got done.

So here I found myself in this incredibly wild and beautiful setting. The local Fort Babine Indian village was still very isolated. There was no bridge connecting the village to the still primitive road to Smithers. There was very poor housing, no street lights, no fire hall, no health services, no sewage treatment, no plumbing but there was a power line which was often damaged, and the power interrupted, by wind storms and fallen trees.

In the late 1940s and early 1950s, Norlakes had traded the first chain saw and outboard engine to Fort Babine so the remote qualities and relation-ship was a daily chal-lenge for both First Nations and Norlakes. In that first season I experienced for myself the sense of remote-ness and dependence on certain ways of do-ing things. You couldn't just go to town when-ever you felt like it to buy something. In fact, Smithers most often didn't have what you needed so planning ahead and then making it work ruled the day.

The other things that impressed upon me were the smells and sounds of the wilderness area where I suddenly found myself. The red-necked grebes were al-ways calling from big packs in the lake. They were waiting for and feeding on the large pods of migrating sockeye smolts. The grebes' calls were more like laughing hyenas. The eagles, ospreys, loons and ducks were all in this mix of waterfowl and raptor noises, plus the sight of aerial battles and manoeuvres. You never get used to it and are constantly stopping what you are doing just to watch and listen.

Every once in a while the big-game animals would show up. One morning Ron, our temporary assistant angling guide, woke up in his tent frame to see a moose poking through the tent door flap. Black bears would come browsing through the lodge grounds, munching the various spring plants. Every once in a while we could hear wolves and coyotes calling, echoing from across the lake or closer. I probably speak on behalf of many tourism operators who live in a wild setting; it grows on you and can never be replaced by anything else.

The whole staff was busy, especially since my wife and I were late in arriving, in preparing for the first guests, and these first guests were something else. One gentleman, Fred Rubra, later passed away in the fall of 1987. He was a long-time guest who booked two cabins for a month. He had requirements for a certain cabin, which had its own dock and a boat with an electric-start outboard motor, which he paid for so it could be available to him during his stay. The second cabin was for his two 'working ladies'. One time he brought three but he was asked to leave when they started offering their services to other guests. One of his gals was more like a personal affairs manager and bridge partner. The other was what I called the trickster in that she was there for what 'working ladies' are best known.

Fred was a real character. Ejnar seemed to like him, perhaps due to the investment advice he provided. He had some oil-rich land in Alberta, which he sold and then invested in gold back when gold was $35 per ounce. Now a millionaire, he was quick to advise invest-ment in gold and land on which a person could survive. He also sub-scribed to various New York-based monthly investment newslet-ters that predicted the crash of the U.S. dol-lar and, of course, the future value of gold. He was married and lived in Nassau when he wasn't traveling the bridge-playing circuit, fishing and playing with his gals.

This was the backdrop to our first meeting when I was called to his cabin af-ter his arrival. Now Fred had cancer and was a very medicated man in his late 70s. He reminded me of Jabba the Hut in Star Wars. He was overweight, out of shape, fat bel-lied, always had an un-lit cigar in his mouth, even at dinnertime. He slobbered his cigar juices and food so his appearance was not going to be approved by most mothers. The trickster wasn't there for the tricks, only the money.

I visited him that first day and he quickly stated that Joy had asked him to leave before because of the prostitutes, so he wanted to know what I thought of the whole situation. Again not knowing what I was getting myself into, I stated, "Fred, you don't really want to know what I think of it, but as long as it doesn't affect the other guests, I'm OK with it."

Things were pretty un-eventful with Fred and the gals in 1986, but in 1987 it was a different story. His last trip to Norlakes before he passed away was anything but forgettable. This time his trickster was a different gal named Pat. She was from Texas and once she realized where Norlakes was and how unhealthy Fred was, she just wanted to "get the hell out of here". I guess she couldn't say 'no' to the money. All I remember about Pat was

she was the horniest woman I had ever met. Like clockwork, after dinner, our then guiding staff of four including me ran for cover because the burning eyes of Pat told us we were fair game if we but smiled at her. I kid you not, she was looking for someone or something to do whatever to and we just hid.

I suppose Fred liked that because he was so drugged up with I don't know how many narcotics. He was having more trouble than usual in navigating his way to and from his cabin, and in navigating his boat to and from fishing the river or on Nilkitkwa Lake. I must admit he was a great angler and fly-fisherman and he knew the lake and Rainbow Alley. In fact to this day, I have caught my biggest rainbow on the Babine while fishing with Fred. That great fish weighed seven pounds and caught right next to Smokehouse Island using a salmon-fry pattern that I tied and still use called the Morley Minnow.

Fred only fly-fished the river on a major or minor period of the sol lunar tables. As far as I could tell it worked, but just about any time in 1986 one could fish since the weather and water conditions were so good, and the fishing always seemed to be good as well.

One day in 1987 he left the Trout Lodge docks with Pat. Pat was yelling as they left the dock that he "didn't know where the f**k he was going" due to all the drugs. Fred told me that day that if he wasn't back by 5:00 p.m. to go looking for him. Late that afternoon a huge black thunderstorm mass developed, of a size and power I have not witnessed since. It was about 5:00 p.m. and, as I looked at my watch and then the massive black mass to the south, I thought Fred was simply dead. I told the staff I was going to go looking for him.

I grabbed a rain poncho and CB radio, told the staff to prepare for the storm to hit the lodge and took off. To the south of the Trout Lodge there is this creek called Nine Mile Creek, which is nine miles from Fort Babine. Over the years this creek has been a good place to troll for rainbows and lake trout. That's what Fred was planning that day so I headed for the creek, meeting the storm about halfway there. I radioed the lodge that I was going in, so to speak, with the storm a dark wall of power rolling down the lake towards the lodge and Fort Babine.

I entered the wall and it was like going into another world. Several minutes into the storm and at one point I could not keep the boat going in the direction I wanted to go. There was sideways rain, high winds and thunder and lightning with no gap in between so I was going around in a circle wondering what I should do next. I banked left and headed for the eastern shore, which I was able to reach, and then motored down the lake close to the shoreline. I reached Cottonwood Point, across from Nine Mile Point and the summer home of a woman named Jean—not her real name.

I beached the boat, which by this time had water over the floor boards, hopped out, introduced myself to Jean, and told her I considered the situation an emergency, and asked if she had spotted a red and green Norlakes boat trolling around recently. She said she hadn't but I noticed something white across the lake near the creek. I asked Jean to make some coffee and find some blankets, and then pushed my boat back into the stormy lake and headed over to the creek area.

When I arrived I could see that it was Norlakes boat #10 completely swamped and being tossed back and forth in the high waves. The top of the outboard, a new 20 hp, electric start model, was visible but not much else. Fred and Pat were huddled under a cottonwood tree looking wet and not happy, but definitely glad to see me. The problem now was what to do. I thought if I wasn't careful, my boat also would be swamped. I circled a few times and the waves were about three feet plus so I decided to gun the boat and run it full speed onto the shore and get it completely out of the water, which I did. I quickly recovered the new engine and then helped Fred and Pat into my boat. I guess I was energized by adrenaline because I was able to push the boat back into the water with the two of them aboard and just got it going before being swamped. We traveled across the lake to Jean's cabin and beached the boat there.

She was ready for us with hot coffee and lots of blankets. We got Fred's clothes off and warmed him up. I used the CB radio to call the Trout Lodge, which had just received the one-two punch of the same storm. I asked for another boat with some of Fred's clothes. Things were going well, maybe too well, in the cabin as Fred and Jean were taking a liking to each other. Pat took me aside and warned me never to visit Jean alone. I asked "why?" and if she thought Jean would "work me over," to which Pat replied "yes". Fred invited Jean over for dinner at the lodge and he went over to Jean's for dinner as well. I'd like to think that he respected her for being the survivalist she is and I'll leave it at that.

The last Fred story has to do with never missing an opportunity. One day I was checking on him at his cabin. When I got there, there he was on his back in half a foot of water. He had fallen off his dock ramp in shallow water but apparently could not get up. When he knew I was there he was saying, "help me, help me," in a barely discernable voice. I helped him into his cabin and summoned his gals to look after him. About an hour later I checked on him once again to make sure he was recovering.

I knocked on the door and entered only to find about $10,000 U.S. in cash hanging around and drying. This cash was in his fly-fishing vest so I asked him why he carried so much money in his vest. He said "you never know when you might meet an opportunity." Fred passed away in the fall of 1987 but will go down in history as his ladies went down on him.

It was such an all-consuming experience to accept the Norlakes goodwill, work with the Madsen family, and serve their guests with the expectation that I would continue all the lodge traditions 100%. And when you are used to being served a certain way for a certain cost, and you've been doing it longer than the new owner has been alive, well you don't want the new owners, as inexperienced as they were, to start changing these traditions first shot out of the bag. These guests were very particular but mostly in such a way as to be great hospitality training for my wife and I.

Since Fred Rubra needed very little guiding at all, the first guest I guided was a 91-year old-named Bill Fife (see also On the River with Bill Fife, pages 143-147). In one of Lee Richardson's books, he referred to Bill as Mr. Babine so I thought it was very meaningful that my first guiding experience should be guiding Mr. Babine. Bill traveled by himself and was mostly blind and

deaf. And don't we live in a small world, as Bill's retirement residence was a place my great grandfather had built in Oakland, CA. In fact Bill would repeatedly ask me if I was related to a particular resident there, and I was but I didn't know this relative even when I once lived close by in my pre-teen youth. Anyway, it was great that Bill could travel annually to the Babine despite his age and physical challenges.

The Ejnar Madsen hand-made wooden coffee tray was and still is one of those Norlakes' traditions that I was to assume. I've seen some things delivering the morning coffee, tea and hot chocolate to guests, who were wondering what took me so long, and to guests that would rather not be interrupted from what they were doing. My first morning waking up Bill was interesting. Usually when entering a guest cabin I would try not to make too much noise...a light knock on the door, setting the coffee tray on the table, making the fire and then politely saying "good morning" and asking if they wanted coffee, tea or hot chocolate. All three items were carried on the tray, plus cups, cream and sugar...sometimes a few marshmallows for the children.

Anyway, when I did all this, Bill did not move nor answer so I raised my voice in saying 'good morning' again. That didn't work so I tried again, louder but still no movement. I thought to myself, oh no, I hope he isn't dead. After a few more much louder pronouncements of "good morning, isn't a great day" and the fire now crackling to help me, I thought I had better place my hand on his shoulder and give it a gentle shake. Still no movement and I was really getting concerned. So I shook him rather aggressively until the bed and his body were all rocking back and forth. Then one of his hands raised into the air and he softly said, "thank you, thank you." That became the morning routine...I would enter the room, make as much noise as I wanted, shake Bill aggressively and see that hand rise with that soft voice, "thank you, thank you."

Another great Norlakes tradition at the Trout Lodge is guiding and fishing from the hand-crafted, flat-bottom, wooden riverboats. These boats are about 21 feet long, four and one half feet wide, made from yellow cedar and marine plywood and are very stable in the water for guests to either stand or sit and cast their flies. The much older guests like Bill could sit down or bring a sturdy lodge chair from which to cast or rest from casting all day. In Bill's case, guiding a mostly blind and deaf angler was even more challenging but the magic and lure of Norlakes and the Babine is that you can be mostly blind and deaf and a few other things and still fish the river and lakes.

For Bill when the fishing or catching was slow he wouldn't say much but was happy to move to another spot on the river. If the catching was good he would exclaim, 'This is just like the good old days.' Another ritual with Bill was to be patient while he reeled up his line and found his own fly in order to secure it on the rod...sometimes this took a while and I would be quietly cheering him on even though his hand would be aimlessly grabbing at the air, so close but yet so far away.

There were so many guests with particular physical and I would say mental challenges and yet they had been enjoying the Babine for so many years that they kept on coming. I used to say they would possibly pass away before their trip, maybe

Tradition plays a big part in the day-to-day life at both Trout Lodge and Steelhead Camp with Pierce or one of the guides waking guests each morning at 7:00 a.m. with tea, coffee or hot chocolate served from Ejnar's original wooden tray.

during their trip and sometimes after their trip even on the way home. They weren't going to be denied their Babine visit even if their family, friends and doctor advised against it. These were the guests that provided and shaped my early guiding training, something unforgettable.

Another fine couple were Jack and Maureen Voogd. Maureen suffered from multiple sclerosis and was confined to a wheel-chair but she could hold a trolling rod and bring a fish to the boat. Norlakes, neither then nor now, is up to code to handle wheel chairs but Jack looked after his wife with a most loving determination to give her what she wanted and what she wanted was the annual Babine experience.

Maureen had a heart of gold for the Babine which included sitting out in the sun all day, burning her fragile skin to the color of a ripe red apple, and enduring whatever weather the Babine had to give. The two of them were a wonderful example of love and devotion to each other and to making a trip to Norlakes work despite the lodge and cabins being a challenge to Maureen's physical needs. We did build a couple of ramps to the lodge and their cabin, and we did devise a means of securing her wheelchair to the floor of the boat, but it was the pure heart of love for the Babine that motivated Jack and Maureen to make the trip.

At a short week's end, they returned home...Maureen wearing her sunburn with pride and paying other physical prices

despite her doctor's concerns. I would only enjoy two seasons of Jack and Maureen as she passed away after her 1988 trip. Jack would soon join her of a broken heart even though he seemed far healthier. We all know the story of a married couple enjoying many years in love and one not lasting long after the other passes on.

There were other long-time guests arriving with multi-generational families. It was the grand or great grandparents who were the family leaders for the angling and fly-fishing in particular. In so many cases they had been guests at Norlakes for the length of my life or longer, something I had to respect and honour. When those grandparents or great grandparents passed away so did the family tradition of Norlakes. These were difficult seasons for us where our annual Christmas letter read more like obituaries and it was difficult to replace the bookings with the same family angling ethics.

There were also peculiar guests that, at the time, we all wished would not return. But the goodwill of any business is hard to mature and perhaps easy to lose if you don't respect what it took to get it in the first place. In my case it would take a number of seasons to learn the trade and to make better decisions. The Babine would also change as well and my attention was divided between fighting against the changes and marketing for new goodwill.

Having older guests is also a fight against change because they don't like change and appreciated that Norlakes stood for not changing a fine tradition of pioneer charm in a wilderness setting. In this day and age it is difficult to find such a tradition in terms of old facilities still maintained, and a relationship between guide and guest that goes beyond the 'how to' fishing experience.

There is also the illusion of a relationship between guiding and anglers where the overall fishing experience can never really reveal the true personality of either guide or guest. I say this because after guiding the same characters for a number of years, I was always surprised to find out who they really were as appearances are always deceiving. I suppose this happens in any people business where the good, bad and ugly personalities make for funny and disturbing memories. Norlakes is probably no different than many other tourism businesses where we can all laugh or cry about the many memories of people versus place.

That first season of ownership was something else because I was lucky to meet the original pioneer guests and experience their goodwill towards Norlakes and was also able to sharpen my guiding skills through attention to detail. I believe that the measure of goodwill is directly dependent on the attention to hospitality details. I also can confim that some of the most successful anglers are the ones who pay attention to every detail of their equipment and technique.

Among the very best are the ones who tie their own flies. One such was Ralph Allen. He was the kind of angler that was both hated and loved. He was hated for his rude bigotry, but he was loved for his wit, memory and attention to angling detail. He could recall the most detail of a time years ago and he was in his 90s. He also carried with him, while angling, about 10,000 flies that he tied himself. I couldn't believe it when I first guided

Ralph. He had all these cheap Macy's shopping bags full of fly boxes containing every fly for every fly-fishing moment or technique under the sun.

And yet he had quality rods, reels, fly lines and all the tools of the trade to exercise the moment of casting, together with these cheap shopping bags. He later brought far fewer flies, say 1000 or so, and in more traditional cloth- and leather-bound tackle bags. Even though Ralph was quite the character, I could always find a fly in his possession, and he knew every one of them, which would catch a great trout on the first cast. First-cast flies are something guides don't ignore and Ralph showed me that it is possible to have such flies…you just had to tie that many.

And what fun to have a group of anglers at the lodge that could drop dead at any moment and not from excessive drinking. Every detail of the day was done in slow motion but with such measured attention from years of experience. There was so much to learn from this and so many stories to enjoy which was a perfect fit for the times in a day where you can't catch a fish on every cast, or where the weather was more conducive to being back at the lodge or in a warm cabin.

Without exception these older Norlakes guests, including the crippled ones, were always the first boat out and the last boat in despite any weather. They had determination to fish all day, to cast all day, to converse all day, and to love every minute of their Norlakes experience. What a witness for a greenhorn guide like myself and I still long for the older guest because of this early years' experience.

I'm glad my first season began when I was just 25 years old. I needed the piss and vinegar of youth since Norlakes had and still does have many needs. The divorce rate for guide outfitters or angling guides is much higher than the national average. This is because attending to a hospitality business as owner and operator leaves little time for family and marital bliss. The work is very physical and the hours are long. One six-month season demands many more working hours than does a full-time, year-round job.

Raising children in this mix is another added challenge. I remember so many times when my children were little…I would come in from a day's guiding before dinner…the kids would be so happy to see me, but not happy to hear I was to guide again after dinner. Kids are full of love, forgiveness and patience but after a while they would just simply say, "no dad, no more guiding, you stay here, that's it, final." If there's no time for children, then there's no time for the wife either so it was or is a challenge to carry on family life as considered normal. But the nature of living and working in a wilderness setting is something most consider the dream life and the lessons and joys thereof make all the sacrifices seem more reasonable.

I think my children have a wiser view of people in general, and I think they will learn to appreciate the unique time they had away from the big city, the hustle and bustle, living in a truly wild ecosystem like the Babine.

The 1986 season, our first, was a remarkable one in that the fishing weather and fishing results were so stellar that greenhorn owners could be forgiven for what they were not. I guess we all get a grace period and the Babine gave us one of enormous proportions. Whether we realized it or not, we were experiencing

Like father like son, Julius Clegg with a handsome hen steelhead from Ejnar's Pool, formerly known as Camp Pool.

a world-class fishing experience complemented by wilderness values still shining to this day.

This took some time to sink in and the best example was a proposed logging bridge that had been planned for construction soon. I had known about this going into the purchase of Norlakes, but I had not known the significance of it. Not until a chopper landed on the river close to the Steelhead Camp did I realize something was seriously wrong. In fact it was not my mind that thought it through but my heart sank, and then raced with un-wanted adrenaline telling me something was very bad about this logging bridge and what it would mean to the wilderness values of the river.

The bridge fight, as it was to become, actually morphed into a full-blown watershed protection issue that eventually led to the creation of the Friends of Babine, then the Babine River Foundation (BRF) (www.babineriverfoundation.com), and the Babine Watershed Monitoring Trust (BWMT) (www.babinetrust.ca). At this time a First Nations interest conducted a blockade of a road approach to another logging bridge proposed on the lower Babine resulting in a landmark court case. Little did I know this was all about to happen and that the Babine watershed would become so hotly contested and protected. To this day the BRF and BWMT still exist and continue to promote the stewardship of the watershed, while First Nations continue to seek ownership and jurisdiction of their traditional territories.

The logging of the Babine watershed has and will have a major impact on the wilderness values. But it is also fair to say that the stewardship efforts by both non-native and native peoples on behalf of the Babine were worth every meeting and lobbying effort. By 1999 a Class 'A' Provincial Park was established and a number of land-use plans and management directions have formed a legacy of protection for the single watershed that is the Babine.

Why did all this happen and why the Babine? I believe I was sent and used to be a catalyst for change. I believe the values contained in the Babine watershed earned her protection and continued stewardship. The First Nation peoples also understood this watershed to be a line drawn in their sand, one concerned with stewardship for a watershed once inhabited by thousands where now there are only hundreds.

I became consumed with stopping the bridge from that fateful day when the chopper landed on the river. No longer was it just a tourism business and raising a family. Now it was the fight of my life for a cost of losing family and almost the tourism business as well. Most of those days are behind me now. There was a second marriage, two more children and we are all happy but will always remember the time when there was no time for each other. If any of you have ever been on some sort of government-chaired committee or committees for years...if you have ever spent ridiculous amounts of time and dollars beating your head against the wall, then you know how easy it can become to be cynical and a burn-out.

I think it is a credit to a free country and a democracy that one or a few people can truly make a difference with an issue of merit. Unfortunately we live in times that may not be that way anymore...I mean issues of merit seem not to hold their influence as once before. Yes, I am cynical about some results, but I must be very thankful to those good guys in government who helped me win some protections for the Babine. There were also some good guys outside of government too, which includes the goodwill of Norlakes. It's a good feeling to know and work with like-minded stewards of wild places. The odds are against wild places which mean the odds are against mankind surviving their greed and disrespect for the ecosystems that provide for life, but if we are going down eventually, I prefer to go down fighting than to do nothing. Apathy is not an option.

I guess the point of all this stewardship talk comes from that first season, 1986, on the Babine in which my appreciation for the wild was born. Born from the education of a wild ecosystem of extreme pleasure and spiritual influence...born from a Norlakes tradition of hard work and hospitality...born from inspirational guests and their generosity, and born from the merits of stewardship. 'Leave it better than you find it' is the fee for the privilege of gaining value from it.

Thus I ended the first season driven to fight the logging interests over the wild values I came to love but did not yet understand. The last day of each season is like saying goodbye to an old friend. The fatigue and exhausted body gives way to the cold and final moments where the weather tells you that you don't have much time left. Back in those early years, the Steelhead Camp closing included returning a huge, non-duplicate set of supplies back to the Trout Lodge before Babine Lake itself froze over. Access around the Federal Fisheries Weir, built in the mid 1940s, was allowed then so we rolled our wooden riverboats on log rollers to get around the weir.

The supplies were carried around and then we proceeded upriver into Nilkitkwa Lake and then into Babine Lake to the Trout Lodge. Often the snow was blowing, migratory ducks and geese were flying and it was a reflective dream state from exhaustion that found the mind staring through the waters dodging weed beds, shallow gravel bars and floating dead salmon. If the

ice started to form on the lakes, the wooden riverboats would be easily compromised by the saw-like ice layers…it was truly time to leave lest staying became far more complicated.

Our last task was to return the boats and supplies to the Trout Lodge and pull out the boats and outboards for winter storage. One boat remained for the trip across the lake where the vehicles were waiting for the last logging-road trip to Smithers. My first wife, Debby, was helping us guides pull the last boats only to damage one of her lower back disks. And while we were unloading the last of the supplies and engines bound for town, we didn't notice that our one untied boat had drifted into the darkness away from the dock.

Maybe it was the dead battery and flat tire that distracted us or maybe we were just too tired. Our assistant guide, Todd Stockner, and I found a canoe with no paddles. We used the two remaining log rollers as paddles and out into the darkness we went and luckily found the boat. Then it was off to town after jump-starting one of the vehicles and changing not one but two flat tires. I think I changed 18 flat tires that first season.

The next morning when Debby rolled out of bed, her injured lower back disk exploded. It was off to Vancouver via medical airlift and so we ended our first season at the Vancouver General Hospital post-back surgery with me leaning over the bed and saying to her, "well, how did you like our first season?"

Everyone knows what a honeymoon period is. Coming to Canada, dropping my life and family in Oregon and moving to Smithers and the Babine could definitely be coined a dream-come-true adventure. Since then I have spoken with many people envious of a life in the wilderness of northern B.C.

They are right but I also think they have absolutely no idea of what a different life it can be. I mentioned earlier that I felt Julius Hansen's spirit at the border crossing and that there would be many more fights ahead. Just running a wilderness tourism business is fight enough. Establishing your own goodwill takes years and there were many other business issues for which I was not really prepared nor educated to address.

My first marriage partner and my father did not see my vision for the business so it was difficult to go through the arguments and disagreements over strategic business planning and decisions. The lodge and camp were run down needing many repairs, maintenance and new capital spending. It couldn't be avoided any longer and this was happening at the same time the older guests were passing away. Revenues dropped from a loss of clientele and costs were increasing from all the necessary replacement of equipment, boats, engines, refrigerators, water heaters and many other maintenance issues.

While these more personal and business-for-self decisions were percolating, the bridge fight and related lobbying was becoming more and more time demanding. There were many lobbying trips to Victoria, the provincial capital, and there were many letters written and the follow-up letters, and research into why three logging bridges were needed to cross the Babine River.

The 1988 and 1989 seasons were where all my piss and vinegar were used up and as my second wife, Anita, put it, I was a man who hit rock bottom without a pot to piss in. Debby and I had separated at the conclusion of the '89 steelhead season, the bridge fight

having been won at what was a tremendous personal cost. The effort involved had totally consumed me and the Canadian adventure was not working out the way we had imagined it would at the outset.

To make matters worse the challenge of being a good judge of character when hiring staff could either make for a good team or a disaster. Either I was a poor judge of character or it was fate and destiny. I don't know which to this day. One particular employee, hired in 1988, I will describe as like hiring the devil himself. The last three digits of his social insurance number are 666. He interviewed like a champion of deception and lies. He was born and raised in the Babine area so I thought that would be an asset. The guests liked him and so did our female housekeepers, one of whom I fired shortly after the start of the Trout Lodge season.

As it turned out later, our devil was a speed addict and had been involved in some drowning incidents on Babine Lake. We were about to be involved in another.

A second assistant angling guide was also hired along with the devil. Perhaps this was like the story of Cain and Abel. In our early years it was very difficult to find and hire employees with prior experience in the wilderness tourism sector so we trained them ourselves. Brian Pol, from Merrit, B.C., was a pleasure to instruct and was very appreciative of the time I spent with him teaching him how to fly-fish, read the holding waters and select fly patterns for different fishing techniques. The devil was much too proud for teaching and thought the rest of us needed to be impressed by him. There seemed to be a bit of competition between the devil and Brian and it was perhaps these competitions which lead to a very dark chapter in Norlakes history.

It was 2:30 p.m. on a beautiful summer July afternoon in 1988. My wife and I had returned from a trip to Smithers for supplies. While were gone, Brian and the devil decided to play hooky from work, grabbed a bottle of booze and took a boat and headed for Tukii Lodge. Back then, Tukii Lodge had a restaurant and liquor licence. Our employees were headed there to order up more drinks. By the time they were done, they were both quite drunk.

Upon leaving the dock at Tukii Lodge, the devil fell in the water. Brian was driving, and for some unknown reason, the devil said Brian jumped out of the boat while he was driving. The devil got control of the boat and by the time he got back to where Brian had jumped in, he was sinking below the surface of the water. At least this was the devil's account of Brian's drowning. A few witnesses at the scene said they saw splashing. Scuba divers found his body days later.

Back at the lodge we were all wondering where our guides were. We decided to set out towards Tukii by boat to find them. Not too long after we departed, we met the devil returning, alone, in boat number 10. The same boat number 10 Fred Rubra and Pat swamped at Nine Mile Point. We asked where Brian was, and the reply was, "he's dead." Utter shock and disbelief set in, as we could not believe what we were hearing.

It was just so difficult to believe that Brian had just jumped out of the boat. He was a great athlete, in good shape, a good swimmer and the water in July was not very cold. The devil said the last thing he saw was a look of shock on Brian's face as he was slipping under the water. The waters of the Babine are dark. The devil said he had jumped in to find Brian at the spot he last saw him go under.

The view from the dock at Trout Lodge across Babine Lake to what some know as Sleeping Indian Mountain.

There was no time to go into this further as we had to return to the lodge where guests were waiting and we had jobs to do. The RCMP had already been to investigate and interview the devil. We discovered that he had already changed his story a few times with the Royal Canadian Mounted Police (RCMP). We had one more week of guests and then we closed the Trout Lodge.

In that time we assembled Brian's possessions and found that several pages of his diary had been torn out, perhaps including some information that had lead to his death. Later it was suspected that the devil had removed the pages from the diary in attempt to cover up relationship problems between the two guides. The devil left some of his possessions at the lodge, among them a large bag of 'speed' pills. Locating the drugs was a clue to finding the devil's eyes so dilated and glazed over in the past summer.

One of the most difficult situations I have ever experienced was to meet Brian's parents in Smithers at the mortuary so they could identify his body. Since it took a number of days for the police to recover Brian's body, it had been hastily prepared for his parents' viewing. It was a chilling scene to see him lying on a stainless-steel table with his head on a brick. Brian's parents, Caesar and Janet Pol, his brother and sister entered the room to see Brian. Words cannot describe the sounds of grief that filled that room. I will never forget the memories of that whole scene.

The tragedy of Brian's death is not so much that his young 24-year-old life was cut short, but that he seemed to have found a life worth living as an angling guide on the Babine River. At one point in his training, he thanked me for the opportunity to be at Babine and learn about the magic of fly-fishing and the tourism business. He was so excited to have found what he was looking for at last.

Another powerful, tragic outcome of Brian's drowning was the effect it had on his family. When they came to Smithers to identify his body, they wanted an inquiry to be held into the cause of his death. There was such a dark shadow over his death; the suspicion of the devil being involved in other drowning deaths on the Babine, the missing diary pages, the number of times the devil had changed his story to the RCMP, the drugs left behind, Brian's forehead marked with a red bruise.

When the autopsy results showed Brian's blood alcohol level to be very high, his father thought he must have some responsibility for his own death. The request for an inquiry was withdrawn. It was a crushing blow to his mother. Brian was the youngest of three. His father retired early.

How do you go on running a tourism business, serving the guests that remain while seeing Brian's footsteps, the projects that he was working on unfinished while remembering the budding friendship and coping with the tragic loss of losing someone on your watch?

I did not fire the devil then but gave him the benefit of the doubt. Steelhead season was upon us and five days into it he finally showed up late. By this time, I was done. A lot of questions remained unanswered and I fired him. During the following off-season I traveled to Merritt to see Brian's family.

My first intention was to pay my respects to his grave. You can see the graveyard from the highway and my eyes were fixed on the gravesites as I approached the cemetery.

As I parked the car and got out I seemed to know just where his grave was. Without knowing ahead of time, I was able to walk right to it. Following that I was able to find his parents' home, visit with them, look at photos and see just what a loving family Brian had. His friends and pals put on a memorial golf tournament for him for several years. I don't know if it isn't going on to this day. We have a memorial plaque on the front porch of the Trout Lodge in his honour.

There were several other dark moments working at Norlakes that saw 'living the dream' kind of feelings lean more towards 'living a nightmare'. The aboriginal young people at Fort Babine were restless with not much to do in the summertime and no prospects for employment. They spent some of their idle time shooting a .22-caliber rifle from the Fort Babine bridge onto the water below. One day they happened to do this just as two of our boats, carrying two young families, were drifting down the river casting dry flies and they experienced a 'bullet hatch', luckily missing both the boats and families. They were scared to death and never returned for another season.

Just when you thought you were really in the middle of nowhere, enjoying a wilderness experience, two young, white-trash males, murderers and drug dealers, arrived from Vancouver Island. They set up a tree fort along the shores of Nilkitkwa Lake on a recreational lease, taking refuge in the wilderness while the RCMP tapped the phones of their girlfriends on the Island and discovered their whereabouts. They were bad dudes, on the RCMP 'most wanted' list having murdered two Island women, execution style. The RCMP used a floatplane, a Suburban and entire SWAT team to get them.

As luck would have it, Anita was transporting a guest from Smithers to Mercury Landing to begin his fishing trip with us when, on her return trip, she was caught in the takedown on the road. A very nervous SWAT team member, who pointed his gun at her and said they had a 'situation' on their hands, stopped her at machine gun point. Having had an adventure or two on that road before, she asked the man to call on his mobile radio to her mother who had our then-youngest, Julius, in her care.

A gunshot went off, she lay on the floor of the van and some two hours later she was driving out of the area in a police convoy. One of the murderers had been shot in the hand while trying to run into the bush to escape. They were apprehended, taken to Smithers and flown by RCMP plane to Vancouver where they were incarcerated. Some years later, inmates murdered one man while drug dealers shot the other immediately after his release from prison. It took a while for the cabin owners on Nilkitkwa Lake, the villagers at Fort Babine and we at Norlakes to put this episode behind us.

There was concern by Fort Babine residents that guns had been left in a home there and there was still food and garbage at the recreational lease occupied by these men. I was asked to contact the RCMP and let them know that their mop-up was not complete.

Then we had to contend with the provincial government's decision to upgrade the lease holdings for the Fort Babine Lodge, granting it commercial operation status and closing off public access there which remains an issue to this day. To get through all that cost our business $30,000.00 to invest in a new transfer boat and motor and change our marshalling point to Smithers Landing at Tukii Lodge where Brian had drowned.

There would be other challenging staff times but nothing can be as challenging as death itself. I have seen other outfitters I know face this through accidents, floatplane crashes and all sorts of events in the bush. I have said we are lucky not to have any planes or horses but we do have the unexpected and unplanned events that are no less devastating to people's lives and dreams.

Giving up is not an option when living the pioneer life. As Brian's memorial plaque states, the lodge exists for people to find what they are looking for while fishing such a unique river in such a unique environment. I found what I was looking for even though I did not really know what it was. My wife Anita found a healing from the death of her husband just as I found healing from divorce and two young children wishing their parents would get back together.

Bridge fights, meetings, committees, good weather seasons and horrid weather seasons. No matter what happens the hospitality show keeps on at a pace from which most would walk away after just months, not years. The beauty and peace of mind that one finds in walking or boating in God's creation, the Babine, did have and still has lots to offer mind and soul while angling.

Perhaps we all get tested in our early years, which then shape who we are or what we become. The adventure of owning and operating Norlakes in keeping with its traditions while adding our own hospitality signature has become priceless. The good relationships with guests, staff and neighbors all have one common bond, a Babine experience that is in your face and soul.

I believe we will always live there in some hospitality capacity and perhaps I too will some day join the growing list of those who have had their ashes lovingly placed there. For now, all I can think of is figuring out how to make another season successful and memorable for the guests whose advance deposits are a down payment on another bonding with the river, our staff and ourselves.

The lifestyle is irreplaceable and I treasure the future where each day is greeted by the sunrise, the birds chirping, the warmth of the morning fire, a hot cup of coffee and a look at the morning sky hoping it tells me another good hatch is possible.

Folks always ask what we do in the winter months and sometime I get into trouble with Anita when I give a smart-ass answer. There's lots of planning to be done, as well as making up for lost family time. And there are always stewardship activities to pull us in as we try to make a difference in a dying world.

The Internet has created a new universe where thoughts and information circulate at lightning speed but a good book and the time to read it remains a precious and rarely found commodity. Study and ask questions and see where it leads.... seek and you shall find and, I have to add, don't stop casting or the end is near.

Steve Rewick plays a fish in Gravel Bar watched by guide Darcy Edwards.
The location is immediately downstream from where the Nilkitkwa joins the Babine.

John Madam's Death Ends First Norlakes' Chapter

The April, 2010 passing of John Madam, in Smithers, brought to a close the opening chapter of Norlakes history for, in the early 1950s, he and his parents, Charlie and Theresa, had helped to build the original lodge and cabins.

"We cut the trees in the bush and skidded them down to where we were working," he recalled. "We were young in those days and that's how we did it. We only had two horses and no chainsaws. You can still see the axe marks on the logs."

John was born in Fort Babine in May, 1926, and raised in a village on the west arm of Takla Lake. "No one goes there now. We stayed until about 1940 and I grew up with Norman West, who worked with my dad on the lodge, and all his brothers.

"I worked lots for Mac Anderson and for Joy's husband, Ejnar. There was only one power saw in the country and Mac got a hold of it and said to my dad 'You are going to have to work for it.' "

John told Pierce a few years back that he still remembered building three of the Norlakes' house-keeping cabins, Rainbow Alley, Aspens and Sunset Cove. As it happens these are the three house keeping cabins that are still rented out to guests during the summer trout fishing season.

Pierce continues: "John and his family did a lot to help Norlakes and others pioneer the fishing on the Babine. Peter Madam, John's late brother, built all the trapper cabins from Fort Babine down to the pool called Huckleberry Hill.

"Peter was very quiet and kept completely to himself, living off the land and trapping. John Madam always wondered how he raised the last logs for the trapper cabins so far above his head. No one knew how he did it since he kept entirely to himself.

"He was still alive when I came on the scene and occasionally could be seen poleing his boat across the river. No matter what the weather was like he would be dressed very lightly. He never spoke but was, like John, a fine singer. The influence of the Catholic Church meant that all the Madam boys learned lots of hymn tunes. When Anita and I attended the funeral for John's wife, Flora, he led the singing and he had a beautiful voice."

Pierce adds: "I employed John from 1986 to build log docks, replace the floor in the main Trout Lodge and also to build a log cabin for my parents on Rainbow Alley. He was always early to start work and was absolutely amazing with a chain saw, cutting all the planks and other wood by eye. He could drop a tree and then cut the lumber from it, a very handy skill to have in the bush.

"When he replaced the main lodge floor, there was a layer of newspapers under the planks dated July, 1953. I saved some of them and made up a collage. It now hangs in my parents' cabin.

"John was a part of a hard working but marginalized generation, influenced by the church and the Hudson's Bay Company. They worked for the logging companies and they helped the guide outfitters and the angling guides break the back of the wilderness. They did guiding and boat building and many other jobs that others would not accept and they did it for cheap since start-up, wilderness-based tourism operations had to have low cost, hard working labor.

"Norlakes' prices were cheap then and so was the labor and John was always there to step up and work harder than most. The next generation is not like John and, with land claims, nothing is or will be cheap again."

—*Pierce Clegg with Peter McMullan*

Anita Clegg on Friendship, Romance and a Happy Place

Anita Clegg stands beside her outdoor clay oven in the garden behind Trout Lodge.

$\mathcal{H}$aving grown up on a dairy farm in the Bulkley Valley, I had only been to Babine Lake once in my childhood. The four families that worked together on the farm shared one vehicle, a milk delivery truck that my father and his brothers used to deliver milk each day to Smithers from the farm in Quick. When my mother's sister and her family came for a visit we were able to make a short trip to Smithers Landing to fish off the government wharf for an afternoon. Trips away from the farm were a rare occurrence for all of us so it was a real treat.

The summer after I graduated from high school, I worked for Trans Provincial Airlines as a dispatcher at the seaplane base at Thyee Lake. One of the pilots had a daughter working for the Madsens on Babine Lake. One night after work I was invited to fly over to the lodge with him and visit his daughter. That was my first trip to Norlakes. I would never forget the charm of the lodge, guests just finishing their dinner and the girls clearing up and doing dishes. We were served dessert and had a visit and left before it was too dark to fly back to Thyee Lake. It would be many years before I was to go back to Norlakes, not so long before I revisited the Babine.

In November of 1974, I married Louis Giovannetti, a geophysicist come farmer. We had an unusual life from the beginning. Following a very small private wedding we set out for the Nilkitkwa, on what was later to be the Nilkitkwa Forest Service Road. We were looking for a travel trailer that the road builder had been living in while working on the approach for the bridge, just downstream from the fish-counting fence.

The road was a slippery, snowy nightmare and we nearly didn't get there. What we discovered, upon our arrival, was that the trailer had no propane, therefore no heat or way to cook. It was below freezing and the water was frozen. While Louis was scouting things outside he ran into a security man toting a rifle. When he asked Louis what we were doing there he said we were on our honeymoon. The man replied, "I did that once. Things ain't been the same since."

While I was looking around inside, it was clear there was also very little in the way of bedding. How romantic. We left early the next morning for Quick to begin a very avant-garde life together that would only span 13 years.

Pierce says it took two men to die so he could be happy. One of those men was my first husband, who had a long and tough battle with cancer, and the other was Ejnar Madsen. He also had a short and intense battle with cancer. As fate would have it they met and became friends before Ejnar died. My husband followed three years later.

While Joy was trying to cope with the loss of Ejnar and run Norlakes, I was trying to get on my feet and resume a career that I had given up to nurse my husband. Widowed and alone at 33, it was hard to focus on going ahead. I was advised to go back to university and finish my degree so that I would be employable. I

was also advised to find a camp job that paid well enough to pay for a year at university. My employment in childcare would not be enough.

I set about applying for camp cooking jobs in the mining industry where I had contacts. When not farming, Louis had taken geophysical contracts in the Arctic. I had gone with him, cooking in the tent camps in which we lived. I also contacted an outfitter I had met while working for Trans Provincial, Bob Henderson. He was not looking for anyone for his operation but suggested that I contact the Cleggs, the new owners of Norlakes. I did, and after an interview in Vancouver, where I was living at the time, I accepted a job as their cook for the 1989 season. It would be a huge job cooking for 25 guests and staff, but I was encouraged by friends and family to go ahead.

Although I was intimidated by the job, I had never felt as at home as quickly and completely as I did when I arrived at Babine that June. The lodge environment was welcoming and the weather was warm and sunny. The work was hard and the days were long but it was very satisfying to be able to serve food that people enjoyed and work with young people that were fun to be with and very light hearted.

I had a very capable and funny assistant in the kitchen, Noelle Lawrence. She really enjoyed making the guests laugh and pioneered 'lunch bag art'. She would highlight the previous day's events pictorially on their lunch bags. Things like 'biggest fish caught', 'cheating at cards', 'last boat out' etc. brought smiles and laughter as did her custom-made lunches. Peanut butter, kale

Pierce and Anita Clegg.

and blueberry sandwiches were an incentive for some gentlemen to learn to make their own lunches at the lunch table. The Cleggs had a nanny for their two young children so there was always a buzz in the kitchen and the lodge during the day. It was the beginning of healing for my broken heart.

During that summer I received word from the University of Victoria that I had been accepted and would be able to begin in September. I had the hard job of letting the Cleggs know that I had been accepted to university and would not stay on for the steelhead season. I would miss the Babine and the routine of the hard work, but wanted to get on with what I believed would be my future.

At 36 it was a nerve-wracking re-entry to university and I buried myself in it to block out my longing for a more rural life. I knew I would never settle in a city. After the steelhead season was over that year I had a phone call from Pierce saying he was sad to say his marriage was over. He was very wounded and worried about how he would be able to continue with the business and maintain an estranged family.

Over the course of the winter and into the spring we traded tales of misery and hope and supported large telephone bills. My dilemma came near the end of my university year when I had to choose between taking a job teaching at the community college and going back to Babine.

Friendship had blossomed into romance and Pierce asked me to return to Babine and work the upcoming season with him. Should we truly be a good team and successfully operate the business together we would go forward together. I had to rethink my feelings and I went to Babine.

The early years were both heaven on earth and desperately hard. We had three children under six, with Julius an infant born after the end of our first complete season running the business together. In the summers we had 21 fishermen coming and going at any given time, and in the fall we had a camp full of eager steelhead anglers, and a staff that ranged from great to dead awful. Experience is everything and I was short of it on a lot of counts.

It was a big adjustment for me to go from being an employee in a business, with which I was unfamiliar, to being part of the management team. To add to that I had years of experience raising other people's children in child-care settings but now I was a stepmother to two very young children and a new mother to boot.

I gave up cooking for a number of years to be with the kids and do the expediting and guest transport from Smithers. While it was good to see the kids grow up on the shore of the lake it was hard to see how much they missed their dad as he went off 'to work' each morning and again after dinner. I was more than a bit isolated, as I was not part of the 'kitchen team' any longer but the manager to whom they answered. It was not an easy adjustment.

When I needed a change of scenery and time away from the Trout Lodge I was always sure to find a smiling face and a cup of tea at the cabin of Louise Kelly on Nilkitkwa Lake. Her gracious hospitality, humor, and tea in a china cup never failed to lift my spirits. In her cabin our kids were always welcome, which was not always the case in the lodge kitchen.

For several years we had interesting staffing, cooks who were good with the guests, not great cooks, great cooks, not great people skills, cooks and housekeepers who were great teams and those who weren't. Living closer than you would with your own families, and having a very relentless routine was not easy for most of the young people we hired in those days.

One season I had a cook that wouldn't cook and a 'child-care helper' who was reluctant to do child-care while I was still trying to expedite and transfer guests. As the business grew and the family increased to four children, it was time once again to re-enter the kitchen and have a more 'hands-on' part in the business. So, when Jesse, our youngest, was able to branch out a bit and not be totally in my care, it was time to make a change.

We were blessed to have Dorelene Pflugbiel come and live and work with us and care for our children. Although she was only expected to care for and guide our children, she happily included the children who came as guests with their families. She was tireless in her efforts to make it a fun and educational time for all. She also was a huge treat for the other staff and organized the most amazing treasure hunts for the housekeeper and guides.

She was lovingly referred to by all of us as 'Nona' because Jesse could not say Dorelene. Her presence and hard work allowed us a very precious four years of fairly smooth sailing for the family and business. Those were the glory days.

It was then that we were able to come to our senses and reduce our weekly guest capacity from 21 to 14. This was a much more manageable workload and made for better service, happy guests and staff and lastly a happy, growing family. Additional highlights were the chances for fun additions to the Trout Lodge kitchen arsenal. My visits with Louise Kelly were always an inspiration. She and her husband, Bob, and their family had dredged clay from the bottom of Nilkitkwa Lake and built an outdoor oven from which, Louise produced the most amazing baked goods and meals.

The seed was planted and I began to research how to build my own outdoor clay oven. That summer I gathered many wheelbarrow loads of rocks and made a crude wooden frame in which to put them. Pierce's dad helped me make a bit of cement to pour over the rocks to form the oven's base. That winter, the pastor of our church asked me if the men's retreat, slated for that coming spring, could help build the oven.

During the winter, Pierce found an old barrel in the California wine country and we ordered the firebrick and bought cement to be mixed with soil for this project. A small cement mixer was also brought out by boat to accomplish the job.

As I cooked in the lodge, I could see the new oven taking shape just outside the kitchen window. Once the cement was cured and the initial firing had been accomplished, I tried a variety of meals and breads. I had success and failures and I was looking for a more consistent outcome. For that reason, most of the cooks we employed were reticent to use the oven for lodge meals.

I was able to get a pyrometer from a local potter and could then see the oven temperature without opening the door and losing heat. In the course of my cooking adventures, I did

manage to burn up three custom-made wooden doors before having a metal one fabricated which is still in current use. We have and continue to enjoy prime rib and turkey dinners, bread, pies and pizza. To quote Pierce: "When the cook is happy, we're all happy."

The second major happiness investment was the greenhouse. I do love to garden and one summer I was tending a vegetable garden that was being demolished by a marmot. Being totally surrounded by testosterone at every turn, I decided this must be a female marmot and named her 'Marmella'. The kids loved to watch her chewing up the kale in the garden. Pierce thought he should encourage her to 'move along' but I foolishly said the kids were enjoying watching her from the washstand where I stood to hang out the clothes. Big mistake. She chewed almost all my emerging garden off, right to the roots.

I started again hoping I would still have some produce for the table. Well, she sure enjoyed my efforts and chewed everything off the minute it poked its head up out of the soil. Apparently I was right about her gender because it wasn't long before there were many marmots around enjoying the abundant greenery and what was left of my garden. When we left that fall, she settled in comfortably under the lodge, with her entire family. The following spring I planted another garden in the hopes I would be successful. I wasn't.

That summer, after seeing me struggle again with the attempt to keep produce in the garden and Pierce's unsuccessful attempts to 'relocate' the family, we had a visit from the pastor. Between relaxing with his family and doing some fishing, he harvested some poles from the bush and put up a frame we would cover with plastic.

The following spring beds were built, soil was dug up in the bush behind the lodge and we planted out first greenhouse garden. It has always been a challenge to keep produce fresh for a full week so a garden of some sort was both a treat and a necessity. Each year the beds were enriched, as was the production of salad greens and herbs.

This greenhouse had a very eventful life of its own. Each time a helicopter landed and took off in the back yard, the plastic would fly off making it look more like a sailboat. Although it wasn't a frequent occurrence, it was the end of the greenhouse walls and roof for the rest of the season. The snow loads during the winter wreaked havoc with the log structure. In the spring of 2007 we arrived to discover the whole frame reduced to a pile of poles. We are now experimenting with an aluminium-frame greenhouse.

Being somewhat isolated from familiar female friends during the spring and summer, it was always a treat to have a group of women come early in June to help plant flowers. Choosing a weekend when they could all get there, they would arrive with a boat load of flowers and spend the weekend planting the window boxes and hanging baskets for the cabins and the lodge.

They have always been referred to as the 'sunshine girls' because no matter what the weather had been the days before their arrival, the sun always came out for that weekend. While I

cooked for them, they planted flowers and we also had time for great campfire visits and a few glasses of wine.

Along with kitchen happiness came the discovery of all the wild produce available for harvest and use. While Dorelene was busy taking the kids on nature walks and identifying plants, flowers and birds, I was also taking the time to pick berries and mushrooms. The lodge garden has a great supply of current bushes, planted by the Madsens, and I added raspberry canes. While the berries are convenient to pick being close to the lodge, it didn't satisfy my gathering instincts to hoard or store.

All the kids have been dumped out of backpacks and rolled over by logs in search of morel mushrooms in the early spring and cranberries in the late summer. Once able to navigate on their own, the kids were issued pails for the hunt and harvest. Along with the gathering instinct is the instinct to hoard or store. Pierce has built me several mushroom dryers over the years, to maximize our supply of dried morels, and had a few calls to add to the grocery list for more canning jars and sugar to make jelly and jam.

For all the years Pierce and I have been together, we have humorous mushroom stories. Very early on in our life together, Pierce took his dad on a spring bear hunt. On their way back to the Lodge, Pierce came across a huge patch of morels. He took off his full-length oilskin coat and began to pick morels and fill this coat. His father was puzzled about this, not knowing how

Pierce with a fine September haul of wild mushrooms.

much I appreciated this treat. When they returned, Pierce said: "Watch this dad, Anita is going to be really excited when she sees all these mushrooms."

When Pierce lay the bulging coat down on the dock, he said: "Bet you can't guess what is in this coat." Because they had been hunting, I wasn't keen to open the coat, fearing what I would see. Once I opened the coat and saw the haul of mushrooms, I was jumping up and down and squealing. Wanting to see this reaction again, he never fails to pick mushrooms for me wherever he might be hiking, driving or guiding on the Babine.

It was cooking that took me to Babine, but I also liked to fish and those opportunities were limited to time away from both the kids and the kitchen. It was a very rare occasion that I was even able to fish with Pierce.

For many seasons, we had the great pleasure of having Kathy Ruddick, one of Canada's best known and most proficient anglers, come to the lodge with groups of fishermen. Each year she would ask me to have a day of fishing with her. I was very anxious to go so one year I made sure all the bases were covered and I was able to spend the whole day out with her. We had a great day of fishing and I was pleased to get some tips on casting and enjoy Kathy's cheerful company. As the day was coming to a close, the weather started to change. Storms develop and intensify quickly on the Babine.

We were just about back to the bridge at Fort Babine when thunder started to rumble and crack, lightning struck, rain started to come down. We slowed down to put our jackets on and the graphite rods stood up in the boat by themselves. Kathy reached for them to get them to lie down again and zap, they stung her hand. She dropped them and they stood up again. Once again she reached to put the rods down again and again, zap! I was driving the boat, Kathy sat down, back to the wind and we headed for home as fast as we could get there.

At the lodge, the air had a burned electrical smell and the storm was about to hit hard. We had other anglers out in boats and all of them arrived back but one. The father and two teenage kids spent the night in a house in Fort Babine, having been lucky to get there during the storm. Esther Joseph, the same First Nations woman who had requested help to have weapons removed from her home when the murderers were arrested, took in our guests. Never before or since have we been in the situation where it was just too risky to go out and look for a guest who did not return after fishing.

As I look back on two decades of life on the Babine, I ask myself why this place is my 'happy place'. Is it the peace, the beauty, the abundance of life? Is it because I have found love and a family? I think more than anything, the Babine has the ongoing ability to recharge my soul. The soul of the angler who never gets enough, the gardener's soul whose season is too short and the mother's soul who has raised her children on the banks of a lake and a river and hopes to be there with her grandchildren. It is home.

When we began our life together we were both broken people struggling to keep the business afloat and raise a blended family. Not for the faint of heart. Blood sweat and tears and the wild of the Babine keep us in the game.

Finally It's Turnover Day

*Pierce was 50 in October, 2009 and his daughter,
Nicole, surprised him with this childhood memory
of a special day at Trout Lodge.*

*B*irds singing, waves rippling and the sound of Johnston 25 hp outboard engines idling. Time to get up. It's usually so hard to get up because that means unzipping the sleeping bag, toes touching the ice-cold wooden floorboards, and stumbling around trying to find matches to light the propane-fuelled lamp in the bathroom.

Today is different. I can always muster the motivation because it is turnover day; no guests and dad is here to stay. Fifteen minutes pass and I'm out the sleeping-cabin door, running down the rocky path, jumping over old roots and flying through the original Trout Lodge door. There he is, moving around the lodge, in and out of doors, doing errands.

"Dad," I exclaim.

"Morning 'Cole." This was his usual greeting.

"Can we go fishing today?" I ask, secretly hoping he doesn't have other things to do around the lodge.

"I'm all yours today," he says with a big smile on his face.

In about 30 minutes, I'll be on a boat with my dad, heading out towards Rainbow Alley on the Babine River. As my dad always says, "on a world-class river for world-class fishing."

After eating French toast, my favourite, and packing a lunch, which must always be in a brown bag with my name ornately illustrated on the front, I am helping dad load up the boat with tackle, fly rods, lunches and other fishing gear. It's clear skies, calm waters; perfect for fishing. We're off, gliding smoothly down the lake, the crisp air brushing our faces and clearing our lungs.

As dad slows the engine to a stop, he reminds me: "OK 'Cole, get your rod out and start fishing."

We drift down Rainbow Alley several times. Talking about life, my dreams when I grow up, dad's childhood memories and how to think like a fish.

Dad helps me to find the fish, "look, there's a rise," and shows me how to cast straight, "two o'clock, pause, 10 o'clock" and "remember to keep your wrist straight."

When I get a fish on he also helps me with landing it in the net and then unhooking it because I am afraid of it jumping out of my hands. I am so happy just drifting and fishing with my dad.

When I feel like giving up because nothing has bit my line in what seems like hours, dad is there to encourage me and

teach me about patience and perseverance. When I get restless and need a break, dad is there to let me enjoy watching nature's miracle all around me while he happily fly-fishes. I learn about the life cycle of fish, the importance of catch-and-release fishing, why we must slow down when we pass other people on the river, what wild mushrooms and berries are safe to eat and how to read the water so I don't hit the shallows when I drive the boat.

I am allowed to keep one fish for dinner. When we return to the lodge at dusk, dad shows me how to gut and clean my catch of the day.

Today I get really lucky when I plead with him to "please show me how to gut the trout with the heart still pumping."

"Alright," he says obligingly, always with a smile on his face.

Dad always explains the steps to cleaning out my fish and the biology behind the heart still pumping. I do not get grossed out. I am fascinated how all those parts of the fish work and wonder how my dad seems to know all its parts.

I can't wait until one day when I can take my children out fishing the Babine to Rainbow Alley. I'll teach them boater's etiquette and safety, about ecology, how to drive and dock a boat, how to read water, how to find food in the wilderness, of course how to fly-fish, but most importantly, to love and appreciate nature.

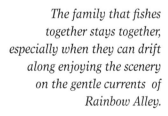

Jake and Ely Schroppel and their friend Whitney Van Cleeve prove yet again that it's not only the adults who have fun going fishing. As it happens their fish was the largest caught by Trout Lodge guests that week.

The family that fishes together stays together, especially when they can drift along enjoying the scenery on the gentle currents of Rainbow Alley.

CANADA'S COMMUNITY FORESTRY FORUM

FOREST *Planning*
CANADA

Volume 4, Number 5 September/October 1988 $4.00

- **Forest Service Attempts Sacrifice Of Fishery, Tourism Values**   *P. 5*

- **$14 Billion At Stake In Forest Privatization Scheme**   *P. 8*

*W*hen I was attending Pacific Lutheran University (PLU) in the late 1970s, I took a logic course from Prof. John Nordby. He had a chance to participate in the House of Representatives JFK Assassination Committee but was turned down. That didn't deter his interest in the case against Lee Harvey Oswald and his logic course was used to apply logical thinking to the case, or lack thereof, against Oswald. It was a very interesting course and one in which my naive opinion of government would be changed forever.

In short, the course taught us how there was no case against Oswald that would stand up in a court of law, and the logical conclusion would be to ask who might have killed the

president if Oswald didn't? There are lots of books on that but what I took from that course helped me apply logic to the upper Babine River bridge fight and beyond. Conspiracy theories, I have some.

Upon completion of the 1987 steelhead season, I began investigating why a proposed logging bridge was needed when there was an existing bridge so close by. Another professor from my PLU days, Professor Ralph Gurke, taught me to ask questions even if you don't get all the answers, that the asking of the questions leads to knowledge. So I visited our local Smithers, B.C. Environment Ministry and spoke with a habitat technician, Gord Wolfe. He gave me some information to study on the proposed bridge and I took it home and began to read.

There was much to learn about the government of Canada and the relationship between what I think are competing provincial ministries, like the ministries of Tourism, Environment and Forestry. There was much to learn about the type of language they used to communicate fish, wildlife and habitat issues, and the forestry jargon was immense. The more information I read, the more questions I had which led to more trips to visit Gord or anyone who would meet with me.

Each report I read sparked my curiosity and Gord was the first to hear me say, "I think this report means this and if it does, we have a problem...do you agree with my conclusion or am I reading this information wrong?" Gord and others would say, "No, you're not reading it wrong."

I was very fortunate to find some friends in government like Gord who were attracted to issues with merit and would help me gather more information and recommend courses of action. These people were Ray Travers, Dave Narver, Frank Hussey, Stuart Gayle and Jack Kempf. They provided information and helped me lobby government at the cabinet level and Jack Kempf was a cabinet-level Minister of Forests.

The basic question and issue was why the need for a new bridge when an existing one was a very short distance away? While I was working on answering that question, First Nation interests were just beginning a blockade of yet another Babine River bridge, proposed for the lower Babine River area near Sam Green Creek. And then to make matters worse, a third proposed bridge was added to the controversy, supposedly to be located extremely close to the Silver Hilton Steelhead Lodge on one of the very best steelhead runs.

Now it was three logging bridges, widespread clear-cut logging of the entire Babine River watershed and the work was to begin as soon as possible. My first winter after my first year of ownership, my wife fresh from back surgery, would begin a long chapter in stewardship efforts that would eventually lead to a Class A Provincial Park, the cancellation of all three proposed bridges and the creation of a multi-layer land-use planning quagmire that still causes one to wonder if issues of merit no longer rule the day.

An issue of merit could get legs quick back in the 1980's, and quickly the Babine gained attention simply because it was and is a truly world-class trophy property for the people of B.C. The steelhead fishery, the river rafting and the grizzly bears became a trio of values which, when combined with the huge salmon run, made the issue attractive and credible. The Babine was the only thing standing in the way of the Hazelton and Smithers sawmills getting to a new source of timber in the Sustut-Takla watershed. It was a race between Prince George area mills and those of Smithers and Hazeleton.

In the end the awarding of the Sustut-Takla timber would be decided by the then Forestry Minister, Dave Parker. Getting the Sustut-Takla timber would have prolonged the over-cutting of timber supply areas particularly in the Terrace and Hazelton areas, so the Babine crossings were a grand plan, a 20-year plan to extend the clear-cutting style of logging that still persists to this day.

Bob Nixon, who then was managing editor of a quarterly publication called *FOREST Planning CANADA*, wrote a great piece on the upper bridge fight in the fall of 1988. Shortly after the writing of that article, the two upper Babine River bridge proposals were cancelled amid suspicion and controversy. It would become a beachhead for the first publicly endorsed land-use plan called the Land Resource Use Plan for the Babine River. This new plan would lead to more plans, a park and the cancellation of all proposed bridges across the Babine River.

First Nations would have victory and a landmark court case over the Sam Green Creek bridge proposal across the Babine River, and the Silver Hilton Steelhead Lodge would also secure protection from a proposed bridge in their guiding area.

The following, reprinted with his permission, is Bob Nixon's article...

Forest Service Attempts to Sacrifice Fishery, Tourism Values on the Babine River
Former Minister Misled, Important Research Data Withheld

By Bob Nixon, Managing Editor, FOREST Planning CANADA, *September-October 1988*

Forest Service Attempts To Sacrifice Fishery, Tourism Values On The Babine River

Bob Nixon

Former Minister Misled, Important Research Data Withheld

"In gathering the facts, it became increasingly obvious that serious forestry mismanagement exists. As far as we can tell, no complete 'integrated' management plan has been developed. The purpose of this report is to further enlighten you to this volatile issue, and get results in favour of true integrated management." *Friends of the Babine, April 1988, a report to Premier Vander Zalm.*

"*In gathering the facts, it became increasingly obvious that serious forestry mismanagement exists. As far as we can tell, no complete 'integrated' management plan has been developed. The purpose of this report is to further enlighten you to this volatile issue, and get results in favor of true integrated management.*" *Friends of the Babine, April 1988, a report to (British Columbia) Premier (Bill) Vander Zalm.*

So began an expose about alleged Forest Service mismanagement, prepared by local business (non-timber) interests in a northern B.C. area which was about to be adversely affected by what they believe is inappropriate and unnecessary Forest Service road development. In some ways, this was a classic conflict between the 'other' forest values and king-timber. Ray Collingwood, a long-time northern guide-outfitter said in a letter to Forest Minister Parker, "What we have here is a unique wild-life area and a river system housing the most magnificent Steelhead fishery in the world. We have been blessed with two major trophy Steelhead rivers—the Dean and the Babine. Before us is one of the most delicate environmental decisions to be made."

In March of 1987, the Forest Minister Jack Kempf visited the site of a proposed bridge crossing on the Babine River. The crossing was recommended to the minister by Bulkley District Manager Guenter Stahl. At that time, the plan was already creating a lot of controversy, at least locally. In a news release prepared for the forest minister after his visit, Stahl said, "We have a mountain pine beetle infestation in the area and it's urgent we get in to log it to control the outbreak." Documents provided to the minister by the District Forest Service Office estimated that the timber to be made accessible by the new road and bridge

would bring in roughly $400 million over the next twenty years. However, as the story unfolded over the following year it became clear that both the beetle scare and data selected to justify the new road corridor were a selected assemblage of misleading facts.

Before getting Victoria's permission to build the new access route and bridge, District Manager Stahl had to convince the Forests Minister to support his plan. Local residents didn't oppose logging, but did want the Forests Minister and his district staff to support the use of an existing road and bridge which would have left the valuable fishery habitat along this section of the Babine River in a natural state—without easy human (vehicle) access which could decimate the fish population.

Selected documents supplied by Stahl claimed the new route would result in over $7 million savings in log hauling costs. Tourism interests feared the new access route would lead to over-fishing and thereby cause the destruction of the wilderness-style businesses operating on the river which is recognized world-wide for its superb wilderness fishing qualities. The complete proposal by the Forest Service district office apparently called for an eventual total of three new crossings over the Babine.

Residents had begun to wonder if Stahl saw it as his sole mandate to find new wood supplies, at any cost, for Westar Timber to run its new $40 million Carnaby mill at Hazelton, and supply two older mills, one of which was subsequently closed. In support of Stahl's bid for the new route across the Babine, Westar employees were asked to write letters to the present Forest Minister, Dave Parker, emphasizing the beetle infestation as cause enough to push ahead. Yet the suspicion remained that

the timber supply for the region had been over cut already. If this were true, forest industry advocates would probably not think twice if they had to destroy other "non timber" forest-related businesses such as the Babine wilderness fishery, in the process of finding new timber to cut.

At the same time, a bit further east in Prince George Forest District, a concentration of lumber mills was also casting about to find new timber outside their traditional 'sustained-yield' supply area. Just over a decade ago, the Forest Service encouraged the Prince George mills to expand capacity to handle another 'insect infestation.' By the time the Forest Service was satisfied the little critters were 'under control', the region's long-term timber supply had been seriously over-cut. In desperation the Prince George mills were looking to the Takla-Sustut, just north of Hazelton and Westar's traditional cutting area, as the place to renew their depleted sustained-yield timber supply. Stahl's new road would have helped Westar expand its timber cutting 'influence area' toward the Takla-Sustat. The price for the successful mills was a new annual timber quota of 400,000 cubit meters, but one which is expected to run out within 20 years.

Pierce and Debby Clegg run Babine-Norlakes Lodge on the Babine River near the site of Stahl's proposed road and bridge system. The Clegg's fishing guide business, along with those of a number of other wilderness outfitters—river rafters, hunting and fishing guides could have been wiped out if Stahl got his new road.

In a letter dated April 8, 1988, to Premier Vander Zalm, Pierce Clegg says of Stahl's handling of the issue, "I must report to you that mandates are being violated, valuable resources degraded, and attempts by the public to correct this situation have been met with concealment of information including unethical, if not criminal behavior." Clegg was referring to alleged acts by Bulkley Forest District staff to pad the transportation/log hauling cost figures used to justify the new access route. The data compared the cost of the new route with that of an alternate, existing road and bridge which already provided access to the timber north of the Babine.

Suspecting that the Forest Service was involved in a cover-up, Clegg got in touch with the former Forest Minister Jack Kempf to find out if he had ever been told by his staff of an engineering study, done by a senior Forest Service engineer, which refuted Stahl's claim of substantial savings if the new route were built. In his reply to Clegg, dated May 11, 1988, Kempf (now sitting in the legislature as an independent) said, "Please allow me to say that on the March 5, 1987 visit to which you referred, I was not made aware (by district staff) of the 'Babine-Nilkitwa Investigation', dated October 30, 1986. Perhaps if I had been, my decisions with respect to the building of a new crossing of the Babine would have been opposite from what it was. One could definitely say that I was not fully informed as to the true viability of the alternative (existing road) and therefore I based my decision (to support Stahl's proposal) on an incomplete story." Kempf further confirmed in an interview with FPC that district staff had never told him of the existence of transportation/cost data which showed the existing road to be a viable option.

Clegg's letter and report to the Premier emphasized, "Those fighting to preserve the Babine river have not been asking the Forest Service to give up significant timber values...previously con-

cealed relevant information strongly suggests that the new upper bridge route is much more expensive in all categories."

The data selected by Stahl showed the new bridge cost savings would be $229,696 annually for 32 years. On the basis of these figures, Stahl pushed ahead. During the summer of 1987, he authorized the clearing of a road right-of-way to within meters of the site of the proposed bridge. Opposition, however, was beginning to build. By the fall of 1987, senior officials in the Forest Service decided to have another look at the proposal. This time, a more "integrated" approach was taken, with the creation of an inter-ministerial committee including fisheries staff from the Ministry of Environment and Parks (EP) and staff from the Ministry of Tourism, Recreation and Culture (TRC). An inter-ministry report was prepared, largely drafted by the Forest Service. EP and TRC committee members refused to approve this new report even though it reversed the earlier Forest Service decision to immediately build the bridge. On an all too familiar note, a committee member from outside the Forest Service was critical of the data used to justify the report's conclusions.

Meanwhile, Stahl again tried to push ahead, claiming his earlier expenditure of public funds to build the bridge approach road was in itself justification to proceed with bridge construction. He also argued that the contract for the bridge construction was already signed and could not be reversed. As it turned out, the accepted bid was too high, exceeding the forest district's authorized budget. So after telling Clegg and other local residents of his inability to cancel the contract, Stahl quietly re-awarded the contract to a bidder whose offer was within the district's budget. The new contractor was Pacific Inland Resources.

In the meantime, higher-ups in the Forest Service finally decided to take the issue out of the hands of the local forest district manager. Bruce Sieffert, Planning and Inventory Officer in the Smithers regional office, was named to head a new investigation. His report was scheduled for completion during June of this year.

After the end of the 1987 tourism/fishing season, Chick Stewart, the new owner of Babine Steelhead Lodge, traveled with Clegg to Victoria to meet with Bruce Strachan, Minister of Environment and Parks, Bill Reid, Minister of Tourism, Recreation and Culture, Ben Marr, Deputy Minister of Forests and Lands, and Mike Wilkins, Assistant Deputy Minister, Operations, Ministry of Forests and Lands. As a result, a new inter-ministerial committee comprising Environment, Forest, Tourism, and Economic Development was formed. Its first decision was a moratorium on bridge construction until it completed yet another review of Stahl's original decision. This committee's recommendations were due April 1, 1988.

The access proposal finally began to unravel when engineering reports, which the District has concealed, were leaked to Clegg and other local businessmen. An October 30, 1986 engineering study, along with a November 14, 1986 memorandum addressed to the district manager, referring to the October report, had, in the words of Pierce Clegg, "...revealed the true colors of unethical and possible illegal behavior on the part of the Forest Service."

The October report concludes there is no significant difference in transportation costs, no matter which access road is used. The November memorandum is from the Smithers regional office,

addressed to Stahl. It also states that two bridge routes, the existing one and the new access proposed by Stahl, would be used in any case to extract timber north of the Babine. Says Clegg, "It is amazing how the bridge issue changes when one has all the facts and considers the 'big picture' in timber extraction."

Stahl had publicly claimed the existing bridge and road were in an advanced state of decay and upgrading would be too expensive. He claimed the bridge timbers on the many creek and ravine crossings on the old access road were too rotten and weak to support logging trucks. This position has since been contradicted by forest engineers employed within the local forest industry.

Early on, Stahl attempted to win over the tourism operators by creating a review committee of his own. He called it the "Babine-Nilkitkwa Resource Committee." At Stahl's invitation, Clegg and other business operators participated. But the committee's terms of reference, set by the Forest Service, would not allow committee members to discuss whether or not to build the new bridge. Instead, discussion was limited, in Clegg's words, to "how and when to construct it (the new route)." Members of Stahl's committee were not told of the existence of the October 30th, 1986 report during the course of its deliberations.

Another report never disclosed by the Forest Service, but subsequently obtained by local residents, was the 1987 Mountain Pine Beetle survey from the Babine area. It showed that in the last four years ending with 1987, the pine beetle infestation was insignificant north and east of the Babine River. This was precisely the area the new route would have made available. Local forest companies, at least privately, admit the bug scare launched by the Forest Service was a fake, an excuse to push the road into new timber.

While this story has a happy ending—the new access route will not be built—there remains, however, a larger question: Is this case typical of the manner in which the Forest Service approaches its integrated management responsibilities?

(Postscript: While both Deputy Ministers—Environment and Forests—have advised Forests Minister Parker to overrule Stahl and announce that the new access route will not be built, a news release to that effect is still sitting on the Minister's desk, unsigned.)

At the time FOREST Planning CANADA, *was published bimonthly in Victoria, B.C. by Woodland Planning Publications Inc., 'to promote the wise use of Canada's forests'.*

Fighting Bridges our only option (continued)

$\mathcal{E}$ven after all the land-use plans and park designation, the true hand of the forestry sector played yet another unethical hand. A bridge was finally constructed across the Babine River very near its confluence with the Skeena. This area was technically outside the park designation and downstream of the Indian Reserve area. This exclusion was done for a reason unrevealed but it was said to the land-use planning tables that the spirit and intent of the land-use plans would extent to the confluence of the Babine and Skeena rivers.

The bridge was constructed without notification to any land-use planning table and later on the Forest Practises Board, a new watchdog board like the fox looking after the henhouse without any authority to penalize, did say the new Babine River bridge violated land-use plans. A slap on the hand, no penalties and since then clear-cut logging has proceeded into the most sensitive grizzly bear habitat identified during the land-use planning phase. And guess where the new logging road direction provided by this new bridge is headed towards? Yes, the Sustut-Takla area, but it has since been blockaded by another First Nation House Territory Chief with the help of a tourism operator.

And what about one of the smallest provincial parks in BC, the Babine River Corridor Park? It is known as the 'weenie park' since it is so narrow and seems functionally ineffective in protecting itself from logging outside its borders. In fact, the most recent land-use plan for the Babine watershed included much debate about the small size of the park and its vulnerability to logging outside its narrow borders. The excuse to log is still the pine beetle so the wilderness values of the Babine, not to mention the extremely high archaeological values, are still on the chopping block.

At issue with all the land-use plans and park status for the Babine, is the implementation and monitoring of the plans and park master plan. All the years spent in planning committees and meetings has taught me that without firm legal standing, fancy land-use plan words like 'maintain the world class angling', or 'maintain the wilderness values', or 'maintain the grizzly bear population', or 'maintain the water quality' are meaningless management guidelines or directions without legal standing. It's a shame and scar upon the spirit and intent of these plans that knowingly weak terminology was signed off in the name of integrated resource management or what is known as a 'win-win' solution.

The Babine River Foundation (www.babineriverfoundation.com) is dedicated to protecting and preserving the wilderness tourism qualities of the Babine River watershed with very limited resources. The foundation is also the only private funder of the Babine Watershed Monitoring Trust (www.babinetrust.ca). The priorities of the forest industry remain logging and clear-cutting the Babine watershed for saw logs and nothing more.

Issues of merit no longer mean that ethical treatment of the same can be expected. The fish farm and sea lice issue of B.C. is case in point. Stewardship of land, water and marine ecosystems is an afterthought even despite the positive economics or net benefit of wilderness tourism or any other economic benefit derived from the wild.

But the call is not to be apathetic and feel one cannot make a difference. The call is to buy precious time for the wild by becoming involved and getting results whether the end game is a total loss or failure. I prefer to go down fighting than to give the bastards an easy way to their greed.

—Pierce Clegg

Press Release a Critical Document

*The faded postmark is dated September 20, 1988, and the letter to Pierce Clegg carries a
37-cent Canadian stamp and the address Office of the Premier, Victoria, British Columbia.
For all who care for the Babine, the enclosed press release remains a critical document to
this day. Issued on September 6, 1988, its headline reads:*

Government Cancels Plan for Bridge on the Upper Babine River

The complete Province of British Columbia release states:

Victoria—Plans have been cancelled for the construction of a bridge on the upper Babine River in northwest British Columbia, Forests Minister Dave Parker and Environment Minister Bruce Strachan have announced.

The bridge was to have provided access to timber stands north and east of the river.

Instead, the British Columbia Forest Service's (BCFS) Nilkitkwa/Horetzky road will be upgraded this summer to provide access to timber in the Bulkley timber supply area east of the Babine, Parker said.

"This decision is the result of a special approval planning study undertaken by the two ministries in recognition of special fishery values of the Babine River," the minister said.

Strachan said the upper Babine River is important for the trophy steelhead fishery and there were major concerns about the impact the proposed bridge might have on that fishery,

In making the announcement Parker noted that the Shedin Bridge, at the Babine's lower end, has been approved and construction will commence shortly. "The Shedin Bridge is critical for access to timber stands and its impact of recreational and fisheries values in the Babine will be minimal," he said.

Parker said planning for the Gail Bridge, mid-way down the Babine, will be undertaken using the BCFS's local resource-use planning process.

Strachan said a special fishery policy for the Babine River—similar to that developed for the Dean River in the mid-coast area in 1987—will be in place for the 1989 fishing season.

To maintain a high-quality angling experience on the river in a wilderness setting, the policy calls for a limit on the number of guide operations and anglers on the river, Strachan said.

He said the environment and forest ministries will extend the local resource-use planning process to develop an integrated resource-use plan for the Babine drainage area.

Meanwhile, the BCFS has closed the recently constructed road to the proposed Upper Babine bridge to all motorized recreational vehicles, Parker said.

"Reseeding the right-of-way will be addressed in the local resource-use plan for the Babine drainage area," the minister said.

-30-

Contact:	Bob Friesen	Bob Hooton
	Regional Manager	Head, Fisheries
	Ministry of Forests	Ministry of Environment
	Smithers	Smithers

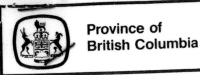

Province of British Columbia

NEWS RELEASE

MINISTRY OF FORESTS
HON. DAVE PARKER, MINISTER

FOR IMMEDIATE RELEASE

MINISTRY OF ENVIRONMENT
HON. BRUCE STRACHAN, MINISTER

September 6, 1988

1988:126

GOVERNMENT CANCELS PLAN FOR BRIDGE ON THE UPPER BABINE RIVER

VICTORIA -- Plans have been cancelled for construction of a bridge on the upper Babine River in northwest British Columbia, Forests Minister Dave Parker and Environment Minister Bruce Strachan have announced.

The bridge was to have provided access to timber stands north and east of the river.

Instead, the British Columbia Forest Service's (BCFS) Nilkitkwa/Horetzky road will be upgraded this summer to provide access to timber in the Bulkley timber supply area east of the Babine, Parker said.

"This decision is the result of a special approval planning study undertaken by the two ministries in recognition of special fishery values of the Babine River," the minister said.

Strachan said the upper Babine River is important for the trophy steelhead fishery and there were major concerns about the impact the proposed bridge might have on that fishery.

In making the announcement Parker noted that the Shedin Bridge, at the Babine's lower end, has been approved and construction will commence shortly. "The Shedin Bridge is critical for access to timber stands and its impact on recreational and fisheries values in the Babine will be minimal," he said.

OFFICE OF THE PREMIER
VICTORIA, BRITISH COLUMBIA V8V 4R3

Mr. Pierce M. Clegg
Babine Norlakes Lodge
P.O. Box 1060
Smithers, British Columbia
V0J 2N0

Ejnar's Old Map No Ordinary Relic

Like all good guides Pierce is an accomplished fly tier,
often working at the bench in his cabin, appropriately called The Gilly.

A fishing guide's cabin is a largely secret, private place, out-of-bounds to all but a very few close friends and guests, a refuge to which he escapes from the very real pressures of his business, if only for a few snatched hours of much-needed rest at the close of each 18-hour day.

Pierce Clegg's Steelhead Camp cabin, aptly named The Gilly, is where he sleeps, ties flies and stores enough spare tackle, waders and clothing to equip a small army of all sizes—in particular those guests who have been parted from their bags by one airline or another. It's also dominated, in the far corner occupied by his bed, by a large and faded wall map of his beloved Babine River.

This is no ordinary relic of a long-ago era. It's a survey map produced many years back. What makes it so special is the fact that, more than half a century ago, it was carefully annotated by Ejnar Madsen, the man who built the Steelhead Camp back in the mid-1960s. Over the years he identified and named 37 of the approximately 75 pools that comprise the upper and middle Babine River steelhead fishery with each name hand printed on his map with black ink.

Later, he used red ink to distinguish the alternate names (*in italics below*), used by the downriver Babine Steelhead Lodge. It may sound confusing, and in a way it is, but Ejnar's map does help the visitor understand better some of the origins of the fishing history of this great river.

He even marks two public-access points as Joe Public #1 and Joe Public #2, both located river right and down from the fish-counting weir, one above and the other below where the Nichyeskwa, a key spawning tributary, comes in river left. Further downstream, river left, a dotted line marks the old trail used by served fishermen staying at the camp. It runs from Olson's Riffle to the head of Trail Drift, now two adjacent, extensive pools called Upper and Lower Trail

Ejnar's widow, Joy (Madsen) Jenkins explains that, as the years went by, he would venture further and further down river to find new pools for the fishermen. "It was always an adventure but Lower Forty was as far as he liked to go. As the days got shorter, running the boats on that treacherous river in the dark was not an option for him," she said.

In the days before the Steelhead Camp was established, Ejnar would bring his lodge guests by boat as far as the weir for their day's fishing.

Joy continues: "He soon had a path cleared along the sides of the river and this allowed the fishermen to walk down to where the Nilkitkwa joined the main stream on the right bank. The first pool to be named was Half Way as that was deemed to be about

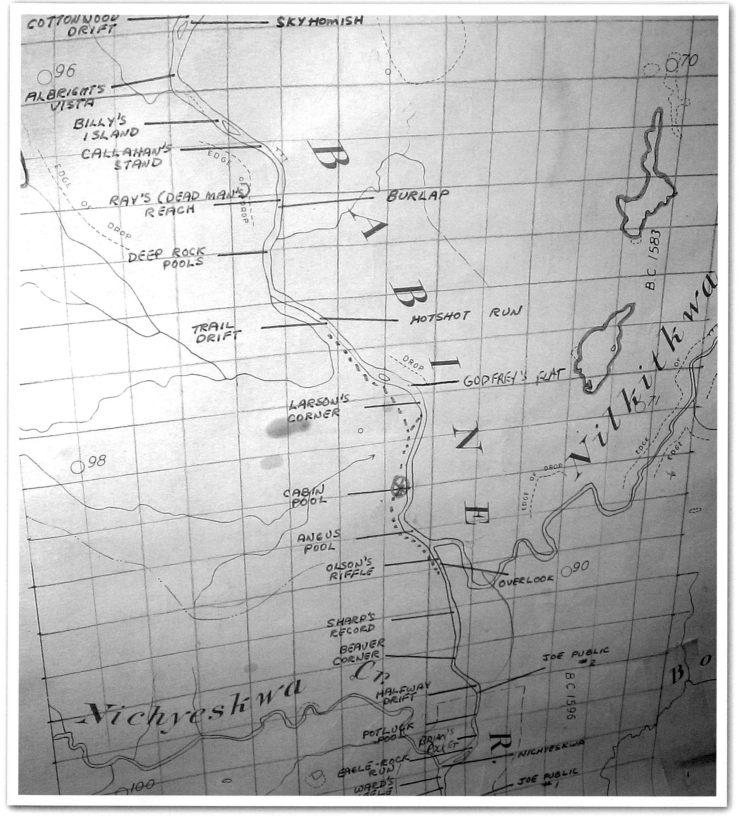

Ejnar's old map, on which he noted all the Babine River pool names, as they were at that time, remains fixed to the wall above the bed in Pierce's cabin—a reminder of a now-distant era when the Babine was still largely unknown.

half way to what later became our Steelhead Camp. Once we began to use the jet unit in place of regular propellers on our boats, the river became navigable and the camp was built.

"The guides would usually drop off two fishermen at each run on the river that seemed likely to produce fish. As the pools and runs were found to be productive, they would be named, usually after the fisherman who caught the biggest fish or the most fish on

the day. This way the guides always knew where the fishermen were and would return by boat to move them to different places.

"Trail Drift, just below the camp, proved to be the best spot and was fished early in the morning while they waited to be picked up by boat and again after they returned to camp at the end of the day. Callahan's Stand, named after a Dr. Jack Callahan from Seattle, turned out to be the most popular place. Each year,

as the same people returned, their names were used for the spots where they enjoyed the most success.

"Brooks Range was named after Joe Brooks, a famous fisherman and author who had traveled all over the world and who had written a number of popular fishing books and countless magazine articles. He usually planned to be at Steelhead Camp for his birthday each year and there was always a raucous celebration with many humorous gifts being presented to Joe by the other fishermen.

"Strom's Pool was where Clarence (*aka* Strom) Stromsness preferred to fish, as did many others (see pages 37-42 and 92-93). He spent three or four weeks in camp for several years and help Ejnar with the many duties that took up precious time. These included filling out the fishing licenses, keeping a tally on the numbers and approximate size of the fish caught and often helping the cook with the dishes.

"The two of them formed a close friendship and were known as the Scandihoovians among the fishermen. When Strom died his family sent his ashes up to us in Smithers and we sprinkled them on the water at Strom's Pool.

"Ray's Reach was named for Ray Bartruff who, one year, after playing and landing a 25-pound steelhead, fell down dead from a heart attack. Forever after, and to this day, that pool has been known as Dead Man's. When I was so distressed over his death, many of the guests informed me that every steelhead

fisherman's dream was to die on the river with a trophy steelhead at his feet. Fortunately the two other fishermen near him at the time were doctors. They pronounced him dead and resumed fishing until Ejnar came by in his boat to check on them. 'We knew that's what Ray would have wanted us to do,' they told Ejnar, and he wholeheartedly agreed with them," she says.

Starting at the weir, less than a mile below Nilkitkwa Lake, the pools Ejnar identified, plus those named since his time, are:

McGuires Riffle, Six-Pound Pool, Ward's Riffle, Eagle-Rock Run, Brian's Pocket (now known as Bear Scare), Potluck Pool, Halfway Drift, Beaver Corner (now Hansen's Corner), Karou's Corner (added later), Strom's Pool (added later), Sharp's Record, Olson's Riffle/*Overlook*, Gravel Bar, Bus Stop (added later), Angus Pool (added later), Bisexual, Cabin Pool/Camp Pool (re-named Ejnar's Pool in his memory), Allen's (named later), Larson's Corner, Godfrey's Flat (now known as The Flats), Jean's Island/*Chick's Chute* (named later), Trail Drift/*Hotshot Run* (now Upper and Lower Trail), Deep Rock Pools, Ray's (Dead Man's) Reach/*Burlap* (now just Dead Man's), Callahan's Stand (now divided into Upper, Middle and Lower Callahan's), Billy's Island, Denny's Pocket (added later), Albright's Vista, Log Jam (added later), Cottonwood Drift/*Skyhomish* washed away and replaced by The Spread, Trappers Pool/*Sunshine Bar*, Trappers Riffle, Brooks Range, Barto's Corner/*Lobo Bar*, Bailey's Triangle, Howie's Run/*Doctor Rex*, (now called Home Run), Ziggy's also called Five Cast (added later), Moose

The cloak of early fall mist starts to lift as a fisherman works his way down Dead Man's Pool.

On a clear day, fishing the pool called Albright's Vista can be a breath-taking experience as the Bait Range Mountains dominate the skyline.

Drift, Twin Flats/*Dislaslie* (also known as Twin Pools and now just a memory), Kinsey's Riffle/*Babine Special*, Joe's Chute/*Spey Run*, Ground Zero (added later), Green Rocks, Laura's Pool/*Big Hole*, Grizzly Bar, Lower Forty and Rempel Pool.

It was left to Pierce, his guides and guests to name the other 24 pools that comprise the middle Babine fishery, extending down as far as rapids which, to all intents, act as a barrier to further progress by boat but not by expertly managed river rafts.

Continuing on downstream from Rempel's, the pools are: Gordon's Canyon, Boat Wreck, Corner Pocket, Rock Ridge, Canyon Pool, Upper Chicken, Lower Chicken, Harm's Way, Sandy Beach, Pubic Pocket, Bomber Bucket, No Name, Last Grab, Huckleberry Hill, Twin Cottonwood, Tokyo Bar, Rock Point also known as Challenge Rock, Rocket Pocket (washed away by high water in 2007 but now showing signs of re-forming), Beaver Flats, Spooled Again, Bitch's Tongue, Ejnar's Last Stand, Rude Awakening and finally Bill's Last Cast.

Incidentally, Pierce says that for years Rocket Pocket, a small area of holding water convenient to the Beaver Flats' satellite cabin, was by far the most productive pool on the entire river, one that provided countless hook-ups with many fish escaping as they powered away downstream. He still mourns its loss but points to more recent hopeful signs that it is starting to re-build.

Below the rapids comes the start of another 20 or more miles of river only fished on a regular basis since 1983, when Silver Hilton Steelhead Lodge was built. Lani Waller, a fisherman and author, whose name is synonymous with both river and lodge, looks back to those early days with great pleasure for, as he says: "It was a lot of fun because no one had really fished there before."

Recounting the names and history of some of the pools, he continues:

Bears and fishermen each going about their own business.

Silver Hilton, like the other two lodges on the river, uses jet boats to move its fishermen from pool to pool.

"Pig Pen is famous for its production of big steelhead. I named it after seeing a 33-pound fish come out of there. Triple Header I named because the first time we ever fished it my friend and I took three male steelhead from 18 to 24 pounds.

"Dead Tree was re-named Esplendido by Silver Hilton owner Stephen Myers. The name means something like 'splendid' in Spanish and it's a good name for the run always produces. It's a great dry-fly run and gave up a 32-pound buck on a Waller Waker dry fly.

"American Run is a two-part run. We fish both parts, the upper and the lower, but in the end, as we like to say: It's all American. Dave's Drift has been re-named Canadian out of respect for the Canadian wilderness through which the Babine runs.

"Dry Fly Diner was named because the steelhead there can easily be taken on a dry fly—especially from the upper part of the run, which is relatively shallow. Sometimes you can see them coming to the fly, especially around a large rock we have named 'Camera Rock' because you better have your camera ready when the fish surfaces for the fly.

"Yellow Leaf was a run I named because I took a large male there one day. After I landed him, I was so excited that on my next cast, I thought I had a soft and very subtle take from another big steelhead but it was only a yellow leaf, which was still impaled on the hook when I brought it in.

"Wounded Eagle was named after we found a wounded bald eagle there and nursed it back to health. We fed it on table scraps for a few days and the bird made it just fine.

"Other great runs fished from Silver Hilton include Eagle, Fergy's, named after one of my best friends, the late John Ferguson, who fished the Babine for over 20 years, Silver Bullet, Wakerville, Paradise, Trotter's Rock, Blue Flag, Goose, Bonanza, Hog Heaven, Cottonwood, Mystery Canyon, Freight Train, Tsunami and Double Header."

Trey Combs wrote extensively about the Babine in his acclaimed book *Steelhead Fly Fishing* and Lani, author of the excellent *A Steelheader's Way: Principles, Tactics and Techniques* (2009), notes some of the Silver Hilton pools Trey mentions have been re-named since the book was first published in 1991. Just as a river will alter its course over the years, washing out pools and creating new ones, so too will fishermen find reason to choose new names for favorite pools and runs. As in nature, nothing is truly permanent.

—As told to Peter McMullan

Silver Hilton guests fly by helicopter to the lodge and enjoy a great view of the densely forested watershed, now preserved from logging as part of the Babine River Corridor Park.

Every Pool's Name Tells a Story

*I*n 1986, my first year of ownership, I still did not know half the upper Babine River's runs and pools. The last named pool was Rempel Pool and I hadn't even been there yet. In 1985 when I visited the Steelhead Camp for the first time, my jet-boating skills didn't allow me to get further downstream from Barto's and Brooks, two great, giant-holding locations. Todd Stockner, who had worked for the Madsens and now for me (see pages 136-142), was very eager to go further downstream than Ejnar had let him venture. It seems that every time Todd had the low boat he would go further down the river. I would ask him, "Alright Todd, how far did you go this time?"

By season's end in 1986, Todd convinced me to consider building a satellite cabin somewhere near where Ejnar's original satellite cabin was. Our only late-season guest, Bus Bergmann (see pages 134-135), joined us on the exploratory trip to locate Ejnar's old cabin and investigate all the runs and pools that had no names. Todd drove the boat, I took notes, and Bus was our fly-fishing angler *extraordinaire*. It seems everywhere we stopped to fish that

looked like decent holding water, we caught fish. To this day we have added little stops to our satellite cabin program. On that trip we found the ash heap and remains of Bob Wickwire's satellite cabin, which looked like the best place to build a new one.

I was very lucky to secure a lease on what we now call Beaver Flats. I was beginning the upper Babine River bridge fight with government and forestry interests, so the eventual watershed protection precluded any more development. I was able to re-open Bob Wickwire's very recently expired lease for the Beaver Flats cabin site thus avoiding re-surveying and other approval details. In the summer before the 1987 steelhead season, the cabin was built in a weekend with the help of Phil Anderson, a local Smithers carpenter.

In the preceding winter months I rebuilt three of Ejnar's 1969 vintage Johnson outboards and these were used to make trips from the DFO weir to Beaver Flats. On our last trip upstream after finishing the cabin, we witnessed a triple rainbow and two sets of grizzly bears, each with three cubs, both sets feeding

*The opportunity to see grizzly bears is cherished
by all Babine fishermen.*

on salmon in the river beneath the triple rainbow in the sky overhead. It was an amazing sight.

Beaver Flats seemed a fitting name for the satellite cabin area since there was a beaver lodge nearby and lots of evidence of beavers doing their thing. In fact, the 2007 and 2008 seasons were more like beaver-watching seasons for trips to the satellite cabin than steelhead fishing; at least we guides sure enjoyed seeing what the beavers were up to in between trips. There is now concern that the beavers will fall some trees on the cabin. When we built the cabin, there were no trees or undergrowth of any kind between it and the river. Now cabin and river are separated by an immature forest of spruce and cottonwood and you can't see the river from the doorway.

The Beaver Flats pool has not changed for the better over the years, but in its early years since 1986, it was a huge tank for holding fish. It was much like Barto's Corner and Brooks just upstream of Babine Steelhead Lodge, both providing great holding water. One day I had some guests from Durango, Colorado fishing Beaver Flats. I had some time to explore a very small pocket of holding water upstream slightly of Beaver Flats.

In those days we were fishing with 30-foot shooting heads and wet flies. I shortened my cast because the water was shallow, so it seemed, and immediately a steelhead hit in such a sudden attack that my fly was immediately snapped off. I waded downstream to a guest named John Flick and said that he better come upstream and try the pocket. While he was doing that I tied on another Green Butt Skunk and flicked about 12 feet of fly line out into the head of the Beaver Flats pool only to be immediately broken off. Then there was some whooping and hollering coming from John and I could see this 18-pound male steelhead rocketing out of the pocket spending more time in the air than in the water.

John named the pool Rocket Pocket and it would become legendary until 2007, when a flood season ruined the lie. Now, two years later I think it is starting to build back. If there was ever a guarantee of a steelhead being caught every time a pool or pocket is fished then Rocket Pocket was such a place. From 1987 to 2006 I believe Rocket Pocket was the most productive and amazing dry-line pocket that God ever created for steelhead.

It's probably the pockets that have provided me with the most intense memories of steelhead below Rempel Pool. These various pockets, when they hold fish, are the most amazing experiences because the angler is so close to the fish attacking and blasting out of the water with a crash down on the dry fly, not very far away from the angler's adrenaline-packed eyeballs. What's so great about the Babine, and contrary to the present double-handed rod craze, is that you don't need to cast long lengths. The angler and steelhead can be very close and the visual action is habit forming.

Most of the new runs and pools named below Rempel's were named as reference points for Todd and I when we were learning all the new holding water in rubber-soled hip waders. Runs like Canyon and Sandy Beach were named for what they were, so not much imagination there. Upper and Lower Chicken were named because we caught only female steelhead in those stretches for many seasons. Boat Wreck was named for a wooden riverboat that ended up there after a huge rainstorm and subsequent river rise washed away an old boat from Babine Steelhead Lodge. Ejnar's Last Stand was named in his honour and is very close to his old cabin site.

There are still some no-name pockets and pools yet to be christened. I don't like naming a pool or changing a name unless something extraordinary happens when angler meets steelhead and all hell breaks loose or something fitting feels just right. One such pool is called Last Grab. Bill McMillan, a well-known Pacific Northwest steelheader, was covering for Lani Waller, who had recently survived a fatal plane crash at the Silver Hilton Steelhead Lodge.

Bill had a particular dry-line technique that wasn't producing much for steelhead. He was on a Beaver Flats trip with me and I had left him in a very large stretch of holding water, as yet un-named. I was returning with the jet boat to check on Bill and he was just releasing a steelhead. I was happy for him since he hadn't landed any steelhead until then.

Running a jet boat on the Babine is never easy, especially in rock strewn spots such as the approach to Gordon's Canyon from Rempel Pool.

Loren Irving took this spectacular Babine fall shot of his friend, Jim Bussard, fishing a pool called Kinsey's.

He went on to tell me landing that fish was quite an experience. It seems his hand-knit sweater had caught on his reel and then he lost grip of the rod and it flew into the river with the fish still hooked. Bill was chasing the rod as it glided toward deeper waters and grabbing at it but missing it several times.

Bill always carries an old camera around his neck and he was making his last grab for the rod with camera held high and his other arm plunged deep into the river with one last chance at retrieving his rod. He said it was his last grab and I thought that's it, Last Grab would be a great name for the pool.

Another great pool called Harm's Way was re-named by Ed Vivona. My father had named it Twisted Gulch since the river twists slightly around a small boulder garden, splitting the pool in two sections. A Japanese guest named Taka landed a 33-pound male steelhead there on a dry line in 1998 and many great bucks have been landed or lost there.

Ed lost one of these massive fish that he hooked in the upper section, watching his line peel out around one of those mid-section boulders turning his rod and reel into useless tools. When he explained what happened, he said he felt like he was standing in harm's way, feeling helpless and defenceless against such a huge steelhead. He was so flabbergasted and in such a mess, not to mention his broken equipment, that I just couldn't resist changing the pool's name. Harm's Way it became.

I could go on and on about the many runs and pools and the many incredible fishing stories surrounding them. I am haunted by the memories every time my jet boat gently glides downstream, maneuvering through the many great holding waters that I was able to enjoy naming and still will name in seasons to come. We are lucky to have over 75 runs, pools and pockets and the mystery of every new season brings excitement to see which ones have changed since the last spring high waters.

Some are lost and some new ones are being developed and it always amazes me to realize that the longer I live the more the river changes, and the more the river changes the more I realize my age and years of guiding. It's hard for the steelhead to hide from my eyes anymore but they always do find the places to hide that no one can see and few can fish with a fly.

Changes in fly-fishing technology, and fishing techniques in general, have made it far more difficult for steelhead to hide from the angler. High catch rates from using bait, now banned, have been replaced by high catch rates from more expert fly-fishing technique and equipment.

I think the fish are happy to see us go at season's end, when the runs and pools can become again what steelhead make the journey for...a place to rest and feed until spawning time so many months distant from when they first return from the ocean.

—*Pierce Clegg*

Working Together Provides Solutions

Smithers forester Gary Quanstrom has a unique view of Norlakes. He cooked at the Madsens' Steelhead Camp as a teenager in 1974 and, more recently, was involved in developing the agreement document for the Babine Watershed Monitoring Trust.

Gary Quanstrom, a Registered Professional Forester (RPF), works for West Fraser Mills Ltd, with responsibility for all license post-harvest issues in the Smithers and Bulkley Valley area and around Fraser Lake. This includes programs that have seen an average of two million trees a year being re-planted (1.4 million in 2009) following logging operations. Over the years the forest industry and the environmental movement have not always seen eye to eye when it comes to the Babine watershed but Gary's view is that both people and their interests have matured over time. He goes on to say:

*V*arious stakeholders are listening to each other and there is much less conflict and more reason on both sides. There will always be a certain degree of risk for any specific resource value for any given space and time period. However, through a clearly defined understanding of the needs of various stakeholders, and of the resource itself, objectives may be created and implemented to meet those needs. All needs may not be met for all people over the same time and space, but the risks to those various resource values may certainly be reduced through sound management.

I worked with others for more than two years on the Governance Design Group, helping to develop the Trust Agreement Document, for the Babine Watershed Monitoring Trust (BWMT)

and I am currently a Trustee of the Trust. West Fraser Mills was one of the original signatories—Settlors—of the Trust, as well as The Ministries of Forest and Range, Environment, (BC Parks), the Babine River Foundation, and the Bulkley Valley Community Resources Board.

This BWMT was established to formalize a Trust that ensures the Trustees act and set monitoring priorities independently from the resource stakeholders, implement projects based on scientific objectivity, and report findings back to the stakeholders and the public.

The key resource-value objectives are set by government through public-participation resource-planning processes to create Land and Resource Management Plans (LRMPs). The

Hand-crafted wooden river boats, like the one in this picture, are used for both trout fishing from the lodge and then again during steelhead season on the river. Pierce has his as a backdrop as he fishes his way down a pool called Rude Awakening.

objectives must be met through the implementation of Forest Stewardship Plans. Monitoring the results and effectiveness of resource plan implementation is now occurring through a more collaborative approach, through government agencies, industry and the BWMT.

I like to take an optimistic view of the present and the future. As far as the risk of forest mortality due the spread of the mountain pine beetle is concerned, I don't see it as a major threat to the Babine system. That's because of the species diversity and distribution of age classes of our forest. Yes, there is some pine but there is also spruce, balsam, cottonwood, alder and aspen in the mix.

There has been a lot of movement to meet the concerns expressed by fishing guides and fishermen. In recent years, the forest industry has taken steps, at considerable cost, to ensure that water quality is maintained, that post-harvest surveys and remediation are undertaken and that we do more in the way of recognizing water and visual quality objectives, as well as other key resources values across the landscape.

Anglers want to catch fish but they also want to enjoy natural rather than man-made sounds. However, these same fishermen are willing to listen to the noise of the guides' jet boats and helicopters transporting clients and supplies to and from the lodges, up and down the river.

The Babine River Corridor Park Plan, states that no logging is allowed within the park boundaries, approximately one kilometre on each side of the river. The Land and Resource Management Plan defines an additional Special Management Zone (SMZ) as a buffer, approximately one kilometre wide parallel and running to the park on each side of the river. Within this SMZ there can be no permanent roads, and harvesting is to occur only during the winter season. This is meant to address concerns regarding noise from harvesting, during the fishing season.

Other values are protected by having portions of the SMZ designated as Landscape Corridor where forest operations must retain approximately 70 per cent of the natural old growth structure. As trees live and die over time, ecological function will be maintained. Implementing this strategy means large clear-cuts will not be created against the park boundaries, animal travel corridors are maintained and concerns regarding public access and visual quality are addressed.

These are some examples of objectives that have been created, and plans implemented and monitored to meet the needs of the Babine River angling community.

The Babine Watershed Monitoring Trust (BWMT) reflects a shift in maturity and attitudes of the various resource stakeholders over time. This shift has evolved from times where people were standing in public meetings yelling at each other, to where some of those same people are sitting at the same table discussing how to work together to reach solutions to the issues.

Making a Difference Despite the Mockeries

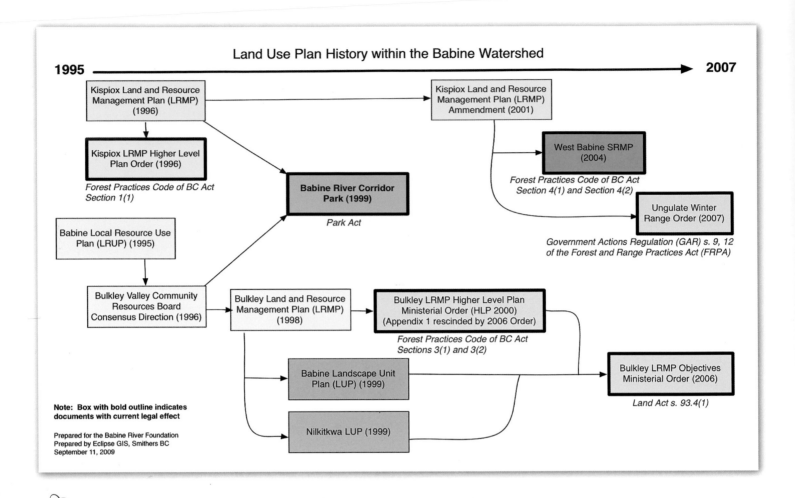

Land Use Plan History within the Babine Watershed

1995 — 2007

Note: Box with bold outline indicates documents with current legal effect

Prepared for the Babine River Foundation
Prepared by Eclipse GIS, Smithers BC
September 11, 2009

$\mathcal{E}$ver since the bridge fights of the late 1980s there evolved a dozen land use plans including land use plan sanctioned ministerial orders. The original plan completed in 1995, was the Babine Local Resource Use Plan (LRUP) which was affirmed by the Bulkley Valley Community Resources Board in 1996...that led to the Bulkley Land and Resource Management Plan (LRMP) in 1998...that in part led to the Babine Landscape Unit Plan (LUP) and the Nilkitkwa LUP in 1999.

While the Smithers-based Bulkley Valley Community Resources Board was doing its work, the Kispiox LRMP was also completed in 1996 except they did not complete the required monitoring framework. Both the Kispiox and Bulkley LRMP's led to the Babine River Corridor Park being established in 1999.

Now if that's not confusing, there were amendments to both LRMP's in 2000 and 2001. Eventually a supposedly higher level planning exercise called the West Babine Sustainable Resource Management Plan (SRMP) would supersede them in 2004. Two further amendments or additions finally followed in 2006, with the Bulkley LRMP Objectives Ministerial Order, and in 2007 with the Ungulate Winter Range Order.

It's amazing to think that stewardship efforts to prevent three bridge crossings to the north side of the Babine River would result in such a land use planning evolution. For a time the B.C. government enjoyed this type of planning exercise since

it collected, corralled and controlled a group of competing interests all under one roof of planning. Participants felt they had some input and collective consensus ruled the day.

Hundreds of meetings, lots of paper tossed around, and a bunch of touchy, feely words on paper made all involved feel like they were doing something for the world-class values they represented. All these plans were signed off and all that participated, at least all the non-government and non-forestry sector participants, felt that the plans would become a reality on the ground.

The sham and mockery of it all was that most of these plans, except the ministerial orders of 2006 and 2007, were never intended to be fully implemented. It became more and more apparent that this was the case as time went on with the realization that there was no budget for implementation or monitoring even though some plans were to require it. I also think the timber harvesting licensees were also left to figure out how to implement the language of the plans in terms of their on-the-ground operations.

This is where it got more convoluted in that not all companies operate under the same stewardship guidelines, and it can be argued that stewardship really only means clear cutting at least cost. The Forest Act and Fisheries Act and much other relevant legislation are always held up as protecting the environment, fish, wildlife and habitat. But when you take a closer look

at how all this legislation relates to on the ground operations, then the ideal world thinking that we are really looking after wild ecosystems becomes seriously flawed.

The original proposal made by the Friends of the Babine recommended a one per cent reduction in the Annual Allowable Cut (AAC) by creating a wilderness designation under the Forest Act. This was a linear line drawn on a map representing a one-kilometre, no logging zone on either side of the Babine River. Dave Goble took the time to map out all the various polygons of timber types through available forest cover maps and the figure of one per cent resulted. This recommendation seemed very reasonable at the time and in the end basically formed the border of the Babine River Corridor Park although the park line became less linear.

The less linear line was basically a grizzly bear fall feeding corridor, proposed by Brian Fuhr, a habitat and wildlife biologist working for the Environment Ministry. Once the bridges were cancelled and this corridor proposal received more political attention, a technical advisory committee was established which finally led to the Babine LRUP of 1995. The point here is that original LRUP became the base document for all the other land use plans for the Babine watershed to follow.

Supposedly the original spirit and intent of the Babine LRUP was to extend throughout all the subsequent land use plans to this day. The problem with that has been that delivering on the spirit and intent, or the actual original language of the LRUP, has presented problems for government, the forestry sector and the wilderness values of the Babine watershed. In short we have not been able to deliver or implement the LRUP according to this original spirit and intent.

For example the population of grizzly bears was to be 'maintained,' but now we see the subsequent plan language say 'emphasis on maintaining grizzly bear habitat,' something much easier to accomplish. Another example is the terminology of most of the plans themselves which use words like 'maintain' water quality or 'maintain' fish habitat or 'maintain provincially significant angling values.' Unfortunately those of us on these committees or land use planning tables did not feel we needed to a have a debate over terminology, and we didn't think that in future years the word 'maintain' would basically become meaningless in terms of actually supporting our values. What does 'maintain' really mean unless it has legal standing. That word is not nearly descriptive enough. We assumed it meant 'preserve'.

The last land use plan in which the Babine River Foundation (BRF) and I participated was the West Babine SRMP of 2004. This new plan was intended to complete the Kispiox LRMP, which had not complied with its own conclusions. This new plan was also considered a higher-level plan in that there would be legal standing given to certain aspects of the plan. This new plan would also supersede to some extend all the other plans while at the same time respecting their original spirit and intent, whatever that really means?

A big Babine grizzly feasts on and guards what remains of a moose.

It was a bitter negotiation with government and the BRF nearly walked away from the table several times. In the end the only thing that kept the BRF at the table was a promise by government to establish a monitoring partnership, which later became the Babine Watershed Monitoring Trust (www.babinetrust.ca). It's funny how this promise was and is a requirement of the land use plans to begin with, but to that date there had been a failure of the only monitoring exercise called the Babine LRUP Monitoring Committee.

There were other concessions given to encourage the BRF to remain committed to the new land use plan that included new 'no logging' zones for the upper Shelagyote River, and a tourism node around the Silver Hilton Steelhead Lodge. Creating new zones only highlighted to me that there was created a new huge zone with no special protections or new considerations on the entire south side of the Babine River, which I called the 'no zone.'

The original Babine LRUP called for a 'no logging' corridor, which later became a park, a special management zone outside the park and an integrated management zone covering the entire watershed of the Babine River. To this day this is the model of management for the watershed with the Smithers Bulkley Valley Community Resources Board looking after the upper half of the Babine River and the West Babine SRMP looking after the lower half of the river. The monitoring trust framework includes an annual monitoring plan, based on risk assessment, subject to an annual budget provided by the BRF and government.

Monitoring to see how well the land use plans are doing in achieving the objectives of the plans is the task of the monitoring trust. Budget constraints provide for only researching compliance with the plans based on what plan objectives is at most risk of failure. This is an excellent model of using limited funds in the most effective way. Richard Overstall, a lawyer in Smithers, must be credited with organizing a group of individuals that came up with this monitoring framework. In the first few years

At the end of the day
Steelhead Camp offers a warm and comfortable retreat
from the elements along with the promise of another fine meal.

The world changes when winter comes to the Babine but the fishing,
while all the more demanding on account of the cold,
can be hugely rewarding.

of monitoring, the trust has spent its limited funds in a very effective way, which has gained it credibility and notoriety.

As it turns out, the areas of more risk due to logging are water quality, road density affecting grizzly bears and wilderness values. I applaud the effectiveness of the trust framework, annual monitoring plan and effective use of limited funds. This model can be transferred to many other watersheds or land use planning type of exercises and is a continuing credit to the BRF and Richard Overstall. The other important aspect of the trust is its independence from influence by the BRF or any other interest. The trust is a legal entity with a set framework for monitoring the objectives of the land use plans...it cannot be told to do anything in particular...we can just fund and support the trust but not influence its work.

The timber companies' reaction to the trust is not to fund it...not one penny has been contributed to the trust from any private source other that the BRF and individual steelhead anglers that fish the Babine. Timber companies and stewardship of the Babine...you decide.

Since 1986 I have participated in and witnessed a great stewardship effort by many people, organizations and government, all associated with the Babine River watershed. If I ever challenge government or anybody else that I am dissatisfied with the stewardship management of the Babine, they are quick to remind me of what has been accomplished. The five-year process (Babine LRUP) after the bridge fight that eventually led to a park, more planning processing and the monitoring trust, are the legacy of stewardship for the Babine River watershed.

About that much I must be happy and proud, but a sober reality also must be given attention. For example, when the corridor park was established in 1999, there were two areas included in the river corridor that did not receive park status. One was the Kisegas Indian Reserve and the section of river downstream

Homeward bound at the end of the day. Pierce and his guests on their way back to Steelhead Camp.

of this reserve to the Skeena River. It's understandable how the reserve was deleted from park status, but the section of river downstream...why? We were told that the spirit and intent of the LRUP and all the other plans would extend to the confluence of the Babine and Skeena rivers.

That was a lie and later a new logging bridge was constructed across the Babine River in this lower section of the river. How did that happen? No public consultation, no amendments to any existing land use plans. Basically the bridge was sneaked in without anybody knowing about it except government and the forestry sector. After the fact the Forest Practises Board reviewed the new bridge crossing and stated that the action violated existing land use plans and decisions...so what, no consequences, no penalties and quickly logging operations followed that continue to this day. It just so happens that these new logging operations have infringed on the most valuable grizzly bear habitats in the entire Babine watershed, as identified by foremost bear biologists.

It's the case of the fox looking after the hen house in that our B.C. government and its Ministry of Forests and friends are still in the business of doing things that are not up front, even given all the land use planning that I have discussed previously. There still is this mentality of arrogance and non-compliance, even in the face of obvious spirit and intent. There is still a plan to get to the Sustut-Takla timber supply areas in order to extend the over-harvest mentality that is basically public policy, our social choice for the management of our forests.

Our values, such as wilderness tourism, salmon, steelhead, grizzly bears and Indians, stand in the way of progress. It doesn't matter if it is un-economic, then we will subsidize it. It doesn't matter what a land use plan says unless the language of that plan is legally binding, which most plans are not. It doesn't matter if the case is made that other values deserve recognition and investment and so we return to the days of the JFK assassination or the bridge fight where reports are concealed and the real agendas are covered up.

If you ever get involved in stewardship of wild ecosystems of world-class value, then you will have to confront these types of mockeries and still be able to find ways of making a difference. I believe it's worth the effort and let the record show that many stewards have tried to represent a Babine watershed as still world-class.

I would like to thank the following people who took the time to make a difference for the Babine and they are: Dave and Shelley Goble, Gord Wolfe, Ray Travers, Dave Narver, Ric Careless and Frank Hussey. They were instrumental during the bridge fight years in keeping me encouraged that the Babine was worth the fight for all the right reasons. Many more individuals would later join to make a stewardship team for the Babine that has left a continuing legacy for years to come.

—*Pierce Clegg*

PART IV

Guest Memories

When Pierce and I decided to work together on this book, and to recount the story of the Babine sports fishery over a period of more than 50 years, we quickly realized that we were not the only ones with great memories of the river and its fish. The following fishermen's accounts, in prose and verse, speak to the very soul of both lake and river, to their steelhead and their rainbow trout.

Anglers are passionate by nature and inclination, gregarious and full of fun and together their written contributions help to give life and colour to the very essence of the Babine, a river that has captured so many hearts to the point that, for some, it has become the final resting place for their ashes. No river could be paid a greater compliment.

Eagle Feathers and Bombers

Loren Irving, from Bend, OR, was the first Norlakes guest to come forward with a contribution to this part of the book. Recently retired from a wood supply business partnership with regular fishing partner Frank Cammack, he is one of a number of great steelheaders from Bend, OR. He is also a terrific photographer and Pierce thanks him for his generous support of many Babine stewardship efforts and for his contribution to the filming of Bubbleheads and Bombers, a Babine dry-line, waking-fly presentation.

*L*et me reflect on a couple of really special experiences from the Babine this year (2006). The first happened the day after we arrived. We were lucky to be the first boat down the river in the morning, headed for the lower runs, and it occurred several times before I realized what was taking place. We sort of 'bumped' a good number of bald eagles while motoring down quietly, almost at a trolling speed.

As an aside here, I think it's great that Pierce and the other guides go down the river very quietly early in the day. In any event, I noticed occasional pieces of what I eventually determined to be fine, little, white feathers, the result of the young eagles' moulting. It even happened a couple of times when I was fishing when no one else was around. There was something about this that just meant so much to me. I just cannot imagine another place where it would happen, or indeed should happen, other than on the Babine. It's something I will never forget.

The second strong memory I have is of fishing a dry fly on the last hour of the last day. Pierce had let me out of the boat

John Hapgood (left) and his good friend, Loren Irving, are a picture of concentration as they watch a waking dry fly.

Loren took this fine steelhead from Rude Awakening on one of his favourite Bubble Bomber patterns.

in mid-stream, at a place where the river broadens out. I have done it in previous years but the wading was pretty challenging. It's actually where Pierce finally convinced me of the benefits of using a wading staff. This time, with the low-water conditions, it was actually easy to wade. It's a stretch where the river is wide and strewn with what I see as likely holding pockets. In previous years it was pretty predictable that you would find a fish some-where in one of those pockets. This time there seemed to be one in almost every conceivable spot.

Using various dries, the majority being my own Bomber patterns, I had seven different fish working in that final hour. I just could not believe it. They were downright playful. I only hooked two and landed just one and, again, that was hard for me

to believe. At one point I stood in one spot and had two distinct pockets 50 feet below me that I thought might each hold a fish. These were about 25 feet apart.

I cast into the one on the left and a steelhead made a swirl at the fly that almost sucked it under. I decided to let it rest and cast to the spot on the right and sure enough was rewarded with another nice follow and a nip. I stayed there and, as you may have guessed, had both fish working alternately with two or three more playful swirls or nips from each before finally hooking the one on the right which turned out to be a small hen of around nine pounds. There was not a soul around to hear me laughing. In 33 years of fly-fishing for steelhead I consider this to be one of my most remarkable experiences.

The Naming of Strom's Pool

Grizzly bears and a camper take equal enjoyment from their wilderness setting just downstream from Strom's Pool.

The late Strom Stromsness, Corning, CA remembers a special day.

*I*n 1971 Bill Winter and some other people from Corning came up to the Babine for the steelhead fishing. I was also going into camp that year so it happened that Bill and I fished together for some of the time.

One day we had been up river, possibly to try Six Pound Pool or Halfway. Ejnar picked us up to return to camp and, on the way down, pointed out a new pool which, he said, had been formed the previous winter and which had not been fished. He suggested we give it a try.

This was in the days when you could use roe, which both Bill and I did. The pool looked good and, on the first or second cast, I had a fish on. While I was playing it, Bill hooked into one. I eventually lost my fish but Bill landed his so I immediately called the pool the Winter Hole. I really thought no more about it until the following winter.

Going down river, again with Ejnar, he said we were coming to a fairly new pool that turned out to be the Winter Hole only Ejnar said it was now known as Strom's Pool. I was completely dumbfounded. Over the years I had fished a lot of places named for people, and these were people who were first-class, if not world-class, fishermen. One pool is named for Joe Brooks, another for Dr. Callahan, Bob Hansen and so on. To think that I would join these people and have a pool named for me was overwhelming.

In succeeding years I fished Strom's Pool many times and almost always caught fish there. The pool changed very little over the years and I know that, as late as 1993, it was still there and producing fish.

Probably the outstanding memory of Strom's is what happened there one day when I was working at the River Camp. I had gone up the river with Kent Williamson. He was from one of the Carolinas and fished a Little Cleo spoon all the time. The river was up from recent rain and, even though high, was still fishable.

The pool was fished from the beach on the left side over to a high bank on the right side. Kent hooked a fish and he could tell it was heavy. He played it for a time and then found his line had caught a snag that, of course, he could not see. The fish did not run but apparently just lay there.

Kent did not know what to do and neither did I but I suggested 'an old Indian trick'. I found a piece of driftwood about three inches in diameter and maybe a foot long and tied it to some monofilament. I put a swivel on the mono, clipped it over Kent's line and put the stick in the water.

Since Kent was well upstream from where the snag was located, the stick was forced out into the current and slid along towards it. By some miracle it floated Kent's line up, the mono came loose and, after some more fighting of the fish, which I netted, he had a beautiful 25-pound buck steelhead on the beach. A great memory.

Fishing at Strom's

*Bjorn Stromsness is the third generation of his family to fish the Babine
and has named his daughter Anna Babine.*

*As Pierce remarks: "Being Chris Stromsness' son and Clarence Strom Stromsness' grandson has
to be both an honour and perhaps an angling curse for Bjorn Stromsness, from Placerville, CA.
Destined by birth to learn all there is to know about the Babine, he has now named his young
daughter, who leads off the family's fourth generation, Anna Babine. These are his words:"*

Out on the water early in the
    morning,
The air is crisp
Hands buried into fleece-lined
    pockets
As the boat takes me up river, to
    the pool,
His pool.
Standing in the clean and cold
    waters
The current rippling around me
I become part of the pattern of
    the river.
Just another seam for fish to
    hold in.
The line dances through the air,
    big loops forming around me

And then shooting tightly through
the air, extending an offering to
    the river.
Mend, mend, rod tip down,
    following the progress of the
    drift
Until it reaches the end... let it
    hang, hopeful
And then pick up and repeat
    the ritual on this bit of
    hallowed water.
Cast, drift, retrieve.
Step.
Cast, drift, retrieve.
Step.
The catechism of the chase.
The ritual passed down.

There, some weight on the line...
Strike!
Serenity shattered as lightning
    explodes from unseen cover,
The steelhead is hooked
And then
It is gone.
The weight is now just water, the
    only head shakes are my own.
The smile just appearing on my
    lips gives way to a gasp,
Twinge of despair, an upwelling of
    hope for another grab.
Back to work,
Sacred work.
The work of a steelheader.

The Story of Gordon's Canyon

Kent Davenport fishes Gordon's Canyon, named in memory of his father.

Dr. Kent Davenport, from Honolulu, HI, is an orthopaedic bone specialist who traveled the world fishing with his father. Pierce recalls their last Babine trip together was to Trout Lodge. "Kent also takes super pictures and has fallen in love with the power, size and beauty of Babine steelhead. He comes to us each year for three weeks in his quest for the big one."

This is the story of Gordon's Canyon. Gordon was my father. He was a good guy and loved rodeos, horses, dogs and kids and didn't like big cities. He talked about the wilderness, trees and the futility of worry, but never about his three Purple Hearts, his Navy Cross or the war. He was an engineer and raised us in a small town in northern California comprised of 50 people, a lumber mill and a bar. It snowed four feet every winter and we were kept busy enough with chores to stay mostly out of trouble.

When Gordon retired he had never been fishing so I took him to Alaska to a nice fly-out lodge where he caught his first fish that happened to be a 25-inch rainbow. He was interested in fishing after that, more because of the interesting places fish lived than in actually catching fish.

Each year we went on an annual fishing trip somewhere in the West. Alaska, Kodiak Island, Canada, Montana, Wyoming,

New Mexico, Arizona—we loved each trip and even caught a few fish. I had been fishing for steelhead on the Babine with Pierce and Anita since the early 1990s and we decided to go there in the summer of 1997 to fish for trout on our fifteenth visit.

It was a great trip. We saw eagles, moose, and bears and caught lots of feisty rainbow trout. The sudden storms that came over the lake added extra spice and the sunsets were always dramatic. "This is the best," he suddenly announced to me. He took his fly off his cast and put it into his hat and sat back smiling. "Maybe we can come here again."

Gordon died that winter of a heart attack. He was 80. My sisters and I divided up his ashes and deposited them in his favourite places throughout the West. My share came with me to the Babine for steelhead fishing in the fall of 1998. I asked Pierce if I could put them in the river and he said 'yes'.

"There is a place we can put them. It doesn't have a name. It's a canyon with a big torrent of water, a boat-killing rock and eagles' nests and lots of bears. We can call it Gordon's Canyon." Gordon's Canyon it was. His ashes went into a wild wilderness spot that he loved.

Over the years I fished Gordon's Canyon occasionally. It was not a great spot for fishing as the water was a torrent, the banks are steep and it was not a good place for fish to hold. I fell in lots but never had a tug while deep in thought about my father.

2006 was a dry year on the Babine, probably the lowest water in 10 years. We had trouble getting the boats up and down the river and the fish moved to different holding areas. Pierce told me that Gordon's was looking good and I thought it might be fun to fish it again. He let me off, gave me an idea off how to wade it and left me to my thoughts.

The boat-killer rock was prominent and the nice slick behind it was the logical place to start. It was easy to wade and I was working my way down the river, staring at the eagles and enjoying my thoughts, when the old Hardy reel gave out a scream like a Monday morning alarm clock. The sunny pool exploded as a huge, bright hen cartwheeled over and over again across the water. The fish was fresh and, at the end of a 10-minute fight, it measured 37 x 19 inches, my largest hen of the year.

It was quite a surprise after no fish for Gordon's Canyon but it wasn't the end and I had another two bright hens by the time I finished the run. The tail turned out to be perfect holding water with boulders and a gravel bottom with a deep slot at the end.

Many other anglers caught fish in Gordon's Canyon that year. The Babine is never without surprises and gifts for the persistent. Sometimes you even catch a fish.

A Simple Man Finds a Chiasm and The Joy

A recently retired hospital trauma specialist, Dr. Ernie Gradillas, from Tuscon, AZ, was introduced to the Babine by a Durango, CO tackle shop called Duranglers Flies and Supplies. Pierce put the welcome mat out for two weeks every year for Ernie and his friend, Bill Jenkins, and always enjoys telling the story of a special experience on the river while dry lining at Laura's Pool. "Ernie has inspired us to look upon the Babine with a more spiritual, natural phenomena point of view," he says.

I'm a simple man. My children recognize it and actively try to exploit it. We once were sitting at dinner and, against the rules of the table, we were (I was) talking about Democrats and Republicans. My point was that there was a passionate gulf, a divide between rational thought and prejudice that was hard for a simple man to comprehend. We were at dinner and we were drinking wine and I called the gap a chiasm. Laughter ensued, and when I was corrected (I should have said chasm), I began to understand the importance of crossings, the beauty of the whole, the reality of the chasm.

Again, as a simple man, my first encounter with the Babine was one of anticipation. I had read *Steelhead Paradise*, John Fennelly's book about the Skeena system (see page 188, Babine Reading List), and really wanted to fish the Sustut or the Morice. Little did I know. A friend who knew we fished the Deshutes and the North Umpqua said he knew a place where one could catch real fish (not Democrats). So, bolstered by the recommendation, I signed on. That was 1991. And I signed on to fish the Babine.

Now, in his book, Fennelly says that if you want to catch steelhead, don't go to the Babine. He really didn't say that, what he said was... "Almost 10 years were required to convince me that the Babine is one of the finest streams in the Skeena watershed for steelhead as well as resident rainbows." Little did he know. My first year there was magical. That year I met (and have grown to love) Pierce and Todd Stockner.

Todd was the first to impart his special brand of what I call 'anthropomorphic mysticism'.

He saw steelhead in a special light. He talked to me about their playfulness, about their anger, about their curiosity and fears. About what they liked, needed and had to have. All concepts about another organism unfamiliar to me (Democrats), but very useful in understanding the Gestalt.

That first year I also met Bob Feist. As a rookie, I was odd man out and on the ride from the weir to the lodge he said "Follow me." I don't usually follow people, but it was really cold and he was a rodeo announcer and had a business card with his picture on it so I said, "Why not?" So we bunked together that year. He also taught me some things. He taught me the pleasure of team fishing.

We fished together the whole week. And we would separate our brief encounters with fish into two phases. The first phase was always a spectator sport. He had a Joy, whooping and hollering, trying to videotape the fish, the scenery, the excitement, the changes of direction, the leaps, the cartwheels, the nosedives.

The second phase was the grind. He reveled in the grind. Always a smile, always encouraging, even when he caught no fish. That's my recollection of the first year on the Babine. Fennelly should have have fished with Todd and Bob Feist. He may have sold more books.

My next year, I met Bill Jenkins. He was much more connected and a better fisherman than me, but we both liked to

Ernie Gradillas has every reason to look happy, beautiful day, beautiful fish.

drink and visit with the guides in the evening. He also had The Joy. We've been team fishing ever since. The next year, we were in Smithers and realized that there was a mountain to the west. Humm... maybe we should look around a little. So, we planned to come a few days early and look around.

We went to the Falls, up to the ski hill, to the Morice and had a memorable day on the Bulkley, when after a night out on the town and after landing a nice little hen behind the school, I just had to lie down and take off my waders. The air, it seems was too thick. Well, we've been looking around a lot over the last 15 years. Team fishing all over the world. Stories for another time.

In the morning, leaving the lodge, when you ride the river to where you're going to fish, you see bears, eagles, waterfowl and, if you're lucky, wolves and moose. I was lucky to see something else. I should say someone else. He was all alone, blowing a whistle at the side of the river. Some of you know him as "...asshole, traitor, gimp and protector of the key": Kent Davenport.

When Bill and I were first introduced to him, he said nothing (for three days) although we were his cabin mates. We were his crosses to bear, his grand impositions. But he has The Joy. He sees things that I see but more composed, more understandable, more universal. I've always enjoyed Kent. Like Todd, he enjoyed

steelhead. In my own subverted, anthropomorphic mysticism I ascribe to him certain human traits unknown to others.

Also, I would be remiss not to mention Big John. Another cabin mate and wonderful man, John Hewitt. John was sleeping for most of the fun times we've had with him. Famous for his formula (or lack thereof) he more than anyone else has The Joy.

Why bore you with the names and perceptions? Because my experience is deeper than chance meetings. What about Pierce? The real keeper of the key. He was witness to my transformation, so was Bill. He was witness to when I found The Joy. He put me there. I'm convinced he knew it would happen and if Fennelly had been there, I know he certainly would have sold more books. The point being that the Babine is a nexus. It's a spiritual place. It's a place where across the chasm we find the chiasm. The crossing, the melding of different paths to make us whole, allowing us to see both ways—all ways.

As they say, raise your hands, bow your heads, read the words written in red (especially the love stories in Corinthians and the last movement of Beethoven's Ninth) and when Pierce has my ashes and is dumping them wherever he wants, he can play Sammy Cahn's, Let it Snow, Let it Snow, Let it Snow.

That's my story and I'm sticking to it.

Of Tadpoles and Butterflies

I love my wife. I'm fortunate and lucky to have met her. If you ever meet her, you would like her too. Like all successful marriages we have nothing in common—except our children who love her more than me. She accepts my passions, but rarely

shares in them. But, sometimes she does. For our 25th wedding anniversary I took her to Christmas Island. For those of you who have gone there you understand why that might not be the best 25th wedding anniversary trip. How could I have known? For our honeymoon (with first child in tow) we splurged and went to Dr. Wilkinson's Hot Springs Mud Bath in Calistoga, CA (before they started putting cucumbers on your eyes). That's why our kids turn to her first.

Well, I wanted to fish for rainbows at Norlakes in the summer. She acquiesced. This time we got it right.

Margie was looking forward to meeting the Cleggs and seeing Darcy Edwards again. However, when we arrived Darcy wasn't there. He had been called away because of a family emergency. Margie and I had previously been on a trip with Darcy to Costa Rica and one night while at dinner, on that trip, she turned to me and said, "Don't you think Anna (our middle daughter) would like to meet Darcy?"

Incredulous doesn't even come close to my response. At the dinner table, I think I blurted out (while spewing my drink from my mouth), "Are you f...ing nuts?" Darcy has been asking me to send him pictures of Anna and calling me Dad ever since. My wife however thought him funny and engaging. I really think Margie was going with me to Canada because Darcy was going to be there. But he wasn't. Because of the accident he had to leave the lodge on the lake and Gary Bailey took his place.

She was mildly disappointed but I tried to tell her that she should just think of it as a natural transformation. The Caterpillar (tadpole) had just turned into the Butterfly (frog)—they really were discontinuously the same. Certainly I am not suggesting one could hold this butterfly responsible for what he might have done as that caterpillar. I don't even know if there is a recollection of experience or thought between stages—same organism, different experience. Does the frog know he was a tadpole and remember it fondly?

In 1997 the lake was very full and the river very high when we were there. And one day Pierce and Gary took us and Darrel Kaufman and his wife to see Steelhead Camp. The sun was out that day and it was a pleasant trip. The river was so high that we had to duck while sitting in the boat when we went under the bridge below the weir. We fished for rainbows and bull trout where the Nichyeskwa meets the Babine and the ladies were introduced to Norlakes Steelhead Camp in its larval form. Weeds as high as a man, water up to the hot tub and the remnants of Curtis Barger's indiscretions still visible (he had apparently been there recently ridding the place of pine martins and ridding Smithers of beer, wine, and other delectables). The ladies couldn't see the butterfly in all of this and I doubt that they really feel any compulsion to travel with us to Steelhead Camp ever again, even if they could get cucumbers on their eyes. How could I have known?

In the summer, at Trout Camp, it doesn't get dark until way after midnight. And one night Gary and I were fishing on Rainbow Alley. It's a great, peaceful spot in the twilight. We had altered our minds and were ooing and awing at the sunset and I asked Gary if he ever thought about changing forms, about dancing with the wolves? No, he hadn't. Well, with the high water, fishing had been pretty slow. I was fishing with some home-made fly that was supposed to mimic a salmon fry. I had never seen a salmon fry, but I had tied up a lot of them and now and then they were catching an odd fish.

One of those caught rainbows disgorged a real 1 inch/2 inch fry and I realized that my fly didn't look anything like it. "Why did the rainbow eat my fly?" I asked Gary. He didn't know. I also asked him if he knew why some rainbows were steelhead and some weren't and how that was possible? He didn't know that either. Did he think in any way that steelhead, but not rainbows, were conscious animals and that might explain the hereditary basis for their life-history differences? He didn't know.

There's not much to talk about while sitting in the boat with a frog, but when I approached it from the standpoint of viewing him as a butterfly (cucumbers et al), things changed. He opened up, so to speak, and talked to me about himself in much more intimate terms, and also started taking pictures of the sunset and the boat and me fishing at the bow. We had a wonderful evening parked on Rainbow Alley and the pictures he sent me are still pasted on my wall at home.

Margie doesn't fish. We talked her into going out one morning. It was raining and the weather sucked, but she was a sport and Pierce parked us in the Alley. I would catch a fish then turn the rod over to her to fight and land the fish. What a kick. Pierce and I had such a good time listening to her scream every time the fish jumped, ducked for cover or made a short run—a 50-year-old kid!

We caught whitefish and fed them to an eagle nearby. We tossed them up into the air and that eagle would swoop down from his perch on a nearby tree and snatch the fish, sometimes in the air, sometimes just as it hit the water. She whooped and hollered like a kid. She never saw the eagle pick up his paycheck at the end of the week, but I don't think it would have spoiled it for her. She had a good time. She had a new experience, learned something and enjoyed herself doing it—shared in the passion.

We humans are conscious animals and remember events like the above that change us. But these things really don't change us in a corporeal sense. How would we remember our night, or our life, if we went to sleep as one thing and awoke with wings as something totally different? Especially if we also had a warm cloth on our forehead and cucumbers in our eyes. Would our memory, our consciousness remain? If we are animals, then when in our resurrection from the ocean did consciousness begin? When did Love begin? Do fish have a little?

How about eagles? Might, like the lives of some organisms, consciousness be discontinuous? Would that explain the differences seen in the same species? One fish that stays in fresh water, the other, genetically the same, but more aware decides to head out to the ocean to live and eat for a couple of years, then decides to return to the fresh to spawn. Is there thought in that? Probably some, don't you think? Thank God for consciousness and thought. Thank all those things before us that have made it possible in us. Especially love.

Rainbow Alley is one of those places that glow in the dark when you cross your eyes. I know because I got pictures. I remember.

That's my story and I'm sticking to it.

—E.G.

No Steelhead in Coalmines

*Carl H. Blowers, from Montour Falls, NY, and his brother Dr. Lewis C. Blowers, another
Babine devotee, have a strong Atlantic salmon background but find time for an annual visit
to the Babine. Pierce appreciates the fact that they are both keen dry line fishermen and
take a special delight in the moment when a steelhead comes to a fly fished on the surface.*

I have spent 12 years traveling to the river to do battle with the steelhead and, although it takes some travel to get there, it is all a part of the steelhead adventure.

The city of Vancouver is the start of the adventure. We land at the marvelous Vancouver International Airport, modern, clean and one that is easy to navigate, with a great hotel and an outstanding restaurant. The city features a list of diverse eateries along with urban parks, rose gardens and urban forests. Or a traveler can just sit at one of the waterfront patios and enjoy the sunset. It is a relaxing place to get ready for the trip north to Smithers and the Babine.

Arriving in Smithers, we check into the Stork Nest Inn; the next stop is to Oscar's Sport Shop to stock up for the river. Then on to the Alpenhorn restaurant across the street, the place to listen to fish stories, sip a beer or two, and have dinner, which needs to be substantial enough to bridge the gap until we arrive on the Babine at 8:30 a.m. the next morning.

The transition to the Babine starts at 6:00 a.m. with Pierce's friend Nick Sikkes, a retired baker, loading the truck and Pierce herding everyone into the van. An hour and three-quarters' drive out to the weir followed by a misty, jet boat ride down river has us unpacking and stringing up fly rods. After strapping on the bear spray and loading up the bear bombs, we are ready for the river.

What is the fly this year? Not any I packed or bought at Oscar's. Is it a Green Butt Skunk? No, it needs to be a waking fly. Try My Shaved Beaver. That is what makes it an adventure. We don't know; we need to get into the water and find out what will bring the steelhead up to splash our fly and maybe get hooked.

When he's hooked, the fight is on, splash, jump, strip line off the reel into the backing, up river, across river. When it looks like the fish is ready for the net, it all starts over again. Now we know the fly of the day, at least, until cocktail time.

The Babine's clear water, magnificent views, wildlife and the wild steelhead makes a wonderful stress reliever. A 10-hour day on the river is turned into what seems to be only maybe an hour while we are strategizing the attack and drinking in the vista.

A trip down river to the Satellite Camp is even more of an experience in nature. The fishing is a change from the up-river fishing but just as exciting. It is a hard two days but very rewarding. The camp is about 10 to 12 miles down river with great fishing on both the up and down river trip. The real treat is to be in the camp cooking over a wood fire, sitting outside as night falls and having good conversation. The night sky there is a thing to behold. We feel that we can touch the stars. They seem only inches away. The only darker place might be down in a coalmine with the lights turned off and there are no steelhead in coalmines.

After the day on the river, it is time to update each other on the day's results and listen, tell and dream fish stories. My 12 years of fishing the Babine has been filled with fish stories. Eight of the 12 years were fished with my brother Lewis (Dr. Lewis C. Blowers) and every year of the 12 with my friend, John Hapgood, one of the most artful fly-casters on any river. John and I have fished around the world together so you can guess there is lots of competition and various versions of the same stories being told. But…the stories grow better from year to year.

The stories started the first year. On our first day we were assigned to a section of the river close to camp noted for great low-water steelhead fishing. The yelling and picture taking started in the first half hour. We were off to a fast start with eight fish that day. Could it be this easy? No! We spent the next three days asking what happened; we never turned a steelhead. The fish had sucked us in and we were hooked. The steelhead have made us believers for all these years.

That first year I was the winner, along with two others, for a two-day, one-night satellite experience. The morning was rain, fog and cold. The three of us and our guide were packed in the guide boat dressed in warm fleece and rain gear, moving down river, when a very unusual sight appeared. An awesome silver wolf stood at the edge of the river staring us down. No question who blinked. Those steel-cold, wolf eyes were riveted on the four invaders of the alpha female's turf. It was a great treat to see her, but also a good feeling to be moving on down river and away from her piercing eyes. I have not seen her again since that meeting.

One day the three of us, Lewis, John and I, were fishing together in the lower river when what took place brought back memories of the wolf's visit. Early in the morning we could hear very faint howling to the north; over the period of an hour the crying grew louder and closer until it was in the woods directly behind us. We waited for the wolf to pop out of the brush and stare us down for the second time. No show, the wolf talk just faded to the south. Just like the wolf pack, steelheading on the Babine sometimes is on, and then fades away to the south.

Another day on the river, sometime in the middle years, Lewis and I were fishing together. John Hapgood was off to another part of the river. There had been some competitiveness building with John, so we all were keeping score of fish caught and released. As the groups arrived back at camp for cocktails and adventure swapping, Lewis and I were very quiet about our day on the river. John on the other hand, had a super day and was relating his fish count, which was three or four nice sized steelhead, when he turned to Lewis and me, thinking our quietness said none or few fish.

He asked: "How did the Blowers brothers do today?" We nearly lost John when Lewis said very softly: "We only landed 19 steelhead but I'm not real sure how many we lost, we stopped counting at about noon time." John was somewhat less talkative at dinner.

It perhaps was that same trip or even the same day. We had eaten lunch on a sunlit sandy spot. Lewis was resting. I had gone up river to cast while waiting for the guide boat to return. I was wading under a tree in water up above my waist and hooked a steelhead. Needing help, I blew my whistle loudly. I am sure my brother thought we had bear company as he was up and out in a shot and not too happy with me when he found out it was a 'fish-on' signal, not a bear warning.

There are hundreds of fish stories, bear sightings, wading experiences, guide wisecracks and great culinary experiences, but I must end. Adventure on the Babine is best lived not read.

On the Babine, fly-casting and taking in the sights, minds wander to the friends and legendary steelheaders whose ashes are part of this historic river. It has been a super 12 years and with any luck, there will be many more great experiences.

Outdoor Life Article Pointed the Way

Walter Russell (left) and his late father, Bill, were an acclaimed father and son fishing partnership over many years on the Babine.

In his tribute to an old friend, Pierce Clegg wrote: "Bill Russell, from Asheville, NC, was 84 when he died in September, 2008. He was and is a Babine legend in terms of the many years he fished here, but especially how he fished. He was a consummate gentleman, a southern type of gentleman from North Carolina. He was a survivor of the Battle of Okinawa, something he didn't talk about and something, as his son Walter has said, that changed him forever. This season I will be remembering Bill, remembering his particular casting and fishing technique, his gentlemanly ways, his son's North Carolina moonshine, his smile, his fishing hat and the many signature Bill Russellisms that have left a huge impression on me. Bill was so pleased to be involved in the book that he sent us not one but four pretty special contributions. Here they are:

I first heard of the Babine around the fall of 1970 or 1971 when I was fishing on the Yellowstone, near Livingston, MT. I met Joe Brooks' wife, who was staying at the same motel, and learned from her that her husband was away fishing with Dan Bailey and a fellow who managed a sporting goods store in Seattle.

A short time later there was an article in *Outdoor Life Magazine* by Ed Zern, a noted humorist and outdoor writer, about the Babine and Norlakes and specifically about Ejnar Madsen, complete with Ejnar's dialect.

The article intrigued me so much about the prospect of steelhead fishing that I called Dick McLean, a friend of mine with whom

I fished for many years, told him about the article and proposed to him that I would try to reach Ejnar and schedule a fishing trip with him on the Babine. McLean agreed.

To make a long story short, Dick and I wound up that fall fishing at the Steelhead Camp. We flew by floatplane to the original lodge, met Ejnar there and he took us down the lake by boat to the weir and then to the camp.

So began my history of 30 years or more annually fishing for steelhead on the Babine. I brought my son Walter with me two or three times when he was a teenager. Thus he became and remains an extended member of the Babine Norlakes family and a steelhead fisherman.

A Conservation Conversation

"After Ejnar Madsen had died and Pierce Clegg was operating the fall Steelhead Camp, I came back for another season of fishing and enjoying the magnificent experience of living in and being a part of what seemed to me to be one of the few wilderness areas left in the world.

By this time, Pierce had established an overnight cabin which he had named Satellite Camp, several miles below our main camp. Early every week it became the custom for the group then in session to arrive at a selection as to who would make the trip to the satellite location. Some people were not interested, wanting to stay close by the main camp for various reasons. Others, myself included, were indeed interested, and there was some competition about who would get to go on a particular trip during that particular week.

One week, I made the cut and, with another steelheader, whose name I do not now recall, set forth with Pierce, fishing from spot to spot for several miles down stream from the main camp to the Satellite Camp where we settled in for the night. The next morning my partner and I set out again toward the various venues available in that area with the understanding that we would fish separately and simply await Pierce's return the next afternoon, whenever that occurred.

I fished during the morning, had a few strikes and I caught one or two medium size steelheads. Having completed what I considered then a successful day of fishing, I decided to return to the camp, a short way in from the river, and rest until Pierce came back to pick us up.

By this time in my steelhead fishing life, I had been fishing the Babine regularly, probably for a period of 25 to 30 years, long enough to observe the gradual change which had come to the river in terms of the attitude of steelheaders, from catch and keep to catch and release, and also the efforts of industry, sometimes apparently aided and abetted by local government, to invade the surrounding wilderness area for timber and mining purposes.

These commercial efforts, of course, brought immediate conflict with steelheaders and conservationists, intent upon preserving the pristine character of the area. By then, Pierce had been operating on the Babine for several years, and had become a noted and effective leader of the conservation movement. He was backed in this by practically all the fishermen who came to his camp every year, as well as by many others in and beyond Canada. There was also strong opposition, led by the timber and mining industries and supported, I am sure, by many local and provincial government politicians more concerned about tax revenues than about conservation, or so it seemed.

In due course, Pierce came down to collect us. My friend was still fishing so he tied up his boat and walked into the camp to join me while we waited for my companion. I had brought a bottle of Scotch and decided that, since I was through fishing for the day, it would be appropriate to declare the sun was over the yardarm at some point in the Universe, and invited Pierce to have a drink.

He joined me and our talk turned to the subject of conservation on the Babine and the substantial opposition then being advanced. Pierce was obviously discouraged at the current status of events, voiced his feelings and indicated that sometimes he felt he should just throw in the towel and let happen what was going to happen.

I was fully aware of the fact that Pierce had been a strong leader in the conservation movement, and reminded him of the many things he had done to protect the Babine. I told him that while I was only an occasional, although an annual visitor, I certainly recognized that the Babine was one of the crown jewels of the entire Province of British Columbia.

I told him he was an excellent speaker and writer, that he obviously had been very effective in his leadership and that he was doing on a voluntary basis what the opposition was spending thousands and thousands of dollars to combat conservation and advance those causes favoured by the business interests. In essence, I told him that, in my view, he had a peculiar responsibility because of his position, abilities and his proven leadership. I was convinced that with his leadership the tide would indeed turn.

Pierce was somewhat non-committal in response, although I sensed that my comments had cheered him up to some extent. Shortly thereafter, my companion returned from the river and we gathered up our belongings, piled into the boat and headed back to the main camp.

In years following that experience at the Satellite Camp, I was pleased to note in the several newsletters and in the annual Christmas letter Pierce sends to all clients (see pages 183—187), that he was continuing the good fight to protect the Babine. I believe he continues to lead that fight, even today. Of course, I don't claim any responsibility at all for whatever successes have come to pass, but I certainly think Pierce is entitled to a tremendous amount of credit.

Having been a lawyer for many, many years, and having experienced my own ups and downs, I could certainly appreciate the discouragement he undoubtedly felt on that afternoon when he and I sat down together, had a drink and talked about the future of the Babine and advancement of conservation interests. All the credit belongs to Pierce Clegg and a few other leaders like him.

—B.R.

The Blue Hole

During one of my early years at Steelhead Camp, I was in our modest cabin quarters, called 'Steelhead Paradise', one evening after dinner. Ejnar came in and told us that as the water was low, he thought we might enjoy spending a day or most of the day above the weir on shore of the lower lake fishing for steelhead and coho salmon at what he called The Blue Hole.

He proposed to select two other fellows of the few of us who were in the camp to make up a party of four. The following morning he would to take us by boat from the camp to the weir and from there transfer us to another boat and go on up the river into the lake and to The Blue Hole. Ejnar described The Blue Hole as a deep depression in the lake that seemed to attract coho salmon and took its name from the distinctive blue color of the water as contrasted with the shallower water surrounding the hole.

Kent Williamson and I readily agreed and the next morning after breakfast, with two gentlemen from California, one from Palo Alto, the other a contractor from San Francisco, we set forth from the camp. We made our way up the river above the weir, probably a distance of one to two miles, to The Blue Hole.

Upon seeing it for the first time, there was no question but it had been happily named. The water surrounding it was clear as indeed was the entire lake, but The Blue Hole, a natural depression measuring perhaps some 100 yards across and dropping down to some unknown depth, was of a distinctive blue color. After wishing us good luck, Ejnar left us to our own devices and set off back down the river to attend to his numerous duties for the other steelhead fishermen in the camp.

The four of us dutifully rigged-up and began casting toward the center of The Blue Hole. Within only a few minutes, one of the California boys, whom I shall call Frisco, hollered in glee. He was obviously into a heavy fish. He fought it for several minutes and the fish showed itself on more than one occasion as a big coho salmon that eventually came to net.

We all gathered around, admiring a magnificent specimen. Frisco looked up at me and said: "Russell, what do you think I ought to do, should I keep this fish or should I turn it back?" I responded "Frisco, it's early in the game and I have a feeling we are going to have a magnificent day. In the interest of conservation, I recommend you turn it back." Frisco looked at me dubiously, saying "Are you sure?" and I responded "Well, as sure as I can be of anything." He then removed the hook and released the coho back to the depths.

It was indeed a beautiful fish. Unfortunately it was the only one caught that day. All four of us fished all the way around The Blue Hole and never had another bite. So the day went, and during the early evening Ejnar reappeared with his boat to pick us up. After helping us in, he inquired "Well boys, how did it go today?" Frisco immediately replied, "The day started magnificently, and I caught one of the most beautiful fish I ever caught in my whole life. But that damn Russell talked me into throwing it away and we never caught another damn fish afterwards."

What could I say? I said nothing. Frisco grouched all the way back, told the story to every steelheader in camp. For the rest of the week he painted me as the pariah who had ruined his day of fishing. I am happy to report that Frisco and I parted friends, although he was never able to resist describing me as the SOB who made him throw away the biggest damn fish he ever caught.

We never went back to The Blue Hole.

—B.R.

A 'World Record' Steelhead from The Corner

The late Bill Russell never forgot losing a really big steelhead at Corner after falling backwards in his boat to find himself fast frozen to the floor boards.

*E*very steelheader, who has ever fished the Babine, knows The Corner, or Corner, as one of the most prolific providers on the entire river for those fortunate enough to be present when a pod of fish is passing through.

When Pierce acquired the Steelhead Camp from Ejnar Madsen's wife Joy and her children, he also secured the services of Gary Bailey, formerly of the Royal Canadian Mounted Police. In addition to his profession of photography, Gary was also an excellent guide.

On this particular fall morning the weather was cold, cloudy with occasional snow, uncomfortable and miserable. Pierce elected to assign The Corner to Kent Williamson and myself and sent us off in that direction. Gary took Kent down to the lower end, put him out there, and brought me back up to the head of the pool.

Those of you who have fished The Corner will recall that the river runs straight for some distance, then makes a distinctive turn to the left going down stream at about a 45-degree angle and continues straight for at least another quarter of a mile before shallowing out into some rapids. The fishing can potentially be good anywhere from the top down to the actual turn itself and on to the very end at the rapids.

Gary apparently had a few minutes between his assignments to take a break so he tied up his boat and watched me as I started to fish. It really was very cold that morning, indeed below freezing, and I had noticed coming down from camp that the wooden bottom of the boat was covered with frost and ice. On this occasion, I was fishing wet and trying to cover the substantial width of the Babine as it ran toward the actual corner itself.

I had been fishing for perhaps 10 or 15 minutes when I had a hookup and instantly knew I was into a big steelhead. In case there was any question about it, I let out a yell. Gary took notice and watched as the steelhead promptly headed off downstream and ran out at least 100 yards of line, intent on going around the corner and heading straight back out to the Pacific, some 200 miles away.

Gary hollered to me: "Bill, hop in the boat and I will take you down to where you can get out and play that fish and you'll have a better chance of landing it." I complied gladly, got in the boat, still holding on to the steelhead, which, after its 100-yard run, had decided to rest for a moment, fortunately, and was sulking near the bottom. Upon entering the boat, Gary promptly motored downstream, pulled in near the shallows and said to me: "Now you can get out and play it from here."

Just as he said that, the steelhead came alive, took off again, and as I was standing up and attempting to slow its runaway progress, my feet slipped on the frozen floor of the boat and I fell flat on my back. At this point, I should add that after many, many years of fishing under many different circumstances, this was not the first time I had ever fallen while playing a fish and I was not surprised or particularly displeased, as I had every intention of getting back up and continuing the fight. Unfortunately, the ice at the bottom of the boat seized my clothes and held me in a firm grip and I could not get up or do anything except move my arms.

Thus I lay on my back and continued to play the fish, still intent upon heading back to the Pacific. Gary Bailey laughed unmercifully at my predicament, but made no effort to help me up, on the theory I had hooked the fish, it was mine, I was playing it, and it was my duty to land it by myself. Unfortunately, my options by then were few and before I could free myself, the fish reached the end of my backing, the line snapped and I lay there with a fly rod, a reel barren of line, a feeling of total helplessness and frustration, enduring the indignity of watching Gary Bailey continue to laugh his head off uncontrollably.

He finally took mercy on me, came over, pulled me off the ice at the bottom of the boat and helped me stand up. In an effort to salvage something out of a total series of frustrations, I exclaimed: "That had to be the world's-record steelhead." Gary mercifully agreed, and commiserated with me.

Since this event, and I have told it on more than one occasion, I have been challenged as to whether my description of 'world's-record steelhead' was indeed accurate, and silenced the challenger by inviting him to prove otherwise.

Time has mellowed my anguish in losing such a tremendous fish and left me with a warm sense of pleasure of having had such an experience on the Babine. I have fished The Corner several times since, sometimes with great success, including one day when I hooked and landed several good steelhead while fishing with Eric Pettine, but never another 'World Record Steelhead.'

—*B.R.*

First Flight into Paradise

Pierce says they all enjoyed meeting Walter Russell, from Candler, NC, when he joined forces with his dad for his last few trips to the river. "He sure follows in his father's southern gentleman footsteps and in his love of life, and no one ever refuses his North Carolina moonshine. And, like his father, he had plenty of stories to tell, like the five on the following pages."

My introduction to the Babine River came in 1973, when my dad, Bill Russell, took me up after I graduated from high school. I fancied myself as a pretty good trout fisherman by that time, but I knew I was heading for a whole new world. When we arrived in Smithers, we stayed overnight, and the next morning caught a flight on a float-plane, which would take us over the mountains and down into Babine Lake, to Norlakes Lodge.

As the junior member of the party, I was treated to sitting up front beside the pilot. I can still see the mountains coming up, closer and higher, to meet the altitude of the little plane. Just as we were approaching the ridge, we spotted a group of Rocky Mountain goats, which sprang into action, running and jumping from crag to moss patch to flee the noisy spectre of the aircraft. A moment later, we cleared the back of the ridge, and watched the valley drop away into oblivion beneath us.

When the plane splashed down into Babine Lake, I thought I had reached a vast inland sea. There is no lake in North Carolina to compare. The plane taxied up to the dock, and a hale, hearty and grinning Ejnar Madsen strode down the pier to help tie up and welcome us to steelhead heaven. Along with our traveling and fishing partners, Dick McLean and Candler (Doc) Willis, MD, we shook hands and made introductions, and then placed our gear on the shore. All, that is, except for Doc. His luggage had missed connections, and flew merrily on to Yellowknife. It would be a few days before Doc and his gear were reunited.

Between ourselves and Ejnar, we were able to outfit Doc with clothes, a pair of waders and shoes, and a wool coat. That and a borrowed fishing rod would have to hold him for a few days. We loaded our gear into wooden lake boats and began the journey down Babine Lake to the weir, where we would transfer gear into riverboats, and enter that most blessed of states...steelhead fishermen one and all.

My first fish of the Babine came not long after. Ejnar put us out not far downstream from the weir for a short session of fishing in the late afternoon before dusk set in, myself in a spot I later learned was called McGuires. I was fishing with monofilament and lures that year, and after drifting and bouncing a 5/8-oz. spoon along the bottom, I had a strike and was lucky enough to set the hook on a heavy steelhead. The fish ran down, up, and finally settled in to sulk on the bottom. I tried all of the tricks that I would use on a big trout back home, but he would have none of it and I could only move him a little at a time. Finally, with the shadows lengthening, I saw Ejnar striding down the bank in his hip boots.

He asked if I was having any luck moving the fish, which I answered in the negative. With a wry grin, he said: "Dark soon, bears will be coming down". With a flash of his Rapala filet knife, my line parted and we walked to the boat. Heady stuff for an 18-year-old...I was hooked for life.

Frosty Starts, Rival Camps and Warm Fires

*S*ome fishing memories do not involve the fish. The same year I was introduced to the Babine River, I also had the joy of experiencing a treat I had only read about until then. The weather was crisp, clear and pleasant during the day, but fell out bitter cold at night. We gladly braved the cold, because we were out watching the Northern Lights in camp. The glowing lights, wavering and darting across the sky, were an experience not done justice by articles or pictures.

Early mornings were frigid, frosty and laden with a fog that froze on all surfaces. In the early days of the Steelhead Camp, there was not yet the gentleman's agreement in effect today about which camp would fish which runs in the mornings. There was a fierce competition between the two camps to see whether the Norlakes anglers or the fishermen from Bob Wickwire's camp downriver would fish the 'choice' runs.

With the perspective of years, allowing that everyone has his favorite spots, I think that there isn't a bad spot on the river. In those days however, both camps wanted to be the first to put their sports out on the plum runs, for the bragging rights and to try to bring in the most action. In order to get the fishermen delivered to the right spots before the other camp got there, we would be awakened in the dark, eat a hurry-up breakfast, grab the lunch pails and Thermos bottles, and climb in the boats to take off in the dark.

We would ride the river upstream or down, and be dropped off at our run with the dark still upon us, the stars still bright overhead, and the icy-cold breeze blowing tendrils of fog about. As first light began to show and spread over the river, we would sometimes hear the motors of the boats from the other camp, and as they would pass by, we would be greeted by stony silence and sullen stares from the guides and sports. As soon as we had fishing light, we would wade out and start fishing. Every now and then we would have to stop to clear the ice from the line guides.

Our wading gear consisted of single-layer latex rubber, stocking-foot Seal-Dri Stream Ranger brand chest waders, topped by a pair of canvas felt-soled Converse-Hodgeman wading shoes. The waders and boots of today are much better at insulating out the cold! With our wool jackets and rubber waders, we counted on hot-running steelhead to help us forget the conditions.

My fishing partner on most of these mornings was Doc Willis. He was a great fisherman with a superb attitude no matter what the weather, but his hands suffered terribly on the cold mornings while waiting on first light. I always carried matches and tinder in a plastic bag in my fly vest, and so my morning routine would be to gather some kindling and strike a small fisherman's fire on the bank and keep it fed, so that Doc could periodically warm his fingers and hands.

I treasure the memories of Doc wading back to the riverbank and thawing his hands over the fire, with the smoke curling up to mingle with the early morning fog.

—*W.R.*

Dad's Fish: It Doesn't Get Any Better

My life has been rich for being able to fish with my dad for the past 42 years. We have shared many good times and watched each other catch a lot of nice fish. My fondest Babine memory is of sharing a day with dad fishing Allen's. The weather that day, to quote Gary Bailey, "looked like a steelhead day to me." The day began with a steady, though at times gentle rain, and periodically switched back and forth from rain to sleet. Dad started out on fishing upper Allen's, and I started about mid-way 100 yards or so below him, working our way downstream as we cast, drifted and swung our sink-tip lines and weighted wet flies through the current.

Dad and I struck and hooked steelhead at about the same time. I got pretty wrapped up with playing mine, as it made some strong runs almost down to and across from upper Larson's Corner. When I could I would look around upstream to watch dad playing his big steelhead. I watched him lean back and pump his rod, gaining a little line now, and letting the fish take line then. I looked back and saw dad stick his rod under one arm (still connected to a hot fish) and with both hands, open the chest pocket of his waders. I saw him reach into his pocket with one hand and take out a small glass bottle. I knew that this was the nitroglycerin he carried to deal with his angina attacks.

As I watched, he balanced the bottle on the back of his rod hand, took off the cap, and shook out a pill on the back of the hand holding the rod which was still attached to a large, strong steelhead with a mind of its own. He leaned back into the rod, gained a little line, placed the pill under his tongue, and went back to playing the big buck. The thought came to me: "You know, the old man is a pretty cool customer."

I went back to dealing with my steelhead and landed it as soon as I could. When I could I would look back upstream at my father playing his big fish and saw him repeat the routine with the nitro bottle. I was able to bring my fish in close and just as I tailed and measured her, Gary Bailey walked up the bank. I showed him my big hen, revived and released the fish, and hot-footed it up the riverbank as fast as you can run/waddle in neoprene waders over round rocks.

I reached the spot where dad was still standing knee deep in the water gaining ground on his steelhead, just in time to wade out, lean over and tail the fish and guide it to shallow water. I held the fish and dad measured it. I had him measure it again, and just as I lifted it to turn and slip it back in the water, the sun broke out for the first time of the day.

Gary snapped a photo of dad and I with the great, dripping hen steelhead with the sun highlighting the green spruce and yellow cottonwood and aspen leaves, the beautiful colours of the steelhead, and the bright red of dad's fishing hat. His fish measured 39 1/2 x 18 1/2 inches, identical measurements to the one I had just released at the bottom of the run.

I had the excitement of playing a great steelhead, watching my dad play its twin sister while juggling a medicine bottle and keeping his calm and staying on track with the fish, seeing the weather change about four times while we played the two fish, seeing the sun pop out at the perfect moment, and having a good friend take a beautiful photograph to remember it all by. As the saying goes, 'It doesn't get any better than that.'

—W.R.

An Ecology Lesson

When I first arrived on the Babine in 1973, I came as a new steelheader. I was right at home on a trout stream, but I knew I had a lot to learn about this new world of big water and strong fish. I asked Ejnar which knot he preferred at the hook. He showed me what he called a double clinch knot, which keeps good line strength and seldom slips. He said this knot was the one Joe Brooks liked when after heavy, strong fish, and that the line will usually break before the knot will slip.

We had been in camp for a couple of days, and were standing by the Home Pool (*now Ejnar's Pool*) before supper one evening. As often witnessed during the salmon runs, the banks were littered in places with the remains of dead salmon, the carcasses often covered with fungus. One of our fishing partners, Dick McLean, looked down at a pile of salmon carcasses that had drifted down and collected around the end of the camp's water intake, which was nothing more than a plastic pipe running out into the water.

He recoiled from the sight as if he had seen it for the first time. Dick looked around in the shock of realization that he had been recently drinking that same water and would be doing so again in the chow hall in a few short minutes. He spied Ejnar and said: "Ejnar, there are dead fish all over the water pipe." Ejnar chuckled and, with his terse Scandinavian humour, grinned and replied: "That's OK, it's all organic."

—W.R.

Practice Key to Breaking Three Rods

On a memorable trip to Steelhead Camp, I arrived to find that the grizzlies were in a season during which many sows had given birth to more than the average number of cubs. Two different sows were known to be working the valley, each with four cubs traveling with her. Now any grizzly is a force to be respected, even more a mother with cubs. We had several sightings of the grizzly families up and down the river during the week. The salmon were plentiful, which brought out the bears, and the steelhead run was good, which brought us out.

Darcy Edwards pulled his boat up with Chris and Stacy Barto, I believe, at Ward's Riffle, to set out Stacy, only to see half of a 30-pound king (chinook) salmon lying on the bank with water and blood still oozing out of it, and wet bear tracks leading up the bank into the thick alders. With a laugh, Darcy said: "Out of the boat, Stacy." We will leave Stacy's reply veiled with a humble "Nothing doing" because the true response blistered the paint off the boat. Later in the week, on the way downstream somewhere close to Sharp's Record, the four-cub sow ran out into the river as the boat went by. As you can see, these gals command respect.

During that week, Gary Bailey dropped off Professor Bob Vadas at Dead Man's to fish dry-line, and ferried me across from Dead Man's to fish my sink tip and weighted wet fly. I was carrying a spare rod rigged for dry-line fishing against the event I wanted to switch over for a while, but I enjoy fishing the sink-tip so much I hadn't used the dry line rod all day. I enjoy fishing across from Dead Man's and when Gary set me out, I picked up my sink tip rod and hopped out, and never gave a thought to the other rod.

The run from river right has a short, steep bank that shelves off pretty quickly, and you can wade knee-deep and roll-cast out and swing the fly down into a gorgeous trough. A short while later I struck and hooked a hot steelhead that had designs on heading downstream to another zip code. I played him up and down and got him close to the steep bank. I was reaching down and had just tailed him when my knee buckled.

I went down, my rod hand went up, I held onto the fish, and the rod snapped from the strain just above the ferrule. I measured and admired the fish, slipped him back into the water and let him swim off when he had rested, and got up to rub my knee and pick up my tackle. At that point I had been trout fishing for 36 years without breaking a rod, and I thought if I was going to break one, it was better on a good fish than in a screen door.

I looked around for my spare rod and remembered it safe and sound in the boat. I did what any fisherman in my situation would do. I cut off the fly, removed the broken tip section, retied the fly, and went back to casting with the remaining half a rod. With a little practice I was shooting enough line to get the fly out over the trough, and I was back in business. From across the run, Bob was hollering congratulations and booming laughter. I had fished that way for a short time when Gary came back down with the boat. I would have given a king's ransom to have hooked a nice steelhead just then. Gary laughed and asked where my extra rod was. I said: "My buddy Gary is looking after it for me."

Later that week, I was fishing Upper Trail, and played in a large buck and slid him partially up on the shingle. I reached down and tailed him, and my knee buckled yet again—darn used parts. Same routine: I went down, rod hand went up, fish went back in the water, hand still on tail, and the dry-line rod, which had now moved up to first string, snapped just below the ferrule.

I got up, measured...I'll spare you the details, but it was a really nice one...and released the fish, shook off the water, and reviewed my options. It was toward the end of the day and the boat was within earshot, so I had a cup of coffee and relaxed. That night I pieced together the usable parts of the two rods, with less than stellar results, from ferrules that just didn't quite match. Pierce magnanimously loaned me a nice rod from his cabin to finish out the week. It was a pretty nine-foot Sage that balanced nicely with my Martin reel and sink tip.

The next morning I was in Pierce's boat and off down the river for a couple of exciting days down the lower river to the Satellite Camp. After two great days with Pierce, Craig Moyer and Rich Spotts we stopped on the way back upriver. Pierce put me out at Boat Wreck and set Rich and Craig out at a couple of nearby runs. I landed a nice steelhead, and a little later struck and hooked a little larger fish. He made some great runs, and I gained and lost line until I got him up close to shore. I tailed him, and slid him over into shallow enough water to kneel in and measure and admire him.

Pierce took a nice picture of me holding the steelhead, which he later sent to me, and took a picture with my camera. I revived the fish, sent him swimming on his way, and stood up to dry my hands. I leaned over and picked up the rod from the rocks on which it was lying. I turned and leaned the rod against an alder branch and, as I did, the top three inches just fell right off. I mean it just fell right off. I looked at Pierce and he looked at me. We both laughed in disbelief and decided that the rod may have picked up a nick from a rock or the boat sometime in the last two days.

That night was the last supper of the week in the chow hall. We all gathered and enjoyed yet another sumptuous meal, and the glasses were lifted in end-of-the-week toasts, laughter, jokes and camaraderie. Pierce strode around the room, got everyone's attention, and asked me: "Just how in the world do you manage to break three rods in one week?" I grinned, and said the only thing there was to say..."Well, it's easy once you get the hang of it."

—W.R.

The Japanese Connection

Pierce credits Fumiya Okuyama, from Tokyo, Japan, with introducing Babine Norlakes' steelhead fishing to the Japanese market in the 1990s through magazines, books and videos. "At one time we had almost 40 guests each season from Japan but then their economy weakened. The Japanese culture of miso soup, eating chinook eggs raw, good humour and the celebration of each fish by sitting down for an hour to discuss it are memories I will never forget. Fumiya now teaches fishing at a university in the Tokyo area."

Fumiya Okuyama (center) and Pierce face the camera with, from left, Tatsu Nishiyama, Yoko Akasaka and Keio Shibata.

*I*n July, 1992 we visited the Babine on our first trip. It was also our honeymoon. Just before I got married, I was looking for a place to fish for wild rainbow trout. I was introduced to Babine Lake and sent a fax to Pierce Clegg, owner of Babine Norlakes Lodge.

My wife, Yukiyo, did not have any experience with fly-fishing at that time but we had very good luck. I was very happy that she could catch some big rainbows thanks to Pierce's guiding. The fish were very beautiful and much bigger than any I caught. And we had never seen that species before. Pierce also took us to the Babine River where the steelhead migrate in September.

At Steelhead Camp, there were many pictures of big fish hanging on the wall, which impressed and amazed us. Before Pierce told us about steelhead, we had very little information about these fish in Japan. But we had seen two steelhead videos about fishing on the Babine so we knew it was a great river.

In September of that year, I visited the Babine again with a video filming crew. We were all very excited during the shooting. Our video ran for 90 minutes and included a lot of beautiful nature scenery with wildlife like a timber wolf, bald eagles, sockeye salmon, and chinook salmon. Directed and edited by Shinji Masuzawa, it was produced for the Japanese market.

Japanese fly-fishermen and women were surprised to watch the video, much more so than we who went there. They gained the best impression of the river itself and realized the Babine is very rich. Rumours began to spread all over our country.

The following year, in 1993, saw the start of fishing tours from Japan to the Babine. In those days, big-fish hunters in Japan

A fisherman balances on Challenge Rock as he fights a plunging steelhead.

The broad expanse of Tokyo Bar provides a suitable setting for Fumiya Okuyama to play his fish while guide Darcy Edwards watches the action.

used two-handed rods and made long casts for our very popular cherry salmon (*Oncorhynchus masou*), a species of Pacific salmon caught on the western side of the ocean. The land-locked type is yamame. Japan also has pink and chum salmon but it's generally illegal to sport fish for them. Recently some rivers were opened for investigative fishing but that is a very special case.

I know I can say that steelhead fishing in Canada is a dream for fishermen from Japan. In the past, many had been to Alaska and Canada to fish for the anadromous species. They could catch salmon and trout but almost no steelhead. Now our dream has come true. All because we found the Babine and we got much information about the river and the fishing.

By the way, there are rainbow trout in Japan. About 130 years ago, rainbow trout were brought from the USA to stock fish farms for eating. And we still do it. In our fishing parks, rainbows are the favorite fish for small children and novice fishermen.

We have also tried to stock rainbows in lakes and the rivers but almost all these efforts have been unsuccessful in terms of propagation. So now, for sport fishing, we fish for stocked trout,

which can grow quite big. It's our only chance in a lifetime to catch fish bigger than 70 cm (2.29 feet) or heavier than 5 kg (11 pounds).

How is it for us on the Babine? The average size of fish in the river is the biggest in the world and we can expect to catch a 10-pounder or bigger. And there are many 20-pounders. That is a dream of dreams. We have so many Babine memories and I have never forgotten my big, no, huge, fish that came up to a Bubble-head fly. It was like a big log.

After we returned to camp, we enjoyed spoon-fishing in the Home Pool (Ejnar's Pool). That was a happy time. With no waders and wearing light clothing, we caught chinook and coho salmon and big bull char. It is impossible to have such a great place in Japan.

It's worthy of mention that our friends from Japan were not only men but also women. Frankly speaking, the cabins, as you know, do not really look suitable for Tokyo city ladies but they stay there for one whole week with no dissatisfaction. That is the magic of the Babine and they all say the Babine is wonderful with one voice.

It also really impressed us that the staff members are so pleased to host the ladies and all of us from a foreign country. There is more. They have named two favorite fishing spots to remember Japanese visitors, Kaoru's Corner and Tokyo Bar. This is a great honor for us.

Kaoru's Corner was named when the river was high after heavy rain. Kaoru Odaira is a small lady, less than five feet tall. One day she was using a two-handed rod and caught a nice buck steelhead on a Bubblehead fly. Her guide, Todd Stockner, commented: "We've never fished here before."

Tokyo Bar is the long pool just above the Rock Point. Soichi Ogura and I fished there with dry flies and beached three steelhead. Todd was surprised and said: "That was unbelievable. We've been fishing there many times but no fish." Later, I hooked a 20-pounder on a dry fly there so it's also a pool of special memories.

We made our second video in October, 1996. In this one we got good footage of a Japanese lady, Tomoko Kawasugi, catching a 15-pound steelhead. By then we had started to understand this mysterious and wonderful fish and were able to capture many fishing scenes for the video.

Year by year we catch more steelhead than on previous visits. Why is that? It's because we get lots of good information from the guides, and from friends we meet on the Babine.

Now we know the steelhead much better than the first time. We have been taught by each other. That is our way of success. At first, when we brought our two-handed rods, we mostly used an overhead cast. But Pierce told us a roll cast was better. So we did that and it gave us more water to cover. Then our roll casts evolved into Spey casts and, now, Spey casting has become very popular all over the world.

As I am writing this story, my heart is not here in Tokyo but on the Babine. My eyes are following a waking fly. I am very excited just imagining the fly as it fishes down the river. I am wondering if a steelhead will chase it. Some of my friends, who have never fished for steelhead, ask me how does this fish fight when it is hooked. I answer that it is like a dolphin in the river showing acrobatic jumps. This dolphin is not the sea animal. It is mahi-mahi, the saltwater game fish.

It is a very valuable experience that we have fishing the Babine. We do not have this spectacular environment in our country. I have fished in many other foreign lakes and rivers for trout and salmon and have caught some steelhead there. However, no other place has made me crazy or moved me like the Babine.

Some of our friends went to another river but they returned to the Babine. Anyway, this reflective writing comes from the other side of the earth. It is far, far away but, despite the distance between us, knowing of the existence of the Babine makes us peaceful.

This is to my wife, Yukiyo and our two boys, Yuki and Naoki. I much appreciate them for allowing me to have several chances to go to the Babine. And I still wonder what she really thought about that first honeymoon visit?

Tmami Sakara's rod takes the strain of a downriver steelhead.

Cast...Mend...Step...

the run starts up there...
you'll want to swing into there.
work that hard...
reach far to those boilers, once you get down farther..
then finish down to the tail out, there... by the alders..

it's a relatively easy wade..
it'll deepen up as you go....
the line will come in and out...
some nice big boulders later on..
nothing too rough though...

you've got your tips, type 8 up top...
then 6 later...
and your bag...
anything else???
see you in few hours...

with the decrescendo of the motor...
the sound of the river takes over;
the soft breaking of water over rock,
and a light breeze through coloured leaves
fills the crisp air...

breathe in....
breathe out...

adjusting my hat and checking knots..
stepping out quietly... as though stalking a brown..
the pressure of the water against my calves and then thighs,
reminds me where I am .....

a fly of last night's tying...
cast... mend...
short at first.... then longer...
working every bit...
cast... mend...
cast... mend... step...

a good bit of working line...
fly turning over nicely...
watch the wind...
watch the anchor...
cast... mend... step...

these colours...
blue into white capping peaks...
yellow into orange..
a bit of lingering green thrown in...
cast... mend... step...

a soulful tune on the mind...
balance in the step
timing of the double Spey..
rhythm in all that surrounds.
cast... mend... step...

I'll try on top first...
then maybe a Blue Moon...
or brighter pattern.
should I tie on another Bomber....
cast... mend... step...

a welcome, warming sun for now...
brightness, illuminating hidden river spaces.
a spot of clouds in the distance...
blue and grey...
watch the waking...
cast... mend... step...

that looks like a young eagle over there...
hmmmm,
this feels like the right spot..
crazy how they can fly like that...
wonder if I should...
cast... mend... step...

the water is so clear..
I can see the label on my boots..
amazing... I am the only one on this run...
what about over there..
cast... mend... step...

cast... mend... step...

—S.H.

The Hook-Up

it seems that sometimes,
when all the grace may have left us...
and found us all at the same time....
at the most inopportune and unexpected moment..
or right where we thought it may happen...
something blows us away...

something beyond a penned word or coined phrase...

you may have reached the limit of your casting length...
or laid down the perfect mend.... thus almost demanding something from the Gods...
or you may be lighting a smoke and futzing with your reel while you wade backwards...
no matter....

when the sun shines on you and the wind blows the right way.
something will happen...

in the middle of a run...
at the top of a pool...
or at that last part of the tail-out...
when the stars align and all is momentarily silent
for a fraction of the skinniest second that ever lived;
all hell breaks loose...
your reel screams...
your rod bends...
and if you're good and lucky enough...
your line holds,
your fly is taken,
and you hook-up...

Both the writer, Steven Hodges and his fishing friend, John Flaherty, are Emergency Room doctors from Chicago, IL. Pierce comments: "We are blessed to have lots of doctors among our guests each season and that has come in handy in keeping the staff upright and working. It can also make for, let's say, interesting conversation at the dinner table. They also have great hobbies, Steven, an Iron Man contestant, and John, the expert on mushroom picking and mastodon bones, and we have both on the Babine."

Dead Man's Never-to-be-Forgotten Jolt

Dr. John Flaherty shares a biography with his medical colleague, friend and aspiring poet Steven Hodges.

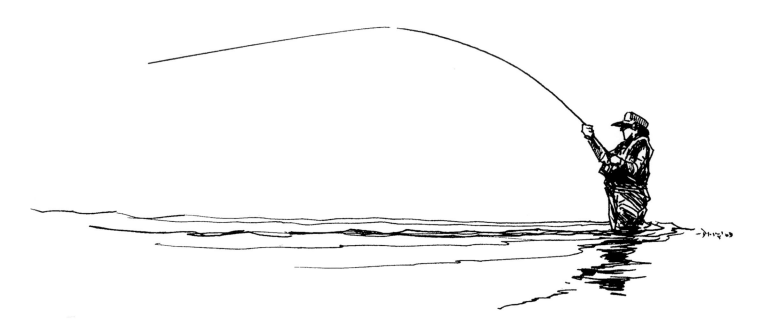

I have been fishing for most of my life, and went through the common phases that fishermen pass through.

First, you want to catch a fish using any means possible.

Second, you want to catch a lot of fish.

Third, you want to catch a big fish.

Fourth, you want to catch a fish on the fly.

Fifth, you just enjoy being out on the water and having a chance to catch a fish. The relaxation and mental clarity that results from the last approach is what I have found on the Babine, and it is what brings me back year after year.

As I approached my 50th Birthday, I came upon a list I wrote 15 years prior. One of my fly-fishing mentors had told me all the rivers I needed to fish in order to 'live a complete life'. Ron Tanouye was a world-class fly-fisherman, and a fellow emergency physician. Ron had traveled all over the world and introduced me to fly-fishing for steelhead, a fish and a way of fishing that would become my passion. I started on the Great Lakes tributaries, learned to Spey cast and maintain a nice long drift. Ron taught me to tie flies, we talked of casting methods and books and he helped fuel the fire.

The year was 2004, and I was determined to fish the East Coast for Atlantic salmon, and Northern British Columbia for Pacific steelhead. The list Ron had given me included the Skeena River with some emphasis on the major tributaries: The Kispiox, Bulkley, Sustut and Babine. He said that these were trophy rivers, remote and unspoiled, and if I had the chance I should fish them. His passion was for the Dean, a river that would take his life in a tragic accident a few years after he gave me the list.

I had some extra time and money that year and began looking for a lodge with some last-minute cancellations in the eastern and western provinces of Canada. Without too much difficulty I found an open late-season trip on each coast. The Atlantic salmon trip was in late September and the steelhead trip in early November. I was a little worried about the cold weather that far north in November but was reassured by lodge-owner Pierce Clegg that, while it was cold, it was not too bad and the fishing was good.

So I jumped on-board both trips, and my life would never be the same. The Malbaie River Outfitters lodge was a wonderful experience for Atlantics, and I hooked five fish and landed three. Most of the others at the lodge didn't hook or land any fish; we could see them but they weren't biting at all. A few of the people had been to British Columbia and told me I would be too late for any steelhead. I laughed and said that it would be just like the Great Lakes steelhead fishing I was used to, where we dodge the ice floes to get a good drift.

However, some trepidation had started to seep into me, and I was beginning to think I would freeze to death along with my young friend, Steve Hodges, whom I had recruited to come with me 'as the trip of a lifetime'. Steve is also an emergency physician, and was part of the training program I have been involved with for the last 26 years. One thing that emergency physicians are aware of is the need to 'go for it' when you have the desire for something. We are acutely aware that there are no guarantees in life.

To get the number of days off needed for both of us to make this trip, we had to work right up to the day we left, which means we both worked the night prior to leaving. Steve got off about 1:00 a.m., I finished at 7:00 a.m. Our flight left at 10:00 a.m. and we made the connection to Smithers and got to our hotel at

8:30 p.m., had some dinner and went to bed. Pierce picked us up at 6:00 a.m, and we headed out on the road. This was definitely a new experience for me. I had always made it to the lodge in one day, and I felt that this must be a very remote place.

The old logging road was not plowed, and we were slipping and sliding all over the place, dodging logging trucks full of logs in the dark morning. We made it to the weir and I was surprised to see three boats and a lot of supplies being transferred. Everybody helped loading stuff into the boats, and we followed as well. The more experienced advised us to sit with our backs facing downstream, to cut the wind as we traveled.

All of the guides and experienced anglers got more excited when we arrived at the camp. They hopped out and told us to pick a cabin so Steve and I walked over to Steelhead Paradise and started to unpack. Everyone was excited and happy, and we then found out that we were supposed to go fishing right away. We expected a little time to decompress and organize, but we were cajoled and prodded to get going right away.

Since we had worked every day right up to leaving, our 'stuff' was in total disarray. But we fumbled around and were able to put together a semblance of a fly line with an assortment of steelhead flies. Of course, we had typical Midwest rigs of floating line and some short sink tips, embellished with some split shot for the two to three feet deep Midwestern streams we were used to fishing.

The guides were chiding us for being so late getting out. First time wading out to the boat in my new neoprene waders with the lug soles, my feet slid out from under me so fast I fell into the boat. Lucky for me I was facing forward. We had so much to learn about this powerful river. Fortunately it wasn't too cold and the guides got us rigged up correctly after having a hearty laugh with us at our lack of experience with the Babine.

The first day was a bit of a blur. I did hook-up with one fish on an egg pattern but it broke me off after about 10 minutes. I was the one that became hooked. The next day we were off early, much more prepared and equipped correctly thanks to the kindness of the guides who loaned us correct-weight rods and longer, sink-tip lines.

Steve was the first to hook a fish, at Upper Dead Man's on an egg pattern. I was fishing downstream and can still hear him whooping and hollering as he landed the fish, a nice hen. I hooked and lost two more and was amazed at the strength and beauty of these truly wild native fish. I almost fell in twice and made a note to myself to get some felt-soled, cleated waders and to use a wading staff. The rest of the day was quiet for us and we were surprised, when we all were discussing how we had done at dinner that night, to learn the other guys were catching eight to 10 fish a day on spoons. They were all spooners and we were the only guys fly-fishing.

The third day started out bright and beautiful, clear and warm for the time of year. I was equipped with an 8-weight, single-handed rod and some Teeny 300 sink-tip line borrowed from Darren Wright, one of the guides. I was dropped off at Dead Man's about 10:00 a.m. and had the whole run to myself. At first I was a little afraid at being alone, but it was so peaceful and beautiful that I quickly lost all fear. I was wading cautiously and

it took me about 20 minutes to get the hang of casting that heavy sink tip. I was fishing a Blue Moon and slowly working my way downstream.

And then on the hang down, after a nice long drift, the fish hit the fly. I saw it turn after feeling the strike, and I almost dropped the rod. This was the biggest fish I had ever seen. Bigger than any salmon I had caught or seen in the Midwest, East Coast or Pacific Northwest. I gripped the rod tightly after almost losing it and lifted the tip sideways toward the bank. The fish took off when he felt the line tighten and I knew I was in for a battle. I braced myself and set the hook again to make sure it bit, and the fish broke the water and headed out to mid-river.

I lifted the rod tip streamside and began to bring the fish in. I began to yell and holler to see if anyone was in earshot to witness this big fish, but I was alone. The fish came back to me until I got him close and then he really took off, broke water twice and headed downstream and I went with him. After 50 minutes of this back and forth he began to tire and I was able to bring him into a shallow beach. I finally got a good look at him, a beautiful double-stripe buck steelhead. It was the largest freshwater fish I have ever seen.

I kept hollering to see if anyone was around to witness this fish of a lifetime, but nobody was within earshot. I was sure that nobody would believe me. I had no tape measure, and only an old, film-based camera. I wanted to take a picture, so I guided him next to the fly rod and tried to take a picture with the fish and rod and reel in the frame. But the fish was too big for my camera so I quickly gathered some flat rocks and stacked them about a foot high to get a better angle and this time it all fit in the frame. I quickly took three pictures and set about reviving the fish. He quickly regained his strength in the cold water and took off to the deep water.

I had to sit down and recover as well; I was still trembling when the guide stopped by about 20 minutes later to check on me. He just smiled and nodded his head when I related the story. "That's the Babine for you," he said, "happens every day." I could just nod back in agreement. Based on my measurements of the picture and the rod, the fish was about 43 inches long with a girth of about 21 inches, at least 25 pounds.

The rest of the week was slow, as a cold front came through and the fishing slowed down, but the memory of that monster fish has brought me back to the Babine every year since. I know now which lines to use, which flies to use, how to read the river, how to cast so far I can carry the river in most places. I have caught many more fish on the Babine since that first trip, as well as on other local rivers, using dry and wet flies, and the guides no longer laugh at me.

I do not feel the need to catch a fish to have had a successful day. Just the opportunities to wade this river, to cast to the areas that I know hold fish, gives me a sense of peace and tranquility even if the fish choose not to bite. I often find myself just sitting on the bank, taking in the changing scenery and being in the moment as much as I can. This is the drug that brings me back to the Babine, but I still get a jolt every time I make the turn into Dead Man's.

Vic Rempel: Bubblehead Pioneer

Pierce describes Vic as a "true pioneer of dry-line and waking-fly techniques on the Babine. His early experimentations were considered more humorous than serious but soon caught on big time. To this day his Bubblehead fly is still one of the waking flies of choice. He and his partner, Chick Stewart, enjoyed lots of trips to the river in the early days."

フライパターン・マニュアル
•増沢信二

Dear
Original Fly Patterns

⑱バブル・ヘッド

山と溪谷社

The illustration of a fly and the front cover of a Japanese fishing book honouring the skills of Vic Rempel, the man who introduced the Bubblehead pattern to the Babine in the mid-1980s (see page 136-137).

$\mathcal{V}$ic Rempel is more than just a legendary Babine fisherman. He was the first to make extensive use of a waking dry fly, the Bubblehead.

He also has to be one of a very few Canadians to find a place in a Japanese book on fly-fishing. Published in 1996 and authored by Shinji Masuzawa, the book's Japanese title translates as *Fly Pattern Manual* with the English alternative *Dear Original Fly Patterns*.

Vic and Shinji came to know each other through Pierce and one of his Japanese guests, Fumiya Okuyama. Flies and tying instructions were sent from Canada to Japan and Shinji commented: "There are two aspects of your flies that have surprised me. First of all they have a real nice wild look to them. I believe this natural feel to the fly should be the origin of fly making.

"Second of all, I think it is rare for the angler who aims for steelheads (cct), like you, to crush barbs. I emphasized these points in my book and I think many Japanese anglers understand your stance.

"I introduced you as a 'saint angler' in my book. I am not sure if you like it or not, but I wanted to express my impression of you whom I have not yet met, in my book. And that is my goal as well."

Shinji's Japanese readers learned Vic Rempel was "born in 1929 and lives in Vancouver. He has an over 30-year career of catching steelhead. A master of rivers in B.C., he introduced the 'Bubblehead' which is famous as a steelhead killer. He has caught thousands of steelhead in his life. He has wonderful casting technique. His style is graceful and elegance. His flies are all barbless. His principle is 'results come after everything'. If I may sum up in a few words 'a saint angler'".

With a forest industry background that included a sawmill business partnership with Babine Steelhead Lodge owner Chick Stewart, Vic started his Babine steelheading with Ejnar Madsen in the 1960s. Twenty years later he was regarded as one of the river's most successful fishermen, sharing his knowledge with the then much younger and less experienced Pierce Clegg.

"Like so many of the earlier fishermen on the river he had started out using gear but when he took up fly-fishing he never looked back," Pierce recalls. "When it came to fishing flies for Babine steelhead he knew the river better than anyone. I learned so much from him and caught some of my very first steelhead in his company.

Vic Rempel, as a young man...

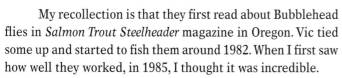

...and in his later years as he continues to excel as a steelhead fisherman.

My recollection is that they first read about Bubblehead flies in *Salmon Trout Steelheader* magazine in Oregon. Vic tied some up and started to fish them around 1982. When I first saw how well they worked, in 1985, I thought it was incredible.

Todd Stockner was guiding for me at that time and we started to push the idea to our guests. Before long we had Bubblehead tying factories hard at it in the cabins at night. In 1986 we had a great steelhead year and the camp went Bubblehead crazy." Earlier Pierce remembers Ejnar commenting: "Well, it certainly creates a lot of commotion."

The Rempel name lives on in Rempel Pool, the last downstream point on Ejnar's old river map and named after Vic's father, Abraham, another early Babine devotee. Fittingly, Pierce spread Abraham's ashes there one fall day, a fine conclusion to a life so closely associated with the river.

Comments Dan Rempel, Vic's grandson: "Interestingly enough, as soon as his ashes were spread there, people started pulling out steelhead. To the best of my knowledge it was pretty slim pickings before that."

And that's not just another fisherman's story. Pierce confirms Dan's impression and continues: "In 2007, which was a record high-water year, Rempel's was fishless until the day the ashes were scattered there. Afterwards there was a bald eagle fly-by from Lower Forty to Rempel's and then on to Gordon's Canyon, all pools that are home to the ashes of former Babine fishermen.

Then I went to pick up two guests who were fishing Lower Forty. They both caught steelhead; one had two, the other one plus a bull trout, which I symbolized as a plug from Vic since he had donated both a steelhead and a bull trout for display at the camp. Lots of meanings and I think the spirit of the event was evident.

For the rest of the year, every time I fished Rempel's it produced. In the last week I caught my biggest fish there, took a video clip of it and sent it to Dan. I'll never forget Rempel Pool for this and a few other memories I have there. It's definitely a special place and pool and, over the years, one of the most challenging to get to know—but now I know."

—*As told to Peter McMullan*
by Shinji Masuzawa and Dan Rempel

Recalling the Early Days

Stacy Barto (left) continues his longstanding friendship with the Cleggs to this day and his annual sea food barbecue is a Trout Lodge tradition. His father, the late Tom Barto, is on the left of the second photo.

The late Tom Barto completed his hand-written recollections shortly before he died coming up to Christmas 2008. His sons Randy, Chris and Stacy all worked for Ejnar in the 1970s. In Pierce's words: "They each have stories to tell and a great and legendary pool called Barto's is named after their father. He made two casts there and landed two steelhead, each weighing almost 30 pounds. Chris and Stacy still enjoy annual trips to Trout Lodge and Steelhead Camp and bring with them memories of the Ejnar work ethic and of the many steelhead that put a bend in their rods."

I made my first reservations for a Babine trip in the last week of October, 1966 in a group made up of myself, Dr. Bill Green, a long-time Mercer Island veterinarian, and Chet Aldridge. Bill Green and I had often fished steelhead together but never got further north than the Thompson. Chet was an ardent salt-water salmon fisher but had never gone after steelhead. All our plans fell apart several weeks before we were to leave and Ejnar and his then-partner, Cecil Brown, said we could apply our deposits to roughly the same time in October the following year.

Towards the end of October the next year there was heavy snow so we stopped in Smithers. There was no airport in Smithers in those days and we had driven up from Seattle. We checked with Joy, Ejnar's wife, to see if we would still be expected at the landing and she assured us we would be picked up. All guests were being picked up there as the road across the lake from the lodge

was on or crossed Indian land and they would not allow any cars to use it.

The drive to the landing was through fairly heavy snow and we were picked up at the appointed time and taken down the lake in an open boat to the lodge.

For our week of fishing that year it was breakfast at the lodge each morning. Then into a boat and down to the weir, change boats and start the day's fishing at Six Pound Pool. Then back to the lodge each evening. During the week we spent one night at the Lower Camp (*now Steelhead Camp*), where Ejnar did the cooking. That was the program for a number of years.

At least for the first year, the outboards were standard, propeller-driven models. If a rock or a shallow spot was ahead the motor was tilted up to avoid shearing a pin or damaging a propeller.

116

When we first stayed at the Lower Camp, and for some years after, Olga Beck was the cook. She was very nice, probably 55 or 60. She was also a well-built lady and we all agreed that, if she heard a bear on the back porch looking for food, she would go out with a slab of firewood in her hand and chase it away.

She was also a Camp Pool addict and, as soon as breakfast was over, and the guests were headed down the river, she was out there fishing in her knee boots. We had great fun teasing her. We even located her hidden cache of cured salmon eggs under the cookhouse, and she always caught fish. Not long after she retired (in 1971) and moved away she was struck by a car and died of her injuries.

Some time during 1969 or 1970 Ejnar said he wished he could find some teenager who could work around the camp. I said I had a 17-year-old son who might like that sort of a job. I added a few praises and stretched the truth a bit, saying he was a good hand with an axe, good with a chain saw and could handle boats very well. The next season Randy was on board as a camp handyman, boat operator, guide etc.—at no pay because he was not a Canadian citizen.

He spent two years there. Then his oldest brother, Chris, was there for three years, along with younger brother Stacy, for one year. I guess they all did their chores OK. Stacy is the really avid fisherman of the family and even then he could hardly wait mornings for guests to leave camp so he could 'test' the Camp Pool. Even today he is an eager 'glow ball' fisher in Camp Pool after dark.

When fishing and staying at the Lower Camp became the routine for the week, there was no way to keep fish iced down or cold enough to take home. It was then that Ejnar and Jim Price dug a fairly large and deep pit in the ground, between the cabins and the river. They made a wooden cover and put a barrel of gas on it to discourage the bears when the fish were cooling.

On occasion a bear would move the barrel far enough to get at the fish so, one night, Randy and Chick Stewart decided to take care of the problem. There was a dusting of new snow on the ground but they still sat for several hours in the doorway of one of the cabins, Randy with a spotlight and Chick with a rifle. After a long wait, Randy spotted the bear moving up the shoreline but Chick couldn't see it, even when it neared the fish box. Randy asked Chick if he knew the location of the fish box. Chick said he did and rested the rifle on Randy's shoulder.

The plan was for Randy to turn on the light when the bear was at the box, which he did. At that point the whole camp was awakened by the rifle shot and the bear was done in. Next morning, Ejnar told Randy he had to dispose of the bear, which gurgled a lot with a stomach full of ripe salmon. I helped him wrestle the bear into the bow of one of the boats and he took off down river.

Randy Barto, then in his late teens, caught this immense fish not far from the DFO weir in 1970. It weighed almost 30 pounds. His companion that day was Strom Stromsness.

On another occasion we were awakened by the blast of a shotgun. Ejnar had leaned out of the door in the sleeping area, above the kitchen, scaring a bear off the porch below. Being soft hearted, he didn't pull the trigger until the bear was out of range.

And let me tell you about what happened one day at what we now call Big Track Drift. It was there that we discovered bear tracks in the wet sand where we could actually stand with both wader boots and still see the edge of the prints outside our feet. *(Tom's son, Chris, thinks that this most likely happened at Dead Man's Pool).*

Often in the evening there would be a poker game under way on the cookhouse table. One of our group, Leroy Kelly, frequently—if he held a winning hand—would drop a $20 gold piece on the table and then quickly pick it up and replace it with paper money. Leroy was somewhat a novice steelheader and had not caught a fish for three or four days.

He asked Mick, a young camp worker, to take him out one late afternoon. They disappeared around the corner and came back a couple of hours later with Leroy all smiles as he had caught a couple of fish. Well, it turned out it was illegal then, and still is, to fish on the river from a moving boat. That evening, at the poker table, Leroy's onetime gold piece came out from Mick's pocket as part of a bet. We finally got them to admit they had been trolling near the mouth of the Nilkitkwa River.

Another time Bill Green and I were going down the river with Ejnar to fish Green Rocks and perhaps Laura's Pool. Before we got to Green Rocks we could hear what was a loud sort of screaming, singing, and passing by we saw Leroy about half way down Laura's Pool singing his head off. When we got near we questioned him and he told us it was to keep the bears away. We cracked up laughing and he said that if we did not believe him, we should take a look out of the windows of the cabin that overlooks the pool. Sure enough they looked as if they had been washed with a muddy mop due to all the bear paw prints on them.

On another Babine trip, three or four of the guests were attorneys in the office of the Washington State Attorney General. That was the year (1970) we discovered that we were no longer allowed to use bait so there we were with lots of illegal boraxed salmon eggs, bait cans and the works. I was at Halfway Drift when one of the lawyers showed up, as I hurriedly tried to get a bit of egg and some skein off my hook before he saw it. Instead, his words to me were: "Don't bother, we're all using the good stuff too."

We enjoyed great fishing then and, in looking back, I think that if bait was still allowed, and we were allowed to kill fish, the Babine would not be the productive river it still is. In fact its steelhead run might have disappeared.

Babine's Spirit Brings Peace

On reading this Pierce commented: "Gene Brenowitz, from Seattle, WA, and his fishing pal, Dr. Gary Williams, from Hawkinsville, GA, are intense, workaholic doctors who are finding some peace of mind and fun at camp and on the river. I think Gene touches on how a brilliant doctor can still find something indescribable but spiritual on the Babine. Perhaps the many peoples that once peppered the landscape still have some sort of spiritual influence or perhaps it's the place and Creator that has always been able to get through all of our busyness (cct) and stresses."

The Babine has a power that grows on you over years of fishing it. Other rivers may have more striking mountain scenery, more magnificent trees, or prettier waters. The Babine, however, has a spiritual presence that is, for me, unmatched.

On my first day on the river in 2008, I waded into Angus and was taken aback by the beauty of the place. I was fishing with a well-balanced Skagit casting setup including a great Spey rod built for me by Bob Meiser. Casting was effortless, my Blue Moon colored Wombat fly was fishing well, and I felt myself relax into a meditative state as I worked my way down the run. The feel of the current against me, the breeze at my face and the sight of the trees and water brought me a great sense of peace.

Slam! Zizzz!! Kapow!!! I can't recall exactly what broke my meditations, the slam on the fly, the scream of line peeling off my reel wholesale, or the sight of a fish up in the air at the tail-out. My fly line reached back across epochs of evolutionary time and connected to a very distant, vertebrate relative and one hell of a hot steelhead. I watched repeatedly as the line seesawed back and forth between the yellow of my running line and the orange of my backing.

Give some, take some and give some more; I was losing ground all the time. Even though I managed to wade into a nice sandy spot to fight from and was wielding a 9-10-weight rod, I was getting soundly beaten up by this fish. As I felt the loop on my sink tip coming past the tip top, I felt the satisfaction of the 'game over' moment. Again, orange backing peeled off. When I am caught in a stalemate, I feel like a clock is running. As time passes, the opportunities for the fish to get off keep mounting. My luck held out. After countless leaps and runs I found myself looking down at a magnificent buck, double racing stripes and all, with my Blue Moon at the corner of his mouth.

I wasn't sure who needed reviving more, the fish or me. I saw to the needs of the fish first. As it disappeared into the river, I felt humbled by the power of the place and the steelhead that live there. The spirit of Babine and a great sense of peace filled me. I was where I belonged and everything was just exactly right.

Memories That Will Never Fade

"Brent Piche, from Okotox, AB, by far and away our youngest contributor, enjoyed his first visit to the Babine in 2008 and already the disease has taken hold. He works for Mike Gifford, owner of Calgary's Country Pleasures Fly Shop, and is dating Mike's daughter. Perhaps a Babine honeymoon? It's been done before," says Pierce.

My first time fishing for steelhead was hardly premeditated. It was during my second year at university, where I realized I had nothing planned for spring break in February 2008. Some pick Cancun; I chose Vancouver Island's Cowichan River. Two weeks before my break, I came to the conclusion that the Island would be my best bet. Temperatures there are far friendlier than on the mainland, and the Cowichan seemed a good choice due to its access and recommendations from friends.

I packed up my Spey rod and headed for five days of fishing. The supposed warmer weather was true, except for the nights I spent sleeping in my car beside the river. I woke up each morning to frosted windows and frozen waders and boots. Those who know me realize the lack of comfort and amenities a two-door Honda Civic offers. The days passed casting with little success, while the evenings were spent in nearby Duncan, drinking litres of coffee at the local coffee shop, watching movies on my laptop, and tying Intruders 'till it closed.

Then it was time to head back to the car for another night of terrible sleep. The weather stayed warm, bright and sunny, without a drop of rain for the week. The river stayed low, clear and very cold. It was great weather for sightseeing, but no fish entered the system. I only hooked one steelhead that trip, the last I saw of it was his red belly three feet out of the water with a pink Intruder in his mouth, heading downstream with four feet of my leader trailing behind it. What some would call a waste, I would call a start of an obsession. That fish haunted me for months.

After realizing that the winter months were probably not my best bet for steelheading, I turned my attention to the late-summer run on the Skeena system, especially the Bulkley River. While chatting in early summer about my failed attempt on the Cowichan and my plans for the 2008 season, I was fortunate enough to be invited by Mike Gifford to the legendary Babine River.

I had read about the Babine, and seen pictures of its impressive steelhead. Suddenly my summer had changed from

Brent Piche was on his first visit to the Babine and eventually came to understand that a steelhead will take a fly when it wants to and not before.

chasing browns with streamers and dry flies, to practicing Spey casting out of the drift boat while my fishing partner for the day would go fish a gravel bar on foot. I was once chastised for throwing a Snap-T to cast a 'hopper to the bank as Mike rowed, and quickly realized fish feeding on Tricos are especially spooked by Double Speys.

Fly tying went from #20 BWO's to six-inch Intruders in black and blue, and my tying bench slowly became a collage of blue, pink and purple rhea feathers. I could only assume that my fellow employees were ready to kill me, after having Lani Waller's steelhead DVD on repeat for the month leading up to my departure. After a short break through the summer, my obsession was back in full swing.

The Babine is very aptly called mysterious. There is very little information about fishing it on the Internet, and the people who have fished it are few and far between. A quick Google search will mention how beautiful and pristine the river is, and includes the obligatory massive-steelhead photos. Most mentions of the Babine are met with a glazed look of remembrance, someone mentioning how they'd love to get out there someday, or someone asking where it is.

The night before going to camp was spent sorting flies into boxes, changing fly lines to different reels, and pre-tying leaders. After having dinner with the group of guys that came out of camp

the day before, who told tales of fish blowing up $5000 reels and donating numerous fly lines to the river, I slept very little.

After the two days of traveling and waiting in Smithers, the morning finally came when we were picked up and brought to the camp. After a drive in the dark to the weir, we all hopped in jet boats for the ride down to Steelhead Camp. This quick trip provides the angler with the first notion of how incredible this river truly is. The air is crisp and cool first thing in the morning and the water is tea-stained, and as clear as can be.

Runs are pointed out, and talk of the river and steelhead fill the 20-minute trip to camp. This also shows how much the guides care for the river, and how well they treat it. The boats are not jetted down river, but idled downstream lest they disturb the banks or the steelhead over which they may be passing. The trip could be done much quicker, but the focus is on sustainability of their resource, and not how fast they can get clients in and out.

We got into camp around 9:00 a.m. and put all the gear in the cabins, made lunch for the day, and had breakfast before setting up rods and getting into the boat. What I couldn't manage to do in a week of fishing on the Island, I managed to do on the Babine in my first afternoon. I had a few plucks in the morning, and had to remind myself not to set the hook till I felt weight, having pulled the fly away. The Spey rod started to work better

for me as the day went on, with the fly going where I wanted it to and the drifts being slowed down nicely.

Just after lunch I put a cast right behind a set of boulders, mended twice, and let the fly swing. I felt my line stop with some weight behind it, I set the hook, and the line was ripped off my reel. A few minutes later I managed to net my first steelhead, a beautiful buck. He was released with a splash to my face, which, as it turns out, seems to be a tradition for Babine steel.

I walked down to the boat, not caring one bit about the few more fish I missed that day. The jet-boat ride back to the lodge was chilly, but the cold wasn't on my mind. Just like the first one I had ever hooked, the pull on the line to the release of my first landed steelhead is engraved in my thoughts. There is nothing quite like the dinners at Steelhead Camp: prime rib the size of your head and steak & lobster to put you fast asleep, dreaming of chrome.

Steelhead fishing is all about routine. You're woken up every morning at seven on the dot with coffee and hot chocolate. Half asleep you wander over for breakfast. Breakfast is of your choice, and I found myself falling into the routine of 'toast and bacon please,' followed by a lunch containing 90% chocolate bars and Smarties and 10% chicken sandwich. You then head back to your cabin, throw your waders on, get all your gear together and head to the beach.

There is no dawdling in the mornings, and you're quickly transported to your first run. You fish all day and hope to remember to eat your lunch, and get back at camp just prior to dark for dinner and the campfire. As it turns out, I'm still asleep until the first fish of the day. It soon became routine that the first fish of the day would wake me out of my slumber by giving me just long enough of a fight to get me awake, before spitting the hook.

I tried my hardest to remove this curse, from having extra coffee at breakfast, casting a little in the pool in front of camp to warm up before the boat ride, and slugging back more coffee on the boat ride downstream, but I was cursed. This did not happen once or twice, it happened every day of the week. Sadly, it seemed that I hooked more fish in the mornings than any other time of the day, usually within the first half hour of reaching the first run.

The biggest fish I hooked all week was first thing in the morning on the fourth day, and it got away due to poor 'ice management,' which had allowed my reel to freeze just enough between casts to prevent the spool from spinning on the first hard pull. Quickly, I realized the first 15 seconds of the fight are everything. You always hook the fish downstream of you, which gives a steelhead the advantage of using the water and angles against you; just a big fish moving his head can usually pull the fly away.

After the first 15 seconds, you find out just how powerful these fish really are. They are blistering fast when they want to be during the fight, and use their body weight extremely well against you. Their leaps are epic and heart-breaking as they dislodge the fly from their jaws and leave you wondering what happened. I even had a big buck crush a forged-steel hook while I only felt the slightest tick—that kind of power.

Steelhead fishing can be aggravating, especially if you are coming from a trout fishing background. You'll go days without landing a fish, or only getting one or two hits, and you start blaming yourself. However, there is nothing you could do that would be worse than taking it so seriously.

You start mending too often, and having no faith in what you're fishing, you react by changing flies too quickly and then repeat this over and over. The most important thing I learned all week, but failed to understand until after the week was over, was to not take it so seriously. The steelhead will bite when they want to, and you just have to hope you're in the right spot at the right time.

I was having a rough mid-week after a great start, hooking fish but not being able to bring any to hand for a couple days. I was fishing one of the runs that I had done well in earlier in the week, going one for three. My fly was tapping and snagging on bottom with regularity when I snagged bottom one more time. I set the hook and then dropped the tip, then pulled back up (a great method for removing flies from snags), to find bottom moving upstream.

This happened for a few seconds before the fish sensed she was hooked. A few screaming runs and leaps later brought a beautiful hen to my guide's net; she was still very chrome, and an extremely clean fish. A few pictures were taken and I released the biggest fish I had ever landed.

The rest of the week was very much the same routine, with fish being caught and lost, followed by much Halloween fun. That night I decided to fish a little later, fishing the Camp Pool after everyone went back to their cabins. I went one for three in half an hour, before having dinner and joining in the Halloween festivities.

Halloween night at Steelhead Camp is celebrated like no other place. You have a massive turkey dinner, followed by filling up the jack-o-lanterns with diesel and setting them on fire in the fire pit. Beers are downed and stories are told, all before the massive fireworks show. You know this is an annual highlight for all the guides and staff due to the sheer number of fireworks they provide.

My final day in camp started just like all the others, hot chocolate mixed with coffee, toast and bacon, and hopping in the boat to head downstream. We were on the river a bit earlier than normal, with hardly enough light to see. Barely awake, as always, I hooked a fish on my fifth or sixth cast, and it spat the hook right away. It seemed that the curse would haunt me right off the river.

Two casts later, I hooked up again, and lost this fish with the leader almost to my rod tip. I had a smile on my face when I was picked up and moved upstream. This stop went a little bit better. I let a buck shake itself off at the beach, and then proceeded to hook another two fish. In my final morning I managed to hook five and land one, but I was beyond pleased.

Every fish I landed that week leaves me a memory to which I can escape, and a feeling of adrenalin that will be hard to surpass. I hope to get back there some day. I will change some of the ways I fish and the flies I tie, but I figure the memories that the Babine generates will never fade.

Meeting the Queen of the Babine

*The final two contributions to this chapter on steelhead fishing
take the reader downstream to waters familiar to guests of Silver Hilton Lodge.*

*Bill Kiefel, from Portland, OR, a senior financial advisor, regards fishing as "not my hobby but my
passion" adding, "I have been fishing for the last 45 years, since I was five years old. Randy Labbe is the
whole reason I know and continue to re-visit the Babine. The fish in the following story was caught on
the second of four trips to date, and on my first visit to Silver Hilton's Triple Header camp."*

*L*ate on the fifth day of our week, a gentle, welcomed rain finally caressed Northern BC. Now the Babine began to look and feel like October. The good rain did not let up. It came down all night, hitting the metal roof of Silver Hilton's Triple Header. I couldn't get to sleep, knowing that tomorrow was the last day of our week and the last chance to land all the fishing hopes and dreams of the entire year. It would be another twelve whole months before I could return to this steelhead paradise.

In the morning, we woke up with great expectations that the water level would be up a few inches. It was our hope that this would do two things: make our boat travel upriver less of an adventure than it had been all week and, most of all, stir up the fish. I needed to rid myself of yesterday's skunk.

Jeremy Dufton ran us up river, maneuvering the big sled, and then the smaller one, as if he had personally laid every rock in its place. Our expert guide picked his way through boulder patch and tail-outs. The river looked great. Although the water was up a few inches, as we had hoped, the colour was still perfect. The water temperature was 47° F, the warmest reading of the week. You could not ask for better conditions. My fishing partner Rod Peck and I kept telling ourselves that this had to be the day.

Finally, the small aluminum sled brought us safely to our destination. We stopped at a short run that had two distinct buckets, both framed perfectly with fishy-looking boils. Named by Lani Waller after a leaf he landed there, Yellow Leaf (see *Ejnar's Old Map No Ordinary Relic*, page 76) is a spot that, in normal water years on the Babine, would usually be ignored. More often,

*Silver Hilton's Triple Header camp, and a pool of the same name, are every bit as famous as the original
lodge built by Bob Wickwire in 1984. Both have undergone extensive renovations since a change of ownership in 1998.*

it was just skipped altogether in favour of the higher producing Hanawald Creek, which is downstream and across.

But 2006 being a record low-water year, Yellow Leaf was Triple Header's top-producing run. It had also been the hotspot of our whole week. Today was my first chance in the rotation to fish it. Jeremy stealthily pulled the boat to shore, well above the first bucket, then jumped out to hold the boat in place:

"Bill, you're up. Take your type six and walk down to where that first big rock sticks out of the water," he said. "I want you just to focus on the two obvious buckets. So don't waste your time on the water between the boat and there. You will not need to wade out any deeper than your knees here. Remember what we talked about yesterday, take smaller steps. Fish it slowly. Radio me if you need any help or get anything. I am taking Rod up to fish Wounded Eagle."

They were off, motoring upstream, around the corner and out of sight.

The rain had glazed the rocks along the bank so that they were shiny black. Sprinkled here and there between them were yellow and pale orange leaves. Slowly making my way down the slippery bank to just above the first set of boils, I waded out to ankle deep.

The setting was very tranquil. With my stocking cap down over my ears and my hood up over my head, I was warm and comfortable. Sounds were muffled. Everything seemed peaceful. I was not in a hurry today, trying to savour the moment. This time tomorrow I would be boarding the helicopter back to Smithers, for the trip home.

I changed what I had on to a black-and-blue tube fly and a sharp new size 1/0 hook. Without pulling any more line off my reel, I made a few short swings with just the leader and tip section out. The current seemed to move at a nice walking speed. My fly had a sexy sparkle from the four or five strands of silver tinsel. We were looking buggy.

The surface film had an oily look to it. Through the clear water, I could make out a gradual sloping bottom with nice sized boulders and various coloured rocks. The great structure, seams and small boils meant steely resting places. It just looked like there had to be a fish here. I started to get that anxious feeling.

Without stepping downstream, I stripped more line off my reel, did my Snap-T and finished with my forward cast. I repeated this process until I had out the entire Skagit head and about eight feet of green running line. I was ready to take my first step downstream.

On the fourth cast, as my line traveled through the top half of the bucket, I felt that familiar tug. There was a pregnant moment between the invitation and the commitment. Then, in a split second, my green running line was peeling off the reel, out toward the center of the river. That wonderful zinging sound came from my reel.

Without moving my feet, I tried to get control of the situation. "OK, that's enough line," I told myself, "time to set the hook." So with a growing confidence from a dozen similar opportunities in the past week, I slowly moved my rod tip toward the bank to consummate the deal. Everything was tight. It didn't seem like a big fish, but it was a hot fish and my first one in two days.

"Come on, please let me land just one more and then I will be satisfied," I thought (the fishaholic's prayer). Excitedly, I radioed Jeremy, "Fish on at Yellow Leaf...do not need any help."

I worked the small hen to my side of the heavy current and started to take a few careful steps backwards, toward the bank. After two short runs upstream and one out toward the center of the river, she seemed willing to let me meet her. The hook had traveled all the way through the roof of her mouth and came out just below her right eye. I quickly tailed her with my left hand. She rested calmly on her side in the surface film.

Finding a safe place to set my rod down, I carefully removed the tube fly from its place with my pliers. She was a healthy, fairly bright, eight-pound fish. Just behind her rosy gill covers were several obvious net marks, like several of the fish we had seen this week. When she was ready to get back on her journey, I gave her a kiss on the forehead and let her explode from my hands back into her world.

I stood there for a moment trying to take in the whole thing. "Man, I am going to miss this place," I said to myself. The rain had backed off into a fine mist. My watch read 8:45 a.m., making that the earliest fish of the week for me. I wondered what else Yellow Leaf could hold, as I had barely scratched the surface.

I made my way back to the scene of the crime and started the whole process over again. As I worked out my line, I could hear the sound of the boat making its way down river. When my cast reached the seam on the other side of the river, I stopped extending it and began stepping downstream. Step, cast, mend, swing, strip...repeat. I was covering the water.

Jeremy eventually motored past me, stopping some 250 yards downstream and across. He put Rod out to fish Hanawald Creek. As I worked my water, I watched Jeremy climb up the high bank to scout the tailout for a really big fish that they had seen there yesterday. Rod had fished to it, but like our whole day yesterday, no takers. They were hoping for a second chance today.

I continued fishing all the way through the first bucket and down to the second big window. At this point, the river was starting to fan a little right, toward Hanawald Creek. I stripped off more line to compensate. Wanting to continue to reach the far seam, I had about 10 full strips of running line out. My cast was at capacity.

Downstream and across, I could see that Rod was reeling up. Jeremy was making his way back to the boat to prepare their move.

I made another cast and then gave it a big mend. The water looked great. My line straightened out for its big sweep. Suddenly, I felt a powerful tug. Line started rocketing off my reel with greater velocity than I had ever seen before. It was like I had no drag at all. The knob on my spool rapped my knuckles hard when I checked my drag. It was fine. This was a big fish and it was leaving Yellow Leaf, headed downstream for Hanawald's.

Within moments, I was deep into my backing and running out of line. I started the first of many prayers, making all kinds of promises to God. With practically all my line out on the water, I thought for sure that it was over. Somehow I needed to turn this fish. The only thing I could think of was to lower my rod tip toward the bank and down close to the water and try to use the

Bill Kiefel's exceptional hen fish weighed an estimated 26 pounds and was hooked in a pool that Lani Waller named Yellow Leaf (see page 80).

current for help. Miraculously, it worked. The fish stopped its run and held.

My rod was bent to the cork, like a palm tree in a hurricane. It had so much pull on it that I had to hold it with two hands. Not being able to radio for help, I gave out a loud whistle for Jeremy's attention. He heard me, looking up at me in confusion. Using his radio, he said to me, "Is that the bottom?" I couldn't communicate back. They were too far away for me to shout and I couldn't let go of the rod to grab my radio.

Again, he came across on the radio: "If that's a fish, raise your hand." As quickly as I could, I let my left hand go from the rod and threw my hand up to signal that it was a fish. They quickly mobilized and headed up to help.

I started to reel in a few rotations of backing. It was a painstakingly slow progress. I would crank three times and then the fish would take it all back. It was like an ongoing giant tug-of-war.

Then, as I started to make a small gain on the fish, it decided to make a long run upstream. Keeping the tip of my rod high, I reeled as fast as I could to keep up, finally getting my running line back on the reel. The silver torpedo was back in Yellow Leaf.

The fish continued on its upstream run, traveling up the far side of the main current, near the opposite bank. Just as it crossed in front of me, it showed itself for the first time. The huge fish surfaced, making a 360-degree boil. I saw a wide body with white and chrome colors. It had to be a hen, but it was so big.

It continued its surge up river. Then, just like before, it stopped. No head throbbing, just constant directional pressure. I started feeling like I was just a passenger here, that this train may never come into the station. I needed her to give me some kind of break.

Jeremy and Rod had anchored the boat by now, grabbed the net and were hurrying down the bank to help out. My mouth was dry and my heart was pounding. This was the biggest fight of my life.

Jeremy told me to keep even pressure on her and try not to horse her. She would come in on her terms. Slowly, between the pressure from my rod and the current, she started to back her way downstream. When she was slightly upstream from me, I turned her head toward the bank and we all finally got a good look at her. You could quickly tell that she was a special fish. Female features to her pretty head but big shoulders and a slab body. She looked like she was in fine shape and a really fresh fish.

When she finally saw us, she wouldn't have any of it. With a quick movement of her forward body and one short, fast flick of her tail, she was back out into the fast current. She ran through the hole, over boulders, between and near sharp rocks. This was crunch time. Someone was going to make a mistake. I tried to let the rod absorb all the pressure. Let her fight with the equipment and not with me. It was all I could do to stay out of it.

This Silver Hilton angler has the pleasure of fishing one of the world's truly great steelhead rivers in surroundings of outstanding natural beauty. The pool is called Triple Header and it's overlooked by Mt. Horetzky.

Eventually, she relinquished control.

Now she was in a safe enough position and Jeremy had me take a few steps back up and out of the water, as he took a few steps with the net, into the water. How much pressure could I put on 15-pound Maxima? I wasn't going to find out today. I would be patient and wait for her.

Slowly and cautiously, she came to her side. With the entire rod, I lifted her head and Jeremy gently netted the big lady. Almost instantaneously, the hook came out of her mouth. It was done. I had cashed in on 1,000 promises. God had blessed me more than I even realized in that moment.

Jeremy, hovered over the net, looked up at me and said repeatedly in his soft-spoken voice: "This is the fish of a lifetime." Laying aside my rod, I came down to the water to see her. She was beautiful, plump and silver. She did not have a mark on her. The largest hen any of us had ever seen.

Acting very ladylike, she let Jeremy take her measurements, length 37 1/2 inches and girth 22 inches. Jeremy figured her weight at 26 pounds. I could barely cup my right hand around her belly to get a safe hold for a picture. Gently lifting her out of the water, I was overwhelmed with her size and beauty. I felt extremely honoured. Without delay, it was time to get this special lady back in the water and on to her purpose. Mine had been fulfilled.

At the time I did not apreciate the significance of Jeremy's words: 'fish of a lifetime.' For, in fact, I had met the Queen of the Babine. It blows me away to think that this resource we know

and love as the Babine can produce such fish. On her fourth return, what a miracle she represents. What a miracle this river is. We must protect it. I have fished Yellow Leaf several times since without a bump. Hasn't mattered. Not really looking for anything more than to pay homage to the Queen of the Babine on her fifth return.

This day Yellow Leaf was full of big surprises. Rod stepped into the spot where I had left off and just a few steps later, he also hooked a really nice steelhead. This time, the run delivered a nice fresh buck of about 24 pounds. Rod's single-hand rod was put to the test. His fish also ran all the way down to Hanawald Creek, taking Rod into his backing. After a heated 40-minute scuffle, he brought the big buck to Jeremy's net.

We both had personal-best fish that morning, within steps of each other. Yellow Leaf gained all of our respect and admiration for years to come. Subsequently a fishing friend advised me: 'A biologist in Smithers estimates that your fish was probably on its fourth return trip and he estimates her age at 14 years. He is comparing it to a hen captured during a radio telemetry study. His comments are as follows: "That is a beauty…. in October of 1994, the B.C. Ministry of Environment, Fisheries Branch captured a female on the Babine River as part of a radio telemetry study. She was a great fish—98 cm nose to fork (38.6 ins), no girth taken, 11.0 kg (24.25 lbs by scale), 14-plus years old and on her fourth repeat."

My Oh My: A Big Fish Takes My Breath Away

Jack Cook, from Carnation, WA, is a former computer programmer and describes himself as a fly-fisherman, fly tier and steelhead guide. He founded The Irish Angler, in Monroe, WA, sold the business early in 2008 and now represents Guideline, the Swedish tackle manufacturer, in the USA and Canada.

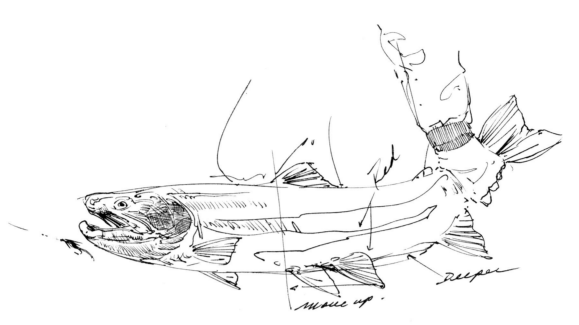

The water was somewhat off colour, like a cup of strong tea. The sky was overcast and it had been raining steadily for the last three days. For the Babine this was really off colour. I selected a nice 3/0 Green Butt Spey, a tie to which I go in off-colour water.

Evans, river right and fished from Silver Hilton, is really two very short pieces of water. There is essentially a large shelf across the middle of the river and a big drop so the water here is really churning as it goes by. The top is a classic piece of water. No more than a 30-foot cast is required, the idea being to set things up in the fast water beyond the seam and then quietly swim the fly into the seam and over the quiet water inside.

As you fish down from the top you come to a point where the bar you are on disappears and so will you if you keep on walking. At that point you cut back into the bank and into the bushes and trees that surround it. A Spey cast works well here; you only need 40-50 feet so being in the trees is not too big a problem. At the bottom of this lower piece is a grouping of medium-sized rocks.

Mark McAneeley told me to start at the top and fish slowly. The top fished like a dream and, although I did not touch a fish, I was sure I would get hammered on every cast. When I made the transition and started on the lower piece I was in the groove and the fly was swimming nicely. I have always been a fan of fishing upstream of rocks so, as I approached the bucket, it was not without expectation. As much as the visibility was poor, I was swinging a four-inch hunk of seal fur and bronze mallard and, if they couldn't see that, they would have to be blind.

As the fly swung 10 feet upstream of the rocks the rod was virtually ripped from my hand. The grab had the power of a bulldozer and made it clear that steelhead be darned, I was securely hooked. The fish was not anxious to go anywhere though.

It stayed in the run, moving powerfully back and forth about 40 feet with some wallowing jumps thrown in.

I knew the fish was big but just how big would have to wait until later. As the beast quieted, I moved him towards the bushes and trees behind me. I found a good tailing spot and, after two or three attempts, managed to get a grip on the thing. It took two or three attempts, for the first time I got him close and saw the size of him I lost all sense of reality and started panicking and worrying about losing him. I never was able to get my hand around the wrist of the tail. It was just too big so I grabbed the fly in his mouth when he floated in and tethered him with it.

I quickly ran the tape over him and saw he was 40 inches, an awesome fish and one I was blessed to be holding. The girth measurement was the killer. As I wrapped that fish in a fluorescent red measuring tape I could not believe it, 24 inches. I measured again and it was the same. WOW. Now my breath was coming in gasps and I knew I was in danger of not surviving the release. I cradled the fish's belly and removed the hook and gave up any hope of getting a picture. I staggered out in the flow, pointed him upstream, and prayed he would survive to spawn an entire race of specimens like himself.

As he twisted from my grasp he did not speed away but powerfully moved back to his lie in slow motion. I fell back and sat in the river, chest pounding, unable to breathe or think or move. When my buddy, Carl Engel, and Mark returned in the boat some time later they found me in this position, my rod tangled in and hanging from a tree, the line running here and there in a mess. I tried to talk but the words would not come. According to Bob Wickwire's Babine-tested formula, this fish would run a little over 31 pounds.

My Oh My.

PART V

Listening to the Guides

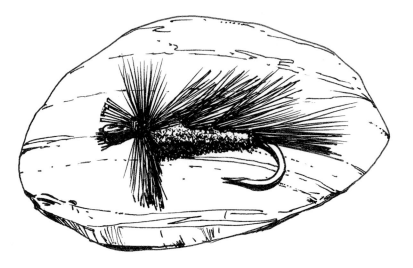

Good guides, reliable, hard-working, knowledgeable and personable, are absolutely essential to the success of any well-run sportsfishing establishment and we were delighted to be able to include these entertaining and informative contributions from men who came to know the Babine as well as anyone can. Their experiences encompass both the Madsen and the Clegg regimes as they spent their working days, and many a long night too, with Norlakes guests down through the years. Together they searched for big trout on Rainbow Alley, and around the weedbeds of Nilkitkwa Lake, and for far bigger steelhead on the river itself, often fish of a size seldom seen on any other watershed.

Fred's Freddie Pattern Hard to Beat

Pierce remembers Fred Watts, from Merrit, B.C., as a Trout Lodge guide in the late 1980s and continues: "He gets the credit for creating a great dry stonefly pattern that we call the Freddie. That fly, and a steelhead version of it, have provided more action than any other dry-fly pattern since he cast the first one on the surface of the Babine."

*I*f you have had the good fortune to experience the rainbow trout fishery on the upper Babine in the last 20 years, chances are you have knotted a Freddie to your line.

I am the Fred after whom the Freddie dry fly is named. Now I can't take full credit for this fly, as it is a compilation of several good ones, most notably the Mikaluk Sedge and the Improved Sofa Pillow."

The Freddie

Hook:	*TMC 2312, #6*
Tail:	Stacked bull elk hair cleaned of under fur.
Body:	Dubbed seal fur: I like a heather mixture of three parts olive, one part radiant gray and half part fluorescent blue. Second choice would be rear one third of yellow seal, front two-thirds fiery brown seal.
Wings:	Stacked bull elk cleaned of under fur with three equally spaced wings.
Hackle:	Metz or equivalent saddle with six or more turns. I will sometimes clip a 'vee' in the bottom or trim it flat if the fish seem picky. Generally though the fly fishes just fine.
Head:	Butts of last wing trimmed approximately 1/16 longer than eye of hook.

One trick I use to improve floatation on the fly is to use Mucilin as dubbing wax. Combine this with dousing the fly in liquid silicone and completely drying before stashing them in your fly box. Hit them with Gink or the like before fishing and you have a fly that fishes like a cork.

I tend to fish this fly down and across with a reach mend while drifting in the boat. It can bring spectacular results on the right days. When it's windy some drag can be a good thing. The naturals tend to get blown all over the water, so why not your fly? Makes for some very exciting takes.

Speaking of takes, don't pull the fly away from the fish at the strike. These rainbows and cutbows tend to hit the natural flies to stun them and then turn to take them. I had one English gent in my boat that missed fish after fish even after I had told him what was happening. I finally got him hooking fish after I made him say, 'God save the Queen' after the strike. Bingo. He didn't miss many fish after that.

I had one large rainbow of 26 inches come for my fly seven times on a single drift before I hooked and landed it. That one will be forever burned in my memory.

I tend to use 2X or 3X tippet with these flies to keep them under control. If things go well you will notice that the bronze of your hook will be replaced by silver as the bronzing wears away from catching so many fish. No, really. It has happened several times to me.

The last time was in late July '07. My wife, Joan, was drying flies for me as I only had two. I had given a couple to Geoff and his father on my way to the boat. I had guided them 19 years previously at the lodge. Half way through the day, Joan noticed the hooks were getting shiny. What a good problem to have.

The other great thing about this fly is that every time I gave one to a guest, there seemed to be a beer or two in the creek under the bridge.

The Untold Story of Jack and the Knot

One of my favorite memories of Trout Camp '89 is of Jack. He and I hit it off well. We talked. Or not. He listened well to instruction, and caught fish.

Jack loved to fish from his feet so he could feel the pull of the river on his legs. There is something about the cool, clean water swirling around as you watch your fly. We both spoke of it. Separated by 50 years.

The only wading fishing was below the DFO weir. I beached the boat on the manicured grassy slope at the DFO camp. We made our way slowly down to the good water below the weir.

Being fairly long in the tooth, Jack's balance wasn't the best and he was a little unsteady. To overcome the instability, I would wade upstream from him to break the current and grasp his shoulder to keep him steady. Luckily we did not

Retired fisheries biologist Fred Jordan provided this very early photo of the DFO fish counting weir.

The Nilkitkwa Forest Service Road bridge, built downstream of the weir early in the 1970s, provides access to Six Pound Pool, still a popular destination for anglers fishing for steelhead, sockeye salmon and trout.

need to wade far to put him in position for a good cast at a nice fish.

It was a picture-perfect day with a few clouds drifting by to break up the warm summer sun. Jack made the deliberate casts of an angler with much experience. Rarely did I need to prompt him to mend.

The fish did their part as well. He duped several nice fish on a standard lodge pattern as we worked down to Six Pound Pool. One was a personal best for him on the Babine. He played it skillfully, but still with the 'fear'. At the head of the pool we stopped so Jack could have a short rest.

While chatting about the great fish landed already I knotted on a Freddie, a dry fly of my own design. I wanted Jack to have the best possible shot at the large rainbow that was at the head of the pool. It may not have been the same fish always, but it was always the best fish in the pool.

Slowly we edged out into the current. Satisfied with his position and footing, Jack paid out line and measured his cast to the slick to which I pointed. The greased Freddie landed right above the target and needed no mend, as the take was immediate and savage. The fish first ran to the tail of the pool and then cartwheeled, drops of water dimpling the pool's surface like raindrops. This was the dry-fly rainbow of a lifetime.

Somehow through experience or luck, perhaps a combination, Jack managed to turn the fish and it bore upstream past him. At this point the fish decided to just sulk and slowly move away from us. Jack put the stick to him and the big trout made one great push and was gone.

My jaw dropped to the water. Our eyes met in disbelief. How could this happen? After we could move again, we made our way to shore.

Jack got to his leader before I did. There was a tell-all 'pigtail'. We looked at each other and I believe I mumbled something. Jack said nothing. The fishing was done for the day.

"Let's head back for happy hour." "OK, Jack."

We didn't talk much. It's hard enough over the outboard, let alone with the pigtail burning into my inner eye. I was dreading the ribbing and razzing I was going to get later. That is what happens when a guide makes a *faux pas*.

Dinner came and went. I tied flies for guests at the lodge. No comments were forthcoming. Not understanding why, but not caring, I kept my mouth shut.

I didn't fish again with Jack, as that was his last day at camp. We said goodbye on the dock as his group's 'plane taxied in to pick them up.

Later when the tips were distributed to the staff there was an extra envelope with my name on it. I decided to wait to open it when I was alone. There were several US 20 dollar bills and a note from Jack:

"Thank you for two great days on the river. If you send me a picture of the fish I landed above Six Pound Pool, I promise not to tell anyone about The Knot. Jack."

I did in fact send the photograph to Jack, along with a couple of flies if memory serves me right. Several weeks later I received a letter from Jack's wife informing me he had passed away. Jack had cancer. The picture, flies and note I sent arrived when he was still lucid. As she showed him the picture and read the note, he smiled.

—F.W.

Nymphing with the Other Joy

*This fine Babine rainbow was fooled by a Freddie,
a deadly pattern by Fred Watts.*

*W*here to start? Perhaps some dry-fly action, or maybe swinging and stripping fry patterns on Rainbow Alley. How about Chironomids down at the weed beds on Nilkitkwa Lake or high-sticking stonefly nymphs on the river below the counting fence?

There are so many ways to fool a fish. How do you pick one? Easy, whatever way best fits the moment.

One that stands out for me is an afternoon where I was showing a guest, and I think her name was Joy, how to high-stick those stonefly nymphs. Here's the fun part: I had never done it myself.

However, thanks to reading books and articles by Joe Brooks, Dave Hughes and Randall Kaufmann, I had a good idea of what to do and where to do it. We were walking below the weir casting big stonefly dries for rainbows and cutbows. The action was very slow but I was sure there were some very nice fish around.

Acting very professionally, I suggested that we try dead-drifting stonefly nymphs through some of the slots in the bedrock of the river. There were several holes, ranging in size from bathtubs to Volkswagens, where the trout just had to be lying.

Joy had never heard about this technique, let alone used it, but she trusted her experienced guide. If only she knew.

I proceeded to rebuild her leader, explaining about the need for a shorter, stouter tippet to turn over the big, heavily weighted fly I was about to knot on her cast.

This technique was not standard so there were no suitable patterns in the box of lodge flies I had with me. What could a good guide do but produce his own personal box and, from it, select a hand-tied specimen for his sport.

"A big, black Brooks Stone should do the trick," I said to her as I carefully tied the knot.

Next came the demonstration of how to cast this rig. What followed was a bit of chuck-and-duck with an open loop upstream, raising the rod to stay in contact without lifting the fly off the bottom. Then, as the fly passes downstream, you lower the tip and follow around to keep it on the bottom for as long as possible.

"Watch your line where it enters the water. If it hesitates, or moves sideways, or just looks funny, then lift the rod to set the hook." It sure sounded as if I knew what I was talking about.

As Joy attempted her first cast, I moved a little further away than usual which was a good thing for otherwise she would have nailed me. "Slow down your casting stroke," I advised her after we had extracted her fly from the brush.

The next cast was perfect. Joy did exactly what I had told her to do and watched her fly line intently while following the fly with her rod. I guess the line looked funny because she lifted to set the hook and immediately was playing a good trout.

Pretty good for being instructed by someone who had never done it before.

Trust is a big thing.

After all the usual hooting and hollering and laughing, and the orders to "keep your tip up," we managed to land an 18-20-inch rainbow. She thanked me for showing her a new technique that she could now use on other fishing trips.

And here is the best tip I ever received from a guest. On the way back to the lodge, Joy asked me if I was going to be guiding there next year as she would like me to teach her grandchildren to fly-fish. That's a day I will long remember.

—*F.W.*

A Novice Guide Learns the Ropes

*In addition to guiding for the Madsens and the Cleggs since the 1960s, Carl McLaughlin, from
Kamloops, B.C., is a talented musician and singer and also a skilled small-engine mechanic. Adds Pierce:
"He has composed and recorded several songs about the Babine and the fierce competition there used to
be between Norlakes and Bob Wickwire's Babine Steelhead Lodge, a few miles downstream. In the old
days he would sleep in what is now our woodshed and he still loves to fish the river."*

*C*arl continues: When I met Ejnar Madsen for the first time in the summer of 1974 I was fishing for rainbow trout just below the DFO counting fence. I was working as an auto mechanic in Prince George and, when we next met, I asked him whether there might be a job for me as a guide. I had lots of fishing background, as I was then co-owner of Suskwa Lodge, cabins and campground on Babine Lake, but had no jet-boat experience.

In time we became good friends and I learned that Ejnar was a very hard worker, quiet with a rather gruff manner and full of dry humour. When there was a job to be done he would get at it.

My first day was at the main lodge, helping him to shut down for the winter and gathering up items that would be needed down at Steelhead Camp. We loaded the boats with propane, wheelbarrows, plywood, you name it and I think we had it. Then down Nilkitkwa Lake we go, unload the boat at the fence, drag it around the fence, reload and head down river to camp.

One other day we had gone down together in one boat and I tried to remember the channel but I hadn't paid enough attention to the details. When Ejnar asked me. "Do you have it figured out?" I, of course, said, "Yes," and away we went.

He led the way and I pushed my boat out from the bank into slightly deeper water. With jet outboards you have to be careful not to plug-up the intake with weeds or with sand and small rocks that will damage the impeller.

First I got hung-up in the shallows and then I got some moss off the bottom and plugged-up. Ejnar saw what was happening and waited for me and eventually we were under way. I was too close to him to start with, riding on his wake, and that meant I could not see the channel so I backed off and stayed at a distance behind him.

Just as we passed a rock called Old Scary, we came to a huge cottonwood tree root in the main channel. We had to go around it very tight in to avoid it and my heart was a-pumping. Before we reached camp my engine quit and I couldn't re-start it. I tipped up the motor, grabbed a paddle and turned the boat around so I could steer it like

*Musician, fisherman and guide, Carl McLaughlin is
a man of many parts having worked for the Madsens
and then the Cleggs over the course of a 36-year
association with the Babine.*

a canoe. Ejnar saw me, came back and towed me in with my anchor rope, as cool and collected as could be.

We quickly found that my fuel line had come undone, simple and I should have seen it. Instead, I was left feeling pretty sheepish and wondering if he felt he had made a mistake by hiring me.

After we had unloaded the boats, Ejnar set me to work varnishing the inside of a cabin he had just finished building. Then to leveling cabins and getting started on the yearly woodpile needed for the airtight stoves in the cabins.

The first guests I guided, Allen and Helen Phillips, were old-timers and long-time guests and said that they had been guinea pigs for all the new guides. I spent the week looking after them and working in camp. Allen's Pool was named after Allen after he caught a 30-pound steelhead there on November 5, 1969.

At the time I stayed in a frame tent and my daily routine was to begin each day by starting the fires to ensure the guests' cabins were warm enough. I would have my breakfast before the guests and make my lunch. Then, while they were at breakfast, I had to fill two water pails for each cabin, fill the wood boxes for the cabins and the cookhouse, make all the guests' beds and get ready to hit the river.

Next job was to get the boats ready and warm the motors before taking the guests to their first fishing holes. Back to camp to finish any un-made beds, clean the cabin floors and put in fresh glasses and drinking water. There was firewood to be cut and split and other chores to do until it was time for the coffee that I would bring to the fishermen in Thermos flasks. They had to be moved to new places and I would spend some time with them on the river until Ejnar came along and said it was time for more chores back in camp.

In the early days there was a lot of competition between the guides and guests at Ejnar's operation and the people at Bob Wickwire's camp further down the river. Now the river is long and there is water enough for all, but it seemed they could not come to an agreement as to how to best utilize the water to the advantage of everyone. In those

The Babine River Song

By Carl McLaughlin

Up and down the Babine River
I spend my life each fall
Taking all the steelheaders
Down to their favourite hole
Hoping that they might catch
The one that they're looking for
Down on the old Babine
Same as the year before.

Up and down the Babine River
Travelling in the fog or dark
With squinted eyes and frozen face
Dodging through the rocks
Trying to get our boys from camp
Down to their favourite hole
Hoping that we might beat
The opposition from below
Down on the old Babine
Same as the year before.

Up and down the Babine River
From the crack of dawn to dusk
Steelheaders from our camp
Beat the waters to a froth
Looking for that certain fish
The one that'll do a dance
The one that'll make that old reel scream
And you can hear up and down
Down on the Old Babine
Same as the year before.

To enjoy to Carl's Babine River Song at its rousing, foot-stomping best go to the
link on the Norlakes' website www.babinenorlakes.com. Carl wrote the song in
1975 for a party of fishermen from Palo Alta, CA. He recalls 'the opposition below'
"was Bob Wickwire at the time. We were always beating him and his crew down to
the best holes early in the morn before daylight."

Still catching steelhead: A happy Carl McLaughlin on a recent visit to the river.

days you could fish from a boat and also use roe as bait. That led to many disagreements and eventually the regulations were changed to prohibit fishing from boats. Then, in 1970, the use of bait was banned completely.

There were still plenty of problems to overcome. If the river was washed out and running high and dirty, the only piece of fishable water was immediately below the counting fence. With both camps at capacity and coming up to join the local bank fishermen, there could be 30 or more people crammed into about 200 yards of water.

Eventually we had the bait ban, followed by single, barbless hooks while the catch limit went from two steelhead a day and two in possession to one per day and one in possession to the present-day catch and release. All these changes are designed to prevent the depletion of this magnificent river's wild stock and to help to maintain its pristine environment.

Before Steelhead Camp was established, around 1965-66, guests would stay at Trout Lodge and come down to the river by open boat, often a long, cold trip. They would then walk down the river along a trail and fish the pools as far as Gravel Bar, where the Nilkit-kwa joins the main river. Then Ejnar decided to build an extra boat that he could leave to fish where the water was more manageable. There were no concerns about theft or vandalism in those days.

There was a temporary camp he used above the weir and it was not long before he had established a downriver tent-frame camp beside a beautiful deep and protected pool. That was the start of the Norlakes Steelhead Camp and the pool, first Cabin Pool and then

Home Pool, was later re-named Ejnar's Pool in his memory after he died in September, 1983.

Building a new camp on such a remote river was a long, hard and slow process. There was no road in so all the supplies had to be brought to the lake from Smithers, which was a good two hours away. Then to the Trout Lodge and on down the lake to the counting fence where everything was unloaded, carried around and reloaded on the other side before the last move down to the River Camp site.

In the early years at Steelhead Camp the staff used this frame tent—not the warmest of spots when the snow came.

A mounted moose head on the wall in Trout Lodge reminds Pierce and Carl of a successful hunt almost a quarter of a century ago.

The trip from Smithers to the lake was an adventure in itself. The 'road' was hardly worthy of the name, flat tires were commonplace, the weather could be a real challenge and the driver could expect to encounter moose and bears and, of course, logging trucks and fallen trees.

Around 1958 there was a big fire in the surrounding area and this led, some 10 years later, to the construction of a new road and a bridge across the river at a point just below the counting fence. That was to allow the loggers access to the timber in that area, burned but still harvestable if cut soon enough, at least that is what the provincial government told us.

A bridge and the new road, while not the most welcome additions to the river, did have good points as they made it much easier for Ejnar to bring in his guests and supplies.

As time went on he built better and better wooden boats but there had to be a more efficient way to power them. The river and its many rocks were really hard on the outboard motors, destroying props and using up so many shear pins that sometimes they had to pull nails from the boat to make it back to camp.

Then he heard about a new attachment for outboards called a jet drive. They were made in California and, with the help of friends and guests, he bought one and fitted it to a 40 hp motor. Now he could get around the river "with hardly any problems".

At the outset a fisherman was allowed to keep a couple of steelhead and many guests did as they liked to have a big one mounted for display. Once a week a guest would be chosen to keep a fish for the cook to prepare for camp dinner. It would be filleted, smothered in dry mustard, brown sugar and onions and wrapped in tinfoil for slow baking. I can taste it now, quite delicious.

The pool in front of the camp was one of the great ones for the numbers of steelhead caught. The camp cook would fish there during a break and was almost always lucky. Most of the fishing at that time was with lures but there was also some fly-fishing. A lure that was particularly effective was a spoon called a Little Cleo, introduced to the river by an early guest from California (see page 45).

At certain times, usually at the start of October, a couple of guests were picked to go up the river and around the fence. They were taken further upstream to a spot called The Blue Hole (See page 101) where the river widened. Coho salmon gathered there and were plentiful at the time and, most always, the fishermen were successful, with the fish averaging five to 10 pounds.

In 1986, when the Cleggs followed the Madsens, I got to know Pierce and his first wife, Debby, and our friendship lasts to this day. By then I had my own repair shop and I looked after all the Norlakes equipment. I worked for Pierce for a season and we spent a lot of good time together when it was over. We got our last moose together on the final day of the hunting season and the head is mounted on the wall at Trout Lodge.

Truly those were wonderful days and my experiences on the Babine enabled me to write a song I call *It's a Steelhead Paradise*, one that I always sing for the guests when I return to Steelhead Camp.

—*As told to Peter McMullan*

Happy Birthday, Bus

Pierce Clegg wrote this piece some 10 years ago as a tribute to Bus Bergmann, a man who became and remains a Babine guiding legend. "He worked for both Ejnar and Bob Wickwire in the 1970s and was already famous on the river when we came along. I give him enormous credit for encouraging the start of a catch-and-release ethic at Norlakes at a time when almost every fish was killed. He excelled as a fly-fisherman and his mastery of the roll cast with a single-handed rod and a 30-foot shooting head had to be seen to be believed. He now lives in Florida and continues guiding both there and in Alaska. What a man."

A young Bus Bergmann was a legend in his time on the Babine, guiding for both Bob Wickwire and Ejnar Madsen in the 1970s.

*N*ews travels fast of a certain legendary Babine angler fast approaching the fifth decade of his life. And since I can only boast of almost ending my fourth decade, I thought only to offer my perspectives of this significant event.

There are two legendary factors to consider, the Babine River and the angler, Bus Bergmann. Just when I thought that Bus might not be extending the legend into the fifth decade, we now have a 1999 reservation.

Even though Bus has not experienced five decades on the Babine River, he certainly has a chance to. And so, the following ramblings come to mind when pondering the real possibility that Bus may end up with over 50 years of steelheading on the Babine. Now, this is truly scary.

The first decade could be described as one of living a dream come true. Most anglers on the Babine during their first decade feel they have really discovered something special. The river captures their wilderness hopes and dreams, and confirms their fears that places like the Babine are very rare and hard to come by. In fact, by the end of the first decade, thoughts of owning a piece of the rock enter the mind. Unfortunately, destiny

The years pass but Bus was still catching and releasing steelhead when he returned as a guest.

takes Bus to another great set of wild waters, Alaska's Chosen River and the Florida Keys.

The second decade of angling the Babine involves the uncovering of secrets. The many mysteries of steelheading a particular river can only be uncovered by those that take and make the time. How many casts and how many different runs and pools before this happens varies between anglers, but Bus made his mark like no other.

The third decade is a perfecting of the secrets of the second decade. This third decade can best be described as one of numbers. Eight for 12, nine for 14, 11 for 21, and so on. It wouldn't matter if Bus followed behind other anglers, or it would not matter if Bus were the last one in Corner at day's end. Other anglers' necks would be sore from turning around suddenly to see yet another hook-up in short order.

The fourth decade is a tough one for many an angler and non-angler, especially of the male variety. Here is when we realize our mortality through sore muscles and easily broken bones. We just can't seem to bounce back the same any more. We heard of this in our first three decades, but denial quickly silenced such talk.

As an angler on the Babine, the secrets once hidden and admired by others are now the shared property of other anglers, especially those slow-to-learn guides that have been watching.

The worst example of this is for Bus to find many more sore-mouthed fish than usual. "What have you done to Angus?" he would ask.

And now we have reached the fifth decade, the return of Bus to the Babine after an absence of several years. Rather than pour salt into your year 50 birthday, I must say that the legend of the Babine and of you, Bus, in my mind, can be described using a sad but true parallel.

The Babine is a great river, this you know. You are a great steelheader, this many know. The things that make the river great are its wilderness, the fish, the bears, the great habitat incomparable. Unfortunately, the plans of progress will stress this greatness, this we all know now. As you grow old too, the stresses of this life will challenge you as never before. "Way up," you've said it before, "way up." This is the way to go in the future, despite what happens to the Babine.

To me, the greatness of Bus the angler is the measuring stick that I look up to as a fellow angling guide. You can bring all the former decades of experience, hard work and knowledge to a level and standard that I admire. Whether it was your military training, or the way you were brought up, one thing is for sure. You may be over the hill now, but you are still on top of it, and most likely always will be.

Happy Birthday, Bus.

How 1986 Introduced Bubblemania

Todd Stockner lives with his wife Kathy, and children, Hannah and Simon, on the banks of the Kispiox River, another famous Skeena system destination, where he has his own steelhead guiding and fine-woodworking businesses. He guided extensively on the Babine for the Madsens and then the Cleggs between 1982 and 1994 and Pierce comments: "Todd helped me turn the Norlakes' tradition of gear-angling into a mostly 'fly-fishing only' clientele. It wasn't easy guiding both gear- and fly-anglers in the same week but Todd taught me how it was to be done in the mid-1980s. He had a great work ethic, learned from Ejnar, and he now has his home, a workshop and his beautifully crafted bed and breakfast, Dawn Chorus Guesthouse, beside the river (www.iwoodfish.com). His following pieces speak to his love of the river and its incomparable steelhead.

*I*t's no exaggeration to say that my years on the Babine were some of the best times of my life. I was 19 when I started there in 1982 and 32 when I finished in 1994. Young, foolish, driving jet boats around a wilderness river fishing for steelhead, coming upon grizzly bears, racing down the rapids, big wild steelhead on dry flies. Beers, stories, and parties back at the camp in the evenings, what more could a young man ask for? I could easily fill a book of my own with my personal recollections of those days, as fueled with passion, friends,

Todd Stockner, who now has his own guiding business on the Kispiox, has many stories to tell of the Babine and its fishermen between 1982 and 1994, working for both Ejnar and Pierce.

and had weaned a few of the regular clientele onto this thrilling way of catching steelhead. Dry flies and a wet fly on the dry line, both were becoming a regular part of the techniques we were using. It must be said that I am not implying that we were the first to use dry lines and dry flies on the Babine, or any other river, but it certainly was early days in the acceptance of the idea that these fish would come to the surface for a fly, and there was much to learn.

No matter how long anyone had been fishing dry flies or using floating lines for steelhead though, it is safe to say that no one had dared to dream that fishing using only those surface techniques could be as good as we found that year.

To be honest, I can't quite sort out each and every week as to who was there during what week and who caught what or how many, especially during the early season, but at some point, likely around the middle of September, the river was so loaded with steelhead that even the most seasoned veterans were at times giddy with disbelief and glee over the numbers of fish; laughing and cackling insanely as they hooked, played, and landed yet another steelhead caught on a floating line. My mind is still brimming over with so many amazing angling moments from that season that it is actually very hard to put them all in order, so I won't even try, but I will recount a few of the most memorable ones.

One of those early weeks, perhaps the second, maybe the third week of September, we dubbed 'Bubblemania'. Since then, we simply refer to the entire season by that title, as we had in camp one particularly keen group of anglers, among them Dr. Nick Rajacich, Jeff Reese, Larry Falk and Jim Shively, who were dedicated—at least that year—to fishing the Bubblehead and the surface with floating lines.

Fishing was so outrageously good, that you could drop someone off at the head of Allen's, or anywhere in Allen's, and if I was not quick enough, by the time I had the boat back out in the current and was heading down to Corner, the angler would have hooked the first fish, and while I was dropping someone at Corner, his partner, down

fish, bears, and excitement as they were; but for the purposes of this book I have three stories to tell from those days during the decade of the 'eighties. Perhaps one day I will get to my book; for now this will have to do.

Those who were there will need no further reminder of what an amazing season 1986 was throughout most of the Skeena system. While, at the time, I had no direct experience or information on the other rivers of the Skeena, I know that the Tyee Index was at a near all-time high that year, and so I presume most of the other tributaries enjoyed fishing similar to what we did on the Babine.

It was, to use a worn-out cliché from more recent times, 'A Perfect Storm' of steelhead fishing that year, for a variety of reasons: record run of fish, including the all-important early component of the run; medium to low, but not at all too low, flows, clear water, and very seasonably warm air temperatures throughout September and well into October. Those conditions, combined with what Jim Vincent called, in an article he later wrote in *Fly Fisherman* magazine, '*The Dry Line Revolution*', made for the fishing of many lifetimes that fall. It was truly the stuff of dreams.

On the Babine we had been playing with dry flies for a few seasons already. Vic Rempel and Ron Crewdson brought the Bubblehead fly pattern to the Babine my first season in 1982, providing steady if somewhat slow results, due mainly to turbid water conditions that year.

I had had fairly consistent results fishing the dry fly for several seasons, not really a lot of fish, but plenty enough to keep me interested, at the lower part of Allen's would have hooked another. All of this with dry flies or wet flies fished in the surface.

Most of the season went like this, especially from mid-September to close to the end of October: double headers even triple headers, were commonplace, more than one fish boiling to a fly was also a common sight; as were instances of people raising a fish up to 10, 11 or 12 times before finally showing it a fly that it would take. Everyone had stories from every day about some outrageous fishing moment.

I can recall arriving to check on anglers to see how they were doing and, in most instances, no one wanted to leave where they were because they were catching so many fish, usually with riffle hitched or dry flies. Most of which would all have sounded like complete fabrication any other year, but because virtually everyone was having similar experiences and seeing similar numbers of fish each day, it was all quite believable and it certainly was real. Although I must say that it all seems a little dream-like from the perspective of 24 years later.

Evenings were spent in the cabins madly tying flies and drinking beer, putting up the next day's supplies of Bubbleheads and Kathleen's Charms, a small, dark, 'closer' wet fly that I had come up with, as we were already experiencing those fish that would show to the big dry fly but not take it.

I can vividly remember one scene that perfectly encapsulated the intensity of the time: One of my camp duties was to light the wood stoves each morning in the cabins. I went into the 'Bubblemania' cabin, since that year known as Bubblehead, which was all dark. Just me and my flashlight quietly laying the kindling in the stove. When all of a sudden, from one of the upper bunks, a flashlight clicks on and Larry jerks up from the bed in a near panic...not because of any kind of emergency, but to immediately check his collection of freshly tied Bubbleheads from the evening before, to make sure that they were 'gooped' just right.

He carefully tended to the wide-flared heads, his eyes burning with a crazed look, his surgeon's hands carefully and methodically tweaking the flies; unable to contain his excitement at getting back out into this steelhead Nirvana of which we were all a part, sleep being minor distraction from the reality of catching fish.

That was the year that Bill McAfee came to the camp. He was without doubt one of my personal angling mentors. It was from Bill

Todd and Simon in a proud father and son picture on the Kispiox.

Todd Stockner and his daughter, Hanna. Both she and his son, Simon, are frequent fishing companions.

that I learned several important things: one was how to cast an efficient, long line, with only one false cast. He also taught us how to release fish using his technique of keeping the fish in shallow water, and when it turned on its side, to throw slack into the line, at which point nine times out of 10, the fish would lie still, to be easily handled and released with the least amount of fuss and harm.

He, more than anyone else, taught me about humility and enjoying the experience of just being in 'special' places like the Babine. On days where, as his guide, I knew that he had hooked and landed fish in or near double-digit numbers, when asked what his day was like, unlike others who would roll out the numbers and strut the beach with their accomplishments, Bill would very genuinely just say that he had had a good day, "Got a few fish, saw a bear," and that was that.

But the prize piece of knowledge that Bill taught me that year and one that is directly connected to that memorable floating line season, was how to riffle-hitch flies. That was a real treasure to me and opened up another door in my dry-line repertoire, one that I found to be so effective, let alone enjoyable, that I spent much of the rest of that season fishing that way and encouraging others to try it.

I spent a good part of the rest of 1986 fishing, or having guests fish, either a riffle-hitched fly or a wet fly on the dry line, often fished in true 'grease line' style: dead drifted across the current, mending it as long as possible to avoid drag. I read the re-issue of Jock Scott's classic *Greased Line Fishing for Salmon (and Steelhead)*. It was like being in 'dry-line steelhead school' I would read a chapter in the evening with interesting bits of knowledge such as, '...if the fish shows to the fly, he is telling you the fly is too big...," and sure enough, with all of the 'boils' we were getting to our big, dry flies, but no hook-ups, we would come back with the small, dark wet fly and right away would get a solid take and hook-up.

It is hard to put into words the thrill of the fishing that season. The stories are simply too many to count, but everyone had them: multiple hook-ups on dead-drifted dry flies, 'a fish behind every rock', ...it goes on and on. All I can say is that I hope that people were having similar experiences on the other rivers of the Skeena, as it just wouldn't have been fair if we were getting it all on the Babine...but on the other hand it wouldn't have surprised me either.

Building the Satellite Cabin at Beaver Flats

This artist's impression of the Satellite Cabin on Beaver Flats, on display in the cabin,
depicts the scene before the dense thicket of trees grew back to hide it from view.

During the season of 1986, I had begun to really push my explorations down the river. In 1983 I had heard from Ejnar, and some of the older, long-time clients, all about the old satellite cabin down in Beaver Flats, about 12 miles below the camp. Being an explorer at heart, this naturally roused my passions for seeing what lies around the next corner. Finding time to boat further and further down the river was not always easy, as we had our 'beats' up and down the better-traveled sections of river around the camps that occupied our time.

But once or twice a week I would take some fishermen down to pools and runs that I had not seen before, each time going around the next corner to prospect fresh water. While this was all very exciting and fun for me, I still had not seen, to the best of my knowledge, the fabled Beaver Flats and the satellite cabins of either Bob Wickwire, or Ejnar.

So, it was with a great sense of excitement and adventure that Pierce, Bus Bergmann and I loaded up my boat with supplies for a possible overnight excursion in late October—it may have even been early November—and headed down the river for 'the promised land'. We fished a little along the way at some of the pools I had already put on my map: Rempel, Boat Wreck, Canyon, Chicken, Sandy Pool. Then a few bends below Sandy we eventually came to where the valley opens up a little more. Bus thought that this was it, Beaver Flats, and he was right. It did not take us long to find the remains of the old Wickwire cabin. Bob had burned it down once his lease had expired and he no longer used it.

Then we went down below the dramatic ledge that spans the entire river below the Beaver Flats run, the one narrow slot up against the bank on river left being the only passage through.

I had heard stories from the older clients about Ejnar running this little slot down to his cabin; about striking a rock as he dropped down the ledge and putting a hole in the side, water coming in. But, as the story was told to me, in the midst of navigating the treacherous rock garden directly below the ledge, the stoic Dane, without batting an eye, took off his glove, jammed it in the hole and just kept the boat on course and afloat.

Just around the corner we found what we thought must have been Ejnar's old camp pool and sure enough, just inside the trees were the remnants of his old cabin, collapsed, crushed by snow, but still there all the same. Coffee pots and a few other rusted trinkets marking the spot, along with the rotting pile of roof and lumber. It was a powerful moment for us: me, having known Ejnar from my first year on the Babine and Bus, who went back before me on the Babine, having worked for Ejnar in the 1970s, and Pierce now carving his own path on this river of destiny.

It might have been right there at Ejnar's old cabin, or maybe it was back up at Beaver Flats, looking over the Wickwire site, that Pierce and I decided to re-establish a presence back at this remote and beautiful part of the river. We decided that Bob Wickwire had had a nicer site, more open and exposed than Ejnar's, which had been tucked into a dark heavily treed clearing in the woods off the river.

So, in the off season that winter, Pierce obtained the lease on the former Wickwire site, and we laid plans to construct a new cabin during August of 1987. He hired Phil Anderson, a carpenter from Smithers, to design and pre-fabricate as much of the building as possible in his workshop, so that when it came to the actual construction there would be minimal cutting and fitting to be done down at Beaver Flats.

I arrived in Smithers that summer in early August and went to work with Phil in his workshop for a couple of days before the three of us loaded up all of the supplies and went out to the river. We got all of the studs cut to length, picked up the trusses from the manufacturing company, got door and window casings measured and cut to length... essentially all of the cabin pre-cut and ready to assemble on the gravel bench overlooking Beaver Flats. I don't remember the date, but it would have been around the end of the first week of August that we headed out in a convoy, hauling everything we needed for a couple of weeks of construction and living at the Steelhead Camp.

The plan was to spend evenings and nights at the main camp and boat down every day to Beaver Flats. This was a great way for Pierce and I to get to know the water better as there are several rapids and boulder gardens along the way that, as the water drops, certainly require a deft hand and knowledge of exactly how to run them.

The first day we got down to Beaver Flats with the first two boat loads and Phil, who then stayed there to prepare the site, while Pierce and I ran back up to the weir for another boat load each. I can't remember how long it took us to run all of the supplies and material down to the cabin site, but it seems to me that we spent at least two days, maybe three, running back and forth, making the 16-mile trip about three times a day to get everything down to Beaver Flats. Meanwhile Phil got going on the cinder-block footings and the floor platform that would form the foundation of the one-room cabin we were to build there.

These were fun times. Pierce and I roaring around the river in the wooden riverboats that Ejnar had built in the early years, using the old 40-hp Johnson motors. We would race hard all the way back to the weir, dodging rocks, climbing rapids, and wringing every bit of power we could out of those old motors to get the edge on each other. Then we had to pick our way back down the river with our heavy, overloaded boats, pointing out bears and wildlife to each other, and refining routes through the rapids and tricky sections. It was exhilarating to say the least.

Once we got all the supplies down the river, I got to work with Phil in the construction of the cabin. As I recall, Pierce had some business in town for a few days, as I think Phil and I were out there on our own for some time, but Pierce came and went, bringing us

A living reminder of the Wickwire family's extensive links to the Babine—in 1979 a young Jud Wickwire carved his name on a balsam tree that still stands not far from Satellite Cabin.

Todd Stockner's semi-vaulted ceiling is a striking feature of the Satellite Cabin.

supplies, food and beer, as needed. We based out of the Steelhead Camp and traveled the river every day to work on the cabin.

I can't quite recall how long it took to build, but I believe that it was around two weeks that Phil was there, essentially until the roof was on and the paneling was up in the interior. So it would have been just before the season started that I was working on it alone to get it finished for use that fall. I still had to do some of the finishing work on the interior: the ceiling had to go in and be insulated, bunk-beds to build, outhouse dug and built, window trims, benches, table; all those little details that as anyone who has ever built anything as humble as a shack will know seemingly takes forever.

The ceiling is something I particularly enjoyed working on, using the tongue-and-groove knotty pine that Pierce and I brought down from the weir, by using the diagonal braces of the truss structure, I created a semi-vaulted ceiling which has proved to be quite popular with those who stay there. It certainly makes lying in the top bunk much nicer, as the ceiling is not right there over one's head as it would be if it were flat.

The rest, as they say, is history. We began right away, the first week of September I believe, running trips down to the cabin twice a week, staying one night. We would fish our way down, spend the night, drop down below the cabin the next morning to fish around Ejnar's old cabin site, eventually naming the run directly below his cabin, Ejnar's Last Stand. Then we would work our way back up to Steelhead Camp to arrive by dinner. All through that first year and subsequent years we refined things as we went along, making a few changes as needed.

It's hard to say enough about how exciting these trips were, down into a part of the river that received little, if any, other angling pressure. There was a sense of adventure about every trip that was always present. Even though at times the fishing was not always great, sometimes it was just plain slow and one might have been better off from a fishing point of view, to stay on the upper part of the river. In one infamous moment, I did make the call to cancel a trip to Satellite Cabin during an extremely slow period in the satellite water when the fishing was very good on the upper part of the river. There is no doubt that every trip to the cabin was, and always will be, something special, often producing some truly magical angling moments.

—*T.S.*

The Great Naval Snowball Battle

It all began as a minor skirmish: a lot of testosterone, easily obtainable projectiles, and jet boats. Is not the history of all of the great wars and battles rooted in such ignoble, masculine beginnings?

When the snow flies on the Babine, the anglers and the guides, like the ravens, come out to play...

This is the story of two boats, two guides and their fishermen, and how one of the greatest naval battles of all times was fought, not on the high seas, but on the magical Babine River in north central British Columbia.

I was one of the guides and Darcy Edwards was the other. Let it be said that Darcy has more than once told the story of how he was once 'scouted' by the Major Leagues for his formidable pitching arm. I am here to tell you that no matter what the exact facts are about that story, no one, and I mean no one who has been on the receiving end of one of Darcy's snowballs, doubts the veracity of his words. And so it began,

quite innocently, albeit stingingly, on the shore of the river in front of camp one snowing morning as we were preparing to head down the river for a day of fishing.

In my boat I had Bus Bergmann, a friend of his from Puerto Rico who had never before seen snow. I think his name was something like Kiko. . . and two others I can't now remember. So, our Puerto Rican friend thinks it would be really fun to start throwing snowballs at Darcy and his four fishermen, Bob 'Super Bowl' Nelson, Brad Moen, and Harry and Stuart Richter. After all, the closest thing to throwing snowballs in Puerto Rico is throwing rocks and they really hurt, so why not throw snowballs when you can?

Naturally, as in any good skirmish, things got perilously close to getting out of hand right then and there and, after a good and earnest exchange of cold-packed projectiles and with a few hard Darcy laser-beam snowballs on our backs, I gunned the motor and headed down the river, already plotting the next retaliation.

The day went on like this, as we each kept leap-frogging the other from time to time as we fished the runs. Every time we passed there was a frantic exchange of snowballs from shore to boat to shore, sometimes the passing boat would even pull over to the far bank and make more snowballs and we would lob them across the river, back and forth. What was noticeable was that each time we passed each other as time went on, the boats were loaded down with more and more snowballs, and the intensity of each battle was ramping up inch by inch; each attack getting more and more impassioned, to say nothing about brazen.

In the mid-afternoon, after we had given them a particularly thorough pasting as we fished Callahan's, we got the distinct sense that the next time we saw them we were going to be in for The Mother of All Battles; something about their beaten looks, the gesticulating, and vengeful language told us so. Eventually we ended up in Lower Trail in the late afternoon, knowing that this is where we would make our stand. With Bus fishing right in the deke of Trail, Kiko decided that he had had enough of steelhead and he was going to make snowballs. He started in and I helped.

We must have made a couple of hundred before I got up to go. It seems to me that I must have gone off to get the other two, who were in the boat with us that day, who might have been in Dead Man's. That part of the story is a little hazy. Once back in Lower Trail, while Bus finished fishing, we made more snowballs.

The boat was now filling up with them, all stacked in the bow, along the sides, on the seats, completely covering the backbench right behind me. There surely must have been upwards of 300 of them...who really knows? All we knew was that this was going to be one hell of a battle.

We waited, making ever more snowballs while we were parked on the side of the river. Eventually, you could hear the drone of the outboard: they were coming. Bus reeled in as the sound of the motor came closer; they had to be down in Deep Rocks. The lumbering boat, heavy no doubt with snowballs as was ours, sure enough came around the corner and began to ascend the fast water below Trail. As soon as they saw us, like drunken gladiators they were all butch and bravado, arms thrusting, holding snowballs in their hands; even from a distance—300 yards—you could see the snowballs stacked in their boat.

I gave my orders: all hands on deck, everyone on board. I pushed off from shore and fired up the motor, moving swiftly and smoothly out into the wide, deep, even flow that is Lower Trail; such a nice wide, slow run, no worries about rocks and obstacles: the perfect place for what was about to happen.

Here they came, all testosterone and no brains; waving their arms in the air, yelling God knows what. I moved the boat up to the head of the run and waited...they were now just in the bottom of the run and closing. With one more pause to let them

get almost to the middle of the run, I revved up the 55-horse Johnson to full power and turned the boat to bear down on them. This was it, the battle had begun: a full-tilt, navel broadside fusillade right there in middle of the Babine wilderness.

We came upon each other, Darcy running full tilt, me running wide open, playing 'chicken' to see how close we would get, veering off at the last minute to put us only a few yards apart. Then we slowed slightly, as we were directly broadside, and there was a blinding exchange as every man in each boat threw snowballs as fast as is humanly possible. If we had had snowball Gatling guns we could scarcely have moved more snow at one time, but we surely would have used them.

We passed, now I was at the bottom of the run and Darcy at the top, but that was just the first pass. We both banked hard and came roaring back for more. Engines howling, the waves crashing on the shore, the two boats closed again for another broadside shelling of snowballs. It was a kind of havoc and mayhem that was at once deadly serious and on the other hand so outrageously funny that none of us could contain ourselves from nearly losing control from laughing so hard. Another intense exchange of snowballs at point-blank range as the boats exchanged positions in the run. Supplies were down but still enough for another round...

Amidst yelling, hysterical laughing, and hard-packed snowballs, we prepared for yet another pass. By this time the wakes the two boats were throwing were rebounding off the shore. The chaotic waves that resulted actually made navigation standing in the back of the boat holding the tiller and controlling the boat, quite hazardous. No matter, the battle was on and nothing was going to stop us now until we were out of snowballs. I banked the boat again, not slowing at all, keeping the engine on full as the boat turned sharply. The turbulence on the water added to the mayhem, splashing over gunwales with outboard jet spray shooting out, me, weak-kneed from laughing so hard...

Here we came again, the closest pass yet. You could almost reach out and touch the other boat, again with so many snowballs incoming and outgoing that it is a wonder we could even see our targets. Every once in a while one of Darcy's throws would hit home and someone would wince. At one point

Winter fishing for steelhead is not for the faint hearted and it will take more than a Babine snowstorm to deter this fisherman.

during that third and final barrage, Bus yells out, 'It's just like the *Monitor* and the *Merrimack*!'

And so it was.

Finally Darcy and his merry gang had exhausted their ammunition and started to make a dash for camp. But alas, I had the faster boat, and we still had about 50 snowballs left. As he was beginning the ascent of the rapids right at the top end of Upper Trail, we caught up and I ran the boat right in close to the stern and we emptied the last of our snowball stores upon those hapless souls as they lay on the bottom of the boat using the plastic milk crates for shelter from our merciless pelting. Finally we too were out, and I pulled away and ran to camp.

So ended what has to be the greatest naval snowball battle that has ever been. I have often wondered what that scene would have looked like to some lost soul staggering out of the wilderness to the edge of the river, drawn by the sound of civilization, only to come upon a surreal scene, one owing more to mythology than reality.

So be it. Let history remember, the Great Naval Snowball Battle of the Babine. And it's good for all to remember that some of the most memorable moments on the Babine were not all about fish.

—*T.S.*

On the River with Bill Fife

Erik Madsen, from San Diego, CA, is the second of Joy and Ejnar Madsen's three children. He was 21 when his dad died in 1983. For the next three years Joy, together with Karl, Erik and their sister Karen, kept Trout Lodge and Steelhead Camp running until the business was sold to the Cleggs in 1986. This is his quite charming, often poignant, recollection of one of the Trout Lodge's regular guests, a gentleman who came back year after year after year, until he was too old and too frail to make the long trip from California.

Trout fishing on Rainbow Alley was an annual and essential feature of Bill Fife's life for many, many years until the frailties of old age finally prevented him from traveling from California.

Bill Fife always wore a suit when he traveled. By the time I knew him he was older and smaller and his suits didn't fit him very well any more, but he still looked good in them. I remember him standing on the dock in his tweed suit with his canvas duffle bags while the float plane idled in to pick him up. I always knew I would see him again the next summer, but still I hated to see him leave.

My family had a fly-fishing lodge on the Babine River in Canada and Bill was one of our guests. Each summer he came up to our lodge for two weeks to fish for trout and I was his guide. After he left there were always other fishermen to guide, great people who came year after year just like Bill, people I'd known as long as I could remember. But still, I hated to see him leave. The lodge was a big part of my life while I was growing up and now, when I want to remember what it was like, I always think of the days on the river with Bill. They were some of the best days.

Bill was an accomplished fly-fisherman, but he needed a guide every day because he didn't see well. He had what he called peripheral vision, which meant he couldn't see anything directly in front of him, only off to the sides. He didn't hear well either. He could carry on a conversation with one person all right, but in the din of a crowd he was lost.

He preferred being out on the river. He fished alone, so it was always just the two of us in the boat. The days could be long if you were guiding someone with whom you were uncomfort-able, but I was always comfortable with Bill. Sometimes hours would go by without him saying more than a sentence or two, and sometimes he would talk for hours. I always liked to listen to him, but when he was quiet I didn't mind because I liked being on the river too.

He was born in San Francisco and survived the great earthquake and fire. He had served in the First World War and been a Rhodes Scholar candidate. He had been a highly respected geological engineer, and traveled the world with his work. After he retired he kept traveling, but then he only went to places where he could fly-fish.

As he got older and his vision failed it was hard for him to keep fishing. He liked the Babine because it was a big river and you fished it from a boat instead of wading like you had to in most places. We used big, flat-bottomed boats that were stable and easy to move around in so, as he got older and couldn't fish anywhere else, he could still get out on the river and fish all day long on the Babine. That's why he kept coming back.

I don't remember the first time I met Bill because I was too young, but I remember the first summer I was old enough to guide him on the river. I didn't know much about the fishing then but my father said it didn't matter because Bill knew it all. He'd been coming to our lodge for years. I just had to run the boat and raise and lower the anchor and Bill would tell me what to do. You'll learn a lot from him, he told me.

Bill and I had good weather that first year, sunny and warm every day. The fishing was good and it was exciting to get away from the chores at the lodge and be out on the river. When I got older I would be on the river guiding fishermen every day all summer long, but that was later.

One morning the trout were rising all around us but none of them were taking his fly. The fish could obviously see his line, he said. He needed a finer leader. He started to reel in, and he asked me if I knew how to tie the barrel knot. I told him I didn't. He said this was a knot I should know if I was going to be a fly-fishing guide, so he would teach it to me.

He cut the fly from the leader, and from a spool in his gear bag, he pulled off a two-foot length of finer monofilament to add to the end of it. He told me to watch closely, and he started to splice them together. It was a hard knot to tie, he said. Some people never learned it. I did not do well with knots, but I watched intently.

Right away he ran into problems. With his peripheral vision he had to hold the lines way off to the side, and his hands were shaky. He said you needed to wrap each piece of line around the other eight times, but one piece would always fall to the floor of the boat before he could finish. And when he tried to feed the end of one piece of line through the gap in the middle, he would miss by four or five inches. One time he thought it was done and he slowly pulled on the two pieces of line waiting for the splice to take hold, but everything unraveled. He kept trying, and I kept watching.

Finally he gave up. He apologized for wasting our time and he handed me the old leader so I could tie the fly back on.

"Never get old, Erik, never get old," he said quietly as he turned to watch the fish rising off the bow. He used to say that to me often, but when you are young you never think you are going to get old.

While he was watching the river I scanned the floor of the boat until I found the two-foot piece of line he had discarded, and I held it up to the old leader and started to wrap. I counted eight times and then, holding the ends in my teeth, I wrapped the other piece the opposite way eight times and fed it through the middle. I pulled the two lines and watched the little barrel form as the splice took hold. I trimmed it close so you could barely see the knot, and then I tied the fly on to the new, finer line.

He turned around. "All set?"

"All set," I said.

The other guests always liked Bill, and he fit easily into the community of fishermen at the lodge. One morning on the river he told me how one of our guests from Seattle had been talking too loud at the dinner table the night before, and telling stories that were inappropriate for the women present. Bill was quiet and dignified, and this obviously bothered him. He was agitated and he whipped his line in the water uncharacteristically as he told me about it. I could tell he had been stewing over it all morning.

I had forgotten about it until later in the day, as we motored through the upper river and I slowed to pass a group of our fishermen in boats a hundred yards away. Bill squinted and turned his head at an odd angle the way he did when he needed to see something with his peripheral vision, and then he leaned forward and said something to me. He spoke softly and his voice was drowned out by the outboard motor, so I slowed down more and leaned forward for him to repeat it. This time he cupped his hands and shouted loud enough to be clearly heard over the motor.

"Is that the horse's ass from Seattle?"

I sat upright and looked at the other boats. Everyone had stopped casting and was turned toward us. I looked back at Bill. He was gesturing toward the boat closest to us and drawing in his breath like he was going to shout it louder still. I held up my hand to stop him and looked away, trying to think of what to say. It seemed like everyone was waiting for me. Then I knew. I turned back toward Bill and drew in my breath deeply and cupped my hands around my mouth to project my voice the way he had.

"No, that's not him," I lied.

The days on the river were usually peaceful and serene, but the days the wind blew were different. An icy west wind sometimes blasted down from the mountains in the afternoons and made the fishing hard. Bill particularly struggled in the wind because it blew the boat at odd angles in the current and disoriented him. It interfered with his casting too.

He had a methodical system for covering the water. When I moved the boat to a new piece of water and dropped the anchor he would start fishing a very short line. Catch the fish close to the boat first, he said. Then he would gradually lengthen his casts and cover a little more water each time. Once he couldn't cast any farther I would raise the anchor and let the current drop us down, and he would start again.

It was on those last few casts that I had to be careful when the wind was blowing. That was the only time our 20-foot boats seemed small. Many times I had to duck as the wind whipped his fly unpredictably over the stern of the boat where I sat. With his peripheral vision he couldn't see his line threatening my face, but he could see my reaction to it and he would look at me oddly. Usually I would bend over as if I had dropped something, or sometimes I would duck and swat at an imaginary mosquito, but he must have known there were no mosquitoes when the wind blew like that.

It was especially daunting when he was fishing a Stonefly pattern, because they are big flies with big hooks. That's what Bill was fishing the day his line whipped across the transom with a terrifying crack and landed violently in a heap at my feet. I helped him get it all sorted out and I realized what made the noise was his fly had impaled the gunnel of the boat near my elbow, and the hook had broken off at the shank. He reeled in the extra line while I looked at the fly. Other than the hook being sheared off, it looked perfect.

"Is the fly OK?" he asked.

I looked at the now-harmless fly in my hand and considered my options. There were two or three hours of fishing left in the day, and I knew the wind wasn't going to die down. The fishing hadn't been good. I looked down at the spot where the hook had buried itself half an inch into the maple gunnel of the boat. Then I looked over at Bill, sitting up on the bow the way he always did, waiting patiently for my answer.

While the fishing today may not always reach the heights enjoyed in Bill Fife's day, Rainbow Alley remains a 'must try' setting for any Babine trout fisherman.

"Is the fly OK?" he asked again.

"No, Bill," I said finally. "I'm going to have to replace it."

The river always changed as the season progressed. In the spring it ran high and fast with the snow melt from the surrounding mountains, but as the weeks passed and the fishermen came and went the water dropped and by the end of the summer the river could get quite shallow. In the high-water years it wasn't a problem, but some years you really had to pick your way through so the motor wouldn't hit the rocks on the bottom. I knew where all the rocks and gravel bars were, but it was a big river and sometimes it was hard to know your exact position.

My father hated us to hit the bottom because it was hard on the propellers, but I didn't like it because it was embarrassing. The engine would lurch and the guests would sit up and look concerned and ask if everything was all right, and you would have to say it was OK and then try really hard not to hit again because you knew they were watching.

One year the water started low in the spring and there wasn't much rain that summer so it just got worse and worse. You could slow the motor to an idle going downstream through the tough spots, but going back up against the current you needed a certain amount of power, especially in the lower river, and that year it was almost impossible to get through without hitting at least once. I got tired of having to navigate it every day.

Bill usually came up in early July, but for some reason he had booked for later that year and by the time he arrived the river was way down. But with his poor hearing he couldn't tell if I hit a rock, so getting up the river was a lot less stressful with him. Just about every time we came up the river that year I hit a rock or two, sometimes pretty hard, but he couldn't hear it. At least I assumed he couldn't hear it, because he never once said anything or looked at me the way the other guests did when I hit the rocks.

The only days when it wasn't much fun being on the river was when it rained. I didn't mind the light summer showers, when the sun came out and dried everything afterwards. But sometimes the rain settled in for days, a cold relentless rain that bore into your face and seeped through your raincoat and ran down your neck. Those were the days I dreaded.

Bill liked them. He thought the rain improved the fishing and that made all the suffering worthwhile. But it seemed to me that it made no difference to the fish if it was raining up where we were or not. Their life went on either way. So did mine.

On one memorable rainy and windy day Bill and I had made our way to the farthest reaches of the lower river, just above the weir, looking for fish that might be feeding. There were none. It was almost the end of the day and the rain had never let up. The current is strong in that part of the river, and the rushing water and the drone of the rain created a monotonous roar. I vaguely heard Bill start to reel in his line and say, "I have to take a leak."

Bill never went ashore to go to the bathroom. Getting in and out of the boat in unfamiliar places was hard with his peripheral vision, and he was too serious a fisherman to lose that much

time from his day anyway. Instead he kept a coffee can stashed under the bow, and soon I could hear it clattering around over the roar of the water.

After what seemed like a long time I heard more stirring in the bow behind me, and then a strange "Uh, oh," from Bill. I had just discovered a way to stand with the wind at my back and my head held at a perfect angle so that the rain ran from my hat down over the shoulders of my raincoat instead of down my neck, so I pretended not to hear.

"It's empty," he shouted over the drumming rain. I had no idea what we were talking about, but I wasn't ready to move yet.

"It's empty," he shouted again.

"What's empty?" I hollered back.

"The coffee can is empty." I still didn't understand. It seemed like the rain was piling up now. I waited.

"I must have pissed in the boat," he bellowed.

Now I understood. After he had finished and picked up the coffee can to dump it overboard, it was empty. He had missed.

I finally turned to look at him. The rain was definitely getting worse. He was kneeling in the bow, still holding the empty coffee can at the gunnel. He looked at me and then he looked down at the coffee can. It was the only dry thing in the boat.

"Oh hell, let's just go home," he said. I don't think he landed a single fish that day.

I could never tell when it was going to rain. My father could look up at the sky over the lake in the evening and tell you what the next day was going to be like, but I never knew how he did it and after he died there was no one else who could. I figured out the fishing well enough, but I never figured out the rain.

One evening, while I was talking with Bill after dinner, outside the dining room overlooking the lake, he looked up at the sky like he had seen my father do so many times and he squinted a bit with his peripheral vision and he looked down the lake to the south and said: "I think it's going to rain tomorrow."

He said the rain always came from the south. I looked down the lake to the south but I didn't understand what he saw.

"Yep, it's going to rain," he said. "We'd better get an early start tomorrow."

It wasn't raining when we set out. In fact, there was something in the air that seemed promising that morning. The past few days had been cold and windy, but as we sped down the lake toward the river I could see that the clouds over the mountains to the west that brought the cold wind were gone, and to the south there were only a few fluffy white clouds far down the lake.

With our early start we were the first ones down the river, and we got into some fish right away. The mayflies were hatching and that brought out the fish. The day warmed up quickly. I took off my shirt and soaked up the morning sun as I moved him around the river in the boat.

I had a feeling that on this first warm day in a while there would be stoneflies hatching in the lower river. The fishing was tiring for Bill down there in the strong current, and it was a long

Wayne and Harriet Coe, Trout Lodge guests of the Madsens for many years, fish Babine Lake with Cecil Brown. Fort Babine is in the background.

boat ride, but if the stoneflies were hatching then the big fish would be there. Like all good fly-fishermen, Bill would rather catch a few big fish than a lot of small ones. It was a risk though, to leave a good mayfly hatch for what would be a big waste of time if I was wrong. And if the weather turned there would be no stonefly hatch, and a long ride back in the rain.

But there was a hatch. The stoneflies were just beginning to flutter around as we ate our lunch in the lower river, and the big fish were starting to feed on them. And because the fishing in the upper river was good everyone else stayed up there, so we had the lower river to ourselves.

I was able to move Bill around to all the places I knew the fish would be as the sun and the hatch moved down the river. I never kept track of how many fish he caught because we always released them, but he caught more big fish that afternoon than I had ever seen him catch in one day. By late afternoon he was exhausted and sunburned and, as I pulled up the anchor for the last time, he said, "that was a good day."

He slept in the boat all the way back. When we reached the dock he thanked me the way he always did, and I carried his gear back to his cabin for him the way I always did. He would get dressed for dinner with the other guests, and they would ask him how his day was and he would say he had a good day, thank you. After my dinner I would be outside again and I would probably talk with him for a little while, but I wouldn't mention the rain. That's not the way I was with Bill.

As I got older and started college Bill was always interested in the courses I was taking and the grades I was getting. He was excited when I told him that I had done well in my first calculus course. Right away he started telling me about a problem from one of his calculus classes that had stumped him for a long time as an engineering undergrad. He outlined the problem for me, and then cast his line out and focused on his fishing for a while so I could consider it. Then he began to explain how to solve it.

I imagined my calculus professor writing the equations on the blackboard while Bill laid it all out in front of me on the river as he fished. It was a beautiful calm, sunny morning without a cloud in the sky. You could see each ridge and snowcap on the Bate Range way to the north, and you could see every rock and pebble down on bottom of the river below us. On days like that on the river with Bill there was nowhere I would rather be, and I liked to think he felt the same. I don't think he could tell that I didn't understand his calculus problem at all.

He wanted me to take Greek too. He had studied it when he was a candidate for the Rhodes Scholarship, and one day while he was fishing he started reciting Homer's Odyssey in the original Greek. He went on for 10 minutes or more without stumbling or pausing to remember a line, timing his casts with the meter of the poem. He fished masterfully while he recited, casting 45 degrees downstream, mending his line into the current, keeping just enough tension in the line to make the fly look life-like without creating a drag in the water.

Bill couldn't see well enough to fish dry flies like our other guests, so he always fished nymphs. Fishing a nymph is much harder than fishing a dry fly because when a fish takes a dry fly it rises to the surface and you can see it so you know when to set the hook. But a nymph is fished just under the surface so you have to feel the fish take it, and they take a nymph very softly. I learned how to do it from watching Bill. As much as I respected him, though, I never studied Greek. It just seemed so esoteric then.

He didn't get the Rhodes Scholarship. He said it was because he was Catholic and the other guy was a Presbyterian. He told me it worked out for the best though because if he had won it he would have become an attorney and he would rather be a geological engineer than an attorney any day. He didn't like attorneys, and I think he held a small grudge against Presbyterians too. He never forgot anything.

Bill lived to be almost 100, and I was able to visit him several times at his home in Palo Alto, CA in the later years. He lived by himself, but he was in a special complex that had staff on hand to help him when he needed it. He had moved in 30 years earlier when his wife needed care, and after she died he just stayed. That was when he started traveling and fishing all the time.

He had two apartments that were joined together so he had plenty of room, and a cleaning service kept the place spotless for him. Each morning there was a special copy of *USA Today*, and he showed me how he could blow it up onto a screen on the wall with an overhead projector. He had a beautiful old Cadillac that he kept downstairs, but he said they wouldn't let him drive it any more.

By this time neither of us was fly-fishing any more. He could no longer keep making the trip to Canada each year, and I had finished college and was starting my own career. We were both finished on the Babine. I guess in a way we'd both grown too old.

For about 12 summers Bill and I had been together on the river, but we didn't talk about it much when we were in Palo Alto. He showed me photos and magazine articles from his life, and he wanted to hear about what I was doing with mine. I walked with him to the post office a couple of times, but he'd never had children and none of his friends were alive any more, so there were never any letters.

Over the years there had been many days on the river, when the fishing was lousy and the weather was terrible, when I used to wonder why Bill didn't just go back to the lodge and sit by the fire with a hot cup of tea. It seemed to me that anything would have been better than suffering through those cold and rainy days when the fish weren't feeding anyway.

After I started visiting him in Palo Alto I began to understand. Maybe Bill never really believed that the rain improved the fishing. Maybe he was just saying that. The river had been a big part of my life, but it had been a big part of his life too. He must have known all along that the day would come when he would no longer be able to fish the Babine. Maybe that's why he always put on his suit when he traveled up there.

We were sitting in his living room in Palo Alto one sunny day and I thought how hard it must be for him, squinting up at the *USA Today* on the wall or making his way home from the post office, knowing that the river was still there but he couldn't fish it any more. That's why I kept going back.

PART VI

Featuring the Babine

Brian Huntington, associate director of the Skeena Watershed Conservation Coalition, took this spectacular shot of the view looking east down the Skeena headwaters valley, about 150 miles upstream from its confluence with the Babine. This is the critical Sacred Headwaters area, the pristine source of the entire Skeena family of rivers and their precious wild salmon and steelhead.

Finally a series featuring the Babine, its people, its fish and the challenges they all face together in the years ahead. Two of these pieces have previously appeared in fishing magazines; the others are published here for the first time.

Steelhead Paradise Under Siege: Steelhead Hell Looms

*By Todd Stockner, Kispiox, B.C., whose background
is to be found with 'How 1986 Introduced Bubblemania' on page 136*

You know it. You have either lived it or you dream it: hours of long casts, heavy lines, big flies into big beautiful waters for big fish, mending and more mending... and casting, again... the hoping, the mind games... then, the pull.

You live for the pull and you know it's all about the pull, the surge, line running, peeling off your reel, a crashing of waters on the surface, red stripe glimpsed through a spray of water, fly line slicing, making a cutting sound as is sizzles through the pool, catching up to the huge buck now jumping way upstream from the direction in which your line seems to be heading... your own little fishy world of mayhem. We love the mayhem, don't we? Paradise is steelhead mayhem. And this is paradise?

The Skeena River and all of her children: The Babine, Kispiox, Bulkley, Sustut and many others that John Fennelly wrote about all those years ago—*Steelhead Paradise*... Because you believe, and because like any pilgrim you either make the journey, or you will, you just know it will be there for you again, be there forever; the fish will always come because they always have. And like your beautiful and strong yet fragile quarry, the steelhead, you will arrive at these rivers of the Skeena ready for whatever challenges will come your way. Ready for the thrill of being here fishing for the fish that we all worship, the amazing wild Skeena steelhead.

Time to re-think Steelhead Paradise.

Like an alarm clock clanging in your head, a rude awakening... me, pouring cold water on your sweet steelhead dreams. I am here writing this to you, my fellow Skeena steelheader, to very deliberately burst your bubble of reverie regarding the magnificent steelhead of the Skeena. If you haven't heard, if you have been sleeping, living under a rock, or just ignoring the issues, thinking it is someone else's problem or that someone else will take care of it or, even worse, that the government of British Columbia will take care of things.

It is time to give your head a shake, time to shed that stale skin of apathy, and join the fight. Because if you don't, you will be telling your kids and grandkids, or your best fishing buddy's kids and grand-kids, about all the good times that you used to have on the old Skeena, or the Kispiox, or the Babine... because it will all be a thing of the past.

In no other place in the world, and at no other time in history, has the plight of wild Pacific salmon and steelhead been more in the balance than now in the great Skeena watershed and all of its many tributaries. The last bastion of great runs of large wild steelhead is now under siege.

Much has already been written about the issues at the mouth of the Skeena: namely fish farming, which thankfully has been more or less beaten back, and the commercial netting, another huge issue, widely written about and needing a chapter all its own. I want to shine the light on the upland issues, so here is a quick, abbreviated run-down of the threats that the Skeena River faces in the coming years, none of these more than five to eight years away:

-- Coalbed methane (CBM) field in the headwaters of the Skeena, Nass, and Stikine watersheds. Royal Dutch Shell has plans for a massive coalbed methane field for an area known on maps as The Klappan, but one that we call 'The Sacred Headwaters.' It is the wilderness, upland plateau where the Skeena, Nass and Stikine all rise.

-- Open-pit coal mines in the upper Skeena/Stikine. Two huge developments right on the banks, and in fact possibly crossing the upper Skeena and one just over the hill, Mt. Klappan to be exact, which will be leveled to get at the coal underneath it, on the Stikine side. Currently, with the global economic crises, these are a distant threat, but that could change very quickly in relation to the global demand for coal.

--The most pressing project on the horizon now is the proposed Enbridge Northern Gateway pipeline that is to link the Alberta tar sands project with a port on the west coast (Kitimat). This project is being vigorously opposed by an "unprecedented" alliance of more than 150 First Nations, envoronmentalists, unions, businesses and Olympic athletes according to the Vancouver Province.

--A huge industrial road all the way up the Skeena, from the Kispiox road, known as the 'SORR', the Stewart Omenica Resource Road: a 'build it and they will come' scheme to encourage as much rampant industrial development in the upper Skeena as possible. This road would open up the last vestiges of the great wilderness of the Skeena to the kind of nightmare industrial developments that would very quickly turn Steelhead Paradise into Steelhead Hell.

--Commercial netting at the mouth of the Skeena. Most of you will know about this, and while it is a very serious issue in itself, I don't want to spend much print on this here as so much has been written about it in the past few years and many others are working on this one now. But all the same it must be mentioned in the context of threats.

Just take a minute to think about all of that. This is all being proposed now for the very near future, not some distant Orwellian scenario and time. The B.C. Government—which is madly promoting all of this in a 'development at any cost' frenzy—and industry, is working at this right now. People in suits, in offices in far-away cities who have never set foot on these or any other rivers, never held a fly rod in their hands, never waded into rivers, never seen or even heard of a steelhead, are working now—likely at this very moment—looking at numbers on a map of the Upper Skeena, planning to make this all a reality, *their* version of reality. The Sacred Headwaters, the life source of the Skeena River, is just a number on a map, another gas 'play' for Shell.

I am a director of the Skeena Watershed Conservation Coalition (SWCC). For more than three years now we have been fighting this battle by raising awareness about the issues that I have listed. At the moment Shell's CBM play in The Sacred Headwaters is under a two-year 'moratorium' on any further development. Be sure though this is no voluntary effort on Shell's part, and they have given word that they want in and will get what they want in time. They have assured some key organizers (with our group) that 'they are patient'. And we can be certain that they don't give a rat's ass about steelhead and salmon. This battle, while undergoing a much-needed reprieve, is far from over. The spring and summer of 2011 may be a long and hard road.

Before anymore is said about this project and the SWCC's role, I have to take a few minutes to talk about the real leaders in this fight. They are a group of Tahltan elders, the First Nations people of the Stikine, who call themselves The Klabona Keepers. 'Klabona' is their word for the Sacred Headwaters area. It is from and on their lands that Shell is trying to gain access to the headwaters.

These are the people who have been on the front lines manning a blockade for three years, keeping first the coal companies and then Shell off the access route. Risking arrest, and at times even being arrested for their efforts, they are the real heroes of this story. It is not too much of a stretch to say that Tahltan grandmothers and grandfathers are keeping the Skeena from destruction so that you can spend your fishing vacation having the amazing experiences you do on this relatively pristine system. So, the time has come for us all to step up.

All of you who have come here, who come here on a regular basis or those who imagine one day casting your hopes and lines into any one of the Skeena's dream steelhead rivers, all of you, all of us... now is the time to act. I realize that these words may sound over-dramatic, a bit of a stretch, but they are not. This is all coming to the Skeena if no action is taken.

What gives me hope is my belief that this is very much about the creating and shaping of reality. The only reality is the one you make for yourself. Other world views are coming into play now in the great Skeena system, views that are very much out of touch with the reality of sustaining steelhead and angling opportunities for now and forever, for us and for our children.

The more of us who connect on this level and express our ideas, who believe in our version of reality, who work to make it happen, then the greater the chances are that this will come to be. Despair and cynicism will not do. Reading this and thinking that you can do nothing will not do.

It is in this way that the Babine, and Pierce Clegg's passion for it, can serve as a prime example of what I am talking about: a vision of reality on the Babine came to pass. What many people have come to take for granted—a wilderness corridor, no bridges downstream of the one at the very top end—was the direct result of people, in large part, Pierce, taking action and making sure that the reality of the logging industry and short-sighted government agencies and ministers, did not come to pass.

It was very 'idealistic' to think that he could have stopped a bridge right there over the beloved Lower Trail run on the beautiful Babine. Impossible, some might have said. But it was because of his ideals, not in spite of them—that Pierce was able to do what he did and make the changes that saved the Babine from a far different fate than the one that we all know and love now.

Let the example of the Babine and what Pierce Clegg did there be an inspiration for all: to allow yourself to be 'idealistic' and let your ideals lead the way, for it is the only way that things ever truly change.

Stepping Into the Same River Twice

Will Blanchard, from Durango, CO, fits perfectly the description 'steelhead bum'. He first came to the Babine as a guide with a group of anglers from Durangler Flies and Supplies fly shop. Now he owns his own guiding business, Animas Valley Anglers, and has produced two late-season DVDs for Norlakes. His outstanding Babine photo albums are to be found at www.gottrout.com.

Will Blanchard (left) and Nate Bronson prepare to return two steelhead to the waters of a pool called Last Grab.

So many moments, over so many seasons. Early season to late season. August to November. High water and low water. Curled cottonwood leaves float down the river like little yellow Japanese junks. An eagle watches them twist and drift away. Golden autumn wanes as grey days out-play sunshine. Rain dimples the eddies. Snow covers the spruce boughs. Deep snow comes, guarded by cold. Rain or snow, we must go. Perhaps we're crazy. Perhaps we're not.

Prepare for battle. The elements ignored with bootfoot waders and hooded parkas. Goose down and Gore-tex. Wool toque warmth under hooded shelter. Snug-up the wading belt; tighten the cuffs, cold digits pull line protected by fingerless fleece. No protection, fingers numb, they feel wooden. Ice crystals burn the flesh. Pushing through it. Eyes on the prize.

Snap-Ts and roll casts, anchored lines as double Speys chase the white mouse. Hidden creatures shifting shape. Leaning spruce and root-wad havens. Wade deep to punch a cast. Countless casts and countless mends, mend again. Slow swing, all the way. Hang-down strip in, take a step, next cast. Fish the deke with hope and focus. Just one more cast, this might be the one. Patience tested.

Lurking steelie slow tugs leech, pulls and plucks. Big grab, hard take, climbed on. Hissing reel as graphite strains. Daydream. Wake up, hook up. Breeching twisted, 20-pounder. Under tension, silence shattered. Beast explodes the tannin water; amber mist rains down—don't falter. Line rips the inky black. Is this the pod? Thank God. Epic battle. Ease him in, grab his wrist, a camera clicks. Keep him wet, send him home. This is it, I'm at the temple.

Broken rods and burned-out reels. Hooks pulled straight. Snapped. Snagged. The ones that got away, the ones we landed, eh. Six-pounders and 30-pounders. Double-striped bucks and frisky does. Big grins and wide eyes peering out from snowy brims. Bloody knuckles and line cuts—battle scars. Badge of honour. No pain. No problem. Spooled again. Comfortably numb.

Bear bangers and pepper spray. Warning shot and shotgun misfire. All things wild. Wilderness. Twig snaps the silence, take a look—you see nothing. From the bush they are watching. Burly boar, silver tipped with twisted claw and gnarled fang. Guarded sow and toy-like cubs take no chances, all alert and with great caution. Give them space, earned respect. Grizzly roams with casual purpose as he sniffs his way through the boat bay. Rotten chum, pink or spring. Salmon carcass oozing stench. Feasting on the rotten meat they consume with gluttony—they need mass, it has to last.

Salmon fin and grizzly fang. All connected symbolically. More salmon spawn on graveled redds and each will die a drawn-out death. Nothing wasted as orange-red eggs incubate. Milt and egg make new life. Small fry, parr and smolts. Back to sea, make the journey. When it's time head home again. Up the river to spawn and die, keeping the cycle so the others can thrive.

Ouzel dips in search of eggs. Golden eagle sits on muscled legs, his talon claws finding purchase. Eagle eats the salmon skein. Scavengers of opportunity. Maggot feasts where others won't and picky crow pecks the eyes. Mergansers fish in troops of 10. Small fry scatter. Camp jay search-

Scott Robinson will always remember his first visit to the Babine after being left with an expensive rod in pieces as the outcome of a violent steelhead 'take' as he fished from Challenge Rock.

es, head-tilt quips, he prefers Old Dutch chips. Raven calls and raven clucks, before he does his air-borne tricks. He clucks once more and tucks a wing. Dollies and white fish—fooled again. Moose on stilts. A wolf pack howls, honking swans head south. Lamprey sneaks, preys on others. Sasquatch shy, like no others. A million dots blur black as a rainbow finds a stonefly nymph.

Jet wash churns; four-stroke power. Quick on plane; wood and metal skims the surface, tries to grip the green-black liquid. Tiller skills. Follow the trail. Follow the smoke and head for camp. Chainsaws and bar oil. Splitting maul and cordwood. Wood smoke lingers, hanging in the cottonwoods—comfort smells. Camp crew cooks are hard at work. Steaks and stews. Potatoes and rice. Upload calories, malt and grape. Roast beast, a steelheader's feast. Grubbed-up—mellowed out. Tilt some Crown or sip some 'shine, now you know you're on Norlakes' time.

Campfire jam sessions as neon marabou rides the fire thermals to nowhere. Popcorn, beers and bacon. Pass the bottle, pass the flask. Hydrate and high-fives. Hockey talk in hot tubs, late-night Babine dips. The matte black night—stars forever. Full moon shadows. Northern Lights—nature's party. Nicotine and gasoline. The human circle roars while the fire rages with reckless control.

Calloused fingers moving fast. Guitar strings strain with acoustic energy. Folksy, bluesy rock-n-roll. In tune and out of mind. Giv'er! Heavy cords with quickened pace. Voices sing homemade songs and made-up phrases as split-shot shakers rattle rhythm in tin cups. Washtub bass and big round drums—manhandled, adding depth. Feet stomp in agreement as a harmonica bends lonesome notes that spring hard from pursed lips and folded hands. The night's alive. Feel the vibe.

Tie a fly, tell a lie. Cigar burns slow. Pass out with your boots on. Hard sleep and hangovers. Coffee and Baileys. Hit the beach. Lunch pails and landing nets. Fly boxes stuffed with stinging steel and bunny fur. Black and blue tied on thick hooks with up-turned eyes. Pink and orange orbs as holographic flash catches light. Arctic fox and Spey hackles. Feather fibres, trailing stingers. Articulated. Dry bag, extra rod. Get in the boat.

Some are gone to far-off waters. Satellite trips in search of tugs. Runs and pools more remote. A quick stop at Grizzly Drop. Bitch's Tongue or Canyon Pool? Alien Rock and Challenge Rock. Boat Wreck and Tokyo Bar. They rolled with purpose at Laura's Pool. Doubleheader. Big buck, Beaver Flats—mowed your lawn. Picked your pocket, pick a fly. Tradition speaks. Boss and Bombers. What's the vibe? Skate it, wake it. Bubbleheads. Foam Freddy got a player, close the deal. Riffle-hitched Green Butt Skunk. Babine Special. Moons are leeches not that pretty. Deke Seekers and Slub-a-Dubs. Egg Suckers and My Shaved Beavers. The Intruder is a lead-eyed monster. Probed deep and hard they get the grabs.

Last cast, bright hen—Ejnar's Last Stand. Snowballs and jet sleds. Jet-boat wars. Guerrilla warfare in your face, snowball stockpile, broken windows, walls tagged white. Guides and guests. Good vibes surging. Night is back. Campfire burning, hot and high; the firelight glows on bearded faces. Sap snaps on glowing embers as flames lick the night sky. Add a log, tell a story. Dark and deep the night rolls on. One last Scotch, just five fingers. Raised glass, giving thanks. Friendships and tall tales of steelie tails and tail-outs. All the stories from all the seasons, mental snapshots, never fading. All the moments melt together, like the river's currents.

When Winter Comes to the Babine

November. Dropping below the clouds, 150 miles south

of our destination, the giddy cabin chatter of seven

steelheaders strapped into The Spirit of Smithers ceases.

Casual glances out the window of this Canadian Airlines

flight become hard focused. The evergreen landscape

below rapidly turns corpse gray. Faces wrinkle.

By Dave Hall

To the locals abroad, the scene is not unusual for this time of year, mid-autumn, give or take a week. But the nervous eye contact among us betrays concern. Memories of another disappointing trip to Skeena country fill our thoughts. That year, 1992, a sudden cold front had pushed in and snatched away a year's worth of anticipation, planning and everything else that's good about old friends coming together for a week of fly-fishing in the wilderness.

These guys are steelhead junkies. Five of the seven have made numerous trips to these waters. This is a special place; it is for all anglers who have had the privilege of wading the Babine River's tea-colored currents to cast for the remarkable strain of wild steelhead that pushed its way up the river each autumn. Our destination now, as then, was Pierce Clegg's Babine Norlakes Steelhead Camp on the upper stretches of this legendary river in northern British Columbia.

In 1992, the November weather had not been kind. Twelve hours after arriving at camp, Mother Nature had reared back and fired the old, high hard one, landing a big donut on the thermometer. Fewer than 24 hours after departure from Oregon we were back at the Vancouver airport. The camp was frozen-over harder than sun-baked concrete. Floating slush rendered our sinking fly lines useless; they lay atop the surface like tipped-over candles on a frosted birthday cake.

Ice in the guides? We had ice slivers in our nostrils. Add ice flakes swirling out of nowhere, sparkling against a cobalt sky with shoulder-high sun glaring down, blown by a brutal northern breeze. Conditions seemed more suitable for hunting seals that steelhead.

It's always a crapshoot. But none of us had thought it would end before it began. We were prepared for cold. The reality of a total freeze-up had jarred each man's sense of Karma.

Now, two seasons later, as we close in on Smithers, the butterflies return. They start churning. It's snowing. The ground appears quilt-like as we pass over patches of clear-cuts dusted with winter. I make a mental inventory of my cold-weather gear.... He had said that he would make changes at the camp to make sure it would remain open in the unlucky event of another freeze. There are definite advantages to coming here this late. Almost 100 percent of the run would be upriver.... other camps downriver would be closed.

Things look dark as we approach landing. It's not even noon yet and, hell, the streetlights are on, brightness turned to dim specks by the falling snow.

"River's in perfect shape," Pierce's smiling, jovial face greets us. "Lots of fish." Snow continues falling as we pack his van. After an hour of last-minute shopping and a quick bite to eat in town, we head east to Fort Babine, two hours away.

Six inches of snow and more can't dampen our excitement. Driving through winter wonderland we hang on Pierce's every word. He expects plenty of action—water conditions are ideal. Still I can't help wondering, *what am I doing in this Canadian icebox, again?*

As we slide in, our old friend, Todd Stockner, is there to greet us with two boats. Todd's experience on the river goes back two decades. He resembles a laid-back Deadhead, his warm and unassuming nature loved by all who have shared river time with him. He worked the original Norlakes camp with the famous Madsen family, who built it in the 1950s, and knows every rock and steelhead lie. He wasn't a fly-fisher when we met in the early '80s—I recall carrying to him his first fly rod and assorted tying materials. Warm handshakes and bear hugs bring it all back. Yes, we're here, and so, we hope, are the fish.

We quickly load the boats. With Pierce and Todd at the helms we head downriver. It will take 20 minutes. Just before camp, appearing out of the snow flurries, a massive sow grizzly and her two bruins scavenge for salmon carcasses. Beautiful. This will be a special week.

With a couple of hours of low light remaining, we hit the river. Within an hour I have two nice fish. As darkness falls, more members of the gang return, all with similar tales. We settle into comfortable, warm cabins. Morning can't come too soon.

What a week. Temperatures in the 20s and 30s, blizzards, snow blanketing the riverbank, broken rods, lost lines, frozen cameras, howling wolves, moose, bald eagles, glowing wood stoves, hearty food, thumping hangovers, and steelhead. All this while wading each day from dawn until dark in 34-degree water, casting 200- to 400-grain shooting heads hundreds of times daily.

And what a sight we must be, stumbling around like seven Frankenstein monsters encumbered with every conceivable piece of cold-weather gear known to man, from long johns made for astronauts to seal caps resembling the famous Himalayan Yeti scalp which are far from glamorous but toasty enough to steam your hair.

The weather holds. Except for some long, dark boat rides, the word 'cold' is rarely mentioned. We stay busy enough playing big anadromous rainbows, freshwater weightlifters that had cast a spell on us many years ago. It is one of those all-too-short times in an angler's life when everything comes together the way it's supposed to.

More than once during our dream week do I spy one of my partners standing still, gawking, rod tip and line dipped in the ice water, amidst a swirling blizzard, seemingly oblivi-

---

Writer and artist Dave Hall, from Glide, OR, and his friends have been fishing the Babine on and off since the early 1980s. Pierce recalls that, for years, he worked in the fly-tying business for the North Umpqua Feather Merchants adding: "He still lives on the North Umpqua River and has fly-tying in his blood. He is an artist and has donated much of his work to the river in support of stewardship efforts. He was the one who got me started on fishing into mid-November, something few considered possible before then. Dave and his friends have made it possible since 1994."

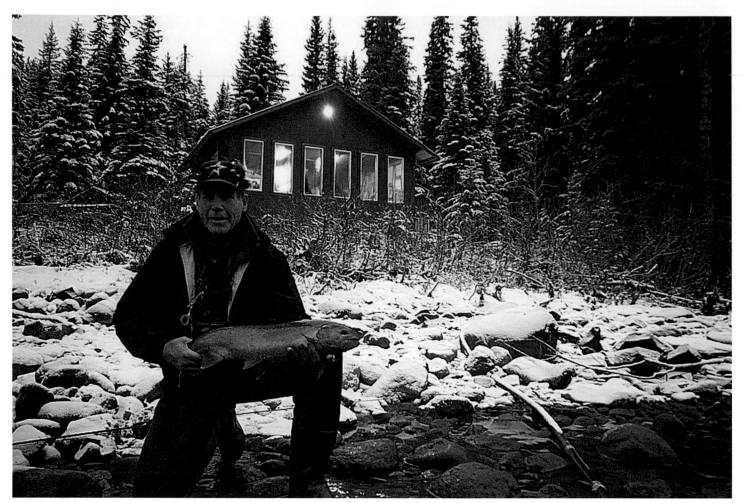

Not his largest steelhead from Ejnar's Pool by any means but big enough to get artist Dave Hall's heart beating a little faster on a frigid November day.

ous to the task of catching a fish yet grinning from ear to ear, dialed-in to the silent splendor of this northern world.

Wackos for sure! I watch as each friend's face lights up, the first charge of adrenaline surging through him as his fly is mauled by a trophy steelhead, transporting him figuratively and literally, his whole experience focused on a throbbing fly line that only moments before was lifeless, now stretched with the heavy weight of a wild creature gone berserk.

It is a many-fish week. It's a shared adventure expressed with the jubilant delight of little boys and a sense of well-being that comes from real companionship. It's rolling the dice and coming up big. It's the way fishing trips are supposed to be. No angler can fish one of Canada's designated trophy steelhead streams and be unimpressed. The rivers are beautiful, flowing through not only scenic but also, for the most part, very wild country.

They are classic and contain everything from long gravel bar runs and ledges to pocket water and spectacular tailouts. Depending on weather and water conditions, fly lines run the gamut from weight-forward floaters to 500-grain shooting heads. Nine-and-a-half foot to 10-foot, eight-weight rods are standard.

Fly selections encompass everything from dries and skaters to lead-eye leeches in many colors and style. Good old patterns such as Green Butt Skunks and other traditional steelhead wet flies should not be overlooked. These fish aren't picky.

Simply put, Babine steelhead are magnificent. The big males with dark, moss-green backs and massive, reptilian heads often have a double cadmium-red stripe covering sides and gill plates. Their huge tails are finely sculpted and perfect. With wide muscled shoulders and deep full bodies they are built for endurance. Their power and strength are legendary. True gladiators—make no mistake—Babine bucks run the show when hooked and can sprinkle one's excitement with a respectful dusting of fear. Male steelhead in this wilderness river average close to 15 pounds. Twenty-pounders are not at all uncommon; fish approaching 30 pounds are hooked every season.

The hens command attention, too—like all females in the animal kingdom. Their robust silvery sides are awash with an opalescent pink hue that extends to their delicate cheeks. They are plump and feisty. Their frenzied, ricochet runs have spooled many a reel over the years. A large female steelhead will weigh 20 pounds; most range between 10 and 15 pounds.

Male or female, a Babine steelhead will test every splice, knot and piece of equipment you fish. If you like big, strong, wild fish, these are the one for you—God bless 'em.

Reprinted by kind permission of Wild Steelhead and Salmon, Winter 1997.

Hooked on the Babine Experience

Pierce counts Gary Flagel, from Prince George, B.C, as a good friend. "He bailed us out big time one season when our Steelhead Camp cook quit on short notice. Gary took leave of absence from his job in the pulp mill and was trained by Anita in one week. That was the only week since 1986 when I was not in camp during the season. He is a great cook and loved by all the guests. When he retired from the mill he became an artist. Most falls he can be found jet boating on his own, painting and fishing the Babine. He's a big guy with a big heart and donates his artwork to various fund raisers for the Babine River Foundation." This is Gary's story.

*I*t's 1956 or thereabouts. My friend Jimmy is showing me an article in *Argosy* magazine. It was about a guy who made his way to the Babine River. That story stuck in my head for he just raved about the fishing and said 10-pound fish were small ones. We thought that would be the place to go when we were older. We managed the older part OK. Jimmy went his way and I mine and, in 1969, my wife and I ended up in Prince George for a job in the pulp industry. During the next few years I again thought about the Babine and about steelhead fishing.

I talked to a few buddies about going there and they thought it was too long a boat trip from Smithers Landing to the fish-counting fence near Fort Babine, not to mention the long bush road in to the landing. So there the thought about the Babine sat and faded once again.

Now it's October 1991 and fate steps in. I and two friends, Gary Bailey and Harry Boyce, a seasoned steelheader, are heading for the Bulkley River. We find the river is blown out when we arrive so head for Oscar's tackle shop in Smithers to see what the word is

on the Morice River. It had been raining for a few days and Steve Hidber told us the Morice was also blown because a lot of the feeder streams were dirty due to the clear-cuts around them.

He suggested the Babine was our best bet as it flows directly out of the lake. We couldn't believe it and then we were full of questions. How far? How bad is the road? It's like a dream. Is he really saying you can drive to the Babine? It's about 140 kilometres, Steve says, most of it gravel road and then he draws us a little map. We can't thank him enough because now we can still go fishing. We drive for what seems like an eternity and finally we are at the logging road bridge over the river and it looks clear.

We are excited to say the least and get out to take a look. The river isn't real big, just nice and full of salmon. Next thing we drive into the DFO fish-counting fence area on the south side of the river to look for a spot to camp. The main DFO base is across the river and there is lots of room to camp on our side. Man, this is great we say. I am surprised to see that this facility spans the whole width of the river and amazed at the numbers of salmon swimming below it.

Once we have had our fill of gawking at all those fish we get ready to go fishing. And fish we did for most of a week. We caught a lot of fish, bull trout, rainbows, cutthroat trout, sockeye, humpies, springs, white fish and even steelhead. We started fishing at the 'no fishing' sign below the fence and on down to the pool under the logging road bridge. It wasn't long before we ventured down the trail to other pools, singing and talking loudly all the way to keep the grizzly bears away.

We fished at the Ledge Rock Pool, now better known as Halfway Drift, the Sandwich Pool (Hansen's), and the Back Eddy Pool (Strom's). I caught my first Babine steelhead at Ledge Rock. It was a wild week of fishing and that was just the beginning. I have been fishing in this marvelous place for 17 years now and it's still like dreamtime. The dreams come in excited flurries and you can't quite make out where you are on the river but it is wild water and crazy fishing and you can't wait to get back.

One day I fished the ledge at Upper Callahan's after going on the Satellite Cabin trip with my friend Gary Bailey and guide Todd Stockner. We are hiking the bank and having a good time when Pierce Clegg stops by in his boat to say hello. We met Pierce during our first year on the river and he always took an interest in us. Then he said: "I'm short of clients this week and, if you are interested, I'll give you a deal for the rest of the week." Well, we couldn't pack our bags fast enough and off we went to Steelhead Camp. We met some of his clients that evening at supper and afterwards there was a draw for three people to go on an overnight trip to the Satellite Cabin.

We didn't win but later that evening, while we were tying flies in our cabin, Carl McLaughlin and his friend Bob stopped by and asked if we would like to do the satellite trip. We couldn't believe they were serious but they explained they had been there before many times and thought we would appreciate it and we sure did.

I never imagined I would get hooked on one place to fish as I was always looking for the next spot to try knowing you could only make a tiny dent in what is out there. But I am hooked on the whole Babine experience and that includes the fishing and sketching some of the runs and different scenes on the river.

This is a wilderness area of wild beauty, not just somewhere you go to fish. It is the wildlife you get to see and hear. Like the first time you see the many bald eagles. Then one of them lifts off the bank. 'Wow' is the word, and not just one do you see. The calls of these great birds skreeing up in the trees stays in your mind like the haunting sound in a dream.

There are the water ouzels (dippers) flitting about, chirping and diving into the water for insects. Let's not forget the whiskey jack trying to steal your lunch, the small songbirds in the alders and the ravens and crows chasing eagles and those great birds sparring in the air. It's all fascinating.

And what about the grizzly bears? You don't want to meet one while you are fishing alone but you really want to see one of these magnificent beasts, their beautiful, shiny fur rippling in the sunlight and, now and then, letting go with a great roar. Over the years I have watched many sows with two to four cubs in tow and Mom reaching out to slap one in the butt for walking ahead. Sometimes you spot a bear up-river from your boat while fishing and scramble back hoping you can close the gap to the boat before the bear does.

It seems you always manage to get back first but, most likely, the bear has already sensed you and has gotten out of the way; neither of us wants a close encounter.

The giant grizzly boars, when you encounter one, are awesome, like the one that came into camp while I was peeling potatoes, a huge bear heading right for the burn barrel. Don't you touch that barrel, I said. He turned and looked in my direction and immediately I felt intimidated, fearing the kitchen window and wall was not a barrier between us. As he headed back for the barrel I said "Hooper has a hunter down here and he will shoot your ass if he sees you." The big bear lit out of there as if he knew what I said but it was most likely the sound of that dining hall talking.

The best one though was last boat out of camp one November with Pierce, Anita, Jesse and myself and the guide, who was Gary Bailey, running the boat. We just got out of the spread between Nicheskwa Creek and Eagle Island when we spotted this huge boar at the pool called Ward's Riffle. We were all dumbstruck. He was so big and Gary went too shallow and bumped into the edge of the ledge rock. That broke the spell for sure.

There was the day I could hear a bear cub bawling and, on checking it out, I could see the sow standing by her cub on the rock point near the Camp Pool. It was obvious she wanted to cross the river but the cub wanted no part of it. After what seemed about five minutes or more of whining, the sow put her big paw under the cub's butt, pushed him into the river and dove in after it. It was too funny and the whining that little cub did when he got to the far bank was hilarious. He sure didn't like getting wet.

The last critter on my list is the lowly mouse. Depending on the year there can be a lot of these pests about but you only need one to drive you mad. The housekeeper would leave the dining lodge door open after washing the floor and I would get after her because mice lived under the building. The cook's room is just off the kitchen, in behind the pantry wall, and the door to the room is always open. One night—I was camp cook at that time—I was awakened by a rustling noise in the kitchen. I lay listening for a few minutes then got up and slowly made my way into the kitchen with flashlight in hand. By the time I made it to the waste paper box the mouse had beat it out of there.

After breakfast I set some mouse traps with a little cheddar on them thinking that should do it. Damn thing didn't like cheese. Second night it wakes me and again he is in the paper box, but tonight I am stealthy, flashlight in hand but off. When the mouse stops rustling in the paper I stop, it starts rustling and I move toward the box. Now I am standing over the box. I hit the light, there it is and I grab the box making a bee line for the door, open it and throw the whole damn thing out then slam the door shut. Gotcha, I think and go back to bed happy.

Up at 5.30 a.m. to start my day and the counter by the paper towel holder is covered with little shreds of paper chewed off the roll. It couldn't have got out of that box, could it? Bacon in those traps ought to do, according to my camp survey, or peanut butter, but who knew that mouse didn't like either. Night three and I wake up with a start; it's scratching around in the air cooler by the back door, just behind the wall at the head of my bed. Gottcha this time you little bugger, I think, as I sneak down the hall stopping when it stops. My hand is on the cooler door now, I

156

Recent counts indicate that upwards of 100 grizzly bears are present in the Babine watershed, feasting on salmon in the fall and providing fishermen with a very special experience, one to be treasured each and every time.

snap the flashlight on as I rip open the door and there it is, bold as brass sitting by the cheese on the top shelf. I'm stunned with disbelief and that split second is all it needs, before my hand even moves.

I can't believe I was so stunned and go back to bed in defeat. Next morning it's peanut butter in the traps, and what mouse could resist this bait, the survey says, but resist it did. The survey now is on about how mice just love beer. After everyone has left to fish I remember some beer that was left outside the front door and went to check to see if it had frozen the night before. To my surprise, there were three dead mice inside an empty bottle. You would have to be crazy for beer to do that.

I decided then to make a bucket trap and, when completed, waited to set it once things had quieted down in the evening. I put six inches of water in the pail, poured some beer in and put some peanut butter on the roller can. Then set the wood ramp up the side and went to my room to read and wait. About 30 minutes later I heard the splash and the deed was done much to the angst of the housekeeper who thought they were such cute little critters.

Then there's the fishing. I am wading down this rock ledge at Upper Callahan's; my whole body is vibrating from the time I first step out and cast. I fish this ledge like it was known to me, cast out downstream, let the fly swing into the ledge and ease the rod tip and line over the top so the current slows the line. Then slowly bring it back to the edge so you can feel the line sink way down to the bottom of the ledge. I can see it in my mind, give the fly a few pumps then mend the line back out into the main current so it will pull the fly away and stop it from hanging up.

Each time I repeat this cast the vibrations in my body intensify. It's a crazy, erotic feeling and hard to believe but, in the back of your mind, you know something is going to happen. Another step down, cast and then another, followed by more and now the feeling is so intense I am shaking. Then I feel it. The fly just stops dead and it's not the ledge. I set the hook and this fish moves hard upstream and he's coming to the surface but doesn't break water and I hear Todd say, 'My God, it's Mister Babine! Then nothing; he broke me off but I'm ecstatic.

I had caught a fish we saw on the way down. We look at the line afterwards and there was the answer. It had broken where it wrapped around the hook eye. To this day I am not sorry I didn't land that fish. The excitement getting there and being on that rocky ledge rock called Callahan's was it and I can still feel that buzz just telling the story.

Not to forget the other fishermen you meet on the river and who I look forward to seeing each season. Some of them I met as a client and the rest as a cook for the lodge for a half season and then a full season. The cooking part was by accident as Pierce had a cook quit halfway through and he was desperate for someone to finish the rest of the year.

My old fishing buddy Gary Bailey, who turned guide for Pierce, convinced him I could cook. As far as I know I have been the only cook to also operate a riverboat and go steal water from the clients. They seemed to get a kick out of it as did I and it was fun cooking for them and fishing with them from time to time. I still get to see some of the steelheaders who come back to fish and also meet the new steelheaders. To hear what they think and say of their experiences on the Babine gives me great pleasure.

Gary Flagel pays
close attention to his
floating fly...

*Gary Flagel pays
close attention to his
floating fly...*

*...and hoists his catch
before returning it to
the water.*

The cooking experience was new for me as far as cooking for a group of people that changed weekly and most never known until that time. Nervous was the feeling but, with a lot of help from Anita, I managed to get over it. After that you couldn't wipe the smile off my face. It was fun learning to bake pies, like double batches at first because the first ones were burnt enough you couldn't serve them to clients (they became great snack food for us late in the evening). Deserts were the things I enjoyed making the most and I had learned a lot about that from my wife, Bernice.

My most memorable one was a cake I made for Piece's 40th birthday. I thought about what I would make for quite a while and then it came to me one day while I was looking at the pictures that covered the walls. There it was a photo of a big bear scat, I mean big. Whoever took that photo thought so because they laid a big three-cell flashlight beside it when they snapped that picture. It struck me like lightning, "A BEAR SHIT CAKE', that's what I will make. It made me chuckle thinking about it but knowing how to do it was another matter.

After a bit of thinking and checking my recipe book, I had it. I will make a few chocolate cakes from a recipe Bernice had found that had chocolate chips in it for some texture and I would cut and put it together using the photo. The topping I decided would be a hot blueberry sauce poured over the top at the time of serving so it would look hot and steamy. Well it was a real hoot when I plopped that in front of Pierce, everyone got a big kick out of it. What fun that was.

It's the experiences there that pull me back. Like six timber wolves cruising out of the woods up over the bottom of the gravel bar at the tail out at Barto's early one November afternoon. Or sitting in the boat by Brooks on the last day of one season, where we went to fish one more time, and listening to them howl, too entranced to even get out of the boat to fish. The days you are fishing and you hear the babbling of the river voices, or when you sit down under that big fir at Larson's Corner on a sunny afternoon and think I could die right here today and that would be OK.

Darcy Edwards is a fun guide who worked for Pierce when I cooked there and it was a joy to watch him with a new steelheader or someone who really tried hard and wanted to know more. He is wired about fishing and all that enthusiasm vibrates into the fisherman. He can be a little devil at times, and could get under a client's skin, but by the time the week was over most went home loving the little bugger. I have watched him with clients and he'd go step for step with them, a smoke in one hand, a beer in the other, enthusiastically talking the client through it—and the client usually hooked a fish while he talked them down the run.

Pierce has always managed to find good guides and now has Darren Wright, who I met a few years back when he and his fiends came from Alberta to try steelhead fishing. I really enjoyed running into him and Daryn McCutcheon from time to time as they love fishing. These guys were so keen they even had a cast-iron Dutch oven on top of charcoal bricks slowly cooking things like a New England dinner so they could fish late into dusk.

My son Lorne comes with me when he can and it's a joy to see him getting into it every time a fish strikes. The fall of 2007 was his first experience of a steely coming up to a dry fly and that sure made him jump. I think that did it for him as that fish came back eight times and even took the fly on the last try. He did not hook that one but hooked he is and that makes me feel proud, knowing how to pass on the knowledge.

So I want to thank people like the Wickwires and Ejnar Madsen, and others never met, and the people of today like Pierce, Lani Waller, Chick Stewart and their clients, plus the many others who come to the Babine to enjoy its wonders. These are the people who keep after our governments and their officials to maintain this wilderness area for all time.

The Greatest Birthday Gift

Pierce Clegg and Bill Herzog on their cherished Babine when both were a good few years younger.

Pierce says Bill Herzog, from Tacoma, WA, has to be one of the river's most enthusiastic fishermen, one who credits the Babine for jump-starting his career as a prolific writer of books and fishing magazine articles as well as this story. "He even pioneered his own very effective spoon after learning about the Little Cleo version that was a Norlakes' favourite for many years. His spoon has now been more or less banned from the river due to its deadly success."

$\mathcal{E}$aster Day, 1978. Standing in my uncle's den, admiring his seemingly countless framed fishing photos, one stood out. Not from the pedestrian, eight-pound female steelhead he was holding, it was odd because my usually clean-shaven uncle was sporting a full beard.

"Oh yeah, you need to grow a beard for warmth before you go there," he said. 'There' was a river which I had never heard of, called Babine. He said something about the superior steelhead fishing he had experienced during that trip, emphasized the large and numerous fish, made a strong suggestion I travel north to sample the place, then dismissed the story and moved on to the next photo. I, however, wanted to hear more.

I was 20 years old, never been to Canada, and thought this Babine might make for an exciting new destination for my budding passion for steelhead fishing. My family bought me a mid-October trip to Babine Norlakes Lodge, where my uncle had stayed—for my 21st birthday. That present, little was I aware at the time, would be the most life-changing gift I would ever receive.

What I found was the true definition of a wilderness river, alive with the life force of bald eagles, grizzly bears, moose, wolves and wild summer steelhead. The Madsens took care of us back then, introducing us to favorite runs, teaching us the nuances of Babine. After my initial visit, I knew—though I was not sure exactly why—this would not be my last trip, but one that would be repeated each and every autumn.

When the Cleggs took over in 1986, Pierce and his wife Anita took the baton well and ran strongly. I categorize them as not just lodge owners but as great friends, who also guided me along this Babine journey. We learned the river's 'vibes', the way Babine talks silently to us. Indescribable how it communicates but knows that all of us who feel the Babine's 'vibes' become aware a second before something special is about to happen.

You truly become one pulse with the river, hydro-psyche, if you will. Something I never could explain, but know that the 'vibes' only occur in chosen few places on this big blue marble. Could be a visit from one of the species of wildlife, perhaps an encounter with a strong spirit from a Babine angler who is no longer with us, most often it was a fish immediately before a take.

And those fish! God's *magnum opus* with fins. Steelhead constructed for endurance, they are fierce, rare and none more

mysterious. Thick bodied like no others, they must be seen—and briefly held—for full appreciation to set in. Elegant metallic pink-gilled, mercury-sided females follow closely alongside the true stars of this Greatest Show on Earth, the double vermillion striped males. Some so large, you dared not tell the truth of their size.

Swift strikes, so violent that excitement immediately turns to terror as a weight like never before felt goes... that away. These 'freight trains,' as Babine regulars passionately name them, can effortlessly diesel off with a spool of 20-pound test or 100 yards of backing before you may swallow your stomach and yet again begin breathing.

My journal notes from so many trips tell of nearly 100 grand fish of 20 to 31 pounds landed, but memory burns brightest for the ones of such impossible size, the ones that took me to task and defeated even the best of rods, reels, lines and hooks. I believe the ultimate challenge in steelhead fishing is to bring one of the Babine giants, those surreal beasts of 40 pounds and beyond, to hand. If your last name is neither Kent nor Christ, I just do not believe it can be done.

Though I could relate dozens of narratives about the ridiculous magnitude of Babine bucks and how they repeatedly beat the shit out of me, I'll share one anecdote from a Monday, October 13, 1987—the Year Of The Giants—and the beast that took me to task.

Back in the day, we primarily swung spoons. Though we now commonly hook many oversized Babine steelhead with flies, we knew back then the shortest distance between us

A warm Steelhead Camp cabin is the place to be at the end of a chilled winter's day on the river.

and a trophy was flashing metal. This cold, clear morning would be no exception. Putting downstream immediately below camp through Allen's, long time Norlakes guide Todd Stockner suddenly began weaving a rapid-fire tapestry of expletives and pointing off the bow.

There in the low, clear water swam a steelhead of such proportion it looked like a tardy chinook. A double red striped chinook, dwarfing the other two 20-plus-pounders swimming alongside. It moved off to the steep bank, just out of sight. Todd has spotted more massive steelhead than any one human has a right, but even he said then and there it was the biggest steelhead he'd ever seen.

"Todd. Let me out!"

"Bill, you are supposed to fish Trail this morning."

"Lemme out or I'll jump out."

Todd and my partner went on down around Corner and out of sight, leaving me alone. Making a mental note approximately where the giant took station, I worked my way along the steep, log-festooned bank to get in position for a cast. My first swing with a brass Little Cleo was met with a thud on the hang-down. Perched 10 feet above the river, looking down into the sunshine-illuminated flows, rose the fish, just a mere foot under the surface, rapidly shaking his Kelly green, alligator head, my spoon flipping in the corner of his jaw. A male so large my rationale had to be overridden repeatedly as this was no way a steelhead.

Twice that of 20, not even close to the few of 30 pounds I've held. Took every bit of concentration not to tumble into the river as my body was shutting down, limb by limb, shaking so badly and so close to vomiting and/or fainting. But I got him. Fresh 20-pound-test spooled on the night before, fast thoughts of a world record flashed. The fish bolted for the other side of Allen's displacing water as if someone had dropped a cow from an airplane. With light speed it returned to my side, swam with singular purpose upriver toward the only trees slanting into the water for miles. Not even heavy saltwater king salmon tackle could have slowed him. The great fish stopped, satisfied with his position under the cat's cradle of limbs and simply sat on a tight line, he and I in a standoff.

I stood there, tethered to my once-in-50-lifetimes trophy, waiting for a Norlakes jet boat to pick me up in the thinnest of hopes that perhaps I would be able to get a change of angle, even pass my rod under the trees and continue the battle. Forty-five minutes later, which seemed like two days, came Pierce downriver, puzzled at my occupation on the crap side of Allen's. I yelled my plight; he came towards me to pick me up. The giant must have felt the motor approaching me, as it woke up and launched upriver faster than gravity would ever allow. Trees and monofilament are poor bed partners, my limp line retrieved and felt as if it had been run over thousands of barnacles. I could not fish the rest of the day.

Fast forward that same year, just before Thanksgiving. My phone rings. It's Pierce, and he has something remarkable

Pierce Clegg and Bill Herzog enjoy a winter day on the Babine.

to tell. Seems as though the Babine First Nations had an unusually large steelhead enter one of the weir traps during one of their fish-counting days. This was one monster to be sure, 54 inches long and 51 pounds. Most curious was the short section of heavy mono attached to a brass Little Cleo pegged in the great fish's jaw.

It is truly a humbling honor to have named two runs on the greatest steelhead river on Earth. Bill's Last Cast, the very last pool below Beaver Flats before the river plunges violently into an un-runnable canyon we call 'Middle Earth', named after landing an average 10-pound female on my last cast of a Satellite Camp trip in 1992. Also Ground Zero, the run between Joe's and Green Rocks, named for the way we used to 'nuke' the then un-named run with spoons. Strom's, Callahan's, Brooks Range, Olson's, Rempel Pool, Bill's Last Cast: some fairly heady company I am blessed to share. Thank You, Pierce.

I am one of the chosen, the very fortunate to have spent much time with Babine and I must admit for the first 10 years I took the extraordinary for granted. I knew that this was a truly special stream, but it really did not begin to trip the amazement lever until 1990. For six consecutive autumn visits, the river revealed more secrets and took up more space in my heart. Late October was my allotted slice of Paradise. However, family and job commitments took over, 11 seasons came and went without seeing my favorite river.

When I returned in 2007, I was afraid it would be so different. The Eagles sang 'once you call a place Paradise, kiss it goodbye.' Fear should have never crept in, as it went beyond the highest standards set by all previous trips. Even after an 11-year hiatus, the Babine still refuses to release my youth. After a thousand winter nights' dreams of my eventual return, each awakening of disappointment, it was as if my last trip never ended. Zero time lapses in surreal wonderment, this place where best friends became brothers.

The Babine lost nothing, still magic, still evoking raw emotions and sheer wonder no river can equal. Trying as I have for so many years, to understand just why this place, this Babine, is far and beyond other steelhead highways, I never could formulate any black-and-white conclusion. I believe the answer is best given from a quote from one G.K. Chesterson: 'Men did not love Rome because she was great; she was great because they had loved her.' Where the rarest ghosts swim, she waited for me.

The next time—or the first time—you are blessed to visit, remember to pause for a moment before you begin casting. Each pool and run has a unique story of its own. Dip your hand into dark, tannin flow, absorb the shocking cold, a reality check telling you that this is indeed actual time and not a dream.

Every riverside feature—from the stump perch in Log Jam, the black wall of Canyon to the irregular ledge undulating along Callahan's—has hundreds of tales to tell. If you stop and listen to the Babine River, you will hear each one.

Chick Stewart: In His 80s and Still Fishing

Pierce remembers guiding and hosting Chick and Marilyn Stewart in his early years on the river. "Chick was a friend of Ejnar's and has always loved the river and adventures. He also still owns Stewart and Rempel Sawmills, in Surrey, B.C., which custom cuts old-growth cedar. Ejnar used to pick some choice pieces of yellow cedar from the sawmill to use as ribs in the river boats he built."

Chick and Marilyn Stewart were special friends of the Madsens and later bought, and still own, Babine Steelhead Lodge, built by Bob Wickwire a few miles downstream from the Norlakes Steelhead Camp.

The 15-year-old boy, who waited around for four days for his first job at a remote Vancouver Island sawmill, has come a long, long way in the intervening 67 years. Today Chick Stewart, now into his 80s and working as hard as ever, and his wife, Marilyn, have their own sawmill along with two superb Arnold Palmer-designed, 18-hole golf courses and impressive club house, all set on over 400 prime acres of former farmland only 30 minutes' drive from downtown Vancouver.

Even more important from the context of this book, and from the perspective of two enthusiastic anglers, Chick and Marilyn and their large family cherish the time they spend each year at their steelhead base, Babine Steelhead Lodge Ltd. They have enjoyed the 12-guest, log-built lodge, located some six miles downriver from the Norlakes property, since March, 1987, having bought it from two Montanans, Drs. Ken High and Vern Horton. In turn, the medical men had

The Stewarts' Babine Steelhead Lodge is located a few miles down stream from the Norlakes Steelhead Camp and was built by Bob Wickwire in the early 1970s.

purchased the two-and-a-half-acre property, then known as Babine River Steelhead Lodge Ltd., from the original builders and owners, the Wickwires, who had come there in the very early 1970s.

Bob and Jerrie Lou Wickwire, another famous pioneering family, owned and ran the lodge for 15 years before going on to construct and operate the third of the Babine's steelhead fishing operations, the air-access-only Silver Hilton Lodge on the lower river. Thus the history of just four families—the Madsens, the Wickwires, the Cleggs and the Stewarts—dating back to the early 1950s, encompasses in so many ways the past, the present and the future of steelhead fishing on the Babine.

Ejnar Madsen's wife Joy and Marilyn Stewart, formerly Marilyn Czorny, have known each other since their early teens, graduated from Langley High School at the same time and were both married the following year, 1956. Inevitably Chick and Ejnar became close friends, enjoying each other's company on countless hunting and fishing expeditions and spending time together in the early days at the Norlakes' steelhead camp and at the Stewarts' saw mill.

"We used to come and help Ejnar and Joy to close up camp in late October and then, when they were still living in Surrey during the winter months, he would work for me in the mill or spend his time building houses to sell later on," Chick recalls.

Having moved as a teenager from Manitoba to British Columbia in 1942—his father was in the Royal Canadian Air Force—Chick had plenty of experience fishing the rivers of the Fraser system but it was not until 1956 that he had his first sight of the Babine.

"Ejnar had invited us to stay at Norlakes that October and we walked down from the DFO fish-counting weir as far as the Gravel Bar Pool, where the Nilkitkwa flows in, fishing with spinning gear for steelhead. I remember it was pretty cold,"

"About 1964, my sawmill partner, Vic Rempel, and I saved up enough to go to the Norlakes steelhead camp as paying guests for the first time. We were getting $1 a load from the truck drivers, who picked up our sawdust, and that was our fishing fund. We drove up from Vancouver to Smithers and on to Babine Lake where Ejnar had left a boat at the dock for us with a note saying: 'Come on down yourselves.'"

S&R Sawmills Ltd., on the Fraser River, has been operating since 1963 with Northview Golf and Country Club launched in 1993. Marilyn is general manager there as well as working in the business side of the mill. These are both family-owned and operated concerns with all nine grandchildren also involved in one way or another.

Recalling Ejnar's famous dry wit, Chick recalls: "Earlier he sent us a risqué illustration from a man's magazine on which he had written 'Don't Miss October.'

"Ejnar later built a much larger boat, almost like a house boat, to bring the fishermen down to the main lodge. I remember one year waiting for him and seeing 12 fishermen get off with 96 frozen steelhead all packed and ready for shipping out. There was an eight-fish-possession-limit in those days and they all had their limits.

"Then there was the time he had to go into Smithers to get a part for the boat motor. He soon found himself forced to drive very slowly behind two moose hunters who simply would not let him past. They did not want him to scare away any game that might be waiting ahead and did everything they could to hold him up. Eventually he did pass the truck and, when he came around a corner, he saw a big bull moose right in front of him. Of course, he laid on his horn and that was that for the hunters.

"Or what about the party of fishermen from Salt Lake City. They were Mormons and drank only water or hot chocolate. One day they asked Ejnar about the source of his water and said they would like to take a sample back home for testing. Ejnar agreed but, when he got the sample, he emptied half of it out and poured in some gin. He never heard another thing from them about the water tests."

Not surprisingly, and like so many of his generation who experienced British Columbia at its wildest best, Chick has a wealth of stories to tell about the early days on the river... of pacing a moose in his truck at a steady 35 miles an hour for mile after mile on the gravel logging road to the lake... waiting up until after midnight to shoot a marauding black bear that had been robbing the underground steelhead camp fish store 'which woke everyone and brought them all out in the snow in their pyjamas'... seeing Ejnar shoot a grouse with his 30/30 rifle and being left with "only two wings and two feet"... how the Indians would come to collect any unwanted pieces following a successful moose hunt... falling flat on his back in the river after jumping too soon out of a boat at Corner Pool only to step and slip on a large and very dead chinook salmon... the abandoned trapper's log cabin near Log Jam Pool with the carved messages on the walls....'Sure miss you tonight, Helen'... 'Sure miss you tonight, Mary'...

When he and Marilyn bought Babine Steelhead Lodge, they found they had their hands more than full getting ready for the start of the 1987 steelhead season in less than six months' time.

"We trucked in two 40-foot-long trailers of building materials and equipment from the coast and had it flown in to the lodge by helicopter. Then we raised the cabins and the main building on skids and moved them all back from the edge of the river. We also added a dining room, drying room, washroom and indoor toilets and got rid of the old pot-bellied stoves.

"Our first guests that September were four doctors from Chilliwack and a party of eight fishermen from Montana. It just happened that was the year when the new steelhead catch-and-release-only regulations were introduced. When we told the guests, who had been booked by the previous owners, about it they were far from happy for they all expected to take home trophy-sized Babine steelhead."

Chick continues: "It was pretty tense at dinner that night and Marilyn was almost in tears. The four Canadians took our side and said the law was the law and I just told the others that, if they were not paid up before 7:00 p.m., I would take them all back to Smithers the next morning. Right after dinner, and just five minutes before the hour, one of the Americans came to our door of our cabin, threw in the cash and checks and said: 'We're staying.'"

While they had a camp manager and two guides at the lodge, the Stewarts were also fully involved in the business over the course of the early-September to late-October season.

"We would be there for the first week and the last week and, in between, we would fly up to Smithers on Thursday night each week and buy all the groceries. Then we would go down to the lodge by boat and bring out that week's guests, take in the next group and fly back to Vancouver on Sunday night," Chick said.

More recently—since 2002—the day-to-day business of running the lodge has been in the hands of the Stewart's oldest daughter, Wendy, and her husband, Barry Chanasyk, with Chick and Marilyn visiting and fishing two or three times each year during September and October. Says Chick: "I like to keep the wood pile full and, of course, I do all the chopping!"

When the two lodges on the upper river both have their full complement of guests, the water is shared on an equitable basis through the day with informal agreements in place among the owners and guides to ensure there is no overcrowding on the many pools.

This was not always the case and there are plenty of stories still told about the 'fish wars' of the early days and the pre-dawn competition to be the first rod in place on the most popular stretches of the river. Chick remembers how Ejnar's guide, Carl McLoughlin, would take them by boat in the dark to a pool, start a fire and leave them in place waiting for Bob Wickwire's guests to arrive with their guide only to find the water already occupied.

He also recalls how a pool now known as Chick's Chute came to be named. "Todd Stockner was guiding us and we stopped at this likely looking spot on the way down to Callahan's. He let us off to have our lunch and remarked 'no one ever catches fish here'. Well, I hooked three steelhead while the others were eating and Todd got another one when he returned and it's been Chick's Chute to us ever since."

—As told to Peter McMullan

A Wild and Pristine River Under Pressure

By Peter McMullan

This picture-bright hen came from a pool called Lower Chicken and weighed around 18 pounds—one to recall for a long, long time.

On the fabled waters of British Columbia's Babine River it didn't take long to rewrite my previously held, lifelong beliefs about dry-fly fishing. Forget dainty Mayflies on #16 hooks, not to mention delicately tapered casts, avoidance of drag at all costs and the old 'fine and far off' dictates dating back to the sport's earliest days. Think instead of working a floating, mouse-sized fly down and across a substantial stream in the hope of raising a trout big enough to be a salmon. These are Canadian steelhead, massive sea-run rainbows that can easily weigh over 20 pounds and, if you are very, very lucky, a great deal more for we know the Skeena system can occasionally produce fish scaling close on or over 40 pounds.

It's dry-fly fishing with a difference and it most definitely works for steelhead on the wild and pristine Babine River, which hooks through the rugged Atna Range in north-central B.C. as it flows west to join the Skeena. It produces so well, in fact, that a floating or waking fly is now the preferred tactic of many of the visiting anglers who come each fall from as far away as Europe and Japan to challenge the majestic steelhead, summer-run fish that amazingly do not spawn until the following spring,

With more than 20 years of fishing and guiding experience on the Babine, my host, Pierce Clegg, was just the person to point me in the dry-fly direction on the last morning of my week-long, early September stay at his Babine Norlakes Fall Steelhead Camp (www.babinenorlakes.com). The fact that the Babine is rated in British Columbia as a Class One water speaks for itself and for the reputation of a river where every fish is treated with the utmost respect and where catch-and-release fly-fishing of the highest quality is the norm, using only single barbless hooks. There can be no better prompt to the virtues of maintaining a tight line between fish and fisherman when the big moment comes.

Earlier in the week I had been making the most of my chances using a #2 Edge Bright Boss on a 7-weight, 13' 6" double-handed rod with a floating line and a 15-foot clear intermediate sink tip. Each day had treated me to at least one fish, sometimes two or even three. The best of them came from a pool called Lower Chicken: a picture-bright hen a few ounces over 18 pounds. Measuring 36 inches x 19.5 inches, the weight was calculated according to the length x girth x girth over 750 formula. That's one to recall for a long, long time.

Flow levels were on the low side for the time of year and, for the first few days, glacial melt in the Nilkitkwa River, upstream of the camp, had made for reduced visibility. Now cooler weather

An Edge Bright Boss proved its worth day after day.

and clearing water told Pierce it was time for me to switch to a full floating line. For the business end we selected one of his own patterns, a well-greased, moose-hair Bubblehead Bomber hand tied on a 5/0 hook, a bulky, pink-tailed beast secured with a half hitch to enhance its waking qualities on a 10-foot, 12-pound-test leader.

Not the sort of offering I wanted sailing anywhere close to my head but definitely the right fly at the right moment as I started down Allen's Pool, just downstream from the camp, for the third time. With two steelhead and a couple of dark, double-figure chinook salmon already landed and released, I knew for sure the fish were there—but catching one on a floating fly was going to be another challenge altogether.

So to work: the buoyant line slides easily down and across the current, the fly swims busily at the end of its tether, the arrowed wake a visual, focal point for fisherman and fish alike. Nothing could be further from all those long-held, dry-fly concepts yet this is every bit as hypnotic with the disturbed journey of the big fly the only thing that matters. Cast, watch and wait for the fish to make the next move, cast, watch and wait. What I now call 'towing the mouse' is definitely a very different approach, one that demands steady nerves and a high degree of concentration.

Over the course of the next hour three offers present and vanish just as fast. I miss the first fish with the fly directly below me and close to the bank in a couple feet of water. It makes its challenge just as I am lifting off, coming from nowhere with a great and audible rush. The second one boils strongly beneath the fly on a dead drift without taking it down while a third one secures only the briefest of holds and is gone. Talk about tension and excitement. With it came a sense of regret that I had not switched tactics a little sooner. We live and learn.

With fishing like this it's little wonder the 61-mile-long Babine and its steelhead are held in such high esteem. Access to this remote and wild river is made both easy and comfortable through lodges like the Norlakes camp, with its main living and dining building and adjacent, cozy cabins for up to a dozen guests. The Norlakes operation looks much the same today as it did in the 1960s. That was when the late Ejnar Madsen, one of the true pioneers of sport fishing on the upper river, built the water's-edge complex after jet drive technology for river boats had opened up mile after mile of previously inaccessible, prime steelhead water.

Using jet boats we were able to reach more than 70 named pools over some 17 miles of rich and hugely varied holding water. For passionate fly-fishermen, it's almost too good to be true with the companionship, experience and knowledge of Pierce and career guides Darren Wright, from Calgary, Alberta, and Shaun Vanderberg, from British Columbia's Vancouver Island, adding to the sense of occasion. By the way, all the fishing on the Babine is walk and wade with the jet boats used only for transportation.

Today nearly all those who fish the Babine come to either Pierce's rustic Norlakes Steelhead Camp, to Babine Steelhead Lodge, another three miles or so downstream, or to the Silver Hilton Lodge, some distance further on down river. Jet-drive boats serve the first two while Silver Hilton is a fly-in operation. There is also limited public bank access to the river just below the federal government's salmon-counting weir. That's where a bridge takes a logging road across the upper river not far from where it leaves Nilkitkwa Lake, an extension of Babine Lake, its huge expanse of water reaching back some 110 miles—the longest natural lake in British Columbia,

Getting there, and to the only boat ramp, located on government-controlled property, entails a two-hour drive from the friendly, Alpine-themed town of Smithers (pop. 6000) on a well-maintained gravel logging road. Privately owned jet boats are an option but only in the hands of a very experienced operator, and there is no nearby, overnight accommodation, while inflatable rafts take four or five days to reach the next take-out point near Hazelton. Smithers is a comfortable two-day drive from Vancouver, 714 miles, to the south, while flying from Vancouver takes less than two hours over some quite spectacular mountain terrain.

Then there are the grizzly bears. Between 75 and 100 of all ages live in the Babine watershed where they gather to enjoy the fall feast provided by dead and dying salmon. The bears are a tourist attraction in their own right but their presence can be an obvious deterrent to the casual visitor who might be thinking in terms of a wilderness camping and fishing trip. Some of our party saw bears during their days on the water, and everyone carries bear spray and bear bangers in the unlikely event of a close encounter, but I saw only large and very fresh tracks, left overnight along the river's edge.

I first met Pierce and his wife Anita during an early summer trout-fishing visit to one of their three Babine Lake house-keeping cabins. The traditional dry-fly fishing on slow-moving Rainbow Alley, leading from the outlet of Babine Lake into Nilkitkwa Lake and to the river itself, was fascinating and productive. So too was Pierce's enthusiastic talk of the huge steelhead that run the Babine and come freely to both sunk and waking dry flies in the fall. I was well and truly hooked and the subsequent invitation to join nine others at the camp in the second week of September was too good to pass up.

Pierce is more than just a generous host. He is a passionate advocate for the river, one who has fought long and hard to ensure it remains as near to possible in its original pristine state, a wilderness preserve to be treasured by all its users. In this regard, Class A Provincial Park status for the whole length of the watershed was definitely a step in the right direction in 1999 (www.env.gov.bc.ca/bcparks). More recently the Babine Watershed Monitoring Trust (www.babinetrust. ca) was established to monitor land-resource management plans. The

Length (in) \ Girth (in)	12.0	12.5	13.0	13.5	14.0	14.5	15.0	15.5	16.0	16.5	17.0	17.5	18.0	18.5	19.0	19.5	20.0	20.5	21.0	21.5	22.0	22.5	23.0	23.5	24.0	24.5	25.0	25.5	26.0
28.0	5.4	5.8	6.3	6.8	7.3	7.8	8.4	9.0	9.6	10.2	10.8	11.4	12.1	12.8	13.5	14.2	14.9	15.7	16.5	17.3	18.1	18.9	19.7	20.6	21.5	22.4	23.3	24.3	25.2
28.5	5.5	5.9	6.4	6.9	7.4	8.0	8.6	9.1	9.7	10.3	11.0	11.6	12.3	13.0	13.7	14.4	15.2	16.0	16.8	17.6	18.4	19.2	20.1	21.0	21.9	22.8	23.8	24.7	25.7
29.0	5.6	6.0	6.5	7.0	7.6	8.1	8.7	9.3	9.9	10.5	11.2	11.8	12.5	13.2	14.0	14.7	15.5	16.2	17.1	17.9	18.7	19.6	20.5	21.4	22.3	23.2	24.2	25.1	26.1
29.5	5.7	6.1	6.6	7.2	7.7	8.3	8.9	9.4	10.1	10.7	11.4	12.0	12.7	13.5	14.2	15.0	15.7	16.5	17.3	18.2	19.0	19.9	20.8	21.7	22.7	23.6	24.6	25.6	26.6
30.0	5.8	6.3	6.8	7.3	7.8	8.4	9.0	9.6	10.2	10.9	11.6	12.3	13.0	13.7	14.4	15.2	16.0	16.8	17.6	18.5	19.4	20.3	21.2	22.1	23.0	24.0	25.0	26.0	27.0
30.5	5.9	6.4	6.9	7.4	8.0	8.6	9.2	9.8	10.4	11.1	11.8	12.5	13.2	13.9	14.7	15.5	16.3	17.1	17.9	18.8	19.7	20.6	21.5	22.5	23.4	24.4	25.4	26.4	27.5
31.0	6.0	6.5	7.0	7.5	8.1	8.7	9.3	9.9	10.6	11.3	11.9	12.7	13.4	14.1	14.9	15.7	16.5	17.4	18.2	19.1	20.0	20.9	21.9	22.8	23.8	24.8	25.8	26.9	27.9
31.5	6.0	6.6	7.1	7.7	8.2	8.8	9.5	10.1	10.8	11.4	12.1	12.9	13.6	14.4	15.2	16.0	16.8	17.7	18.5	19.4	20.3	21.3	22.2	23.2	24.2	25.2	26.3	27.3	28.4
32.0	6.1	6.7	7.2	7.8	8.4	9.0	9.6	10.3	10.9	11.6	12.3	13.1	13.8	14.6	15.4	16.2	17.1	17.9	18.8	19.7	20.7	21.6	22.6	23.6	24.6	25.6	26.7	27.7	28.8
32.5	6.2	6.8	7.3	7.9	8.5	9.1	9.8	10.4	11.1	11.8	12.5	13.3	14.0	14.8	15.6	16.5	17.3	18.2	19.1	20.0	21.0	21.9	22.9	23.9	25.0	26.0	27.1	28.2	29.3
33.0	6.3	6.9	7.4	8.0	8.6	9.3	9.9	10.6	11.3	12.0	12.7	13.5	14.3	15.1	15.9	16.7	17.6	18.5	19.4	20.3	21.3	22.3	23.3	24.3	25.3	26.4	27.5	28.6	29.7
33.5	6.4	7.0	7.5	8.1	8.8	9.4	10.1	10.7	11.4	12.2	12.9	13.7	14.5	15.3	16.1	17.0	17.9	18.8	19.7	20.6	21.6	22.6	23.6	24.7	25.7	26.8	27.9	29.0	30.2
34.0	6.5	7.1	7.7	8.3	8.9	9.5	10.2	10.9	11.6	12.3	13.1	13.9	14.7	15.5	16.4	17.2	18.1	19.1	20.0	21.0	21.9	23.0	24.0	25.0	26.1	27.2	28.3	29.5	30.6
34.5	6.6	7.2	7.8	8.4	9.0	9.7	10.4	11.1	11.8	12.5	13.3	14.1	14.9	15.7	16.6	17.5	18.4	19.3	20.3	21.3	22.3	23.3	24.3	25.4	26.5	27.6	28.8	29.9	31.1
36.0	6.9	7.5	8.1	8.7	9.4	10.1	10.8	11.5	12.3	13.1	13.9	14.7	15.6	16.4	17.3	18.3	19.2	20.2	21.2	22.2	23.2	24.3	25.4	26.5	27.6	28.8	30.0	31.2	32.4
36.5	7.0	7.6	8.2	8.9	9.5	10.2	11.0	11.7	12.5	13.2	14.1	14.9	15.8	16.7	17.6	18.5	19.5	20.5	21.5	22.5	23.6	24.6	25.7	26.9	28.0	29.2	30.4	31.6	32.9
37.0	7.1	7.7	8.3	9.0	9.7	10.4	11.1	11.9	12.6	13.4	14.1	14.9	15.8	16.7	17.6	18.6	19.6	20.7	21.8	22.8	23.9	25.0	26.1	27.2	28.4	29.6	30.8	32.1	33.3
37.5	7.2	7.8	8.5	9.1	9.8	10.5	11.3	12.0	12.8	13.6	14.5	15.3	16.2	17.1	18.1	19.0	20.0	21.0	22.1	23.1	24.2	25.3	26.5	27.6	28.8	30.0	31.3	32.5	33.8
38.0	7.3	7.9	8.6	9.2	9.9	10.7	11.4	12.2	13.0	13.8	14.6	15.5	16.4	17.3	18.3	19.3	20.3	21.3	22.3	23.4	24.5	25.7	26.8	28.0	29.2	30.4	31.7	32.9	34.3
38.5	7.4	8.0	8.7	9.4	10.1	10.8	11.6	12.3	13.1	14.0	14.8	15.7	16.6	17.6	18.5	19.5	20.5	21.6	22.6	23.7	24.8	26.0	27.2	28.3	29.6	30.8	32.1	33.4	34.7
39.0	7.5	8.1	8.8	9.5	10.2	10.9	11.7	12.5	13.3	14.2	15.0	15.9	16.8	17.8	18.8	19.8	20.8	21.9	22.9	24.0	25.2	26.3	27.5	28.7	30.0	31.2	32.5	33.8	35.2
39.5	7.6	8.2	8.9	9.6	10.3	11.1	11.9	12.7	13.5	14.3	15.2	16.1	17.1	18.0	19.0	20.0	21.1	22.1	23.2	24.3	25.5	26.7	27.9	29.1	30.3	31.6	32.9	34.2	35.6
40.0	7.7	8.3	9.0	9.7	10.5	11.2	12.0	12.8	13.7	14.5	15.4	16.3	17.3	18.3	19.3	20.3	21.3	22.4	23.5	24.7	25.8	27.0	28.2	29.5	30.7	32.0	33.3	34.7	36.1
40.5	7.8	8.4	9.1	9.8	10.6	11.4	12.2	13.0	13.8	14.7	15.6	16.5	17.5	18.5	19.5	20.5	21.6	22.7	23.8	25.0	26.1	27.3	28.6	29.8	31.1	32.4	33.8	35.1	36.5
41.0	7.9	8.5	9.2	10.0	10.7	11.5	12.3	13.1	14.0	14.9	15.8	16.7	17.7	18.7	19.7	20.8	21.9	23.0	24.1	25.3	26.5	27.7	28.9	30.2	31.5	32.8	34.2	35.5	37.0
41.5	8.0	8.6	9.4	10.1	10.8	11.6	12.5	13.3	14.2	15.1	16.0	16.9	17.9	18.9	20.0	21.0	22.1	23.3	24.4	25.6	26.8	28.0	29.3	30.6	31.9	33.2	34.6	36.0	37.4
42.0	8.1	8.8	9.5	10.2	11.0	11.8	12.6	13.5	14.3	15.2	16.2	17.2	18.1	19.2	20.2	21.3	22.4	23.5	24.7	25.9	27.1	28.4	29.6	30.9	32.3	33.6	35.0	36.4	37.9
42.5	8.2	8.9	9.6	10.3	11.1	11.9	12.8	13.6	14.5	15.4	16.4	17.4	18.4	19.4	20.5	21.5	22.7	23.8	25.0	26.2	27.4	28.7	30.0	31.3	32.6	34.0	35.4	36.8	38.3
43.0	8.3	9.0	9.7	10.4	11.2	12.1	12.9	13.8	14.7	15.6	16.6	17.6	18.6	19.7	20.7	21.8	23.0	24.1	25.3	26.5	27.7	29.0	30.3	31.7	33.0	34.4	35.8	37.3	38.8
43.5	8.4	9.1	9.8	10.6	11.4	12.2	13.1	13.9	14.8	15.8	16.8	17.8	18.8	19.9	20.9	22.1	23.2	24.4	25.6	26.8	28.1	29.4	30.7	32.0	33.4	34.8	36.3	37.7	39.2
44.0	8.4	9.2	9.9	10.7	11.5	12.3	13.2	14.1	15.0	16.0	17.0	18.0	19.0	20.1	21.2	22.3	23.5	24.7	25.9	27.1	28.4	29.7	31.0	32.4	33.8	35.2	36.7	38.1	39.7
44.5	8.5	9.3	10.0	10.8	11.6	12.5	13.4	14.3	15.2	16.2	17.1	18.2	19.2	20.3	21.4	22.6	23.7	24.9	26.2	27.4	28.7	30.0	31.4	32.8	34.2	35.6	37.1	38.6	40.1
45.0	8.6	9.4	10.1	10.9	11.8	12.6	13.5	14.4	15.4	16.3	17.3	18.4	19.4	20.5	21.7	22.8	24.0	25.2	26.5	27.7	29.0	30.4	31.7	33.1	34.6	36.0	37.5	39.0	40.6

Uses formula of Weight in lbs = (Length x Girth x Girth)/750

This faded old chart for calculating a steelhead's weight from its length and girth dates back to the Madsen years.

work of the trust, which has an annual budget of over $56,000, is supported by the owners of the three fishing lodges on the river and by matching funding from the government of British Columbia.

The bulk of the financial support for the work of the trust comes from a foundation (www.babineriverfoundation.ca), established as a joint enterprise by the three lodges in 2003 to help preserve the river in its natural state. In the winter of 1986, the precursor Friends of the Babine had vigorously battled against forest industry plans for one or more additional bridge crossings,.

The allies then were the Cleggs, the Stewarts, from Babine Steelhead Lodge, the Wickwires, from Silver Hilton Lodge, and the Gobles, owners of a Smithers-based river-rafting company. Today each lodge guest pays a surcharge of between $200 and $250 and the provincial government contributes $1 for every $2 raised by visiting anglers, the large majority of them American. With over $100,000 raised already, the importance of the visitors' and other private donors' generosity cannot be overstated. All monies raised from the sale of this book will also go directly to the trust.

In an era when potential conflicts seldom find co-operative resolution among the competing users, the trust is setting an example that's of great significance to those with similar concerns. It's only been in place since 2004 but already there are many who would like to see a similar model adopted for the entire Skeena system.

Nothing is plain sailing when it comes to conservation and land-use decisions, and the Babine, like so many rivers, is under considerable and constant pressure. Pierce worries that sooner rather than later the appalling pine beetle invasion, which is relentlessly sweeping north and east through British Columbia's forests, will strike the Babine watershed leading to pressure for increased logging in areas that would otherwise be left untouched.

In the Skeena estuary, proposals for a number of new fish farms were recently strongly and successfully opposed (www.friendsofwildsalmon.ca), all the more so on account of the devastating impact that sea lice, associated directly with farmed Atlantic salmon, have on migrating wild Pacific salmon smolts (www.raincoastresearch.org). The North Coast Steelhead Alliance (www.northcoaststeelheadalliance.ca) is another powerful advocate on behalf of the precious wild steelhead in northwest British Columbia.

Add to these concerns the ongoing impact of the commercial salmon nets in the ocean approaches to the Skeena system, with the headwaters of the Babine river more than 275 miles from the sea, and the proposal for coal bed methane gas extraction in the Bulkley Valley—another important Skeena tributary—and you can appreciate why friends of the Babine are now working to speak with a collective voice through the Babine Watershed Monitoring Trust and the Babine River Foundation. This is truly a special river and they are determined to ensure it remains that way for future generations.

At the end of each remarkable day on the river, with the forked flames of the nightly campfire warming the cold night air, those of us fortunate to have fished the Babine talk not only about the thrill of watching big steelhead come up for a towed mouse, of mighty fish that can crush strong hooks in an instant, but also about the challenges of keeping this great river safe and secure for generations to come. There on the river's bank we pledged our support for this most worthy of causes.

—Reprinted with kind permission of Finland's quarterly
Chasing Silver *Magazine, issue # 2, 2008*

Who Hears When the Stones Cry Out?

By Pierce Clegg

Harou Hikawa fishes Canyon Pool from the spot where Pierce first noticed an 'alien head shaped rock' attached to an underwater peninsula that offered a good casting position. This rock was later washed away in a spring flood before he found another one very similar in appearance further upstream.

We have this guest named Dr. Ernie, a good doctor from Tucson, Arizona...you know, the kind of doctor you wish to get when you arrive at the Emergency Room after a bad traffic accident. Anyway, he finds himself on the Babine River one fall and is persuaded to try the dry line and wake a fly. It's October and not too many seasons ago, it was difficult to convince anglers to try the dry line or wake a fly when the snow or fall leaves were flying. It's Laura's Pool, river right, and a beautiful glassy-surfaced tail-out, the kind that makes you think surface fly since any slight break of the surface waters would shatter the mirror.

Ernie is casting and watching intently, the sun breaks through the trees up to his right or is it the sun, he now wonders...he becomes disoriented and dizzy...the shaft of light beaming through the trees so far away...what is it really...he must retreat from the wading before wading becomes swimming...no he must retreat before he is beamed up into the source of the light beam. Wow, what a story and to this day we can't get Ernie to dry line and probably never will again at Laura's Pool, river right.

For years I thought Ernie was just being funny about the whole thing. We often prodded him to tell the story. Funny descriptive words like 'the aliens are here', or 'something's out there watching'...these types of conversations with Ernie would become common.

Then one season Ernie took his wife to the Trout Lodge. There was another couple there, the Kaufmans, and the husband had also been a regular at the Steelhead Camp. One evening we were all on one of the log cabin porches and I asked Ernie to tell his dry-line, alien story. Well he did and I listened and then realized after years of hearing this story that Ernie really seemed to be telling the truth, at least I had to ask, "Ernie, are you serious?" He was.

We had a great housekeeper/cook's assistant, Curtis Barger. One season we were raising funds for the Babine River Foundation through a silent auction and other activities. One of these activities was to auction off Curtis's hair, beard and other body hair which we did over a number of weeks to the tune of around $5,000 U.S. in total. Some of his hair went to the fly-tying vise

and I tied up a Curtis beard fly as well. At a large run called Lower Trail I had two October guests from the Duranglers Flies and Supplies Shop and they were fishing sink tips. They would not try the dry line no matter how many stories we told. I had the Curtis fly ready to go and asked if they wouldn't mind me fishing downstream of them and they said "yes" as if to say "go ahead and fish your silly little dry fly."

As soon as that Curtis fly hit the river with its bulging, water-soaked wake, the steelhead were on it. The next 20 minutes was mayhem with six or so steelhead rising to it, getting hooked, getting un-hooked, getting landed. Every time one of them would come up to the surface I would look upstream and yell at those sink-tip jockeys and say: "Did you see that, did you see that?"

Well finally those bottom-dredging disbelievers waded to shore and started changing their fly lines to floating fly lines. I guess my excitement or sheer unintelligible ravings influenced them enough to give the waking fly a try. They waded back into the river and started casting waking flies and sure enough the steelhead began to boil on their flies. A couple were hooked and some half dozen surface takes were missed.

Then, for whatever reason they became dizzy, and disorientated to the point where they had to wade back to shore or fall in. I immediately thought of Ernie and the aliens or whatever super natural force was at work. Maybe and simply it has something to do with staring intently upon waking flies and the waters near them...maybe somehow us dry liners staring at waking flies get mesmerized? Ernie said to me later when I told him what had happened, "there's something out there."

For many seasons after these events, and mostly out of having fun with Ernie, I would look for alien head rocks on the river or in the river. Ernie spent a good portion of his time on the riverbank looking for heart-shaped rocks to bring back to his wife. Being a guide, I have lots of time to wander the riv-   er-banks and examine all sorts of things. While cruising in the jet boat, idling downstream, we guides are always searching for steelhead and the rock structures of the bottom can be interesting. I also like to search for grizzly tracks that are under the water.

One of our satellite cabin trip pools is called Canyon, basically because there is a small canyon section with tall walls of rock separated and sliced by the eons of time as the river cuts its way downstream. The head of the pool has always been a huge challenge to fly-fish. After many seasons trying to roll cast from the bank, I noticed an underwater peninsula of rock. Wading to the extended point of this peninsula was a little nerve-racking because to fall off it would mean swimming for sure.

At the end of the peninsula and to my laughing surprise, there was an alien-head-shaped rock attached to the peninsula. It had big eyes, as you can see in the picture. Once you were near it there was back-casting room or an easy roll cast to the best holding water of the pool. Since finding that peninsula and the alien head rock, we named this part of the Canyon Pool, Alien Rock. I was excited to tell Ernie and ever since we have been able to fly-fish this pool better and catch lots of great steelhead.

Now jump to the year 2008 and two significant things happened both relating to Ernie, alien rocks and the future of the Babine. Every spring we guides enjoy witnessing the river changes from the previous spring runoff. Some seasons we have lots of changes and some not. The last two seasons, 2007 and 2008, we had above-average spring runoffs. In fact the 2007 season was perhaps a 200-year flood event.

Guests will remember how much more difficult the wading and fishing was in that flood-year season of 2007. But in 2008, on my first return trip to Alien Rock, I immediately noticed it was gone. I mean totally gone, ripped off or broken off by something. Was it a chunk of ice or a tree or what...I don't know? The peninsula is still there but the Alien Rock is not, gone forever I assumed.

Or maybe not...early in the 2008 season I was guiding on a run upstream from Canyon Pool called Brooks Range, named after noted outdoor writer, Joe Brooks. He had written for *Field & Stream* magazine and has two Babine runs named after him. Anyway I was strolling along the shoreline while my guest was casting away...and there it was...a rock with very noticeable eyes staring at me. The rock was oval in shape about the size of a human head only the eyes were prominent. Upon closer examination, it seemed evident that the rock was man-made. So into my boat it went and later at camp I placed this rock upon an old tree stump adjacent to our campfire pit.

Every once in awhile a guest would notice and the more discerning ones would pick the rock up for a more detailed study. Ernie was one of these guests and he quickly pronounced it man-made. He also stated that I should put it back to wherever I found it, implying that the rock may be more important than we realize...that the rock could be somehow too important for us to have it in our possession.

Above: The origins of the Alien Head rock remain shrouded in mystery but this much is known. It is definitely man-made and has been identified as being of a frog's head with a possible link to a local clan. Archaeologist Rick Budhwa, research program manager with the Bulkley Valley Research Centre, in Smithers, consulted with various colleagues and with carvers and artists and it's generally agreed that it almost certainly predates what archaeologists call 'first contact,' thus strongly suggesting a First Nations association going back hundreds and perhaps thousands of years.

The newcomer walking into the main Steelhead Camp building for the first time is greeted with a unique display of photos and other memorabilia that echo the history of steelheading on the Babine over many, many years.

Other guest/physicians also examined the rock over the course of our 2008 season and they all concurred that the rock must be man-made. At season's end I took it home to Smithers and then gave it to a local archaeologist for further and more professional examination. So far the feedback from this archaeologist is confirming that this rock is indeed very interesting, man-made and further investigations are underway. This same archaeologist was involved in a recent archaeological investigation assessment on the Babine River near the present-day Federal Fisheries Weir.

Competing interests who, in turn, have recommended new development in the area are hotly contesting this area. Before development plans were to be authorized the archaeological investigations were needed since we know this weir area was once a prominent Indian village inhabited by thousands of people. As it turns out the very first shovel pushed into the ground revealed multiple layers of historical habitations.

One quick conclusion is that not even an outhouse shall ever be constructed on such high-value archaeological real estate. This made me think that the recently discovered rock was also stating the obvious...that the Babine River and its salmon and steelhead were a lifeline to a people once firmly entrenched in the watershed.

Perhaps the prophet Ernie is right that the rock should have been put back where it was found. I have been thinking about this as the time rolls on and more and more significance is derived from the rock.

Once again I have been reminded of my late grandfather, Rev. Julius Hansen, who told me about a great king that was riding a donkey into Jerusalem with hordes of people of competing interests who were praising this king. The rulers of the day questioned the king, suggesting he should instruct the people to stop praising him, and the reply was that if the praising people kept quiet, then the stones would cry out.

This story has some great parallels and symbolism to our newly discovered Alien Rock and the Babine watershed. For years we have been pushing for protection, conservation, zonation, special management of, and basically a very careful logging of, or not at all, of the Babine watershed. But not until confirmation of the weir area's cultural value, plus this newly discovered rock, do I now realize that if we do not let the people praise this great river, then the stones will cry out and now they are.

The different historical cultures of the Skeena watershed, which we now describe politically as those of the First Nation peoples, are slowly but surely becoming more of an influence in the watershed through political, legal and fishery management means. Their spiritual influences cannot be understated. This rock also represents a time when the First Nation peoples were firmly attached to a social system and holistic method of viewing the wilderness and nature.

I have often listened to this perspective in various land-use meetings and committees in which the First Nation peoples did participate until they felt they were not being listened to or taken seriously. What I liked from these perspectives was the notion of respect for the wild ecosystems and to keep that balance functioning. Our Second Nation notions seem to progress to this holistic management perspective more and more as time moves on. I think this is happening because we realize, like the culture before us, that a healthy environment is our future if we expect this planet to survive us.

How do we practise good logging, mining and overall development of the wilderness and still 'maintain' that ecosystem balance intact? Is it possible to do this or are we just too idealistic to even imagine it would be possible. If we fail to achieve a balance what are the consequences? Supposedly the spirit and intent of land-use plans is to find such a balance. The devil is in the details and that's where the word 'maintain' has become functionally meaningless. And so now we enter a phase where the stones and rocks cry out and will we hear them?

It's so obvious we are not listening to these cries. The salmon runs slowly depleting...the bears becoming more and more habituated...the wolves and predator-prey relationships dramatically changing as we increase the road densities in order to access saw logs...the siltation of creeks and streams... the pine beetle infestations partly created by putting out too many fires...it's all starting to add up and we still claim we are professionals doing our jobs much better than ever.

I think the word they used was a 'higher level' land-use planning process. Another term used is 'acceptable limits of change' where agreement can be found to change the zebra's stripes to spots. There are tradeoffs to protect one zone and have no protections somewhere else. A great and measured fragmentation is thought to be so thoughtful that even the wilderness values can't understand it. Build a road and guess what, the animals use it. Massive change to wilderness is status quo and changing that status quo in the name of a 'higher level' plan is still massive change plus further fragmentation.

I remember what seemed to be a great land-use planning method called Functional Integrated Resource Management but the acronym FIRM suggested too aggressive a stand for wild ecosystems so it was scrapped. So far it's the only credible land-use method I have ever seen on paper.

In a recent 2007 Forest Stewardship Plan prepared by West Fraser Mills Ltd, a Pacific Inland Resources Division located in Smithers, we read that an Archaeological Overview Assessment (AOA) identifies high archaeological potentials. Trouble is nobody is doing them unless they completely and obviously stumble upon a value indicating that there is some sort of cultural-heritage resource present. And no forest-

You don't see many split cane rods on rivers these days but Dr. Kent Davenport has a favourite 12 ft. Winston, made for him by Glenn Bracket about six years ago, that he puts to good use on the Babine each time he visits. He took this photo while he was playing a fish on The Spread, just downstream from Log Jam, and comments: "I always carry my small digital compact camera from a lanyard around my neck. If you don't have a camera where it's easy to get at, you could miss many great photos."

harvesting company in their right mind would go looking for cultural-heritage values or spend the money to do an AOA.

The Babine watershed is probably full of cultural-heritage values, particularly where salmon and steelhead values are found. But fish may be the tip of the iceberg of values. The point of bringing this example up is that there are many values in the Babine that don't overlay or complement clear-cut logging. Land-use plans were and are intended to recognize these values and where appropriate, reduce the cut, change road routes, delete areas from the cut altogether and a myriad host of other management prescriptions that are intended to protect things like wilderness values.

Competing values is not the solution. One industry should not be allowed to cancel out another in the name of land-use planning. Deliberate non-implementation and pathetically supported monitoring will not produce credibility. Maybe we should start listening to the stones since we seem incapable of truly and holistically managing world-class values...internationally recognized values layered in double-speak land-use plans.

The values of wilderness always lose in the face of unsustainable clear-cutting and road density overkill. And what is wilderness anyway...if we can't agree on what that is, then we aren't really capable of looking after it...even when competing interests say we should be. Lastly, wilderness tourism is no match for heavy industry and a public policy that doesn't value the wild. We use the wild until it is used up, that's what we do best.

The future of a wild Babine rests with groups like the Babine River Foundation and the Babine Watershed Monitoring Trust although their investment in the watershed pales in comparison to that of heavy industry. This David and Goliath battle has always been worth the time and effort spent slinging stones, so don't expect the rock or rocks to remain silent.

Part VII

Babine Briefly

by Peter McMullan

Two Huge Skeena Steelhead

*V*isiting fishermen arriving in Smithers Airport are inevitably drawn to the display case holding two huge Skeena steelhead. Unfortunately, for so many reasons, they were caught not by an angler but in the Department of Fisheries and Oceans (DFO) Tyee Test Fishery gillnet on August 1, 1998.

They weighed an estimated 41 pounds and 40 pounds respectively, not far off the world-record steelhead (42 pounds 2 ounces) captured at Bell Island, Alaska.

Scale readings, taken on behalf of the Fish and Wildlife Branch of the then B.C. Ministry of Environment, Lands and Parks, showed the larger fish was in its thirteenth year and was returning to spawn for the fourth time while the other fish was in its ninth year. Their respective measurements were 44.5 ins. x 26 ins. and 43.5 ins. x 26.5 ins.

It could be that their final destination was the Babine but without DNA analysis, there is no easy way of knowing which of the formidable family of Skeena tributaries produces a particular fish taken in the main river.

Outlining the life history of the steelhead, another Environment Ministry airport display tells visitors about summer steelhead:

"Ten thousand years ago, when most of Canada was blanketed in ice, steelhead swam in the ancient seas. As the ice retreated, steelhead moved farther and farther inland, colonizing the Skeena and her tributary streams.

Today, steelhead return to the streams of their birth after spending one to four years in the North Pacific Ocean, where some migrate nearly as far as Japan. Once in the river, these remarkable fish may travel more than 500 kilometers to reach the streams where they were spawned.

Returning steelhead may stay in the river for up to 10 months before spawning occurs, in May and June. The young hatch later in the summer and spend as many as five years in fresh water before reaching about 20 centimeters in length, after which they make a perilous journey to the sea to feed on marine life. Once at sea, their weight can increase by 100 fold or more— if they survive the many predators that seek them. Skeena steelhead are the largest on the planet and may exceed 20 kg [44 pounds] in weight.

Unlike other Pacific salmon species, steelhead are relatively fewer in number and may spawn as many as eight times.

Due to their arduous spawning journeys and long fresh water residency, these fish are especially vulnerable to predation and habitat changes. Their presence and abundance is an indicator of a healthy environment."

DFO Fence Enables Babine Sockeye Count

*The weir across the Babine has been in place since 1946 and allows the DFO to obtain an accurate count
of the sockeye salmon entering Babine Lake. It also provides a fishery for local First Nations.*

The Babine River Counting Fence, often referred to as the weir, occupies the full width of the river and has been operated since 1946 by Fisheries and Oceans Canada, also known as the Department of Fisheries and Oceans (DFO). It is located less than one mile downstream from Nilkitkwa Lake and 223 miles from the commercial fishing boundary at the mouth of the Skeena River.

The fence is used to provide an accurate escapement count of sockeye and other species of salmon entering Babine Lake. It is usually installed in early July and is opened to allow fish to move on upstream between 6:00 a.m. and 10:00 p.m. Counting is performed over a series of two-hour shifts by teams of up to four people, depending on the strength of the run.

Joy (Madsen) Jenkins recalls how, in the early days, Norlakes sports fishermen would come down as far as the fence by boat from Trout Lodge and then walk around it and on down the river casting for steelhead. "Ejnar soon had a path cleared along the banks and they could go as far as the Nilkitkwa River where they had great stretches of water to fish."

She adds: "The DFO established what was a little government town on the hillside, building a cook house and three cabins for the young men to live in for the summer while they counted salmon as they swam through the wooden channels of the fence."

The counting fence is located at or very close to the site of a fishing weir that was used by First Nations for thousands of years. In 1906 Fishery Officer Hans Helgerson described it as having "the most formidable and imposing appearance... constructed of an immense quantity of materials, through which not a single fish could get through. People were catching and processing three quarters of a million fish."

Today members of the Lake Babine Nation use the DFO counting fence for a dip-net fishery when there are sockeye and pink surplus to what is required for spawning. In 2008 this fishery, for both food and profit, produced 104,585 sockeye worth some $300,000.

Pierce Clegg observes that the emphasis at the fence now appears to have more of a commercial than a research basis. "This fishery is non-selective in that there is no way of knowing if the sockeye being taken there are from the enhanced stocks or from wild stocks on their way to other Babine Lake spawning areas. More controls are needed to ensure these vulnerable stocks are not fished-out altogether."

There is also an August 1-31 fly-fishing sports fishery for sockeye from a boundary sign about 80 meters below the weir—there is a no sports fishing zone upstream from there to the weir—to a sign near the confluence of the main river and Nichyeskwa Creek, downstream from the Nilkitkwa Forest Service Road bridge. This second sign also marks the boundary of the fly-fishing zone between June 16 and September 30. The sockeye sports fishery has been in place since the mid-1990s with a 2003 survey by the Babine Nation showing a catch of just over 6,400 fish.

*—With information from DFO,
BC Ministry of Environment and First Fish Consulting*

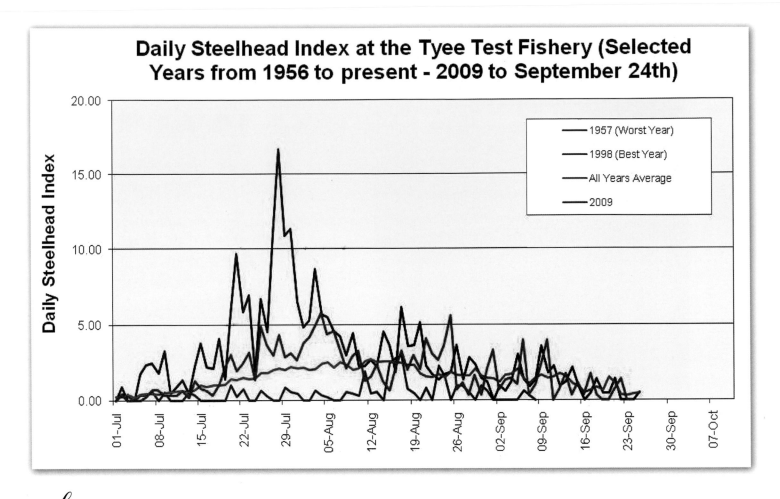

Daily Steelhead Index at the Tyee Test Fishery (Selected Years from 1956 to present - 2009 to September 24th)

Since 1955 the federal government's Department of Fisheries and Oceans (DFO) has operated a test gillnet fishery at Tyee, in the lower Skeena River, half way between Terrace and Prince Rupert. This fishery provides a daily in-season estimate of the numbers of salmon and steelhead returning to the Skeena system.

The 1200-foot net is set at high and low water slack during daylight hours, every day from early June to late August or early September, and is allowed to drift for exactly one hour. It is usual to make three sets a day but sometimes only two sets can be completed. The net is allowed to drift within a channel, between one and a quarter to just over three miles in length and approximately 260 feet wide, that runs parallel to the northern shoreline of the river.

According to the DFO: "The program was developed to provide daily estimates of sockeye escapements through the commercial fishery. The data obtained from this operation, combined with estimates of the commercial catch in Area 4, provides a complete picture of the sockeye and pink runs as they develop each year."

Daily returns from the Tyee Test Fishery are available through the Internet and are of great interest to Skeena system steelhead anglers in that they give a good indication of the strength of the run at any given time through August and September. The figures also enable comparisons to be made with previous years' statistics.

Pierce Clegg explains the methodology as follows: "It provides the only and best rough estimate of the salmon and steelhead runs of the Skeena system. How it works is based on a mathematically adjusted index number for each species of salmon and steelhead.

For example, for every steelhead caught in the net, they estimate 245 steelhead were passing the net at that moment. A count is kept of the daily catch of steelhead. This tells us how many have managed to avoid the commercial nets and are continuing on their way to the rivers that make up the Skeena system.

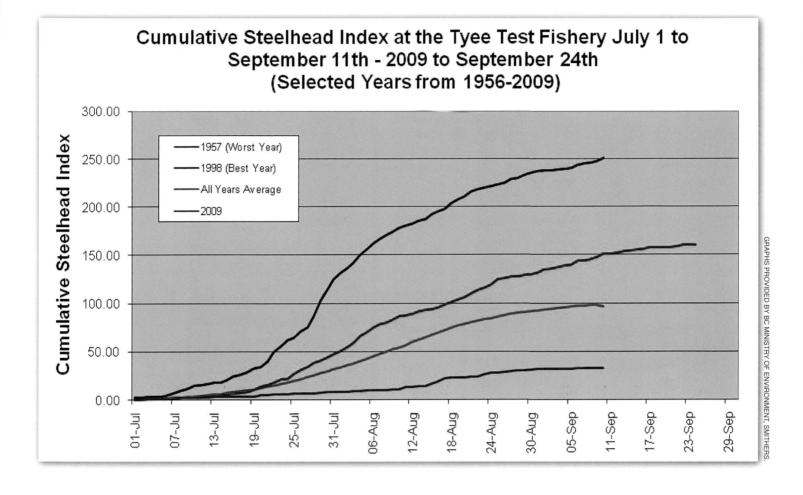

Cumulative Steelhead Index at the Tyee Test Fishery July 1 to September 11th - 2009 to September 24th (Selected Years from 1956-2009)

Legend:
- 1957 (Worst Year)
- 1998 (Best Year)
- All Years Average
- 2009

Y-axis: Cumulative Steelhead Index (0.00 to 300.00)
X-axis: 01-Jul to 29-Sep

The accuracy of the Tyee index is debated, and we know there was an overestimate of 38% in 2008, but it still provides a fair indication of the abundance or lack thereof of the runs. It's the only indicator we have and the DFO uses the index to manage the commercial net fishery at the mouth of the Skeena and in the approach waters. In 2009 the final Tyee figure was 166.20 on October 12. That translates into a run of 40,719 steelhead into all the Skeena rivers.

There have been years when the index was poor, but certain tributaries had good runs, and there have been years when the index was generally accurate for most tributaries. Recent DNA sampling and analysis studies are providing scientists with a much better idea of the contribution each of the Skeena rivers make to the overall stock each year.

I believe the Tyee index is fairly accurate but I think the most important factor is water conditions, optimally clean and dropping. There could be a huge run of steelhead but poor angler success if the water is dirty.

Also, we know from experience that increased angling pressure makes the fish harder to catch in the upper reaches. There are more active sports fishermen, more skilful fishermen, and the equipment they use has been greatly improved and that's another issue to be considered. If the fishermen catch more fish does it mean they will become staler earlier?

Provincial steelhead biologist Mark Beere adds: "Although Tyee speaks to trends in steelhead escapement, we still do not know the catchability of the net or how efficient it is at catching steelhead and therefore many assumptions are made (i.e. the catchability is 1/245, for instance).

My opinion of the Skeena steelhead escapement this year (2009) was that it was better than average but not quite as good as one would expect looking at individual stock-assessment projects. Tyee data suggests that this year (2009) was a little under last year's escapement and I believe this to be true."

—*With information from DFO and the B.C. Ministry of Environment*

Park a Precious Wildlife Sanctuary

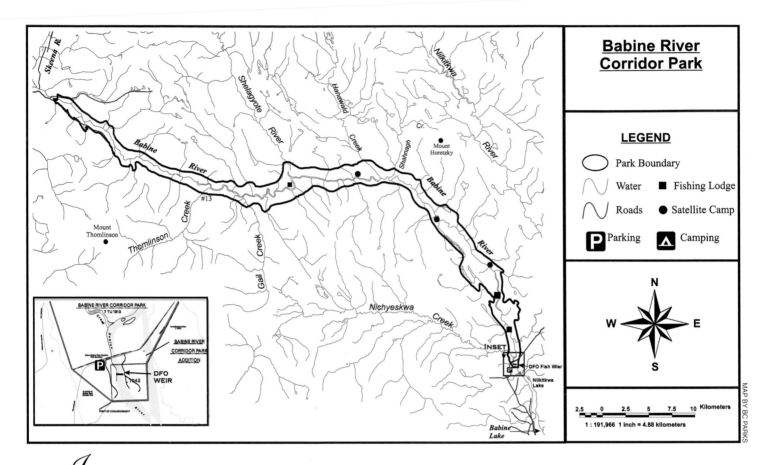

$\mathcal{I}$magine, if you will, a pencil-thin, green line snaking its way north and then west for 60 miles through some of the most spectacular country in Canada

That's the essence of the 36,936 acre Provincial Class A Babine River Corridor Park, a linear fish and wildlife sanctuary created by the Government of British Columbia in June, 1999 to preserve the heart and soul of the watershed from any further incursions by the forest industry or others intent on exploiting the natural resources of the area.

The park extends downstream along both banks of the river from the Nilkitkwa Forest Service Road bridge crossing to Kisgegas, a First Nations Reserve some six miles from the confluence with the Skeena River.

It's home to significant populations of grizzly bears, wolves, moose and bald eagles and many other smaller wildlife species while the river supports runs of chinook, coho, pink and sockeye salmon along with some of the largest steelhead in the world, as well as Dolly Varden and bull char.

These steelhead are a magnet for discerning catch-and-release fly-fishermen who gain access to the river by way of three remote fishing lodges. Drive-in, day anglers can fish from below the Department of Fisheries and Oceans' fish-counting weir, just upstream of the bridge crossing. In total it's just over 80 miles from Smithers to the bridge, including 36 miles of active logging road.

No overnight camping is permitted in the bridge area, as large numbers of grizzly bears are commonplace, especially in late summer and early fall at the height of the salmon runs. Up to 100 grizzlies visit the Babine River during the salmon season, making this river first and foremost in the world for its concentration of fish, eagles and bears. To reduce the risk of bear encounters, visitors are advised to view them only from the bridge walkway.

BC Parks describes the grizzlies as 'wild and respectful, and thus safe as long as you do not surprise them or threaten them.' Every effort continues to be made to ensure the animals do not become habituated to human presence.

To give the bears time to fish undisturbed during daylight hours, the day-use portion of the park is closed from one hour before sunset to one hour after sunrise.

The Babine also offers internationally significant rafting and kayaking opportunities, both guided and unguided, with around 18 miles of Class 3 and Class 4 category rapids. It is highly recommended that white-water runners have a leader who is familiar with the river with knowledge of its hazards. Contact BC Parks for names of experienced individuals.

A rustic, serviced campground with 10 moderate-sized campsites is located less than three miles west of the park entrance. Wilderness camping is allowed for park users traveling down river but no facilities are provided.

—With information from BC Parks

Skeena Steelhead Regulations Chronology: pre-1953-2010

Unspecified period up to and including 1953—40 fish annual limit on Lower Mainland rivers only.

1959   Season limit of 40 fish in all districts, daily limits of two fish in all districts except the North (still three), possession limit still three days' catch.

1970   Babine added to roe ban list.

1981   Province-wide annual quota of 10 steelhead. Annual limit of two on Babine and Kispiox.

1986   10 steelhead per year, two steelhead per month.

1987   10 per year, two per month; in-season notice, issued Aug. 17, going to one per year; in-season notice, issued Nov. 20, restoring two per month in main stem and tributaries downstream from Terrace.

1988   10 per year, two per month; in-season notice, issued June 10, going to one per year, effective July 1; in-season notice, issued July 8, going to zero quota in Babine, Bulkley and Kispiox and select other areas for remainder of season.

1989   10 per year, two per month; in-season notice, issued June 5, effective July 1, going to one per year; in-season notice, issued Aug. 28, going to zero quota in main stem and all tributaries upstream from Terrace, effective Sept. 1.

1990   One steelhead per year in effect for entire season.

1991   One per year; in-season notice issued effective Aug. 1 going to zero quota for remainder of season.

1992   One per year: in-season notice issued mid-summer going to zero quota.

1993   One per year; in-season notice issued Jan. 18 going to zero quota pending assessment of run strength around Aug. 1. No change thereafter.

1994   One per year; BC Freshwater Sportfishing Variation Order, issued July 11, going to zero quota, effective immediately.

1995   One per year; BC Freshwater Sportfishing Variation Order, issued June 5, going to zero quota, effective July 1.

1996   One per day, two per month; BC Freshwater Sportfishing Variation Order, issued June 14, going to zero quota, effective July 1.

1996   To present: Zero quota.

— BC Ministry of Environment
provided this information

Facts and Figures

The Babine River is a tributary of the Skeena River, which it joins 32 miles north of Hazelton. The watershed extends over 4,045 square miles making it the largest of the Skeena's sub-basin tributaries.

While the Babine is some 61 miles in length, its steelhead face a journey of around 275 miles if they travel, as some do, all the way from the mouth of the Skeena, just south of Prince Rupert, to their historic spawning grounds in tributary streams and in the Babine itself above and below the federal Department of Fisheries and Oceans' sockeye-counting weir.

This weir is located not far from where the river leaves Nilkitkwa Lake, a narrow extension of the huge Babine Lake, which is 110 miles long with a surface area of 85 square miles. The elevation at the weir is 2,250 feet above sea level while the elevation of Babine Lake is 2,333 feet.

The weir, which extends bank to bank, is located about three miles upstream of the Norlakes Steelhead Camp and is the site of the only boat-launch ramp on the upper river.

Babine steelhead start to arrive in the river in July and August with the Norlakes' sport-fishing season running from the second week in September into November when the demands of early winter weather can be considerable.

The steelhead over-winter in the river and lake before spawning in April and May, in the river and in its tributaries, among them Nichyeskwa Creek, Nilkitkwa River, and Shelagyote River.

Almost 17 miles or 28 percent of the lower third of the river is high-grade canyon water through which passage is only advised for the most experienced and well-equipped river rafters. There is also some lesser canyon water between the two lodges on the upper river, Norlakes' Steelhead Lodge and Babine Steelhead Lodge, and Silver Hilton Steelhead Lodge further downstream.

Access to the two upper lodges is by way of a two-hour drive, on mostly gravel roads, from Smithers to the launching ramp at the DFO fence, and then by outboard jet-powered boat, while Silver Hilton Lodge uses helicopters to bring in guests and supplies.

All steelhead anglers must have in their possession (1) a British Columbia freshwater angling licence, (2) a Steelhead Conservation Surcharge Stamp and (3) where appropriate, an additional British Columbia Classified Waters Licence.

The Babine is rated as a Class One River between September 1 and October 31 and a special Classified Waters Angling Licence is required. The river is closed to all angling between January 1 and June 15.

Licence fees vary for residents, non-residents and non-resident aliens (NRA), e.g. those fishermen from a country other than Canada. NRAs face other restrictions as detailed in the B.C. Freshwater Fishing regulations.

Sport fishing for wild steelhead throughout B.C is on a catch-and-release basis. The use of bait, usually salmon or steelhead roe, has been banned on the Babine since 1970.

The three lodges operating on the river promote fly-fishing over all other legal methods and Norlakes Steelhead Camp introduced a fly-only rule for its guests, starting September 2009.

Facts and Figures

It's not easy to obtain accurate estimates of the total number of steelhead entering the Skeena and its tributaries each year. The runs fluctuate and the total for the entire system—a watershed extending over 4,045 square miles—can be up to 55,000 with the Babine's share a conservative 2,500 to 4,500 and perhaps more. Those numbers were likely at least doubled in the era before enhanced sockeye runs.

DNA sampling at the Tyee Test Fishery in 2007 and 2008 showed that the Babine provided 13.2% and 11.2% of the total Skeena steelhead stock. In both years it was the Morice that made the biggest contribution to the annual run, 18.65% in 2007 and 23.6% in 2008.

The B.C. Fish and Wildlife Branch creel survey reported that, on average, 474 anglers caught 3,678 Babine River steelhead each year between 1985 and 1995. These totals are based on responses to an annual questionnaire and may be on the high side. They also include fish caught and released more than once.

In 2007/08 Babine River angler effort statistics indicate 425 rods fished 2,574 days for a recorded catch of 3,092 steelhead. This was the second highest number of steelhead reported since 2000/01 with the 2001/02 figures leading the way: 738 anglers fishing 5,329 days and landing 7,332 steelhead.

Province-wide creel survey figures for the 2006/07 season (1996/97 figures in brackets) show 11,948 (13,296) active anglers, 7,569 (8,329) of whom were successful, kept 3,629 (6,280) steelhead and released another 61,417 (85,081) in 103,841 (149,730) angling days. In 1996/97, 19,608 steelhead licences were issued compared to 17,494 in 2007/08 and 30,198 in 1989/90.

There would be many, many more steelhead in the Skeena system today were it not for the deadly toll taken by the commercial seine and gill-net fleets operating in both Alaskan and British Columbian waters. They mainly target sockeye and pink salmon but continue to account for very significant incidental catch numbers of steelhead as the various stocks intermingle.

It is estimated that the annual commercial catch of steelhead in Alaskan and B.C approach waters accounts for over 40 percent of the total Skeena steelhead run each year.

This remains a huge concern to all with an interest in the future of Skeena steelhead. The economic value of the steelhead sports fishery to the local economy, as a generator of tourism income worth upwards of $52.8 million annually, far exceeds the value of the commercial salmon catch, most recently estimated at $15.2 million a year.

Federal government spawning channels were built between 1968 and 1971 on Fulton River and Pinkut Creek following a steady, historic decline in Babine Lake sockeye runs. This enhancement effort, and the commercial fishery it supports, continues to place tremendous pressure on Skeena steelhead, especially the early-running July and August stock, which are present at the height of the commercial sockeye fishery.

Babine Lake, the largest naturally occurring lake in B.C., accounts for approximately 90% of all the sockeye returning to the Skeena system as a whole, supporting enhanced runs that, in peak years, can be measured in millions of fish: 6.9 million in 1996, almost 4 million in 1998 and 2.5 million in 1999. In 2008 the figure was well over 2 million.

Down through the years it has been the intense commercial response to these runs, involving hundreds of boats, the large majority of them (300 and more) gillnetters, that has depleted not only the steelhead but also weaker and smaller stocks of sockeye from other Skeena system rivers, including the Babine tributaries, along with annual runs of coho and chinook salmon.

In 2009 the Skeena sockeye run was forecast at 2.1 million but only 886,352 returned resulting in the all but complete curtailment of the North Coast commercial sockeye fishery and improved steelhead numbers at the Tyee Test Fishery.

PART VIII

The Letters at Christmas

The annual December letters span 30 years of history, both personal as it relates to the two families—the Madsens and the Cleggs—who between them have owned and operated Babine Norlakes Lodge and Steelhead Camp since the very early 1950s, and from the perspective of the fishing for the system's abundant rainbow and steelhead trout. Those fortunate enough to be included on a mailing list, now numbering in the hundreds of addresses, wait eagerly for their annual letter, hoping perhaps to see their own name in print or to read about the adventures of friends made on previous visits. Regrettably, and almost inevitably, the passage of time has accounted for the correspondence from the early years but we have managed to collect every letter from 1978 to the present, a priceless assembly of news and views, humor and opinion. The first Madsen letters required only a single sheet; the most recent from the Cleggs, recalling the events of 2009, show at least a sevenfold increase in content and are presented on glossy, four-color paper complete with illustrations. Together, they paint a striking and fascinating picture of day-to-day life on the Babine system while also telling the story of a quite extraordinary quality of fishing, especially in those early days. The letters total over 50,000 words with the following just a small sample of the complete collection now assembled at the Babine Norlakes website (www.babinenorlakes.com).

Madsens, 1980

It is December now and the snow-white Hudson Bay and Babine Mountains stand out sharply against a bright, blue sky in the clear, cold air. The lodge has been tucked in for the winter and all is quiet with the lake frozen over.

The season just past was, for us, a good start to the 1980s and seldom in years gone by have the piscatorial rewards on the Babine been greater. Spring came early and the lake was free of ice by the beginning of May. The trout were big and hungry and there were plenty of them, both in river and lake. Except for a few cool days, the first half of summer was pleasantly warm and ideal for fishing and fly hatches. 'It gets better every year,' said Bill and Solly Smith who were celebrating their 20th annual fishing work-out (they call it a vacation) at the lodge by catching more than ever before. After the middle of July, the weather cooled and with it for a while, came the good fly-fishing in the river. Trolling in the lake continued at a hot pace with many trophies boated. Al Leonard, the headhunter, brought in the largest on a Muddler. It weighed 11 3/4 pounds and had reached the ripe old age of 10 years.

It was with some apprehension that we opened the River Camp for steelhead fishing on September 6. Was it going to be another slow fishing year as in 1979? We need not have worried. The steelies were there in numbers from day one and Vic Rempel landed 26 of 33 hooked in the first week. Several others did even better during the fall but Vic took all of his the hard way, on flies. Fishing continued as it began and everyone was catching steelhead.

The big turkey, those over 20 pounds, were not always prominent but perhaps that was because the small fry, weighing between 10 and 16 pounds, beat them to it. However, there were a few landed measuring over 40 inches. And why were the steelhead so plentiful this year? Well, it was probably a large run anyway but, because of more restricted commercial fishing, a bigger percentage got through. Everyone appreciated the excellent fishing, whatever brought it on. Marie, our precious cook, also took her daily swing at them with good results.

Beside Marie, our able kitchen help at the Lodge included, at various times, Gail, Janie, Karen 1 and Karen 2 and Bandit, our bear dog. Brent and Erik were the fish finders, fly tiers and wharf builders. Brent was also the official bear finder although sometimes the roles were reversed.

Norlakes Lodge
1980

Merry Christmas

Dear Friends:

It is December now and the snow-white Hudson Bay and Babine Mountains stand out sharply against a bright blue sky in the clear, cold air. The lodge has been tucked in for the winter and all is quiet with the lake frozen over.

The season just past was, for us, a good start on the 80's and seldom in years gone by have the...

1983, Ejnar Madsen's death from cancer in September left Joy, Karen, Karl and Erik to write:

The buildings along the Babine are silent now. A gentle snow muffles even the winter bird song as the Lodge and River Camp wait for another season to begin. Time to reminisce about the season past. 1983 was a year of sorrow for all of us as Ejnar lost a gallant battle with cancer. Our loyal and dedicated staff, as well as understanding, compassionate guests gave us the strength to carry on in this difficult time.

The lake was free of ice by May 1, the earliest break-up the local Indians ever remember. Karl and Erik were opening up by May 10, joined briefly by Ejnar who was able to enjoy spring in the country he loved so dearly. It was a warm May and the dry-fly fishing was at its best by early June, a great bonus to the wet-fly fishing more common at that time of year. Then the rains came and continued for most of the summer, until the local wildlife started pairing off and heading for higher ground. Mayfly hatches were spotty, depending on the temperature, and the lake weed beds showed very little throughout with most of the action in the river.

In mid-June, Larry Tripp had some of the finest fishing he could recall in a long life of angling and Bill Fife charmed staff and guests alike, as he has since 1957. Young Kyle and Evan Johnstone hooked some good fish and began to exhibit fine fly-casting technique under the watchful eye of their grandfather. As June drizzled into July the fishing declined, a disappointment after the exciting days enjoyed earlier.

Some large trout were hooked during the stonefly hatches but most managed to leap free. Dwayne and Tunney McClendon were so successful that the guides started watching them in an effort to learn their secrets. Ralph Allen didn't know until Father's Day that his daughter, Mandy, would be up here too, a fine family surprise for him. We were pleased to welcome back Ed and Lura Struve after a long absence and to meet Mr. and Mrs. John Congreve and Tom Speir, who traveled from England to try the fishing in North America.

We opened the Steelhead Camp on September 1 with Karl at the helm in place of Ejnar. It was a year with many bears, both black and grizzly, but not so many steelhead. Fisheries reported a poor run throughout the Pacific Northwest but, so far, have not come up with an explanation. Ejnar passed away September 13 and, at the request of the fishermen in camp that week, the Camp Pool was renamed Ejnar's Pool. In the absence of Karl, the following morning Dick Andersen took the coffee around to the cabins and, on the day of the funeral, Bob Tindel played taps on his horn for the last time. It was the end of an era and Chick Stewart gave a touching eulogy at the service.

In spite of the slow fishing, Hugh Benton landed a 42-1/2-inch buck at Log jam, Gene Tennyson had a 42-inch buck on a fly and Dave Hunter wrestled one of equal size before releasing it. The weather was mild and overcast most of the fall, making it pleasant to be on the river with water conditions fairly stable throughout. Joe Ferguson had the distinction of hooking a beaver on a dry fly while Dean Skorheim caught a 22-pound buck on a fly above the weir. Bill Herzog and Shawn Mills continued the tradition of the initiation swim and Chuck Davis did so well with flies that he has given up the casting rod. It is gratifying to report that most of the steelhead were released to spawn and thereby ensure the continuation of this magnificent race of fish.

We feel as deep gratitude for a job above and beyond that call of duty from Marie and Todd for the season at both camps, and from Kathy Robertson in the summer and Cathy Peterson for the fall. Without them we would have surely faltered.

Madsens, 1986

*The final Christmas letter from the Madsen family—Joy, Karen, Karl and
Erik—announced the sale of Norlakes thus severing a link stretching all the
way back to 1953, when Ejnar joined Mac Anderson and Tom Stewart to build
a two-storey lodge and cabins on the shore of Babine Lake. The letter explained;*

*Ejnar and Joy with their three children and Trout Lodge staff member Coleen Wall,
far right. Karen is seated beside Ejnar with Karl, in the life jacket and Eric.*

As many of you already know, the kids and I have sold Norlakes Lodge to Pierce and Debby Clegg. They plan to operate it much as we did and we encourage all of you to continue your annual trips and enjoy the wonderful fishing on the Babine. They will do a good job.

As you can imagine, it was no small decision for us to sell and we already miss the wonderful way of life we enjoyed there but we decided it was time for us to give it up and go on to new things. Karl, Erik, and Karen have many plans for the future in the education and business fields and they must be free to pursue these interests. As for me, I am getting older and I think it takes young people to run the lodge the way it should be done.

We will miss all of you very much but we have kept the Phillips cabin and five acres of land on Babine Lake and I am sure we will find ourselves out there for a good part of the summers. It will not be possible for me to know when you are coming up, so for those of you who would like to see us, please let me know in advance. I am happy in my home here and I will live here for the present. All three kids live in Vancouver. We are in close touch and they hope to be free to come up in the summers.

Not everyone can write a book, but I have decided to give it a try. When I look back on the 31 years I have spent living in the wilderness, in what must be one of the most beautiful spots in all the world, and the experiences that Ejnar and I shared as a young couple, meeting there, getting married and raising three children; running it as a family business as the children were big enough to help, I feel a great desire to write it down and share it with others. I have no expertise as a writer but I am willing to give it a try. I am asking you to help—will you share some of your experiences at the lodge with me? Ejnar had such wonderful dry humour and I know that many of you shared some funny (and sad) times with him that would be worth putting in the book. I would be very grateful if you would take the time to write down some of these things and send them to me. I would like the book to be a tribute to Ejnar. He was a unique man who loved what he did and did it so well. What a great legacy he built and left for all of us.

Please do not think of this letter as goodbye. The meaningful friendships that have developed and grown between us over these many years are a very important part of my life and the kids feel the same way. I would like to keep in touch with you and know that we can see you when we return to Smithers. We look forward to hearing from you.

Have a happy holiday season with family and friends and drink a toast to the Madsens as we each embark on a new life. The four of us will be together here for Christmas and will drink to all of you and the wonderful times we shared at Norlakes.

Cleggs, 2009

The snow is falling, the holidays are calling and we wish you all the best for the New Year and beyond.

Memories of the feelings created by a place, a moment, a smell, a sight and the connection: inexplicable, unbelievable…a huge fish strikes and all of a sudden we know why we are here. Whether it's a trophy rainbow trout or the close cousin, the steelhead, there is a 'blood brothering' that is sometimes literal. I picture countless memories of guests wrestling with a huge, lifetime-sized male or female steelhead with its sharp teeth and the live eye…then a quick move and the angler is cut, blood flowing into the river, fish released…it's a rush.

Back to the lodge or camp, back to the Babine family; a cast of anglers and friends…one week to share, laugh and try to figure out a few things about fishing, casting, rods and lines, then a few beers or your favourite brew. Maybe you'll go back to your cabin, prepare for another day, repair the waders, revisit your fly-line strategy, dry off your fishing clothes and try to be ready for another day in a wild place, a wild river and very wild fish.

Veteran guests and veteran guides marvel at the newcomer. Do you recall that first trip, that first day on a river you've never fished before? It's hard to believe it but it's your arrival day, a great first day of a much-looked-forward-to holiday. Counting the days, even years, communicating the excitement through mail, e-mail, the website photos and video clips, or maybe a friend has you over for dinner just to tune you up.

I began writing this letter during the Yankee Thanksgiving holidays with 24 seasons of thankfulness to think about. Nearly a quarter century of the Babine is enough to make me realize just how fortunate we all have been. My mind is always in debate after a season with memories of Babine, the river, and the ever-pondering question of why this river does to us what it does.

The Norlakes 2009

Season's Greetings

The snow is falling, the holidays are calling and we wish you all the best for the New Year and beyond.

Memories of the feelings created by a place, a moment, a smell, a sight and the connection: inexplicable, unbelievable…a huge fish strikes and all of a sudden we know why we are here. Whether it's a trophy Rainbow trout or the close cousin, the Steelhead, there is a 'blood brothering' that is sometimes literal. I picture countless memories of guests wrestling with a huge lifetime-sized male or female Steelhead with its sharp teeth and the live eye… then a quick move and the angler is cut, blood flowing into the river, fish released…it's a rush.

Back to the lodge or camp, back to the Babine family; a cast of anglers and friends…one week to share, laugh and try to figure out a few things about fishing, casting, rods and lines, then a few beers or your favourite brew. Maybe you'll go back to your cabin, prepare for another day, repair the waders, revisit your fly-line strategy, dry off your fishing clothes and try to be ready for another day in a wild place, a wild river and very wild fish.

Veteran guests and veteran guides marvel at the newcomer. Do you remember that first trip, that first day on a river you've never fished before? It's hard to believe it but it's your arrival day, a great first day of a much-looked-

Babine Norlakes Management Ltd.
SMITHERS, BRITISH COLUMBIA

I began writing this letter during the Yankee Thanksgiving holidays with twenty-four seasons of thankfulness to think about.

Nearly a quarter century of the Babine is enough to make me realize just how fortunate we all have been.

My mind is always in debate after a season with memories of Babine, the river, and the ever pondering question of why this river does to us what it does.

Whatever the cards or fate that came together, you are now here maybe never even fly-fished before or ever caught a steelhead in your life. Suddenly your waking fly is no longer just gliding across the surface undisturbed. Eruption of water, large head, and jaws clenched on the fly, rod flexed, reel heating up fast and adrenaline flowing...it's your first steelhead ever landed and it's over 20 pounds..." I did not expect this," she exclaimed. Yukari Watanabe, all the way from Japan and her first steelhead is 40 inches long by 22 inches girth. The guide did not expect the tingling sensation moments before the strike. He did not expect this river once again to connect and surge the message, "get ready." But the river does this time and time again... the newcomer's experience, the seasoned guide's surprise...this is a river of greatness beyond words, as Peter McMullan puts it, "beyond belief."

Why so great? A local biologist and young father of two sons recently commented from much research and expertise on steelhead: "The Babine is the greatest wild steelhead river in the world." That big lake, 110 miles long, the longest natural freshwater lake in B.C....the natural slow tail waters flowing into another nursery called Nilkitkwa Lake...the relationship between rainbow tout and steelhead, and then there is the habitat. The finest of natural habitat grows the interrelationship of fin and forest, first the old culture—where once there were thousands are now only hundreds at best. Now we discover it all over again only to use our new technologies to alter the course of history, of habitat, of species and ultimately ourselves.

It's all too easy to imagine the size of this grizzly as it marked its passage through the riverbank mud.

I dedicate yet another annual letter to the family Babine. These are hardcore lovers of the wilderness and its values who met the same fate as I. "We didn't expect this. We didn't know what a real or reel love for a river could be. We've had our ups and downs in life and on the river too, but we keep coming back. Neither terrorism nor the economy can keep us from making our annual pilgrimage to a river connection, a fix we need, a place to mind-rest, a place to have way too much fun and leave it there. I lift my rod to those that scrimp and save the dollars. I lift my Molson Canadian beer to those who travel against doctor's advice and for the love of the place, show up. I rise up early in the morning to prepare the sacraments of the coffee tray for those that honour the memory of Ejnar and what he did at great personal expense. In a new age of longer rods and deadly flies I still applaud the simple satisfaction that comes from a grin on the face of a guest who didn't expect what they caught.

After all these seasons I have found myself finally venturing out away from the river. Not pouring over maps or reports from afar or going to countless meetings battling over the obvious, but wandering amongst the giant pine trees so much larger than normal...no wonder the clear-cutters wanted them so badly. Follow a grizzly bear trail and stumble upon old-growth wonders, not just the huge trees but also the old broken-down and rotting pieces of archaeology telling a much different story of survival and prosperity. Old growth also means old souls and old living things like Mycelium, a threadlike, interconnecting, living organism that is the producer of mushrooms, but only old-growth Mycelium produces very large mushrooms. I am no longer wondering why old-growth watersheds produce large trees, large fish, and large bears, large anything. Large lake, large habitat, old growth...it all adds up to one hell of a significant feeling in our minds and to experience it is to be a part of its spirit and intent. As the Order of Canada-winning rock band Rush said, "Catch the spirit...catch the drift."

Where in the world can you find a steelhead river where almost daily a 20-pounder is landed? And where can the angler go who has never been or has never caught, and be the one this day to say, "I did not expect this?' There is only one Babine, so the slogan says, but the evidence speaks for itself. As Mongo from the movie "Blazing Saddles" said, "I am just a pawn in the game of life." I say never underestimate the pawn in game of life. And so we fight for wild watersheds, we fight against open-net-cage fish farms, we fight against so-called selective gillnets, we fight against coalbed methane mining proposed for the upper Skeena watershed and 'we keep on keeping on' even if it seems like we might lose in the end. There is no loss for those who fight for clean water, air, land and spirit, and look what victories we have that buy us precious time to pass on to our children. It's never futile to make one more cast in a Babine pool where for the last four hours no fish has cared. It is futile to believe that no one will ever care and that in the end nothing will change. Individuals throughout history have changed much.

Look at the work of Alexandra Morton or the thoughtful strategies for the Skeena watershed by Richard Overstall. These are just two individuals changing history in watersheds and ocean environs. Look at Save Our Salmon and the passion of one man, Eric Hobson, to change the status quo. The Babine River

A familiar sight every morning after breakfast at Steelhead Camp as fishermen
prepare to leave for another full day on the river.

Foundation and the Babine Watershed Monitoring Trust, these are two legacies that the Babine family as individuals can be proud of and continue to support. Through partnership with outside funds or from within, there has been victory over expanding fish farms to the north coast. The battle on the south coast continues, but many cracks in the fish-farm dyke have weakened the idiots of government who think they know better.

Ali Howard swam the Skeena to highlight a great watershed and to link the historical cultures of the watershed with the present-day modernism of economics and development. What kind of watershed do we want for future generations? I think not the kind planned for. We seem to be a watershed of individuals full of discontent with the *status quo* who rise up and fight, and we all can be a part of the victories and efforts. There are huge efforts of individuals with a different vision for the future, one in which the old-growth values that I have mentioned will survive well into the 21st century. Every penny from our guest surcharge has been well spent with far-reaching influence throughout B.C. The Babine family has given back and we thank you dearly for it.

So there is hope for the future and I am still filled with excitement to renew my own bond with the Babine beginning each spring. Larry Hartwell and I were pushing the limits of excitement as we tried to reach the Trout Lodge early this spring and were stopped by too much ice. Our transfer boat, loaded with our first supplies, bashing and crashing through the ice, met its match around Nine Mile Point where the ice became too thick to

break through. So we returned to Tukii Lodge at Smithers Landing, unloaded the boat and drove to Fort Babine Lodge and found no ice from there to the Trout Lodge, a first since 1986. It was a long day of loading and unloading the transfer boat and we both fell into our respective cabins, early to bed, exhausted, but early to rise the next morning.

It was a strange season for weather, water conditions and fishing. There was above normal snow pack, a late spring with unusually colder lake-water temperatures followed by a record heat wave and drought conditions. We were lucky not to have much lightning, but some fires were close to the lodge and attacked by firefighting crews. The cold winter months made the deep waters of Babine Lake much colder than my memory could recall and even after the record heat wave the lake was slow to warm. As a result the hatches were late, but they were good when they arrived. Rainbow Alley, the Nilkitkwa Lake weed beds, the lower river stonefly hatch and the below-the-weir trout fishing were all stellar most of the time. But after the Trout Lodge was closed for the season, Larry and I looked back and agreed that "it was not what we expected."

From heat stroke in July to snowing in November, a full season on the Babine is always an adventure and this season was no less surprising or rewarding. Soon I will be sending out confirmations for the 2010 season and soon we will all be reliving a countdown to a river experience of a lifetime. I enjoyed my 50th birthday last season and Anita and I realize that the future for us

will be different. If we are to continue on serving the Babine family, we realize we must downsize our two operations in order to still serve the fantastic goodwill that is the Babine family. For the first time in Norlakes history the Trout Lodge will offer just a 30-day season from mid-June to mid-July. This will include a return to the grill by Anita which you won't want to miss. There will be a couple of housekeeping cabins, unguided, and it will be great to once again provide meals, accommodation and guiding to four lucky guests per week at the main lodge. The Steelhead Camp will also be downsized to a maximum of 11 guests per week with perhaps some more downsized weeks for the future. Many of you know that we are planning on selling the Steelhead Camp in the future, but until we actually get an offer, we plan to continue on with the same energy and drive to enjoy possibly many more seasons with our Babine family.

It won't matter how many seasons I am graced to experience the Babine; I always love the beginning at the Trout Lodge. It was here that the sportfishing story began, and it was here that a pioneering of the Babine River for fly-fishing began. And when I arrive and smell the grounds as they thaw and walk the paths, I am renewed just as the springtime renews so many living things. The old log cabins and the various colours that their age gives in the evening light, bring back my memories and I wonder about memories before my time here. Getting old things to work again and getting new things to work like old things, Larry Hartwell and I know what needs to be done and we just start in on it all. The fresh air, the sounds of the creek growing in size as the snow melts, in fact, all the sounds seem heightened because they are different than the sounds of a typical city home. No electronics and so many city noises are replaced by the wind, the leaves crackling, the lakeshore waves lapping or the birds looking for some seed. That old friend wilderness cannot be replaced by the TV or a drive in the country. I cannot recreate what is renewing itself each spring and I love it.

It's always interesting to watch the breakup of lake ice and to sit on the porch one sunny afternoon and listen to all the sounds of spring. The days grow longer and the sunsets seem to creep further into a day's fatigue. So it's time to do the first campfire of the season and stare into the flames once again. The old lodge fireplace needs extra attention too, since a winter of frozenness takes time to thaw, and Larry is always stoking the fire so he can sleep without seeing his breath. One great way to warm up the lodge in the spring is to cook a turkey, which also makes for a great meal and leftovers. Anyway you cut it, a fire in the wilderness, inside or outside, is always appreciated in the spring.

Summers in the wilderness are full tilt with enjoying it, for all living creatures know that summertime in the north is short and fleeting. The insects know it too, so don't be bothered by itching and Deet. I don't care what other products or advertising that tries to get us away from that dreaded, supposedly cancer-

Sunshine, high clouds and dense forest frame the durable aluminium boat and jet drive outboard that are key to Babine River mobility for steelhead guide and fisherman alike.

causing Deet...don't buy into the go-green bug crap and get the real deal. But with bugs come bug-eating fish and the Babine fish begin with the T-bones-like stoneflies and mayflies and not the midges. So it doesn't matter if you live beneath the surface of the waters or above, summer is the time to make hay while the sun shines and we all do. The 2009 summer set records for heat and I mean heat-stroke-producing heat. And when you are drifting on the surface waters enjoying that reflective heat on top of record-breaking heat, well, I never dipped my hat and poured it over my head so many times as last summer.

Cottonwood trees are the suckers of water. It is incredible how much water they drink and hold but it was hot enough last summer that even the cottonwood trees had trouble supplying water to their leaves so some of the leaves burned up. I thought the drought would spell challenges for certain things like berries or low water for the fall but trying to predict the future in the wilderness seems futile. In the end the berry crop was a banner yield and the low water never materialized as the fall rains came and the mushrooms grew. Just as the fisheries managers can never seem to predict the salmon or steelhead runs, so are those living in the wilderness ...they cannot predict the weather, the hatch or the number of fish to be caught. But to be in the wilderness in the summertime is when the earth is the friendliest to the people and critters that make their lives there.

And then the season changes again in the fall. The colors are amazing, the salmon and steelhead are running and it's time to eat, drink and be merry for tomorrow the winter comes. To be on a river of life due to its salmon run is like being on the mother lode of diversity. Calling all small and big-game animals plus the wings of the air, come and get it, share it, fight over it and fill your stomachs. Even the flora and fauna benefit when the bear drags a carcass far off the river and into the forest...nature's best fertilizer is optimum under the water and above water. The richness of a salmon run is directly related to the richness of the forest and land around it and you can see this, document this, and live with this even into the winter. A recent archaeological examination of the Babine River weir area uncovered such richness and multi-layers of human history that the archaeologists were stunned. Once upon a time, not very long ago, the salmon could support thousands of people living in the weir area all winter long. Now, I am not so sure.

Late fall or late-season angling on the Babine is another season unto itself. I have been trying for years to develop a late season for steelheading. I guess it's not for every angler, but if more anglers knew how special it is, then maybe it wouldn't be so special. The 2009 late season on the Babine was no less amazing than most in recent memory. We had snow on the fall colors of cottonwood and poplar leaves, leaves way late in falling. We had lots of dying or dead salmon and few bears wanting them which was puzzling. The river had few anglers and lots of big steelhead. We had lots of fun with some of our favorite late-season guests. Despite challenging economic times the Babine called even louder to a cast of late-season steelheaders that once again renewed their bond with a wild river. So many times the words "unbelievable" were called out to the river, the trees and spirit there. Big buck steelhead and again some that couldn't be landed...One

As the season progresses the fall foliage is ever more colourful.

angler exclaimed, "I had no chance," after losing a battle with a huge buck in Upper Callahan. We can see the world-record steelhead in the waters of this river but it doesn't mean we can land them when hooked. Some have over the years and it's best to let those stories just be stories.

Rivers can get loved to death and we are constantly reminded by so many guests of how underloved the Babine still is. This is extremely rare and special and really few anglers out there realize it. I say to family Babine, keep the faith and spread the word only to those whom you think would someday realize what you know. In trying to express why this river does what it does, well, good luck. Perhaps just before next steelhead season there will be a new book about the Babine authored by many. And perhaps an attempt will be made to capture the 'why' of this river. It probably won't be the last book trying to explain this Babine spirit, but I want to thank all those who took the time to contribute to the book and also thank all of you who keep visiting Norlakes and keep the memories alive each season.

Until then, keep up the good fight for things like wild salmon and steelhead and thanks again for any time you take to support the foundation, the trust, Alexandra Morton, Eric Hobson, Ali Howard, Richard Overstall and the many individuals dedicated to preserving the experience and the fish. The three wise men from the east did not expect to find a baby king, the fishermen on the Sea of Galilee did not expect the catch they received and I know many guests will not expect the catch glided to the shore by the guide's net in 2010 so all the best for the new year, new season and beyond.

Babine Reading List

For those interested in learning more about the Babine, both its early days and its present fishing outcomes, the following reading list covers a great deal of ground and a significant span of time, from 1955 to 2009.

Books

—*Steelhead Paradise*, by John F. Fennelly. Published in 1963 by Mitchell Press Limited, Vancouver, B.C. See Chapter Three, *The Babine*, pages 24-30.

—*You Should Have Been Here Yesterday,* by Lee Richardson with a preface by Roderick Haig-Brown, limited edition of 1200 copies. Published in 1974 by The Touchstone Press, Beaverton, OR. See Chapter Five, British Columbia: Hail The Babine, pages 73-85.

—*Steelhead Fly Fishing*, by Trey Combs. Published in 1991 by Heritage House Publishing Company Limited, Surrey, B.C. See Chapter Twenty, Babine River, pages 267-278.

—*To Save The Wild Earth, Field Notes From The Environmental Front Line*, by Ric Careless with a foreword by Maurice Strong. Published in 1997 by Raincoast Books, Vancouver, B.C. See Chapter Seven, Babine River, The Economics Of Preservation, pages 149—164.

—*Fly fishing British Columbia*, various writers edited by Karl Bruhn. Published in 1999 by Heritage House Publishing Company Limited, Surrey, B.C. See, Two Northern Trout Streams, pages 71-72, also pages 36 and 67.

—*Angling In The Shadow Of The Canadian Rockies*, by Jeff Mironuck. Published in 1999 by Jeff Mironuck. See Rainbows and Steelhead of the Babine, by Pierce Clegg, pages 117-121.

—*Skeena Steelhead And Salmon: A Report To The Stakeholders* (46 pages), by Adam Lewis. Published in 2000 by the Bulkley Valley Branch of the Steelhead Society of British Columbia, Smithers, B.C.

—*Famous British Columbia Fly-Fishing Waters*, by Art Lingren. Published in 2002 by Frank Amato Publications, Inc., Portland, OR. See Chapter Twelve, The Skeena and its Famous Tributaries, pages 104-121.

—*There's Only One Babine: An Introduction to the Babine River Foundation*, soft cover, spiral bound, 76 pages. Published by the Babine River Foundation, Box 5016, Smithers, B.C. V0J2N0

—*River Of Dreams*, by Lani Waller with a foreword by John Randolph. Published in 2004 by West River Publishing, Grand Island, NY. See Trotter's Pool, pages 21-34, River of Giants, pages 115-129, Playing the Numbers, pages 185-198.

—*Skeena River Fish And Their Habitat*, by Allen S. Gottesfeld and Ken A. Rabnett. Published in 2008 by the Skeena Fisheries Commission and Ecotrust, Portland, OR. See Chapter 15, Babine Watershed, pages 183-198.

—*A Steelheader's Way, Principles, Tactics And Techniques*, by Lani Waller. Published in 2009 by Headwater Books, New Cumberland, PA and Stackpole Books, Mechanicsburg, PA. See Index for Babine River, numerous references.

Magazine Articles

There are sure to be others in this category but these are among the ones that have come to our attention, the first six from the library of Chris Stromsness.

—"Crimson Steelhead", by Charles McDermand, *Field and Stream*, October 1955.

—"Heaven Is A Steelhead", by Joe Brooks, *Outdoor Life*, October 1968.

—"Those Wild Babine Steelhead", by Edna and Ann Skinner, *Western Outdoors*, September 1969.

—"Angler's Choice ... Steelhead or Atlantic Salmon? ", by Joe Brooks, *Outdoor Life*, September 1971.

—"Home of the Super-Steelhead", by Ed Zern, *Field and Stream*, April 1973.

—"The Superstar of Steelhead Streams", by Dave Whitlock, *Outdoor Life*, 1978 (month unknown).

—"Splendid Skeena", by Thomas R.Pero, *Trout*, Autumn 1990.

—"Northern Exposure, Babine Lake Rainbows On The Fly", by Karl Bruhn, *BC Outdoors*, January/February 1992.

—"Cutting The Babine", by Jim and Carolyn Shelton, *Flyfishing, April 1994.*

—"Steelhead Paradise Revisited", by Bill Herzog, *Salmon-Trout-Steelheader*, April/May 1994.

—"Rafting for Babine Steelhead", by Andrew Williams, *BC Outdoors*, November/December 2005.

—"The Tragedy Of Steelhead", by Dylan Tomine, *Wild on the Fly, Issue #12,* Winter 2007/2008.

—"When Winter Comes To The Babine", by Dave Hall. *Wild Steelhead and Salmon*, Vol.3, Issue #2, Winter 1997. Reprinted on pages 152-154.

—"Legendary Rainbow Alley", by Jeff Minoruck, *Fly Fishing the West*, Fall/Winter 2005.

—"Meet the Deke. Steelheading the Babine is never easy, just worth it." By Tosh Brown, *The Drake*, publication date unknown.

—"The Babine's Steelhead Stewards", by Peter McMullan, *Fly Fusion Magazine*, Winter 2006.

—"A Wild And Pristine River Under Pressure." by Peter McMullan, *Chasing Silver Magazine*, Issue #2, 2008. *Reprinted on pages 165-167*

Skeena Region Scientific Reports

These are too numerous to list but almost 150 of them, including a number related directly to the Babine, are available on the Internet through the B.C. Ministry of Environment site: http://www.env.gov.bc.ca/skeena/fish/skeena_reports/sk report_index.htm

Credit to the Illustrators

Just as the contributions collected to create this book echo many voices so the paintings, drawings and photographs represent the talents of a number of different people, all fishermen and all sharing a love of and respect for the river, its fish and its wildlife.

We would like to thank the following individuals whose work so greatly enhances the pages of *Babine*:

Dave Hall
for the cover, endpapers and for the illustrations on
pages 2 and 3, 8, 10, 12, 21, 25, 26, 38, 39, 46, 50, 81, 90, 100, 101, 104, 110, 111, 112, 125, 126, 131, 140, 152.

Gary Flagel
for the illustrations on pages 1, 53, 155

The photographs, graphs and maps were contributed by:

Dust cover photos by Loren Irving, back and front flap, both, and Peter McMullan; pages 4-5, Loren Irving; 6-7, Mike Gifford; 9, Babine River Foundation; 11, Wayne Davidson; 13, both, First Fish Consulting; 15, Dr. Kent Davenport; 17, both, Madsen Family; 18, both, Madsen Family; 19, Madsen Family; 20, top, Madsen Family; 21, both, Madsen Family; 22, Madsen Family; 23, Stromsness Family; 24, Madsen Family; 27, Al Ducros; 29, top, Madsen Family, lower, Andersen Family; 30, lower, Madsen Family; 31, Madsen Family; 32, Washington State University; 34, Barto Family; 37, Stromsness Family; 43, Will Blanchard; 44, Andersen Family; 61, Loren Irving; 64, Dr. Kent Davenport; 78, Loren Irving; 79, lower, Dr. Kent Davenport; 80, both, Ken Morrish (Flywater Travel); 82, top, Dr. Kent Davenport, lower, Brad Bailey; 83, Loren Irving; 84, Gary Quanstrom; 85, Dr. Kent Davenport; 87, Dr. Kent Davenport; 88, lower, Will Blanchard; 89, Gary Flagel; 91, both, Brad Bailey; 92, Paul Robinson; 93, Stromsness Family; 99, both, Russell Family; 108, top, unknown photographer, lower, Fumiya Okuyama; 109, Okuyama Family; 110, 111, backdrops, Brad Bailey; 114, both, Shinji Masuzawa; 115, upper, Andersen Family; 116, right, Barto Family; 117, Barto Family; 119, Darren Wright; 121, Ken Morrish; 123, Jeremy Dufton; 124, Ken Morrish; 127, Fred Jordan; 128, Fred Jordan; 132, lower, Bob Miller; 134, Madsen Family; 136, Will Blanchard; 137, top, Larry Falk, lower, Will Blanchard;141, Josh Nowlin; 143, Madsen Family; 146, Madsen Family; 148, Brian Huntington; 150, Paul Robinson; 151, Dave Robinson; 157, Dr. Kent Davenport; 158, right, Darren Wright; 159, Herzog Family; 160, Josh Nowlin; 161, Herzog Family; 162, both, Stewart Family; 163, Ken Morrish; 166, Loren Irving; 171, lower, Dr. Kent Davenport; 172, BC Ministry of Environment; 174, 175, BC Ministry of Environment; 176, BC Parks; 177, Josh Nowlin; 178, backdrop, Loren Irving, photos l to r from top, Ken Morrish, Gary Flagel, Joel Nowlin, Brad Bailey, Josh Nowlin, Loren Irving: 179, backdrop, Loren Irving, l to r, Pierce Clegg, Brad Bailey, Mike Gifford, Gary Flagel, Peter McMullan; 181, Madsen Family; 182, Gary Quanstrom; 184, Loren Irving; 185, Dr. Kent Davenport; 186, Brad Bailey; 187, Dr. Kent Davenport.

Pierce Clegg and Peter McMullan provided the following photos: Pierce Clegg, 30, upper; 41; 42; 47; 49; 57; 62; 67; 68, upper; 69; 71; 79, upper; 88, upper; 94; 96; 102; 107; 115, lower; 116, left; 129; 130; 132, upper; 135; 139, lower; 142; 145; 154; 168; 169; Peter McMullan, pages 16; 20, lower; 45; 55; 59; 63; 66; 68, lower; 76; 77; 133; 138; 139, upper; 158, left; 165; 171, upper, 173.

Index